Malcolm M. MacFarlane
Editor

Family Therapy and Mental Health

Innovations in Theory and Practice

Pre-publication
REVIEWS,
COMMENTARIES,
EVALUATIONS . . .

"This anthology brings together an impressive collection of contributors whose essays describe efforts to combine family therapy with the more traditional individual approach to mental health care. I have never understood the polarization exhibited by those who staunchly support one or the other of these approaches as the sine qua non of treatment. A movement toward integration rather than prolonging a theoretical turf war has always made much more sense. MacFarlane is to be congratulated for undertaking a readable and practical effort to bring the two viewpoints to a common ground.

This collection of essays will make a valuable addition to courses in family therapy programs as well as in courses training therapists to do individual therapy for such disorders as OCD, panic disorder, schizophrenia, or depression. Especially important for those who hold fast to the idea that individual therapy works best is the first chapter, which gives an overview and discusses research findings that clearly spell out how family therapy can not only augment individual therapy, but can often make the difference between successful recovery or failure."

Marcia Lasswell, MA
Professor of Behavioral Science,
California Polytechnic University,
Pomona

More pre-publication
REVIEWS, COMMENTARIES, EVALUATIONS . . .

"This 'best practices' text is a must for clinicians who seek to be maximally effective in the treatment of the major psychiatric disorders. Driven by current understanding of how the family influences and is influenced by serious mental and emotional disorders, this book goes well beyond the psychoeducational approach to schizophrenia, bipolar, panic, obsessive-compulsive, and borderline personality disorders. It offers integrated multi-modality, multi-level approaches for understanding these processes and their assessment and treatment. Solid literature reviews, illustrative case applications, indications, and caveats make this book valuable to those practicing in a variety of mental health settings. This text also will be an important addition to traditional psychopathology assessment and treatment courses."

Robert E. Lee, PhD
Professor,
Michigan State University,
East Lansing

The Haworth Clinical Practice Press
An Imprint of The Haworth Press, Inc.
New York • London • Oxford

Family Therapy and Mental Health
Innovations in Theory and Practice

HAWORTH Marriage and the Family
Terry S. Trepper, PhD
Executive Editor

Propagations: Thirty Years of Influence from the Mental Research Institute edited by John H. Weakland and Wendel A. Ray

Structured Exercises for Promoting Family and Group Strengths: A Handbook for Group Leaders, Trainers, Educators, Counselors, and Therapists edited by Ron McManus and Glen Jennings

Making Families Work and What to Do When They Don't: Thirty Guides for Imperfect Parents of Imperfect Children by Bill Borcherdt

Family Therapy of Neurobehavioral Disorders: Integrating Neuropsychology and Family Therapy by Judith Johnson and William McCown

Parents, Children, and Adolescents: Interactive Relationships and Development in Context by Anne-Marie Ambert

Women Survivors of Childhood Sexual Abuse: Healing Through Group Work: Beyond Survival by Judy Chew

Tales from Family Therapy: Life-Changing Clinical Experiences edited by Frank N. Thomas and Thorana S. Nelson

The Therapist's Notebook: Homework, Handouts, and Activities for Use in Psychotherapy edited by Lorna L. Hecker and Sharon A. Deacon

The Web of Poverty: Psychosocial Perspectives by Anne-Marie Ambert

Stepfamilies: A Multi-Dimensional Perspective by Roni Berger

Clinical Applications of Bowen Family Systems Theory by Peter Titelman

Treating Children in Out-of-Home Placements by Marvin Rosen

Your Family, Inc.: Practical Tips for Building a Healthy Family Business by Ellen Frankenberg

Therapeutic Intervention with Poor, Unorganized Families: From Distress to Hope by Shlomo A. Sharlin and Michal Shamai

The Residential Youth Care Worker in Action: A Collaborative, Competency-Based Approach by Robert Bertolino and Kevin Thompson

Chinese Americans and Their Immigrant Parents: Conflict, Identity, and Values by May Paomay Tung

Together Through Thick and Thin: A Multinational Picture of Long-Term Marriages by Shlomo A. Sharlin, Florence W. Kaslow, and Helga Hammerschmidt

Developmental-Systemic Family Therapy with Adolescents by Ronald Jay Werner-Wilson

The Effect of Children on Parents, Second Edition by Anne-Marie Ambert

Clinical and Educational Interventions with Fathers by Jay Fagan and Alan J. Hawkins

Family Solutions for Substance Abuse: Clinical and Counseling Approaches by Eric E. McCollum and Terry S. Trepper

Couples Therapy, Second Edition by Linda Berg-Cross

Family Therapy and Mental Health: Innovations in Theory and Practice by Malcolm M. MacFarlane

How to Work with Sex Offenders: A Handbook for Criminal Justice, Human Service, and Mental Health Professionals by Rudy Flora

Marital and Sexual Lifestyles in the United States: Attitudes, Behaviors, and Relationships in Social Context by Linda P. Rouse

Psychotherapy with People in the Arts: Nurturing Creativity by Gerald Schoenewolf

Clinical Epiphanies in Marital and Family Therapy: A Practitioner's Casebook of Therapeutic Insights, Perceptions, and Breakthroughs, by David A. Baptiste Jr.

Family Therapy and Mental Health
Innovations in Theory and Practice

Malcolm M. MacFarlane
Editor

The Haworth Clinical Practice Press
An Imprint of The Haworth Press, Inc.
New York • London • Oxford

Published by

The Haworth Clinical Practice Press, an imprint of The Haworth Press, Inc., 10 Alice Street, Binghamton, NY 13904-1580

Names and other identifying information have been altered in all case examples to preserve client confidentiality.

Cover design by Anastasia Litwak.

Library of Congress Cataloging-in-Publication Data

Family therapy and mental health : innovations in theory and practice / Malcolm M. MacFarlane, editor.
    p. cm.
    Includes bibliographical references and index.
    ISBN 0-7890-0880-7 (hbk. : alk. paper)—ISBN 0-7890-1589-7 (pbk. : alk. paper)
    1. Family psychotherapy. 2. Mental health. 3. Family—Mental health services. I. MacFarlane, Malcolm M.

RC488.5. F3342 2000
616.89'156—dc21

00-066457

CONTENTS

About the Editors   xii

Contributors   xiii

Foreword   xvii
Dorothy S. Becvar

Preface   xxi

Acknowledgments   xxvii

PART I: OVERVIEW

Chapter 1. Family Therapy and Mental Health:
Historical Overview and Current Perspectives   3
William C. Nichols
Malcolm M. MacFarlane

Introduction   3
The Road to the Twenty-First Century   5
Family Therapy   7
Families and Theories of Causation of Mental Illness   9
Families and Treatment of Schizophrenia   11
Recent Events and Trends   12
Future Directions   20

Chapter 2. The Partnership Model: Working with
Families of People with Serious Mental Illness   27
Eric D. Johnson

Introduction   27
Setting   30
Treatment Model   31
Case Example   40

Strengths and Limitations of the Model   45
Integration with Psychiatric Services and the Role
    of Medication   47
Cultural and Gender Issues   48
Future Directions   50

PART II: TRADITIONAL POPULATIONS

**Chapter 3. Family Treatment of Schizophrenia
    and Bipolar Disorder   57**
      Kim T. Mueser

Introduction   57
Setting   59
Treatment Model   60
Case Example   68
Strengths and Limitations   72
Integration with Psychiatric Services and Role
    of Medication   73
Cultural and Gender Issues   74
Future Directions   76

**Chapter 4. Family Treatment of Depression
    and the McMaster Model of Family Functioning   83**
      Wilson McDermut
      James W. Alves
      Ivan W. Miller
      Gabor I. Keitner

Introduction   83
Setting   84
Treatment Model   85
Case Example   95
Strengths and Limitations   102
Integration with Psychiatric Services and Role
    of Medication   102
Cultural and Gender Issues   103
Future Directions   104

Chapter 5. Family Therapy for Panic Disorder: A Cognitive-Behavioral Interpersonal Approach to Treatment   **109**

Kristie L. Gore
Michele M. Carter

Introduction	109
Setting	116
Treatment Model	116
Case Example	119
Strengths and Limitations	126
Integration with Psychiatric Services and Role of Medication	127
Cultural and Gender Issues	128
Future Directions	129

Chapter 6. Family Treatment of Borderline Personality Disorder   **135**

Ira D. Glick
Emily L. Loraas

Introduction	135
Setting	141
Treatment Model	142
Case Example	147
Strengths and Limitations	149
Integration with Psychiatric Services and Role of Medication	149
Cultural and Gender Issues	150
Future Directions	150

Chapter 7. Systemic Treatment of Obsessive-Compulsive Disorder in a Rural Community Mental Health Center: An Integrative Approach   **155**

Malcolm M. MacFarlane

Introduction	155
Setting	160
Treatment Model	161

Case Example   167
Strengths and Limitations   173
Integration with Psychiatric Services and Role
    of Medication   174
Cultural and Gender Issues   176
Future Directions   177

**Chapter 8. The Psychoeducational Model and Case
Management: The Role of Marital and Family
Therapy in the Treatment of the Chronically
Mentally Ill   185**
    Joan Keefler

Introduction   185
Setting   194
Treatment Model   195
Case Example   198
Strengths and Limitations   202
Integration with Psychiatric Services and Role
    of Medication   205
Cultural and Gender Issues   206
Future Directions   208

**Chapter 9. Family Treatment of Borderline Personality
Disorder Through Relationship Enhancement Therapy   215**
    Marsha J. Harman
    Michael Waldo

Introduction   215
Setting   219
Treatment Model   221
Case Example   225
Strengths and Limitations   229
Integration with Psychiatric Services and Role
    of Medication   230
Cultural and Gender Issues   231
Future Directions   232

Chapter 10. Treatment of Suicidal Clients and Their Families   **237**

       Peter D. McLean
       Lynn Miller

Introduction	237
Setting	244
Treatment Model	245
Case Example	253
Strengths and Limitations	256
Integration with Psychiatric Services and Role of Medication	257
Cultural and Gender Issues	258
Future Directions	258

Chapter 11. Family Therapy in Walk-In Mental Health Centers: The Eastside Family Centre   **261**

       Arnold Slive
       Nancy McElheran
       Ann Lawson

Introduction	261
Setting	262
Treatment Model	266
Case Examples	272
Strengths and Limitations	276
Integration with Psychiatric Services and Role of Medication	279
Cultural and Gender Issues	281
Future Directions	283

PART III: SPECIAL POPULATIONS

Chapter 12. Behavioral Couples Therapy for Comorbid Substance Abuse and Psychiatric Problems   **289**

       Rob J. Rotunda
       Jane G. Alter
       Timothy J. O'Farrell

Introduction	289
Setting	290
Treatment Model	291
Case Example	299
Strengths and Limitations	303
Cultural and Gender Issues	305

Integration with Psychiatric Services and Role
    of Medication   306
Future Directions   306

Chapter 13. Family Therapy of Brain Injury:
Basic Principles and Innovative Strategies   **311**
    Laurence Miller

Introduction   311
Setting   316
Treatment Model   317
Case Examples   322
Strengths and Limitations   324
Integration with Psychiatric Services and the Role
    of Medication   324
Cultural and Gender Issues   325
Future Directions   325

Chapter 14. Women and Mental Health:
A Feminist Family Systems Approach   **331**
    Carmen Knudson-Martin

Introduction   331
Setting   333
Treatment Model   337
Case Example   349
Strengths and Limitations   353
Integration with Psychiatric Services
    and Role of Medication   354
Cultural and Gender Issues   355
Future Directions   356

Chapter 15. Family Therapy and Issues of Aging   **361**
    Jonathan G. Sandberg
    Jason J. Platt

Introduction   361
Setting   369

Treatment Model   370
Case Example   374
Strengths and Limitations   377
Integration with Psychiatric Services and Role
    of Medication   378
Cultural and Gender Issues   380
Future Directions   384

Index   **389**

ABOUT THE EDITOR

Malcolm M. MacFarlane, MA, is a graduate of the California Family Study Center in Burbank California (now renamed the Phillips Graduate Institute in Encino, California) with a Master of Arts in Marriage, Family, and Child Therapy. He is a Clinical Member and an Approved Supervisor with the American Association for Marriage and Family Therapy (AAMFT), and is a Registered Marriage and Family Therapist with the Registry of Marriage and Family Therapists in Canada and the Ontario Association for Marriage and Family Therapy.

MacFarlane has worked as a frontline mental health clinician for fifteen years and is currently employed as a mental health therapist with Ross Memorial Hospital Community Counselling Services in Lindsay, Ontario, a rural community mental health center funded by the Ontario Ministry of Health. He has been a contributor to a number of professional journals as well as contributing to the text *What Works! Innovation in Community Mental Health and Addiction Treatment Programs.* He was a presenter on family therapy with brain-injured clients and their families at the AAMFT annual international conference in Toronto in 1996, and presented a workshop entitled "Family Therapy and Mental Health: 2000 and Beyond" at the AAMFT Millennium Summit Conference in Denver in 2000. He has qualified as an expert witness in the area of social work practice and family dynamics in family court.

CONTRIBUTORS

Jane G. Alter, LICSW, CAS, is Clincial Director, Harvard Counseling for Alcoholics' Marriages (CALM) Project, Harvard Medical School Department of Psychiatry and Veteran's Affairs Medical Center, Brockton, Massachusetts.

James W. Alves, MSW, LICSW, is Senior Clinical Teaching Associate, Department of Psychiatry and Human Behavior, Brown University, and Director of Outpatient Department, Butler Hospital, Providence, Rhode Island.

Michele M. Carter, PhD, is Associate Professor, Department of Psychology, American University, Washington, DC.

Ira D. Glick, MD, is Professor of Psychiatry and Behavioral Sciences, Department of Psychiatry and Behavioral Sciences, Stanford University School of Medicine, Stanford, California.

Kristie L. Gore, MA, is a Doctoral Candidate in Clinical Psychology, Department of Psychology, American University, Washington, DC.

Marsha J. Harman, PhD, is Associate Professor, Departments of Curriculum and Instruction, and Psychology and Philosophy, Sam Houston State University, Huntsville, Texas.

Eric D. Johnson, PhD, is Assistant Professor, Family Therapy Program, Hahnemann University, Philadelphia, Pennsylvania, and Director, Consultation/Education Associates, Lawrenceville, New Jersey.

Joan Keefler, MSW, is Lecturer and Doctoral Student, McGill School of Social Work, Montreal, Quebec, Canada, and Staff/Lecturer, Argyle Institute of Human Relations, Montreal, Quebec Canada.

Gabor I. Keitner, MD, is Professor, Department of Psychiatry and Human Behavior, Brown University, and Chief of Adult Psychiatry and Director of Mood Disorders Program, Rhode Island Hospital, Providence, Rhode Island.

Carmen Knudson-Martin, PhD, is Professor and Director of Doctoral Programs in Marriage and Family Therapy, Department of Counseling and Family Studies, Loma Linda University, Loma Linda, California.

Ann Lawson, MASc, is Program Manager, Wood's Homes, Calgary, Alberta, Canada.

Emily L. Loraas, BA, is Research Coordinator, Department of Psychiatry and Behavioral Sciences, Stanford University School of Medicine, Stanford, California.

Wilson McDermut, PhD, is Assistant Professor of Psychology, Department of Psychology, William Paterson University, Wayne, New Jersey.

Nancy McElheran, MN, is Director, Wood's Homes, Calgary, Alberta, Canada.

Peter D. McLean, PhD, is Professor, Department of Psychiatry, University of British Columbia, Vancouver, British Columbia, Canada.

Ivan W. Miller, PhD, is Professor, Department of Psychiatry and Human Behavior, Brown University, and Director of Adult Psychology and Research and Associate Director, Mood Disorder Program, Rhode Island Hospital, Providence, Rhode Island.

Laurence Miller, PhD, is in Independent Practice, Boca Raton, Florida, and is Director of Psychological Services for Hartland Rehabilitation Centers in the South Florida area.

Lynn Miller, PhD, is a member of Sessional Faculty, Department of Educational and Counselling Psychology and Special Education, University of British Columbia, Vancouver, British Columbia, Canada.

Kim T. Mueser, PhD, is Professor, Departments of Psychiatry and Community and Family Medicine, Dartmouth Medical School, New Hampshire–Dartmouth Psychiatric Research Center, Concord, New Hampshire.

William C. Nichols, EdD, ABPP, is Adjunct Professor of Child and Family Development, University of Georgia, Athens, Georgia.

Timothy J. O'Farrell, PhD, is Professor of Psychology, Harvard Medical School Department of Psychiatry and Veterans' Affairs Medical Center, Brockton, Massachusetts.

Jason J. Platt, MS, is Clinical Supervisor and Adjunct Instructor, Department of Applied Behavioral and Communication Science, University of Oregon, Eugene, Oregon.

Rob J. Rotunda, PhD, is Assistant Professor, Department of Psychology, University of West Florida, Pensacola, Florida, and Harvard Medical School, Department of Psychiatry, Brockton, Massachusetts.

Jonathan G. Sandberg, PhD, is Assistant Professor, Marriage and Family Therapy Program, Department of Child and Family Studies, Syracuse University, Syracuse, New York.

Arnold Slive, PhD, is in Independent Practice, Calgary, Alberta, Canada, and is Clinical Consultant, Wood's Homes, Calgary, Alberta.

Michael Waldo, PhD, is Professor, Department of Counseling and Educational Psychology, New Mexico State University, Las Cruces, New Mexico.

Foreword

As I was reflecting on how best to introduce *Family Therapy and Mental Health: Innovations in Theory and Practice,* I was reminded of the chapter written twenty-five years ago by James Framo, titled "Chronicle of a Struggle to Establish a Family Unit Within a Community Mental Health Center." This chapter was included in the edited book *Family Therapy* (Framo, 1976), one of the early classics in the field. In it, Framo describes his efforts, his frustrations, and ultimately his decision to leave the community mental health center following a valiant attempt to establish one of the first units focused on families and family therapy in such a setting. When comparing this chapter with the present volume, I could not help but think about the well-known maxim, *plus ça change, plus c'est la même chose.* Indeed, the more things change, the more they remain the same, which is the essence of first-order change (Watzlawick, Weakland, and Fisch, 1974).

What certainly has changed over the past quarter of a century is the fact that, in many ways, marriage and family therapy has come of age. To a significant degree it has become a recognized discipline within the mental health professions. Many colleges and universities throughout Canada and the United States now offer specialized training at both the master's and doctoral degree levels. Today, licensure as a marriage and family therapist is available in some of the provinces and most of the states. Also, a vast body of theory and research specific to the field and a growing amount of data that document and support the effectiveness of endeavors in this area is emerging.

Also changed is the context within which the majority of marriage and family therapists work. Unlike the early days of the movement, private practice is fast becoming a phenomenon of the past. Given the current domination of the economic arena by large managed care companies, more and more marriage and family therapists are faced with the necessity of seeking employment in agency or group settings.

What continues to remain the same, however, and seemingly more and more so, is the struggle described by Framo for those who choose to think and work from a family systems perspective. That is, then, as now, the systemic paradigm upon which the field of marriage and family therapy is built is inconsistent with the mainstream medical model approaches to the treatment of mental illness. Those trained in traditional approaches to mental illness—consistent with the medical model—often have a difficult time either making a shift to or understanding the benefits to be derived from a systemic approach. Those working from a systemic perspective often find themselves having to fight an uphill battle as they attempt to remain consistent with the paradigm according to which they were trained and in which they believe. At best, they may feel torn between models; at worst, they may find themselves having to abandon one or the other. Adding to the dilemma is the fact that marriage and family therapy services still do not have parity with traditional mental health approaches, e.g., they are not eligible for reimbursement from third-party payers. Practitioners working from a systemic perspective, therefore, often find they must compromise some of their basic beliefs in order to survive in business.

Nevertheless, as each of the chapters in this book attests, despite continuing struggles many practitioners have found ways to incorporate family therapy into their work with clients who are receiving treatment for problems falling within the traditional mental illness diagnostic categories. Implicit in their work and the approaches they describe is a recognition of the reciprocal influence between families and family members who are experiencing serious challenges. Also significant is the recognition of the interplay between the biological and the social, between the intrapersonal and the interpersonal. In addition, there is an awareness of the advantages to be gained from a perspective that is inclusive, as the family is enlisted as an ally rather than as an adversary in the treatment process.

Particularly noteworthy, however, is that the models and approaches described herein were created and/or evolved within the real world of mental health practice. In fact, a common lament among practitioners is that the academicians and researchers whose articles and chapters tend to fill most of the journals and books that are published are not in touch with life in the trenches. On the other hand, those who are manning the trenches rarely can spare the time to write about their experiences and/or are not particularly inclined to document what they do. Thus, in both the choice of orientation for this book and in his ability to recruit practitioner-authors, what Malcolm MacFarlane has done is certainly worthy of praise.

Accordingly, what the reader will find is a fine collection of essays that illustrate various attempts to include both individual and family therapy approaches aimed at the achievement of mental health in a variety of populations. What is more, it seems to be a book whose time has come. That is, we have described the last part of the twentieth century as a time in which much energy began to be focused on transcending models and developing collaborative and respectful therapeutic dialogues (Becvar and Becvar, 2000). In attempting to transcend polarities, by finding examples that bridge differences and in describing unique integrative frameworks, the book stands as a valuable contribution to this ongoing tradition. One hopes that it may also contribute to a change of change, which is the essence of second-order change (Watzlawick, Weakland, and Fisch, 1974).

Dorothy S. Becvar
St. Louis, Missouri

REFERENCES

Becvar, D. S. and Becvar, R. J. (2000). *Family therapy: A systemic integration.* Boston: Allyn & Bacon.

Framo, J. L. (1976). Chronicle of a struggle to establish a family unit within a community mental health center. In P. J. Guerin (Ed.), *Family therapy: Theory and practice* (pp. 23-29). New York: Gardner Press.

Watzlawick, P., Weakland, J., and Fisch, R. (1974). *Change: Principles of problem formation and problem resolution.* New York: W. W. Norton.

Preface

Despite the fact that family therapy has at least some of its roots in the mental health field and early attempts to find a more effective treatment for schizophrenia, many would argue that there has always been a certain tension between the two disciplines. Family therapists have long been critical of the more traditional individually focused psychoanalytic and biomedical approaches to treating mental health problems. They rightly argue that individual mental health problems are often symptomatic of disturbances in interpersonal relationships, and that effective treatment requires attention to the context in which the symptoms occur. This emphasis on context, and the complex interactions between individuals and their social environment, has long been a strength of the family therapy field.

Many traditional mental health practitioners are equally critical of the family therapy field. They also rightly argue that family therapy purists often ignore clear research evidence that many mental health problems (such as depression) have a biological component to their origins, and that pharmacological treatments are often a necessary and appropriate treatment approach. Although individual psychopathology may be played out in relationship dynamics, an exclusive focus on treating relationship issues while ignoring the influence of individual pathology is counterproductive to effective treatment. All problems do not have their roots in disturbed relationships.

Unfortunately, this polarization between the two disciplines has resulted in less than optimal service for many clients and their families who are struggling with mental health issues. Mental health problems are complex and require intervention on a variety of levels: biomedical, psychological, family, and social. As family therapists are well aware from their systems training, there is a reciprocal relationship between each of these levels, and events occurring at each level impact the other levels. A coordinated and integrated treatment approach that addresses the needs of mental health clients and their families at each level will inevitably be more effective than treatments that focus on any one level alone. It is time for family therapy approaches to be more fully integrated into the mental health field.

For the past fifteen years, I have found myself in an ideal position for observing both the mental health and family therapy fields. I work as a frontline mental health therapist in an adult outpatient community mental health center attached to a rural hospital. My professional affiliation and training is as a family therapist, and I approach my cases from a family systems perspective. At the same time, I work closely and collaboratively with a number of psychiatrists, as well as within a broader mental health system, which tends to focus on individual diagnostic labels and sees individuals rather than families as the focus of treatment. I have been fortunate; the agency where I work has valued my family therapy skills and systemic perspective and has actively embraced a more systems-oriented approach to the treatment of the center's clients. I feel our clients and their families have benefited from integrating family systems concepts with more traditional mental health treatment approaches; and we are able to address clients' mental health issues on a variety of levels, including the impact of their illness on other family members and the ways family members may feed into the individual's problems.

The idea for this text originated from my curiosity about the ways that other mental health treatment providers might be integrating family therapy approaches into their work with adult mental health problems. I believed that there might well be more going on in the way of integration than the current literature suggested. I also believed that it was important for the experiences of those who were working to integrate family therapy with traditional mental health practices to be shared. Through this sharing, we could all learn from what was being done, and family therapists and mental health practitioners could begin to get a sense of what models and treatment approaches were being used successfully to treat various mental health problems. This book is the end result of my explorations, and I believe it demonstrates a wide range of family therapy treatment approaches which are successfully being used to treat a variety of mental health problems.

In designing this book, I tried to think about what I, as a practicing frontline clinician, would like to see in a text on family therapy and mental health. I have tried to incorporate chapters on the typical problems that I see in a mental health practice in a community mental health center. These problems include depression, anxiety disorders, personality disorders, suicidal clients, obsessive-compulsive disorder, and comorbid substance abuse problems. They also include the more serious mental illnesses, such as schizophrenia and bipolar disorder.

Each chapter includes a case example that illustrates how the treatment approach is applied. In my experience, medication is routinely used as a treatment modality in most mental health settings, so each chapter also includes a section on integration with psychiatric services and the use of medication. In keeping with the current emphasis of the American Association for Marriage and Family Therapy on clinicians being sensitive to the gender and cultural contexts of their clients, a section on gender and cultural issues has been incorporated into each chapter. The use of a standard format of chapter headings for each chapter helps to ensure uniformity and permit comparison between treatment approaches. The headings for each chapter after the first are: Introduction, Setting, Treatment Model, Case Example, Strengths and Limitations, Integration with Psychiatric Services and Role of Medication, Gender and Cultural Issues, and Future Directions.

This text is loosely organized into three sections. Part I: Overview is intended to provide a broad examination of issues related to family therapy with adult mental health populations. This section includes a chapter by William C. Nichols and myself that reviews historical and current perspectives on family therapy and mental health. It also includes a chapter by Eric D. Johnson on the Partnership Model. Although Eric's chapter describes a specific treatment model, he also does an excellent job of emphasizing the importance and benefits of a collaboration among mental health providers, the mentally ill client, and the client's family. I felt his chapter provided an excellent depiction of the importance of family therapy for mental health populations, and so I have included it in the Overview section.

Part II: Traditional Populations includes nine chapters that deal with what are often considered the traditional or core mental health problems including schizophrenia, depression, bipolar disorder, panic disorder, borderline personality disorder, obsessive-compulsive disorder, and suicide. The treatment models in this section include a broad cross section of family therapy approaches ranging from behavioral and cognitive-behavioral family therapy approaches to systemic therapy and communication skills training. Also included in this section is a chapter by Slive, McElheran, and Lawson outlining a creative single-session, walk-in mental health program.

Part III: Special Populations includes several chapters dealing with specific special issues that clinicians working with mental health populations may encounter. In my experience, comorbid substance abuse disorders are a common occurrence in mental health populations, and Rotunda, Alter, and O'Farrell outline a comprehensive behavioral couples therapy approach for dealing with this issue. As our population ages, increasingly we will be dealing with mental health issues in the elderly. Sandberg and Platt describe a contextual and life review approach to dealing with mental health issues in later life. Also included in this section are chapters by Laurence Miller on family therapy after brain injury, and by Knudson-Martin on understanding women's mental health issues through a feminist family systems approach.

Although the chapters in this text clearly indicate that an array of useful family therapy treatment approaches for adult mental health problems is available, it is also clear that the integration of family therapy modalities into the traditional treatment of mental health populations is in its infancy. In their comments regarding future directions, the contributors almost uniformly indicate a serious need for further research into the effectiveness of the different models in treating mental health populations. Although some approaches seem to have some solid research supporting their effectiveness, many of those approaches that have the greatest research support appear to be those which incorporate behavioral or cognitive-behavioral components into their treatment approach. In many cases, the research seems to support the behavioral component of the treatment, but further research is needed to validate the family therapy components of the models.

Gore and Carter in Chapter 5 of this text suggest that perhaps the reason that research is focused on cognitive and behavioral approaches lies in the fact that cognitive-behavioral interventions, which rely on objective measures to assess therapeutic change, are easier to study than interpersonal techniques. Although this may be the case, the chapters in this text clearly indicate that families and mentally ill individuals receive many benefits from family interventions, which enhance their quality of life. These benefits may not be readily apparent from research that focuses on behavioral measures alone. An argument can be made that family therapy research in the mental health field should take a broader stance rather than focusing on simple behavioral measures and instead focus on the many ways in which family interventions enhance the client's quality of life and assist families in coping with the stresses and demands of living with a mentally ill family member.

I believe that family therapists and mental health practitioners will be encouraged by the material in this text. There *are* effective family therapy approaches for working with adults with mental health problems, and there *is* movement toward integrating family therapy approaches with traditional mental health treatment models. It is my sincere hope that these chapters will inspire family therapists to work more closely with mental health populations and encourage mental health practitioners to increasingly incorporate family therapy approaches into their work with mental health clients and their families. This increasing integration can only benefit the clients we serve, improving their quality of life and enhancing their emotional well-being.

Acknowledgments

No work of this nature comes together without a great deal of input and effort from many individuals. Unfortunately, it is not possible to acknowledge each and every person's contribution. Although those individuals and organizations mentioned here have played a special role in bringing this work to fruition, I appreciate the efforts of all those who have worked to make this text a reality, and I offer my deepest thanks.

I would like to thank The Haworth Press for making this text possible. They were willing to take a chance on the untried editorial skills of a relatively unknown frontline clinician. I am grateful for the opportunity they have provided, and I hope that the resulting work has justified their faith in my abilities and their openness to new authors.

I would also like to thank Haworth Senior Editor Terry Trepper, who has been an unfailing source of encouragement and support throughout this process and a pleasure to work with. I have always found his guidance and comments helpful, and appreciate his respectful confidence in my ability to find my own solutions to the challenges of editing.

The backbone of any edited work is the contributors, and I have been fortunate to work with some of the best in the field. I would like to thank all of the contributors for their energy and enthusiasm for the project, as well as their patience in responding to my many queries and requests for revisions. This was a collaborative process throughout, and I am honored to have had the chance to learn from each of them.

I would like to thank my wife, Valerie Cunningham, and my mother, Mary MacFarlane, for proofreading the manuscript and for their valuable comments. Any errors that remain are my responsibility alone.

Finally, I would like to thank my wife, Valerie, and my daughter, Rebecca MacFarlane, for their patience and understanding throughout the very long process of editing this book. They have both sacrificed hours of valuable family time and have been supportive and understanding throughout. I look forward to the opportunity of spending many delightful hours with both of them now that the project has reached completion.

PART I:
OVERVIEW

Chapter 1

Family Therapy and Mental Health: Historical Overview and Current Perspectives

William C. Nichols
Malcolm M. MacFarlane

INTRODUCTION

In North America, dealing with the mentally ill traditionally has been marked by a preference toward focusing on the individual and largely ignoring the family or treating it with indifference, ambivalence, or sometimes outright hostility. Although a small number of texts and other writings emphasize the importance of integrating individual and family perspectives in major mental illness (Hatfield, 1994; Lansky, 1981, 1985; Perlmutter, 1996), the important role of family therapy in the treatment of mental health problems continues to be underrepresented in the literature.

As Keefler notes in Chapter 8 of this text, the lack of attention to family therapy approaches is somewhat surprising, since ample research exists to indicate that family interventions have many positive effects in the treatment of mental health problems, including reducing relapse rates, reducing hospital admissions, encouraging compliance with medication, improving outcome, and reducing family burden and the cost of outpatient treatment (Azrin and Teichner, 1998; Droogan and Bannigan, 1997; Goldstein and Miklowitz, 1995; Penn and Mueser, 1996). Indeed, even if family interventions were not beneficial to family members with mental health problems, the beneficial impact of family therapy for families of the mentally ill would likely justify greater attention to this modality. Caregivers who live with a mentally ill relative indicate that caring for the relative can be a major burden. Gallagher and Mechanic (1996) and Song, Beigel, and Milligan (1997) have reported a variety of negative effects on the physical and psychological health of caregivers. Research indicates, however, that the coping abilities of families improve with the quality and quantity of social support from both professionals and their own social support system (Jutras and Veilleux, 1991; Solomon and Draine, 1995).

Eric Johnson, in Chapter 2 of this text, notes that many mental health professionals continue to overlook a rich resource for improving the community functioning of individuals with mental illness by not including family members' information and insights into the problem. In his interviews with family members, Johnson found that many family members felt ignored by the mental health community and felt that their experiences were disregarded or dismissed as irrelevant by mental health professionals. Family members seemed to attribute this poor treatment to professionals being overinvested in a medical model of illness as an intrapersonal biological phenomenon, which seemingly exists without a social context.

Johnson's findings fit well with recent research by Dixon and associates (1999) on the utilization of family therapy in the treatment of schizophrenia. Dixon and colleagues found that only .7 percent of a Medicare sample, and 7.1 percent of a Medicaid sample received family therapy. Further, only 30 percent of the field study participants affirmatively answered the question, "Did anyone in your family receive information about your illness or your treatment, or advice or support for families about how to be helpful to you?" These findings are very disconcerting given that psychoeducational family therapy for schizophrenia has been demonstrated in research to be an effective treatment approach (Goldstein and Miklowitz, 1995).

The current picture, in terms of the integration of family therapy approaches with traditional individually focused mental health treatments, appears to be very mixed. Although there are a few encouraging signs of an increasing recognition of the important contributions family therapy can make in the treatment of mental illness, it is obvious that the historical struggle between individual and family orientations in diagnosing and assessing mental disorders and psychological problems, and in providing treatment, continues into the present.

THE ROAD TO THE TWENTY-FIRST CENTURY

A brief look back to the eighteenth century and forward to the present seems essential for understanding what is occurring today in the treatment of the mentally ill and psychologically disturbed. During the colonial days and into the early years of the United States as a nation, virtually no facilities were provided for the severely mentally ill, who largely lived with their families, were homeless, or were in prison (Hatfield, 1987).

The Asylum Period of Institutionalization

Taking the mentally ill out of the home and placing them in special facilities began in the mid-eighteenth century. When America's first general hospital, the Pennsylvania Hospital in Philadelphia, opened during that period, it provided housing for the mentally ill in its basement. The first state "asylum" for the mentally ill in the United States was opened in 1773 in Williamsburg, Virginia (Hatfield, 1987). The asylum pattern prevailed until approximately the 1860s, with psychotics, in particular, often housed in such institutions. Some continued to live in poorhouses with other individuals, including dependent children. Efforts to provide treatment were launched in the United States around the beginning of the nineteenth century. The most popular approach was "moral treatment," which referred to the application of psychologically oriented therapy in an effort to return the disturbed individual to a state of reason. Introduced from Europe by Dorothea Dix, Horace Mann, and others, it involved placing the person in an asylum in a controlled atmosphere of "moral" sensibility or reason, in which he or she received a combination of somatic and psychosocial treatments. This approach was expected to restore mental health and avoid the development of chronic mental illness, but it did not prevent chronicity (U.S. Department of Health and Human Services, 1999; Grob, 1983, 1991, 1994).

The Mental Hospital Period of Institutionalization

The "mental hygiene" or public health movement appeared near the end of the nineteenth century. As the states were given the responsibility for providing care for the mentally ill, local communities tended to send them, along with some dependent persons, to state institutions. The asylums were renamed mental hospitals. Their development coincided with growing urbanization and, in light of the problems created by and for the mentally ill in cities, the hospitals were largely placed in rural areas (as were prisons), separating the patients from their families. Presumably the hospitalized mentally ill were to receive treatment as well as housing in the hospitals. In reality, the picture was quite mixed; large numbers continued to receive primarily custodial care and remain "warehoused" in mental hospitals once they were admitted. By 1955, there were approximately 559,000 psychiatric patients in state and county mental hospitals (Adamce, 1996). The National Committee on Mental Hygiene (currently the National Mental Health Association) advocated for moving mental health care into the mainstream of health care in a variety of ways, including outpatient treatment (U.S. Department of Health and Human Services, 1999).

The Community Mental Health Movement and Deinstitutionalization

During the 1940s, the concept of community mental health developed. Within a few years, partly due to the introduction of antipsychotic drugs that significantly reduced symptoms, state hospitals began to reverse the perpetual institutionalization pattern and to release some patients into the community. The recent surgeon general's report (U.S. Department of Health and Human Services, 1999) indicates that "The advent of chlorpromazine in 1952 and other neuroleptic drugs was so revolutionary that it was one of the major historical forces behind the deinstitutionalization movement" (p. 7).

With the passage of some state legislation on community mental health services and the 1963 enactment of the Community Mental Health Act, the deinstitutionalization period arrived full force. Some state mental hospitals were closed, others were downsized, and the movement to place the mentally ill in community placements (halfway houses and group homes) was fully underway. Community mental health centers were opened on a wide-scale basis to provide care not only for the seriously mentally ill who formerly had been hospitalized but also for others suffering from mental and psychological difficulties that impaired their functioning.

Graham (1988) describes a similar movement toward a community mental health focus in Canada. He notes that as a result of the continuing process of deinstitutionalization that began in the 1950s, in combination with improved treatment methods, the majority of people with chronic mental illnesses now live in the general community. He further estimates that in Ontario two-thirds of all psychiatric patients admitted to inpatient units stay for less than two weeks, and 90 percent stay for less than a month. With the implementation in Ontario of the Adult Community Mental Health Services Program in 1976, there was a major and positive shift toward locally based care and support of the mentally ill in the community.

In the United States, the mentally ill hospital population dropped to 193,435 by 1976 (Hatfield, 1987) and below 100,000 by the 1990s (Bachrach, 1996). Patients were outside mental hospitals, but families were not significantly involved with them. As Adamce (1996) has pointed out, "large numbers who were not in the care of their families were homeless or in prison," as had been the situation in the eighteenth century (p. 13).

The Community Support Movement

During the mid-1970s, a new reform movement emerged out of the community mental health movement. The new community support movement (U.S. Department of Health and Human Services, 1999) advocated acute treatment and prevention and added the new dimension of providing for the social welfare needs of individuals incapacitated by mental illness, with a view to returning them to adequate functioning as citizens (Goldman, 1998). The concept of recovery became an important part of the picture. Beginning in the late 1970s, as former mental patients and their families became active regarding mental illness, new organizations such as the National Alliance for the Mentally Ill (NAMI) began to advocate for adequate services to help the most seriously mentally ill.

FAMILY THERAPY

The conscious emergence and flowering of family therapy also marked the 1950s and 1960s. Family therapy, therefore, began to attract many professionals at approximately the same time that the community mental health approach was adopted. During the period in which family therapy was developing, professionals generally were reluctant to acknowledge that they were working with families. The individual was the focus of treatment. Psychoanalytic theory largely shaped the therapy world and provided strictures against working therapeutically with more than one person at a time. It was in the late 1950s, particularly after some disclosures at the 1957 annual conference of the American Psychiatric Association in Chicago, that many psychiatrists and psychologists began to acknowledge openly that they had been working with families, instead of simply with individuals.

Family therapy, which has a much more varied and complex background than is frequently recognized, developed and emerged from several different sources. It came from marital therapy roots, the child guidance movement, the social work emphasis on working with families, family life education and counseling developments, and—the source typically cited—researchers and clinicians seeking a cure for major mental illnesses, especially schizophrenia (Broderick and Schrader, 1981, 1991; Nichols and Everett, 1986; Nichols, 1996). Many family therapists were working with a wide range of other types of mental illness and psychological and relationship disturbances; they were not primarily or even incidentally, in some instances, concerned with schizophrenia.

One of the major pioneers of family therapy, counseling psychologist John Elderkin Bell, began working with total families after mistakenly concluding from a conversation with a colleague in England that John Bowlby at London's Tavistock Clinic was working with complete families at all sessions. (Bowlby actually was working with family members individually and seeing them together for an occasional conference.) Some who had been working with families and family systems under the rubric of "counseling"—the term "psychotherapy" being largely restricted to psychiatrists prior to that time—nevertheless were doing serious therapeutic work with problem populations, although they were not attracting much attention.

The early days of trying to introduce family therapy into the treatment programs of community mental health centers and other outpatient treatment facilities were marked sometimes by tremendous conflict. Some of these are reflected in the trenchant article of Jay Haley (1975) titled, "Why a Mental Health Clinic Should Avoid Family Therapy." Others have described, in informal anecdotal accounts, being ordered to refrain from working with families and to destroy films and recordings they were using to train therapists. At the core of many conflicts were disagreements over focusing on an individual versus a family systems orientation.

In 1970, the committee on the family of the Group for the Advancement of Psychiatry (GAP)—which included Murray Bowen, Ivan Boszormenyi-Nagy, Norman Paul, and Lyman C. Wynne— highlighted part of the issues with a reference to diagnostic evaluation in family or conjoint marital treatment:

> The traditional terminology used for individuals in individual psychotherapy does not apply to a group of patients. One cannot label the psychological maladaptations with one term; the malfunctioning and problems may vary sharply from one member to another. What is needed, then, is a new nomenclature, a new method whereby the problems of an entire family can be diagnosed systematically and validly. (pp. 545-546)

Unfortunately, support for the development of such a nomenclature has been slow in developing. Other sources of conflict pertained to medical versus nonmedical therapy and therapists and political (i.e., power) issues.

FAMILIES AND THEORIES OF CAUSATION OF MENTAL ILLNESS

According to Walsh (1996), opinion in the field of mental health has tended to alternate between dichotomous assumptions of biological and social causation. Walsh indicates that simplistic either/or arguments for genetic versus environmental explanations have been common regarding the transmission of schizophrenia and have bred controversy regarding the family's role in its etiology and course as well as family involvement in treatment. In this polarization, some argue that schizophrenia is a myth, symptomatic of a problem family that has caused or needs to maintain schizophrenia to serve a family function, and oppose diagnosis, hospitalization, or medication. At the opposite pole, biological determinists have relied primarily on psychopharmacological treatment and tended to keep families out of treatment.

Families and Etiological Explanations

Starting with psychoanalytic theories and assumptions that produced such ideas as "the schizophrenogenic mother" (Fromm-Reichman, 1948), a considerable amount of professional opinion moved along to a more general blaming of the family for illness among its offspring. Socially, also, the family tended to be viewed in pathological terms. A variety of illnesses and disorders manifested by individuals came to be viewed as stemming from family deficits and negative influences.

In the 1950s, schizophrenia was defined by some theorists and researchers as a learned pattern of communication instead of an illness of the mind. The now familiar double-bind hypothesis set forth by Bateson, Jackson, Haley, and Weakland (1956) in an influential article titled "Towards a Theory of Schizophrenia," attracted a considerable amount of attention and elevated hopes for a breakthrough in understanding and treating that disease. Eventually scholars and clinicians concluded that double-bind communication was no more prevalent in families of schizophrenics than in other families (Hatfield, 1987, p. 11); the theory was dropped as an etiological explanation.

Other attempts to explain schizophrenia in terms of family patterns and interactions that were advanced included the constructs of marital schism and skew (Lidz, Fleck, and Cornelison, 1965), other family communication disorders (Wynne, 1978), and disorganized family behavior and hierarchical incongruities (Haley, 1980; Madanes, 1981). Optimistic claims on the part of some early family therapists regarding a presumed discovery of the etiology of schizophrenia were not supported.

Biopsychosocial Model of Disease

George Engel (1977) offered the biopsychosocial model of disease, a framework which theorizes that biological, psychological, or social factors may be causes, correlates, and/or consequences in relation to mental health and mental illness (U.S. Department of Health and Human Services, 1999). Engel disputed the prevailing view of disease: that biological factors alone were sufficient to explain illness and health. This broad framework helped to change the view that families were to blame, or, as Walsh (1996) has put it, to move much of the field from "deficit to resource models" of the family.

FAMILIES AND TREATMENT OF SCHIZOPHRENIA

Family therapists understandably backed off from the idea that family therapy was the treatment of choice for schizophrenia. It is likely that the majority of family therapists were seldom, if ever, in volved in attempting to treat schizophrenia or dealing with hospitalized populations. There was additional change in the 1970s. According to Pinsof and Wynne (1995), two factors at that time renewed family therapist's interest in mental illness. In addition to deinstitutionalization, which forced families to deal with members who were affected with schizophrenia, the research on expressed emotion (EE) linked a family variable to the frequency and length of hospitalization. High expressed emotion (emotional overinvolvement, critical comments, and tone of voice) in families was shown to be associated with high relapse rates among released mental patients (Brown, Birley, and Wing, 1972; Vaughn and Leff, 1981; Leff and Vaughn, 1985). Organizations such as NAMI have been critical of EE studies, suggesting that they continue to "blame" families for mental illness by suggesting that family emotional characteristics contribute to schizophrenic episodes (Hatfield, 1991; Lefley, 1996). Despite concerns from organizations such as NAMI, the EE concept has proved useful in providing an opening for increased family involvement in the treatment of schizophrenia, and, in particular, through psychoeducational family therapy.

Psychoeducational Therapy

Psychoeducational therapies, which directly involve the patient's family and view the family as critical in the management of schizophrenia, were developed as a result of the emerging research findings regarding EE. Practical attempts to help families through psychoeducational approaches "absolve families of being causative in the illness but . . . say or imply that families are a factor in perpetuating it" and train families to become effective caretakers with the aim of preventing relapse and rehospitalization (Hatfield, 1987, p. 15). In addition to "deblaming" the family as a cause of the illness and creating a "no-fault" atmosphere, psychoeducational approaches engage families early; educate families about the etiology and prognosis of the illness and available treatments; provide communication training and recommendations to help the family cope with the situation; and provide problem-solving training and crisis intervention as needed (Goldstein and Miklowitz, 1995). The psychoeducational approaches also involve the use of psychopharmacotherapy. Current approaches, therefore, are grounded in a stress-diathesis model—stress from the environment and diathesis from a genetic predisposition (Hatfield, 1987).

One of the best sources for understanding the relationship between family therapists and schizophrenia in the psychoeducational approach is the work of Anderson, Reiss, and Hogarty (1986) at the University of Pittsburgh Western Psychiatric Institute and Clinic. It sets forth a considerable amount of information stemming from a lengthy project, the Schizophrenic Research Project, and provides a detailed guide for implementing the psychoeducational approach. The authors give the families of schizophrenic patients credit for devising many of the interventions used with schizophrenic persons and their families.

Research studies indicate that psychoeducational interventions with families of schizophrenic patients that are integrated with pharmacotherapy are decidedly more effective than the use of medication alone, and also more effective than routine care consisting of medication management with crisis intervention as needed (Pinsof and Wynne, 1995).

RECENT EVENTS AND TRENDS

During the past two decades or so, the mental health field has become more closely allied with the medical model and the psychiatric profession and seemingly more focused on individual than family formulations of mental health problems. What has been largely missing is a recognition and acknowledgment of the complex interactions between the family and the mentally ill individual, which is a hallmark of the family therapy approach. Whether recent research and political developments will alter this situation remains to be seen.

The U.S. Surgeon General's Report on Mental Health

An event that is bound to affect how mental health and mental illness are regarded and dealt with in the United States is the recent publication of the first surgeon general's report on mental health in late 1999 (U.S. Department of Health and Human Services, 1999). Mental illness is described as a term that refers collectively to all of the diagnosable mental disorders, which are characterized by abnormalities in cognition, emotion, or mood, of the highest integrative aspects of behavior, such as social interactions or planning of future activities. A major message of the report is that mental health conditions are fundamental to health; that mental disorders are real health conditions that have an immense impact on individuals and families. Some major points of the report follow:

- The Congress of the United States proclaimed the 1990s the decade of the brain, and this theme was essentially carried through in the report. The brain has emerged as the central focus for studies of mental health and mental illness. Mental functions are all mediated by the brain, and symptoms of behavior or mental life clearly reflect variations or abnormalities in brain function, according to the report.
- One in five Americans has a mental disorder in any one year, and 15 percent of the adult population use some form of mental health service during the year, according to epidemiological surveys. Approximately 28 to 30 percent of the population has either a mental or an addictive disorder.
- With respect to etiology, the report indicates that although the precise causes of most mental disorders—or of mental health—may not be known, it is known that they are shaped by broad biological, psychological, and sociocultural forces. It emphasizes that the causes of both health and disease are generally viewed as a product of the interaction among biological, psychological, and sociocultural factors. Most mental disorders lie in some combination of genetic and environmental factors, which may be biological or psychosocial.
- A review of research supports two main findings: (1) the efficacy of mental health treatments is well documented, and (2) a range of treatments exists for most mental disorders. Two broad types of intervention are available: (1) psychosocial treatments, e.g., psychotherapy or counseling; and (2) psychopharmacologic treatments. These treatments are often most effective when combined. Studies also demonstrate that treatment is more effective than placebo, and placebo is more effective than no treatment. The report focuses on individual psychotherapy and also men-

tions couples therapy and various forms of family interventions, particularly psychoeducational approaches. Psychodynamic, interpersonal, and cognitive-behavioral therapy are most commonly the focus of treatment research mentioned throughout this report.

- The most prevalent mental disorders in adults are anxiety disorders (Regier et al., 1990).
- Effective treatment of schizophrenia extends well beyond pharmacological therapy; it also includes psychosocial interventions, family interventions, and vocational and psychosocial rehabilitation.
- The major types of psychotherapy for children are supportive, psychodynamic, cognitive-behavioral, interpersonal, and family systemic. A range of efficacious psychosocial and pharmacologic treatments exists for many mental disorders in children, including attention deficit hyperactivity disorder, depression, and the disruptive disorders.
- Families have become essential partners in the delivery of mental health services for children and adolescents.
- With regard to marital or couples therapy, the best-studied interventions are behavioral couples therapy, cognitive-behavioral couples therapy, and emotion-focused couples therapy. A recent review article in which the body of evidence on the effectiveness of couples therapy and programs to prevent marital discord was analyzed found that approximately 65 percent of couples in therapy did improve, and 35 percent of control couples also improved (Christensen and Heavey, 1999). Couples therapy ameliorates relationship distress and appears to alleviate depression. The gains from couples therapy generally last through six months, but there are few long-term assessments. Similarly, interventions to prevent marital discord yield short-term improvements in marital adjustment and stability, but insufficient study of long-term outcomes has been done.
- The consumer movement has produced powerful agents for change in service programs and policy, with increased involvement of both individuals with mental disorders and their families in advocacy, consumer-run services, and mutual support services. Self-help groups are a rapidly increasing part of the

scene; the percentage of adults using such groups grew from 1 percent in the early 1980s to 3 percent a decade later.

- The idea of recovery signals a renewed optimism about the outcome of mental illness, including results achieved through an individual's own self-care. The concept was introduced by consumers who had recovered to the degree that they were able to write about their experiences of coping with symptoms, getting better, and gaining an identity (Deegan, 1988; Leete, 1989; and in Canada, Capponi, 1992), and also was propelled by longitudinal research covering a more positive course for a significant number of patients with severe mental illness (Harding, Strauss, and Zubin, 1992).
- Mental illness and mental health problems must be understood in a social and cultural context; services should be designed in a racially and ethnically sensitive manner.
- Public understanding of mental illness had increased significantly by the 1990s, but the stigma was still strong. The reason for persistence of the stigma appeared to be the fear of violence by the mentally ill (Phelan et al., 1997).
- Normal aging is not characterized by mental or cognitive disorders. Disability in individuals over sixty-five years of age caused by mental illness will become a major health problem in the near future because of demographic changes, with dementia, depression, and schizophrenia presenting particular problems.

The Efficacy of Marital and Family Therapy

A convincing body of empirical research has developed to support the efficacy—that is, the power to produce intended results—of marital and family therapy (MFT), according to Pinsof and Wynne (1995), the editors of a special issue of the *Journal of Marital and Family Therapy* on the effectiveness of MFT. Among the major conclusions reached by Pinsof and Wynne are the following: MFT works. They state that a clear and consistent body of evidence has been accumulated and reviewed that indicates that MFT (MT/FT) is significantly and clinically more efficacious than no psychotherapy for the following patients, disorders, and problems (p. 604, adapted):

- Adult schizophrenia (FT)
- Outpatient depressed women in distressed marriages (MT)
- Marital distress and conflict (MT)
- Adult alcoholism and drug abuse (FT/MT)
- Adult hypertension (MT)
- Elderly dementia (FT)
- Adult obesity (MT)
- Cardiovascular risk factors in adults (FT)
- Adolescent conduct disorder (FT)
- Anorexia in young adolescent girls (FT)
- Adolescent drug abuse (FT)
- Child conduct disorders (FT)
- Aggression and noncompliance in ADHD children (FT)
- Childhood autism (FT)
- Chronic physical illnesses in children (asthma, diabetes, etc.) (FT)
- Child obesity (FT)
- Cardiovascular risk factors in children (FT)

MFT is more effective than standard and/or individual treatments for the following patients, disorders, and problems (p. 604, adapted):

- Adult schizophrenia
- Depressed outpatient women in distressed marriages
- Marital distress
- Adult alcoholism and drug abuse
- Adolescent conduct disorders
- Adolescent drug abuse
- Anorexia in young adolescent females
- Childhood autism
- Various chronic physical illnesses in adults and children

MFT is more cost effective than standard outpatient and/or residential treatment or placement for schizophrenia and severe adolescent conduct disorders and delinquency, according to data from a small number of studies.

Marital and family therapy is not sufficient in itself to treat effectively a variety of severe disorders and problems but is a critical and necessary component in their treatment. Psychoeducational therapies for schizophrenia involve medication and educational components, in addition to family therapy components; and the most effective treatments for childhood autism, severe adolescent conduct disorders, adult and adolescent drug abuse, and adult alcoholism involve additional treatment (group and/or individual and/or medication) and education components. It is hypothesized from the data that "multicomponent, integrative, and problem-focused treatments may be necessary to treat severe behavioral disorders effectively in adults, adolescents, and children [and that] . . . the more severe, pervasive, and disruptive the disorder, the greater the need to include multiple components in effective treatments" (Pinsof and Wynne, 1995, p. 605).

Current Role of Marriage and Family Therapists in Treating Mental Health Problems

Although the full extent of marriage and family therapists' involvement with mental health populations is not known, we can get some indication of it from the American Association for Marriage and Family Therapy's recent Practice Patterns Survey (Doherty and Simmons, 1996). This study surveyed 526 marriage and family therapists from fifteen states, and explored a wide range of variables pertaining to marriage and family therapists, including therapist and client demographics, areas of competency, presenting problems, fees, and so forth.

The research found that MFTs treat a wide variety of mental health and relational problems. In terms of traditional mental health issues, the authors found that depression and anxiety were among the top five presenting problems treated by survey participants. Personality disorders represented 5.1 percent of presenting problems, and the more serious mental illnesses such as bipolar disorder and schizophrenia represented 1.2 percent and .4 percent of referrals respectively. MFTs also viewed themselves as trained and competent to treat a wide range of mental health problems, including: anxiety disorders (93.2 percent), mood disorders (88.4 percent), personality disorders (72.9 percent), phobias (54.7 percent), schizophrenia (23.8 percent), and other psychotic disorders (15.9 percent).

These findings indicate that MFTs are already extensively involved in treating a wide range of mental health issues as well as bringing to this treatment their unique recognition of the impact of these problems on interpersonal and family relationships. As MFTs become increasingly involved with treating these mental health issues from a relationship perspective, the need is becoming apparent for a broader diagnostic system than that provided by the current individually focused DSM-IV. Such a diagnostic system would recognize the impact of mental health problems on marital and family relationships and the importance of addressing relationship issues as well as individual symptomatology, which is often treated from a psychobiological perspective.

Relationship Diagnosis and Dysfunctional Family Patterns

A significant start has been made recently by family therapists under the leadership of Florence Kaslow (1996) toward developing a classification system for assessing both distressed relationships in close interpersonal systems and the individuals within those relationships. This work provides a foundation for the conceptualization and formalization of relational diagnoses. To date, family therapists have lacked a basis for communicating clearly about their dynamic evaluation of relational difficulties and thus have been severely hampered in their efforts to communicate with other professionals and to convince insurers that marital and family therapies are cost effective with positive outcomes. Kaslow's (1996) *Handbook of Relational Diagnosis and Dysfunctional Family Patterns* is a definite step in the direction of constructing the nomenclature called for by the Group for the Advancement of Psychiatry (1970) three decades ago. In the interim, some work had been done toward such a goal by the American Psychological Association's Division of Family Psychology (founded in 1987) and an interorganizational Coalition on Family Diagnosis (established in 1988). The various relational diagnoses offered are grouped under three headings:

Child and adolescent focused. Child and adolescent depression (Kaslow, Deering, and Ash, 1996); learning disabilities and attention deficit hyperactivity disorders (Culbertson and Silovsky, 1996); oppositional behavior and conduct disorders (Alexander and Pugh, 1996); and children with life-threatening illnesses (Kazak and Simms, 1996).

Couple focused. Anxiety disorders (Rosen, 1996); borderline disorders (Solomon, 1996); sadomasochistic interactions (Glickauf-Hughes, 1996); antisocial and histrionic personality disorders (Nichols, 1996); personality disorders (Young and Gluhoski, 1996); affective disorders (Gollan, Gortner, and Jacobson, 1996); abusive spousal relationships (Walker, 1996); and sexual and gender identity disorders (Stayton, 1996).

Family focused. Relationship conflict inventory conceptualization (Bodin, 1996); intrafamily child sexual abuse (Trepper and Nieder, 1996); incest survivor syndrome (Kirschner and Kirschner, 1996); dissociative identity disorder (Koedam, 1996); mood disorders (Keitner, Miller, and Ryan, 1996); substance abuse and addictive disorders (Williams, 1996); eating disorders (Levine, 1996); evil in human personality (Charny, 1996); chronic illness (Barth, 1996); and panic disorder (de la Gandara and Pedraza, 1996).

Although the Kaslow volume offers a considerable amount of assistance for clinicians, it is recognized that it is not a definitive product. A primary goal was to "foster ideas about relational classification and stimulate further dialogue" leading toward a definitive manual of relational diagnosis. The editor views the work as congruent with the work of others that have recently sought to "go beyond the somewhat narrow focus of the DSM-IV" and to lift relational problems above second- or third-class status (Kaslow, 1996, p. vii). It provides some basis for conducting the research that is required to solidly establish diagnostic categories and proposed criteria for a more definitive relational diagnosis approach.

A large amount of work remains before individuals and groups outside the family field are persuaded of the importance of family issues in classification. Noted psychiatrist and family therapy researcher David Reiss, in a foreword, writes:

> Concepts and approaches, such as those in this book, will form an attractive foundation for a systematic approach to classification that could receive wide acceptance among family therapists.
>
> But a deal should be struck. Family researchers should not formulate and disseminate systems of classification unless clinicians agree to participate in field trials of these systems. . . . Extensive field trials would test the reliability and clinical utility of these systems. This pattern of transaction, within the family field, may be the most important factor in influencing clinicians outside of it. (Reiss, 1996, p. xv)

FUTURE DIRECTIONS

The Need for an Integrated Approach

The need for a truly integrated biopsychosocial approach for treating mental health problems would seem to be strongly suggested by the material outlined previously. The surgeon general's report on mental health emphasizes that the etiology of mental disorders is shaped by broad biological, psychological, and sociocultural forces. As such, it makes sense to treat these disorders from a biopsychosocial perspective. This report also indicates that effective treatment of illnesses, such as schizophrenia, extends well beyond pharmacological therapy and must include psychosocial interventions, family interventions, and vocational and psychosocial rehabilitation. It emphasizes that families have become essential partners in the delivery of mental health services.

The importance of an integrated approach is further emphasized by Pinsof and Wynne (1995), who note that marital and family therapy is not sufficient in itself to effectively treat a variety of severe disorders and problems but is a critical and necessary component in their treatment. They write that, "the more severe, pervasive, and disruptive the disorder, the greater need to include multiple components in effective treatments" (p. 605).

There is also an increasing recognition that interpersonal relationships and family dynamics may contribute to the maintenance of certain mental health problems, and that family interventions may contribute to the maintenance of gains and the prevention of relapse with many disorders. This appears to be particularly the case with depressed women (Pinsof and Wynne, 1995). Gore and Carter, in their chapter in this text on family therapy for panic disorder, note the importance of interpersonal interventions in the successful treatment of anxiety and panic disorders. MacFarlane, in Chapter 7 of this text, suggests that family therapy may assist in the resolution of obsessive-compulsive disorder (OCD) symptoms, which are embedded in problematic interpersonal relationships, and which do not improve with standard individual behavioral treatments.

Family therapists working from a systems perspective may be uniquely suited to implement an integrated approach. Therapists working from a systems perspective will quickly grasp the reciprocal relationships between biological, psychological, and social levels of mental illness and recognize the importance of addressing all levels of the problem system in their treatment planning. Their familiarity with negotiating the complexities of family systems can translate well in dealing with the complexities of treatment systems where different mental health professionals work from different models or constructions of reality, whether individual, biomedical, or social. Working from a metaperspective that includes an awareness of their own place in the treatment system, they can assist in resolving treatment impasses and facilitate increased understanding and communication among members of multidisciplinary treatment teams.

The chapters included in this text present a broad range of family therapy approaches for intervening in mental health problems. The models outlined include behavioral and cognitive-behavioral approaches, communication skills training, contextual therapy, systemic therapy, and brief therapy interventions, among others. All of these approaches are relationship focused and involve significant family members in the treatment process. The authors have found that these approaches can provide effective treatment and enhance the quality of life for clients and families struggling with mental health problems. We hope that these chapters will inspire more family therapists to work with mental health populations and more mental health professionals to incorporate a family systems perspective into their work with individual clients.

REFERENCES

Adamce, C. (1996). *How to live with a mentally ill person.* New York: John Wiley and Sons.

Alexander, J. F. and Pugh, C. A. (1996). Oppositional behavior and conduct disorders of children and youth. In F. W. Kaslow (Ed.), *Handbook of relational diagnosis and dysfunctional family patterns* (pp. 210-224). New York: John Wiley and Sons.

Anderson, C. M., Reiss, D. J., and Hogarty, G. E. (1986). *Schizophrenia and the family.* New York: Guilford Press.

Azrin, N. H. and Teichner, G. (1998). Evaluation of an instructional program for improving medication compliance for chronically mentally ill outpatients. *Behaviour Research and Therapy, 36,* 849-861.

Bachrach, L. L. (1996). What do patients say about program planning? Perspectives from the patient-authored literature. In B. Abosh and A. Collins (Eds.), *Mental illness in the family* (pp. 7-25). Toronto: University of Toronto Press.

Barth, J. C. (1996). Chronic illness and the family. In F. W. Kaslow (Ed.), *Handbook of relational diagnosis and dysfunctional family patterns* (pp. 496-508). New York: John Wiley and Sons.

Bateson, G., Jackson, D. D., Haley, J., and Weakland, J. (1956). Toward a theory of schizophrenia. *Behavioral Science, 1,* 251-264.

Bodin, A. M. (1996). Relationship conflict—verbal and physical: Conceptualizing an inventory for assessing process and content. In F. W. Kaslow (Ed.), *Handbook of relational diagnosis and dysfunctional family patterns* (pp. 371-393). New York: John Wiley and Sons.

Broderick, C. B. and Schrader, S. S. (1981). The history of professional marriage and family therapy. In A. S. Gurman and D. P. Kniskern (Eds.), *Handbook of family therapy* (pp. 5-35). New York: Brunner/Mazel.

Broderick, C. B. and Schrader, S. S. (1991). The history of professional marriage and family therapy. In A. S. Gurman and D. P. Kniskern (Eds.), *Handbook of family therapy* (Volume II, pp. 3-40). New York: Brunner/Mazel.

Brown, G. W., Birley, J. L., and Wing, J. K. (1972). Influence on family life on the course of schizophrenic disorders: A replication. *British Journal of Psychiatry, 121,* 241-258.

Capponi, P. (1992). *Upstairs in the crazy house: The life of a psychiatric survivor.* New York: Viking.

Charny, I. W. (1996). Evil in human personality: Disorders of doing harm to others in family relationships. In F. W. Kaslow (Ed.), *Handbook of relational diagnosis and dysfunctional family patterns* (pp. 477-495). New York: John Wiley and Sons.

Christensen, A. and Heavey, C. L. (1999). Interventions for couples. *Annual Review of Psychology, 50,* 165-190.

Culbertson, J. L. and Silovsky, J. F. (1996). Learning disabilities and attention deficit hyperactivity disorders: Their impact on children's significant others. In F. W. Kaslow (Ed.), *Handbook of relational diagnosis and dysfunctional family patterns* (pp. 186-209). New York: John Wiley and Sons.

de la Gandara, J. E. and Pedraza, A. (1996). Panic disorder and the family. In F. W. Kaslow (Ed.), *Handbook of relational diagnosis and dysfunctional family patterns* (pp. 509-522). New York: John Wiley and Sons.

Deegan, P. E. (1988). Recovery: The lived experience of rehabilitation. *Psychiatric Rehabilitation Journal, 11,* 11-19.

Dixon, L., Lyles, A., Scott, J., Lehman, A., Postrado, L., Goldman, H., and McGlynn, E. (1999). Services to families of adults with schizophrenia: From treatment recommendations to dissemination. *Psychiatric Services, 50,* 233-238.

Doherty, W. J. and Simmons, D. S. (1996). Clinical practice patterns of marriage and family therapists: A national survey of therapists and their clients. *Journal of Marital and Family Therapy, 22,* 9-25.

Droogan, J. and Bannigan, K. (1997). A review of psychosocial family interventions for schizophrenia. *Nursing Times, 93,* 46-47.

Engel, G. L. (1977). The need for a new medical model: A challenge for biomedicine. *Science, 196,* 129-136.

Fromm-Reichman, F. (1948). Notes on the development of treatment of schizophrenics by psychoanalytic psychotherapy. *Psychiatry, 11,* 263-273.

Gallagher, S. K. and Mechanic, D. (1996). Living with the mentally ill: Effects on the health and functioning of other household members. *Social Science and Medicine, 42,* 1691-1701.

Glickauf-Hughes, C. (1996). Sadomasochistic interaction. In F. W. Kaslow (Ed.), *Handbook of relational diagnosis and dysfunctional family patterns* (pp. 270-286). New York: John Wiley and Sons.

Goldman, H. H. (1998). Deinstitutionalization and community care: Social welfare policy as mental health policy. *Harvard Review of Psychiatry, 6,* 219-222.

Goldstein, M. J. and Miklowitz, D. J. (1995). The effectiveness of psychoeducational family therapy in the treatment of schizophrenic disorders. *Journal of Marital and Family Therapy, 21,* 361-376.

Gollan, J. K., Gortner, E. T., and Jacobson, N. S. (1996). Partner relational problems and affective disorders. In F. W. Kaslow (Ed.), *Handbook of relational diagnosis and dysfunctional family patterns* (pp. 322-337). New York: John Wiley and Sons.

Graham, R. (1988). *Building community support for people: A plan for mental health in Ontario.* Toronto: The Provincial Community Mental Health Committee.

Grob, G. N. (1983). *Mental illness and American society, 1975-1940.* Princeton, NJ: Princeton University Press.

Grob, G. N. (1991). *From asylum to community: Mental health policy in modern America.* Princeton, NJ: Princeton University Press.

Grob, G. N. (1994). *The mad among us: A history of the care of America's mentally ill.* New York: Free Press.

Group for the Advancement of Psychiatry (GAP) (1970). *The field of family therapy* (GAP Report No. 78). New York: Author.

Haley, J. (1975). Why a mental health clinic should avoid family therapy. *Journal of Marriage and Family Counseling, 1,* 1-13.

Haley, J. (1980). *Leaving home: The therapy of disturbed young people.* New York: McGraw-Hill.

Harding, C., Strauss, J. S., and Zubin, J. (1992). Chronicity in schizophrenia: Revisited. *British Journal of Psychiatry, 161,* 27-37.

Hatfield, A. B. (1987). Families as caregivers: A historical perspective. In A. B. Hatfield and H. P. Lefley (Eds.), *Families of the mentally ill: Coping and adaptation* (pp. 3-29). New York: Guilford Press.

Hatfield, A. B. (1991). The national alliance for the mentally ill: A decade later. *Community Mental Health Journal, 27,* 95-103.

Hatfield, A. B. (Ed.) (1994). *Family interventions in mental illness.* San Francisco: Jossey-Bass.

Jutras, S. and Veilleux, F. (1991). Informal caregiving: Correlates of perceived burden. *Canadian Journal of Aging, 10,* 40-55.

Kaslow, F. W. (Ed.) (1996). *Handbook of relational diagnosis and dysfunctional family patterns.* New York: John Wiley and Sons.

Kaslow, N. J., Deering, C. G., and Ash, P. (1996). Relational diagnosis of child and adolescent depression. In F. W. Kaslow (Ed.), *Handbook of relational diagnosis and dysfunctional family patterns* (pp. 171-185). New York: John Wiley and Sons.

Kazak, A. E. and Simms, S. (1996). Children with life-threatening illnesses: Psychological difficulties and interpersonal relationships. In F. W. Kaslow (Ed.), *Handbook of relational diagnosis and dysfunctional family patterns* (pp. 225-238). New York: John Wiley and Sons.

Keitner, G. L., Miller, I. W., and Ryan, C. E. (1996). Mood disorders and the family. In F. W. Kaslow (Ed.), *Handbook of relational diagnosis and dysfunctional family patterns* (pp. 434-447). New York: John Wiley and Sons.

Kirschner, S. and Kirschner, D. A. (1996). Relational components of the incest survivor syndrome. In F. W. Kaslow (Ed.), *Handbook of relational diagnosis and dysfunctional family patterns* (pp. 407-419). New York: John Wiley and Sons.

Koedam, W. S. (1996). Dissociative identity disorders in relational contexts. In F. W. Kaslow (Ed.), *Handbook of relational diagnosis and dysfunctional family patterns* (pp. 420-433). New York: John Wiley and Sons.

Lansky, M. (Ed.) (1981). *Family therapy and major psychopathology.* New York: Grune and Stratton.

Lansky, M. (Ed.) (1985). *Family approaches to major psychiatric disorders.* Washington, DC: American Psychiatric Press.

Leete, E. (1989). How I perceive and manage my illness. *Schizophrenia Bulletin, 8,* 605-609.

Leff, J. P. and Vaughn, C. E. (1985). *Expressed emotion in families.* New York: Guilford Press.

Lefley, H. P. (1996). *Family caregiving in mental illness.* Thousand Oaks, CA: Sage.

Levine, P. (1996). Eating disorders and their impact on family systems. In F. W. Kaslow (Ed.), *Handbook of relational diagnosis and dysfunctional family patterns* (pp. 463-476). New York: John Wiley and Sons.

Lidz, T., Fleck, S., and Cornelison, A. R. (1965). *Schizophrenia and the family.* New York: International Universities Press.

Madanes, C. (1981). *Strategic family therapy.* San Francisco: Jossey-Bass.

Nichols, W. C. (1996). Persons with antisocial and histrionic personality disorders. In F. W. Kaslow (Ed.), *Handbook of relational diagnosis and dysfunctional family patterns* (pp. 287-299). New York: John Wiley and Sons.

Nichols, W. C. and Everett, C. A. (1986). *Systemic family therapy: An integrative approach.* New York: Guilford Press.

Penn, D. L. and Mueser, K. T. (1996). Research update on the psychosocial treatment of schizophrenia. *American Journal of Psychiatry, 153,* 607-617.

Perlmutter, R. (1996). *A family approach to psychiatric disorders.* Washington, DC: American Psychiatric Press.

Phelan, J., Link, B., Stueve, A., and Pesocolido, B. (1997, August). *Public conceptions of mental illness in 1950, in 1996: Has sophistication increased? Has stigma declined?* Paper presented at the meeting of the American Sociological Association, Toronto, Canada.

Pinsof, W. M. and Wynne, L. C. (1995). The efficacy of marital and family therapy: An empirical overview, conclusions, and recommendations. *Journal of Marital and Family Therapy, 21,* 585-613.

Regier, D. A., Farmer, M. E., Rae, D. S., Locke, B. Z., Keith, S. J., Judd, L. L., and Goodwin, F. K. (1990). Comorbidity of mental disorders with alcohol and other drug abuse. Results from the Epidemiologic Catchment Area (ECA) Study. *Journal of the American Medical Association, 264,* 2511-2518.

Reiss, D. (1996). Foreword. In F. W. Kaslow (Ed.), *Handbook of relational diagnosis and dysfunctional family patterns* (pp. ix-xv). New York: John Wiley and Sons.

Rosen, A. (1996). Anxiety disorders as they impact on couples and families. In F. W. Kaslow (Ed.), *Handbook of relational diagnosis and dysfunctional family patterns* (pp. 239-250). New York: John Wiley and Sons.

Solomon, M. F. (1996). Understanding and treating couples with borderline disorders. In F. W. Kaslow (Ed.), *Handbook of relational diagnosis and dysfunctional family patterns* (pp. 251-269). New York: John Wiley and Sons.

Solomon, P. and Draine, J. (1995). Consumer case management and attitudes concerning family relations among persons with mental illness. *Psychiatric Quarterly, 66,* 249-261.

Song, L. Y., Beigel, D. E., and Milligan, S. E. (1997). Predictors of depressive symptomatology among lower social class caregivers of persons with chronic mental illness. *Community Mental Health, 33,* 269-286.

Stayton, W. R. (1996). Sexual and gender identity disorders in a relational perspective. In F. W. Kaslow (Ed.), *Handbook of relational diagnosis and dysfunctional family patterns* (pp. 357-370). New York: John Wiley and Sons.

Trepper, T. S. and Nieder, D. M. (1996). Intrafamily child sexual abuse. In F. W. Kaslow (Ed.), *Handbook of relational diagnosis and dysfunctional family patterns* (pp. 394-406). New York: John Wiley and Sons.

U. S. Department of Health and Human Services (1999). *Mental health: A report of the Surgeon General.* Rockville, MD: U. S. Department of Health and Human Services, Substance Abuse and Mental Health Services Administration Center for Mental Health Services, National Institutes of Health, National Institute of Mental Health.

Vaughn, C. E. and Leff, J. P. (1981). Patterns of emotional response in relatives of schizophrenic patients. *Schizophrenia Bulletin, 7,* 43-44.

Walker, L. E. A. (1996). Assessment of abusive spousal relationships. In F. W. Kaslow (Ed.), *Handbook of relational diagnosis and dysfunctional family patterns* (pp. 338-356). New York: John Wiley and Sons.

Walsh, F. (1996). Mental illness: What have we learned? In B. Abosh and A. Collins (Eds.), *Mental illness in the family* (pp. 26-37). Toronto: University of Toronto Press.

Williams, T. G. (1996). Substance abuse and addictive personality disorders. In F. W. Kaslow (Ed.), *Handbook of relational diagnosis and dysfunctional family patterns* (pp. 448-462). New York: John Wiley and Sons.

Wynne, L. C. (1978). Family relationships and communications. Concluding comments. In L. C. Wynne, R. M. Cromwell, and S. Matthysse (Eds.), *The nature of schizophrenia* (pp. 534-541). New York: John Wiley and Sons.

Young, J. E. and Gluhoski, V. L. (1996). Schema-focused diagnosis for personality disorders. In F. W. Kaslow (Ed.), *Handbook of relational diagnosis and dysfunctional family patterns* (pp. 300-321). New York: John Wiley and Sons.

Chapter 2

The Partnership Model: Working with Families of People with Serious Mental Illness

Eric D. Johnson

INTRODUCTION

Family therapy with families who have a member with serious mental illness (i.e., those diagnosed with schizophrenia, manic-depressive, or schizoaffective disorders) has a long but not necessarily glorious history. The beginnings of family therapy in the United States, in fact, involved families with schizophrenic members, most of whom were interviewed in the context of the ill member's hospitalization. Based on earlier psychodynamic ideas such as the "schizophrenogenic mother" (Fromm-Reichmann, 1948), many of these family therapy pioneers speculated that family communication and affiliation dynamics were responsible for causing schizophrenic symptoms (Bateson et al., 1956; Lidz and Fleck, 1960; Wynne and Singer, 1963). These theories were tested in research studies during the 1960s and found wanting; those studies concluded that the theories of family etiology of mental illness failed to produce any variables that could be clearly linked to the development of schizophrenia (Meissner, 1970; Mishler and Waxler, 1965). However, long before they had been adequately tested, therapeutic interventions based on these theories were already taking place, often to the detriment of families of the mentally ill, who felt blamed by family therapists for causing their family member's illness (Hatfield and Lefley, 1987).

In the 1970s, the focus of attention shifted to examining the course, rather than the cause, of serious mental illness. British researchers developed the concept of expressed emotion (EE), and found that high

EE levels (especially negative emotion) of family members correlated with patient relapse or rehospitalization (Brown, Birley, and Wing, 1972; Vaughn and Leff, 1976, 1981). They concluded that people with schizophrenia may be especially sensitive to too much stimulation (physical or emotional), and seem to function best in environments that are structured, not extremely complex or demanding, and are neutrally stimulating (Brown, Birley, and Wing, 1972; Wing, 1978). These findings suggested that there were steps that could be taken by families to lessen the likelihood of relapse (Goldstein, 1992; Miklowitz et al., 1989).

In the late 1970s, a grassroots organization of professionals and family members developed into the fledgling National Alliance for the Mentally Ill (NAMI). Initially conceived as a self-help support movement for family members struggling with the problems of having a mentally ill member, this organization has achieved remarkable political influence over the past two decades in the areas of mental health legislation and funding of community resources in the deinstitutionalization process. NAMI has been critical of the EE studies, feeling that they continue to "blame" families for mental illness, and suggesting that "unusual" family characteristics might be the *result* of having to cope with a family member who behaves in unusual ways (Hatfield, 1991; Lefley, 1992).

In the 1980s, clinicians began to develop the possibilities suggested by the EE researchers into a new approach to helping families with a mentally ill member. This new approach sought to avoid blaming and attempted to lower emotional expression through the use of a "psychoeducational" methodology (Anderson, Reiss, and Hogarty, 1986; Bernheim and Lehman, 1985; Falloon, Boyd, and McGill, 1984). The approach was based on a "stress-diathesis" theory; some people have a genetic predisposition (diathesis), which makes them more vulnerable to break down under stress. If the vulnerability is a heart condition, these people are more likely than others to have a heart attack under stressful conditions. If the vulnerability is a mental condition, they are more likely to have a psychotic breakdown under stressful conditions (Falloon and Liberman, 1983; Zubin, 1986). The focus of psychoeducational approaches has been to help normalize the experience of the family, avoid reference to family etiology, identify biogenetic influence factors, provide information about medication use, and train family members in reducing emotional expression while dealing with problematic situations. This has usually been done in a group format, either through day-long workshops or an ongoing series of topic-focused meetings (Lefley, 1996; McFarlane, 1991; Miklowitz and Hooley, 1998).

Although psychoeducationally focused groups, led either by community mental health professionals or families in the NAMI movement, have been very successful in helping families to better understand and deal with the illness of their family member, these groups have generally been limited to the kinds of families who are attracted to NAMI (predominantly white, suburban, and upper middle class). The engagement of lower-income families, urban families, and minority families in voluntary psychoeducational groups has been extremely limited to date. In addition, for many families group psychoeducation has not been enough to help them overcome the problems they experience in trying to cope with an illness that presents a chronic but uneven pattern. Therefore, it is important that a model for working with families with a seriously mentally ill member be utilized that can take advantage of the gains made in psychoeducational group formats, while adding other possibilities that will help to engage previously under-served populations, as well as combining psychoeducational and psychotherapeutic help for families.

The Partnership Model presented in this chapter was developed after interviews with over 200 families in Mercer County, New Jersey. All families had at least one member with a serious mental illness having had at least one previous hospitalization for a psychotic episode involving mood or thought disorder. The ill members were fairly evenly divided by gender and urban/suburban residence and distributed by age and length of illness. The families represented a cross section of ethnic groups (European-American, African-American, and Hispanic-American) and socioeconomic status (upper-middle class, lower-middle class, and lower class) in the community, which runs the spectrum from suburban Princeton to urban Trenton. Referrals of families came from a wide variety of sources, including the community mental health center case management unit, a clinician-led family support group, outpatient clinics, inpatient programs, the county jail system, and the local NAMI chapter. The study, which is more fully described elsewhere (Johnson, 1998, 2000, in submission), found that both environmental stressors and illness-related stressors had significant negative effects on the community functioning of people with mental illness, but that this was buffered somewhat by general family functioning, and considerably buffered by the family's sense of competence in managing problems related to the illness. This is of some significance because it suggests that the lives of mentally ill members, as well as other family members, can be improved if the family feels more confident and competent in handling the illness.

SETTING

The Partnership Model is a way of thinking about and working with families and their ill members, rather than a specific program. As such, elements of this model can be incorporated into a variety of programs and settings, depending on the extent of resources. For example, in a number of community mental health settings in New Jersey, several mental health clinicians are designated as "family support staff." The family support personnel work with both families and the other mental health program personnel to integrate the concerns of family members, as well as to provide support directly to family members. The elements of psychoeducation and family therapy are combined by family support staff in both the group format and with families separately. The group format is preferred, since it is more cost effective and requires less time; useful meeting places for the groups have included churches and libraries, as these are often less intimidating settings than mental health clinics or hospitals. They also have the advantage of being located in people's neighborhoods, which adds to the convenience factor, since most of these meetings are in the evenings.

However, the family support staff who are working in these mental health programs have found that some families are not comfortable with the group format. This affects some middle-class families who are feeling stigmatized, minority families who feel out of place, and lower-income urban families who feel burdened and overwhelmed by having to go out to a meeting. These families have sometimes been seen in individual family meetings (which most families prefer in their own homes). A second solution has involved small group meetings, in which the family support staff member combines two or three families from his or her own caseload, so the staff member represents a "common denominator" and families are not asked to join a group of strangers with an unknown group leader. A third option involves the use of small groups organized by ethnic or neighborhood similarity (these have been most effective when they involved staff or family leadership of the same ethnic or neighborhood identity).

Community mental health centers have had to organize a "dual thrust" approach to incorporating the model, with one thrust gearing programs to the suburban (largely European-American) population, and a second thrust gearing programs to minority families and to lower-income urban families. Particularly when dealing with low-income families, it has been useful to provide transportation, child care, and food if they are going to be involved in group meetings. Agency commitment to providing the resources to ensure that families can get to meetings, or to provide staff availability to them at home, is essential to the success of the urban thrust. A major component of the Partnership Model is the recognition that families with a mentally ill member represent a wide range of experiences, and their uniqueness deserves respect. Rather than forcing families to fit into a program, it attempts to mold programs to fit the families.

In addition to the family support staff in the mental health centers, other community mental health program units have also been able to benefit from the model by incorporating family and mental health "team" meetings into day-treatment and residential programs, especially those which work on the "clubhouse" model. Although these programs do not routinely provide ongoing family contact (families who express an interest in this are referred to the family support staff), this allows for increased sharing between family and mental health providers, and the family support staff help provide continuity among programs.

TREATMENT MODEL

The Difference Between Mental Illness and Emotional Disturbance

The first important distinction made in applying the Partnership Model is the difference between biologically based mental problems and emotionally based mental problems. Most diagnoses of mental problems rely on the classifications of the *Diagnostic and Statistical Manual of Mental Disorders,* Fourth Edition, the DSM-IV (American Psychiatric Association, 1994). However, the authors of the DSM-IV have explicitly avoided references to etiology, opting to present clusters of symptoms to define categories of problems. This presents two dilemmas for clinicians: there is no useful way of assessing dimensionality within a category (i.e., less severe to more severe symptoms), and there is no useful way of differentiating conditions that have a demonstrated biological basis from those which are situationally or emotionally based. In light of advances in medical technology (Torrey, Bowler, and Taylor, 1995; Whybrow, 1997), NAMI has argued successfully in several states to get insurance coverage parity for people with biologically based mental illness. Thus, it is important that clinicians separate in their minds those problems that are related to a biological illness and those problems that are emotionally based. The emotionally based disorders might best be thought of as "survival strategies" or ways that people have developed to cope with a stressful, dysfunctional, or dangerous environment.

The importance of this for people with a biologically based disorder is that there is almost by definition an overlay of emotional disturbance in coping with a biological deficit. (The same phenomenon can be seen in families with a chronically ill member, a severe acute illness, or a biologically based learning deficit.) Many of the most troublesome behaviors of people with a thought or mood disorder, both for family members and for mental health clinicians, are behaviors related to their emotional disturbance (e.g., personality disorder) features, rather than features of the biological illness. It is important to distinguish whether a particular pattern of behavior requires increased medication to control psychotic symptoms or whether the ill member needs help adjusting survival strategies in the current situation. A key component of this model is the recognition of the type of problem encountered, so the most useful solution can be found; otherwise, the three components of the team (the person with a mental illness, his or her family members, and the mental health professionals) will be working at cross-purposes.

This issue of attribution of the problem is a significant one for family members. We have found that family members who understand the implications of having a biological illness have an easier time dealing with problematic behaviors than family members who attribute the illness to other problems or to "lack of willpower." This has been the basis of much of the development of the psychoeducational approach over the past two decades. However, without an understanding of both the biological components of the illness (e.g., hearing voices, becoming more grandiose) and the emotional disturbance overlay, family members are likely to misinterpret problems or to become frustrated and annoyed at those behaviors which were not identified to them as part of the illness (e.g., lack of motivation, blaming others for their troubles).

The Developmental Approach: Understanding Individual and Family Growth

The second key component of the model involves understanding that the normal developmental progression of the life cycle is interrupted both for the person experiencing a mental illness and for the family. This presents a number of difficulties related to normative expectations. If the ill member continues to believe that he or she can pursue the goals previously envisioned, frustration will lead to an increase in the symptoms of emotional disturbance. This is particularly a problem for people who were reasonably high functioning before the effects of the illness limited their life prospects; they are often caught in a dilemma in which the work they would like to do is too stressful and the work they can manage is too boring. The problem of reconsidering expectations is compounded if family members continue to harbor their original hopes and dreams for the ill member and are themselves unable to change their expectations. This will lead to demands of performance or behavior that are unattainable by the ill member and increase the expression of negative emotion in frustrating conflict between the ill member and other family members.

This model approaches problem solution from a developmental perspective, which suggests that there are very few behaviors (other than the extremely psychotic or sociopathic) that are not appropriate to some level of development. For example, a forty-year-old man may be behaving in a manner that is inappropriate for a forty year old, but may be a perfectly normal temper tantrum for a five-year-old child. The problem is that a large person can throw a large (and frequently intimidating) temper tantrum. When this happens, both family members and mental health professionals often make the mistake of assessing the mentally ill person on the basis of his or her chronological age rather than the developmental (socioemotional) age. One of the cruelest things done to people with mental illness, often out of a misguided sense of kindness or respect, is to treat them as though they were their chronological age rather than their developmental age. This has resulted in increased homelessness and the inability to commit people to a hospital when necessary. This problem is further compounded by the uneven socioemotional development demonstrated by people with mental illness, so that they are not *consistently functioning* at a particular age. This leads to a confusion over capacity versus motivation for both family members and mental health professionals.

In our work with family members, we have encouraged them to rely on their previous experience in child rearing in order to assess the appropriate age for the behavior *of the moment* and respond with the appropriate parental response to a person of that age exhibiting that behavior. In the example given above, the response to the forty-year-old man throwing a five-year-old's temper tantrum would be: "This is unacceptable behavior; you will have to go to your room now." Family members are often surprised that when they respond this way, the ill member stomps off to his room, usually saying something like: "You can't boss me around. I'm not a kid, you know." The intervention works because it is syntonic with the ill member's level of development at that moment. The worst thing that a family member (or mental health program staff) can say at that moment is: "Act your age!" If the ill person were able to act his or her chronological age, we would not be seeing the behavior. Therefore, other members of the team need to respond in a way that is congruent for the ill member at that moment and within his or her repertoire. Failure to appreciate the developmental component will leave family members and mental health professionals frustrated and unsuccessful in helping the mentally ill with their community adjustment.

We have also found that siblings have a difficult time accepting the behaviors of the ill member, largely because their developmental framework is different. They operate from a frame of reference that suggests that once you have mastered a task you should be capable and responsible for continuing to perform that task. However, the ill member is likely to be affected by developmental inconsistencies that are difficult for the sibling to appreciate. Thus, siblings are likely to need more help than parents in understanding and dealing with the developmental differences between themselves and their ill sibling.

Psychoeducation and Family Therapy

The third component of the model involves the recognition that psychoeducation and family therapy need to be combined in a plan that allows for the uniqueness of each family and situation. Although some families will find additional information sufficient to cope with the demands of mental illness, most families will need a greater level of support. Through a cooperative effort of NAMI and the community mental health professionals, especially the family support team, we have found that it is possible to tailor a plan for each family. Most psychoeducation frameworks include the following components: understanding the diagnosis of mental illness; understanding what causes (and does not cause) mental illness; appreciating the effects of mental illness on the ill member, as well as on other family members; understanding the role of medication in treating the problem; dealing with common problems; and getting help from the mental health system. In our area, the local NAMI chapter offers a repeated course called "Family to Family," which is led by trained family members in a group format. A similar course is offered by the family support team at various locations around the county. However, for families who are not ready for or interested in a group format, the same information can be provided individually. We have found that family members often forget what they learned in the courses and need "refreshers," which might be structured as follow-up groups or done in the context of individual family work.

Just as families differ in the amount of educational input they need to feel confident in their knowledge of the problem, families demonstrate many differences in their levels of function and dysfunction and their abilities to handle problems. While the psychoeducational component focuses primarily on the biologically based disorder, family therapy focuses primarily on handling the problems of emotional disturbance. The family therapy component of this model has been strongly influenced by the structural family therapy school of thinking (Colapinto, 1991; Minuchin and Fishman, 1981). Structural interventions are often necessary to help the family find a new direction when they are bogged down repeating an unproductive pattern. Integral to the structural model is the importance of the functioning of the family to its members. This is nowhere more important than in work with people with serious mental illness, for whom the family represents their greatest resource—and often their greatest sense of frustration. Because of the developmental issues mentioned earlier, many people with a mental illness are functioning at a much younger level than their chronological age. They both recognize their dependence on their families and resent it. Because this pattern is very similar to the developmental needs of children, situationally oriented family therapy approaches that are designed to fit families with minor children will also be adaptable to the needs of the seriously mentally ill and their families. Structural family therapy appears well suited to this, as it utilizes decision making and boundary setting in the immediate situation to reorganize the system for problem solving.

There are certainly some differences in how decision making happens if all (or most) of the family are currently adults, as is the case for many families with a mentally ill member. It is important that (where possible) both parents and siblings of the ill member be involved in decision making and action. Nevertheless, we have found that the connection between parents and their ill child is very different from the connection between siblings and their ill sibling. Siblings tend to feel less obligated than do parents, and they often present as peripheral and uninterested in becoming more invested. In this situation, we have employed a strategy of asking each family member to do something with or for the ill member on a regular basis (e.g., help out with shopping, go to a movie, have the ill member over for a meal, provide respite care on a periodic basis, take the ill member to appointments). When the strategy of defining and containing contributions is utilized, siblings often demonstrate that they are more connected to the ill member than it initially appeared—that their frustration and distance have more to do with the fear of the illness taking over their lives than alienation from their sibling. This is one of many examples we have found in our work that demonstrates the importance of the clinician getting to know the individual family well enough to know what kinds of structural interventions are within their "range of change." If intervention strategies are employed that are outside the family's perceived range, they will fail, and the family members will be seen as "resistant."

Structural family therapy interventions are utilized to support and enhance the competence of the family in solving problems, as well as for the clinician to help families reorganize their ways of problem solving. The ability of the mentally ill member will vary considerably in this process. Generally, people with manic-depressive (bipolar) illness retain a higher level of functional ability during periods of remission and can be expected to contribute more to the changes in pattern than can people with schizophrenia or schizoaffective disorders. Also, within a given family, the ability of the ill member to contribute to decisions will vary in accordance with the shifting developmental differences mentioned earlier.

It is important that as many members as possible become involved in this psychoeducational/family therapy component. The more people in the ill member's family, extended family, and community network who can be enlisted, the better. In this way, each member can take a small but clearly defined piece of responsibility, freeing the central caregiver from an excessive load, and increasing the workable social network for the ill member (who may have few social connections outside the family). For this reason, it is often useful to include "network therapy" as well as family therapy, having meetings that involve church members, neighbors, or other members of the community who are willing to be helpful in a defined way.

The Partnership Team: Complementary Roles of the Patient, Family, and Mental Health Professionals

In contrast to the previously described experience of families feeling "blamed" by mental health professionals for the illness of their family member, the families we interviewed did not express this concern. It appears that the professional community has embraced an illness understanding that has allowed the door of cooperation with families to open. Unfortunately, to date, this cooperation has rarely taken place. Instead of feeling blamed for the illness, family members now feel largely ignored by the mental health community, as professionals become overinvested in a medical model of illness as an intrapersonal biological phenomenon, which seemingly exists without a social context. Despite significant research in many areas of physical illness which suggests that family interventions can be helpful (McDaniel, Hepworth, and Doherty, 1992; Rolland, 1994), many mental health professionals continue to overlook a rich resource for improving the community functioning of people with mental illness by not including family members' information and insights into the problem. Families we interviewed often discussed the experience of being disregarded or dismissed as irrelevant by mental health professionals—and this experience was described by families of all ethnic groups and socioeconomic classes. Family members felt that their opinions and knowledge were rarely requested by mental health personnel; they felt particularly disregarded by the staff of crisis centers and hospitals and by psychiatrists in all settings. Although families are frequently expected by the mental health community to fulfill housing and case management functions once the ill member is released from the hospital, they have generally not felt included in developing the treatment plan.

The Partnership Model is intended to correct this problem by understanding the patient, the family, and the mental health providers as a triangular partnership team. Like any team, if the members are working together, impressive things can be achieved; but if one of the team members is omitted from the game plan, it is difficult to be successful. Worse, if two of the team members are working at cross-purposes, the results are likely to be ineffective at best and disastrous at worst. When the ill member starts to decompensate, family members tend to blame the professionals, professionals tend to blame the family, and everyone tends to blame the patient. To prevent this from happening, it is imperative that each of the three team components be regarded as an *equal partner* in planning and executing the plan. If mental health professionals see treatment as something they do *to*— or even *for* the patient—they operate with a sense of noblesse oblige which provides them with a sense of superiority and makes cooperation as a team impossible, even when the intentions are good. In order to be truly effective in managing a problem as difficult as mental illness, all of the team members must have a respect for the contribution of the other members.

This partnership has certain implications in addressing realistic goals and helping people with a mental illness achieve and maintain as much independence as possible. Previous research suggests that the critical goal for the first year posthospitalization is maintenance (Hogarty et al., 1991; McFarlane et al., 1995). This is best achieved by compliance with a medication regimen, providing social skills training for the patient, and preserving a "holding pattern" in the family. Beyond the first year of sustained community adjustment, incremental changes are appropriate. One of the problems we have observed in this regard is lack of attention to transition and misconstruing a drop-back position as a failure. In family therapy, the most useful frame of reference is a spiral—a pattern in which we make progress, followed by a drop-back period, followed by renewed effort at progress. Unfortunately, the drop-back is often interpreted as a setback and therefore cast as a failure, rather than as a normal part of the developmental process.

As an example of this, we observed that patients in a community housing program were often "graduated" from a closely supervised group home, which was run much like an extended family, to an independent apartment complex with reduced supervision and attention. Many of these patients subsequently relapsed and had to be rehospitalized after making this shift. In consultation with this program, I suggested that patients be allowed to return to the group home to visit for several months after their transition, and be invited back for special occasions (e.g., holidays, birthdays). Most families do not send their children off to college and tell them not to return, but frequently mental health programs operate without this sense of people's developmental need for continuity in transitions. Similarly, people with a mental illness are often first moved to a program that provides greater independence than family life, and *then* provided help with activities of daily living (ADL) skills. In the normal course of family life, we first learn new skills, then go out into the world to try them out. Lack of attention to basic family-oriented developmental needs has handicapped many professional programs; further, it has sometimes been overlooked by the families themselves due to focus on the chronological, rather than socioemotional, age of the ill member.

These examples illustrate the importance of shared goals among the partnership team and how these goals are defined. Just as in a family, things look different from each person's perspective, so the triangle looks different from each corner. Because the experience of people with a mental illness is outside the experience of most of us, it takes considerable effort to appreciate how scary it must feel not to be able to limit and control your thoughts or actions. It is also difficult for those in positions of power to appreciate the experience of powerlessness. Because mental health professionals are often in the position of making decisions about hospitalization, treatment protocol, admission to programs, and so forth, it is often difficult for them to appreciate the helpless feelings of family members who wish to aid their ill member, but are told that they are too intrusive in the program or too protective of the ill member. Mental health professionals will *never* have the power that the family has for a person with a serious mental illness. Not to make use of that power is not only ineffective, it is foolish. The therapeutic job for mental health clinicians in the Partnership Model, therefore, is to help enhance and utilize the competence of the family to help its own member. Families generally underestimate and misperceive their own significance in the lives of those with a mental illness. By understanding the biological component of the illness, attending to the differences between the biologically based problems and the emotional disturbance overlay, recognizing developmental needs and limitations, and combining the informational component of psychoeducation with the restructuring opportunities of family therapy, mental health professionals can provide families with the tools to understand and change things. This will allow families to normalize their experience, recognize their own strengths, appreciate the value of their family connections, and make changes that can enhance the lives of both the ill member and the family as a whole. These changes enable the ill member to make a meaningful contribution to the family, rather than simply being "taken care of" by the family. Above all, the Partnership Model is about respecting the differences of the team members and valuing the contribution of each.

CASE EXAMPLE

In order to provide a picture of how the Partnership Model can be utilized, a case study is provided. To protect the identity of the family, names and other identifying information have been altered.

The Family Interview

The Baileys are an African-American family. They live in a modest house in a largely lower-middle-class neighborhood in the city of Trenton. Mr. Bailey, sixty-five, worked as a prison guard for thirty years, and has been retired since he was sixty. His wife, who was a clerk in a state office building, died three years ago from cancer. Mr. Bailey is the primary family caregiver for Johnny, thirty, the youngest of his three children, who lives with him. Mr. Bailey's oldest son, Ben, thirty-eight, is married, and has three children; he is the manager of a construction firm. Mr. Bailey's daughter, Sally, thirty-five, is married, has two children, and works as a teacher's aide in a local public school. Both of Johnny's siblings live in nearby suburbs of Trenton and stop by the house at least once or twice a week. Mr. Bailey has two siblings, as well as a brother of his late wife, living in the area. Several other siblings and in-laws of his are in touch periodically but live in other states.

Johnny was first hospitalized at age twenty-two. Like his siblings, he graduated from high school. He went into the military service, but it became increasingly difficult for him to stay focused, and he expressed concerns that other soldiers were picking on him and making fun of him. Eventually, service personnel had a meeting with Johnny and his parents, in which they agreed to grant him an honorable discharge and release him early due to "medical reasons." Johnny then returned to his parents' home and got a job in his brother's construction firm. However, he had similar difficulties with other workers and began to accuse them of plotting to steal his tools and poison his lunch. He was hospitalized when the police had to be called to his work site because other workers were fearful that Johnny might attack them.

Johnny spent a month in an inpatient unit at a local hospital before being returned to his parents. He was diagnosed as "paranoid schizophrenic" and referred to a local clinic for medication and therapy. However, Johnny refused to believe that he had a problem, kept insisting that others (including his brother and sister) "got all the breaks," and soon stopped going to the mental health clinic. He spent his time "hanging out" with other unemployed young men in the neighborhood, many of whom were heavily using street drugs. His mother tended to interpret his problem as being overstressed by the demands of modern life and trying to compete with his siblings, while his father tended to feel he was often "faking it," and did not really want to have to work for a living.

During the next several years, Johnny went through additional hospitalizations, at the rate of about once per year. Initially, these were one-month stays in the local hospitals, but they later involved stays of several months at the state psychiatric hospital. Although stable when he came out of the hospital on medication, his condition worsened when he stopped taking medication and started using street drugs again. During his periods of hospitalization, he was visited frequently by both parents and his sister. His brother, who was angry at him for embarrassing him at the workplace and tended to attribute his problems to "drugs and laziness," came occasionally, but the visits often resulted in arguments.

With the advice and support of his family members, Johnny gradually came to realize that his symptoms became more problematic when he used street drugs, and he stopped taking them altogether, although this resulted in the loss of his primary reference group. Once he stopped taking street drugs, Johnny's relationship with his brother improved considerably, and Ben began to realize that Johnny was suffering from a mental problem separate from drug use. All family members noted a significant improvement in Johnny's functioning when he was taking medication; his father reported that he could tell when Johnny had stopped taking medication because he started pacing around the house and mumbling to himself.

Both Ben and Sally brought their partners and children over to the house on a regular basis. Johnny looked forward to seeing the children but had difficulty staying in a room when too many family members were there. He often went to his room and listened to music on his headphones. The children found him odd but looked forward to seeing him. Occasionally, they would go on walks with him around the block, and he appeared to be quite protective of them. When his mother became ill with cancer, Johnny got very anxious and attentive. After she died, his pacing behaviors and paranoid fears increased, and Johnny had to be hospitalized for several months.

Johnny's last hospitalization was six months ago. He was hospitalized voluntarily after he reported that "the voices were telling me to hurt myself." It took two months in the state hospital to restabilize him on a new medication. Since then, he has been living with his father while attending a daytreatment program. Mr. Bailey monitors his son's medication, and makes sure he gets to his program and appointments. He gets assistance in this from his other son and daughter, when they are available, but Mr. Bailey does not like to impose on them. He thinks that the mental health people generally do a good job, but does not believe they are interested enough in hearing his own views on what Johnny needs. He is not in touch with other families of the mentally ill.

At times, Mr. Bailey feels quite overwhelmed by Johnny's needs and the limitations that this imposes for doing things with his own friends. He worries about the limited life that Johnny will be able to live and what will happen to him when he (Mr. Bailey) passes on.

Johnny is currently getting Social Security Disability (SSD) because of his work history, but it is very limited; Mr. Bailey is afraid that Johnny will not be able to afford to live independently. He believes his other children will take care of Johnny, but does not like to burden them with this, because "they have their own lives to worry about." Mr. Bailey would like to see more subsidized housing and supervised living arrangements available for mental health patients. He would also like to see increased case management services and respite services to take the burden of case management off himself and to provide continuity for Johnny if Mr. Bailey is no longer there. He misses the help he got from his wife, but currently feels that he gets a great deal of support from the Baptist church he attends, from the men's club he belongs to, from his children, and from the memory of his wife.

The Partnership Model Intervention

The Bailey family demonstrated a number of significant strengths, but also had some difficulties in managing the problem of mental illness. Over time, they came to realize that Johnny had an illness that affected his behavior. They noted that this condition got better when he was on prescribed medication and worse when he was using street drugs. Thanks to the power of the family, they were able to persuade Johnny to leave street drugs alone, which meant that he did not need a dual-diagnosis program. The three remaining members of his nuclear family had a positive attitude toward helping Johnny and were actively involved. Mr. Bailey had some good support not only from his children, but from his social and faith contacts as well. And Johnny had developed a recognition that he had a chronic illness which required the ongoing use of medication for containment.

However, although the family had some understanding of the illness, they had difficulty differentiating between the emotionally based and biologically based symptoms, and they had some difficulty sorting out capacity versus motivation issues because Johnny was so inconsistent in his ability to function outside of the hospital. His brother, in particular, tended to get frustrated with him and expected him to perform more consistently.

In addition, although the family had access to several extended family members, they were not making use of this part of the family system to help with the problem. They were isolated from other families struggling with the problem of serious mental illness, and lacked a reference and support network in the community. They had encountered gaps in the mental health services system, as well as lack of attention from mental health professionals when they had attempted to provide information.

A family support staff member was assigned to the Bailey family after Mr. Bailey indicated that he thought this would be helpful. The staff member met with Mr. Bailey individually, with Mr. Bailey and his other children, and with the whole family at different times in their home in order to answer questions about the illness, address attributional concerns, provide clarification on developmental and motivational issues, and help them develop solutions to some behavior problems. Mr. Bailey was informed of the existence of the local NAMI chapter, which met biweekly in the evenings at a suburban library branch. He and his children Ben and Sally went one time, but found that there was only one other African-American family there. Mr. Bailey and his son Ben felt it would be difficult for them to reveal personal information and felt embarrassed asking questions in that context, so they did not return, although they had positive things to say about how they were treated at the meeting. After several months of contact with the Bailey family, the support staff person suggested the idea of meeting with the Bailey family and two other African-American families also living in Trenton. These meetings were enthusiastically attended by Mr. Bailey and his two other children; however, Johnny attended only sporadically. The Baileys reported that they liked these meetings because they could relate to what the other families were experiencing, often got helpful ideas from the other families, and felt good about their ability to help the other families as well.

During the course of these multifamily meetings, the Baileys worked out a system for "dividing up the work." This was particularly helpful to Ben and Sally, who found that they were feeling guilty about not helping their father more, but at the same time were overloaded by the demands of their own work and family obligations. In taking responsibility for specific activities with Johnny, they both found that they spent more time with him, yet they reported feeling less burdened.

The support staff person also encouraged the Baileys to convene a "network meeting," which involved extended family as well as the pastor and some members of their church who had been particularly close to Mrs. Bailey prior to her death. Several of the people in this network expressed that for some time they had wished to be of assistance, but did not know how they could help. Taking on limited responsibilities for Johnny's functioning in the community allowed them to feel that they were doing something tangible to honor the memory of Mrs. Bailey.

The support staff person found that Mr. Bailey was reticent to approach the day treatment program about ideas he had, for fear he would say the wrong thing and jeopardize his son's acceptance in the program. In fact, the day treatment program (and particularly the prescribing psychiatrist) had not been very available to input from family members. In a series of meetings, first with the day treatment staff, and then with staff and Mr. Bailey, the support staff person helped address these concerns and arranged for a member of the Bailey family to attend treatment planning meetings. Staff from the day treatment program then helped Johnny and his father get connected to a housing program for people with mental illness. To date, Johnny continues to live with his father but is cautiously positive about the idea of moving out to a supervised shared apartment. He is currently working on his independent living skills—especially transportation, cooking, and taking care of household responsibilities. By clarifying who will help Johnny with various aspects of his life, the day treatment staff and members of the Bailey family are supporting one another's efforts. Johnny recently expressed the opinion that "it seems like I got more friends now than ever."

STRENGTHS AND LIMITATIONS OF THE MODEL

Strengths of the Partnership Model include the integration of patient, family, and mental health professionals into a "team" that is able to get more done with less effort. It is both an effective and an efficient model. When mental health professionals see only themselves as the members of the treatment team, they miss valuable opportunities. When the patient is included in the treatment plan as well as the treatment, compliance is fostered by the patient's commitment to make his or her own plan work. If it is someone else's plan for your life, how much investment are you likely to make in it? When family members are included in treatment planning, it is possible to improve patient compliance because of the power of the family's influence and the personal investment that only they are likely to make in the patient's life.

At first glance, the Partnership Model may not appear to be a more efficient model. After all, it requires the investment of staff resources in providing a family support staff; administrative commitment to the resources and flexibility to allow the support staff to make home visits, provide transportation, and offer other supports to allow families to attend meetings; structure meetings among staff of various programs; and involve staff in additional time negotiating with family members. However, when one considers the considerable time, energy, and other resources involved in the process of decompensation (which should be understood as a several-week period of increased attention from outpatient, day treatment, or residential programs, as well as the resources of the crisis center and hospital), it should be apparent that a model that minimizes these efforts over the long run will be more cost-efficient.

The effectiveness of the Partnership Model relies heavily on administrative support and funding. Without adequate funding, the necessary investment of resources described earlier will not be possible, and the project will be doomed to mediocrity. Similarly, without a commitment to this approach from administration, the needed collaboration will not occur. If administration encourages program staff to cooperate with family support staff, but penalizes them for spending time in "nondirect" services or fails to allocate time for staff training, this type of model will not work.

In addition to the problems of limited administrative support and funding, there is another major factor that will limit the effectiveness of the Partnership Model: viewing conflict among the team members as an indication that the partnership is not working. As in the management of any team, conflict presents difficulties. People with a mental illness are often annoyed with family members and may externalize blame for their troubles onto family members, wishing to exclude them from participation. Mental health professionals have generally been too ready to accept the patient's view of reality, rather than personally communicating with others in the family to obtain perspective on the problem. Just as in family therapy, it is important that "everybody knows what everybody knows." I generally tell my clients with mental illness, just as I tell my clients who are minors, that it is my job to act in what I consider to be their best interest—which will not always be the same as what they consider to be in their best interest. This will undoubtedly set up conflict situations, but, as in family therapy, conflict is not the problem; lack of resolution of conflict is the problem. When team members come into conflict, there needs to be provision for discussing it together among the team, and coming to a particular plan of action. This process will not always result in consensus. If the dissenting member of the team has the experience of having been heard and has the opportunity for future input, the team can continue to function adequately even without consensus; however, if one or more members consistently feel disregarded, the team will become dysfunctional. Many times in working with people with a mental illness and their families, I have recommended a course of action that the other two team members rejected. If I remove myself from the team because of this, I lack any future opportunity to be helpful. As family therapists have observed, a functional system needs to maintain the flexibility to continually adjust to new circumstances. A chronic yet uneven course of illness—as is usually seen in mental illness—demands that all three team members recognize that being "outvoted" on one decision does not mean the team is unworkable.

INTEGRATION WITH PSYCHIATRIC SERVICES AND THE ROLE OF MEDICATION

As described, the Partnership Model can be integrated into most existing mental health/psychiatric service systems quite readily, as it dovetails with services already being provided to the patient and expands both the range and effectiveness of those services. Regarding the integration of medication, in our interviews with families we found almost unanimous support for psychotropic medication as well as the recognition that the ill member functioned better when compliant with prescribed medication. Family members were readily willing to be involved with mental health professionals in monitoring medication, providing information about medication compliance and observed side effects, and being instructed on the best ways to encourage compliance.

However, we frequently found that mental health providers (especially psychiatrists) were extremely reluctant to enter into any communication with family members, often viewing them as irrelevant to the treatment of a biological disorder or potentially harmful to the patient's interest, since they had been portrayed negatively by the patient. Those familiar with family therapy will recognize this as a common problem for therapists who work only with individuals. It is a curious example of cognitive dissonance that a mental health professional, who is generally skeptical of the ability of a patient with a thought disorder to be an accurate informant, will nevertheless take without question the patient's description of other family members. Lack of attention to following through on this, or the deliberate decision not to do so, is often done in the name of "confidentiality." However, this is yet another case of disregarding the developmental level of the person with mental illness and responding as though they are functioning at chronological age. In this regard, "confidentiality" often serves to protect the mental health professional from having to deal with systems issues, rather than serving the best interests of the patient.

A further problem in this regard is the misguided emphasis in many mental health programs on "rehabilitation," such that the goal is moving the patient to a "higher level of functioning" with some vague ideal of restoring the person to a fully independent life. Viewed this way, achieving failure is almost assured because we fail to factor in the power of the illness to affect progress. Programs would do better to assess the current functional levels of the patient, and provide opportunities that are congruent with that level of functioning. If the patient moves to a higher or lower level of functioning, other opportunities should be provided. Thus, the goal is not to "rehabilitate" the patient, nor to "empower" the patient, but to "enable" or make change possible. Rehabilitation in mental health is something we do *to* the patient; empowering is something we do *for* the patient. Although both of these goals are well intentioned, it is important that mental health professionals shift the focus to *doing with* the other members of the partnership team. If we see our job as "making things happen," we will frequently encounter failure. If we see our job as "enabling things to happen," we more often experience success and, in the process, recognize the critical role of the other team members.

CULTURAL AND GENDER ISSUES

In our interviews with families, we found some significant differences across ethnic groups and socioeconomic classes (Johnson,

2000). Minority families often had greater extended family help available, although it was often not being utilized as the nuclear family continued to struggle with the problems. Families with extended family available and willing to help have an excellent opportunity to extend the "division of labor" discussed in the section on the Treatment Model, so that the social network expands for the ill member, while demands on these other family members are kept limited and predictable. We have found that the predictability factor is important, because it is this that allays the fear in the minds of family members about the illness taking over their lives. The predictability factor also works well for the ill member, as constant change and uncertainty are likely to be major factors in precipitating relapse.

Lower socioeconomic-class families were usually experiencing multiple problems, both material and psychological, and often were simultaneously coping with significant problems of other family members, leaving fewer resources for helping the ill member. Given these increased needs, we have found that these families may require considerable help for an extended period of time. Often they are only able to make structural shifts in patterns of behavior slowly and with repeated drop-backs. They are often unlikely to show up for or benefit from either educational or therapeutic groups and tend to require an additional investment of case management and advocacy help from family support staff. In the absence of a designated family support clinician, they are likely to do poorly because the level of family investment in most mental health programs is not sufficient for their needs. For this reason, the Partnership Model works best in areas of the urban or rural poor by utilizing the "dual thrust" approach described in the Setting section of this chapter.

This problem is further compounded in the case of minority families whose members either do not speak English or do not know the language well; in the absence of agency commitment of resources specifically for these populations, it is impossible to make use of family resources in any consistent way. In our work, this has been a problem for Spanish-speaking families. It has often been difficult to recruit minority or bilingual, bicultural staff for family support positions, and it can be difficult to engage families (especially poor urban or rural families) without this.

Finally, we have found significant differences between men and women in handling the problem of mental illness. As in most caregiving situations, we found that the primary caregiver was most often a woman and usually the mother of the ill member. We found that men have generally had more difficulty in accepting the emotional disturbance problems than women, particularly when the ill family member is also male. There appears to be a male definition of self that involves productivity ("doing" rather than "being"), which makes it harder for male family members to accept lack of productivity in an ill male family member than in an ill female family member. Male family members often initially appear peripheral and difficult to engage, which has encouraged mental health personnel to deal only with the primary caregiver. However, once the particular individuals in the family are known to the family support person, it has usually been possible to involve males in the partnership by emphasizing what they can *do* to help, rather than asking them to *be* more emotionally available. In this way, we can optimize the family's resources for problem solving, as well as increase the bonds between the family and the ill member.

FUTURE DIRECTIONS

Results of our study indicate that the functioning of people with serious mental illness in the community is strongly impacted by the negative effects of both environmental and illness-related strains, but that these can be significantly buffered by how the family perceives the problem and helps the ill member to manage the illness. Possibilities for improved family satisfaction and ill member functioning through the support and development of a family sense of competence are considerable and are achievable by utilizing the resources of the patient, family, self-help supports in the community, and the mental health community in a partnership.

In order to achieve this vision, funders of mental health services will need to work collaboratively with consumer groups and with NAMI to design plans that can be tried in specific situations. As we have discovered in attempting to implement this model in various places in New Jersey, each setting has its unique requirements and possibilities. If the effort is made to coordinate efforts from the top down, planning is likely to be effective. However, to date there have been many grassroots efforts to involve family members that have met with very limited success because of resistance or inertia within the larger system of mental health providers or funders.

Pilot projects developed for specific locales should include both qualitative and quantitative research components that will allow administrators to assess the relative success of the project, both to ensure ongoing funding and to see which elements can be replicated successfully. Documenting cost-effectiveness and efficiency savings of this program would also be an important focus for future research. In the current economic climate, it is important that mental health services be provided that are both meaningful and efficiently delivered. Incorporating a research element into programs will also allow for the further development of the model, helping to make it more applicable to a variety of settings.

The Partnership Model involves both a conceptual framework and practical application component. It allows persons with mental illness, their families, and mental health professionals to work together collaboratively. This collaboration makes it easier to achieve the goal of providing the best possible adjustment in the community for the patient and greatest sense of satisfaction for both the ill member and his or her family. The Partnership Model requires some reconceptualization by mental health providers, including questioning certain assumptions previously made about persons with mental illness and their families. If mental health professionals can "step out of the box" of previously defined services and create services that incorporate all three members of the Partnership Team, they are likely to find that the end result is more satisfying for all concerned.

REFERENCES

American Psychiatric Association (1994). *Diagnostic and statistical manual of mental disorders* (Fourth edition). Washington, DC: Author.

Anderson, C.M., Reiss, D.J., and Hogarty, G.E. (1986). *Schizophrenia and the family*. New York: Guilford.

Bateson, G., Jackson, D.D., Haley, J., and Weakland, J. (1956). Toward a theory of schizophrenia. *Behavioral Science, 1*(4), 251-264.

Bernheim, K.F. and Lehman, A.F. (1985). *Working with families of the mentally ill*. New York: Norton.

Brown, G.W., Birley, J.L.T., and Wing, J.K. (1972). Influence of family life on the course of schizophrenic disorders: A replication. *British Journal of Psychiatry, 121*, 241-258.

Colapinto, J. (1991). Structural family therapy. In A.S. Gurman and D.P. Kniskern (Eds.), *Handbook of family therapy*, Volume II (pp. 417-443). New York: Brunner/Mazel.

Falloon, I.R.H., Boyd, J.L., and McGill, C.W. (1984). *Family care of schizophrenia.* New York: Guilford.

Falloon, I.R.H. and Liberman, R.P. (1983). Interactions between drug and psychosocial therapy in schizophrenia. *Schizophrenia Bulletin, 9,* 543-554.

Fromm-Reichmann, F. (1948). Notes on the development of treatment of schizophrenics by psychoanalytic psychotherapy. *Psychiatry, 11,* 263-273.

Goldstein, M.J. (1992). Commentary on "Expressed emotion in depressed patients and their partners." *Family Process, 31,* 172-174.

Hatfield, A.B. (1991). The National Alliance for the Mentally Ill: A decade later. *Community Mental Health Journal, 27,* 95-103.

Hatfield, A.B. and Lefley, H.P. (Eds.) (1987). *Families of the mentally ill: Coping and adaptation.* New York: Guilford.

Hogarty, G.E., Anderson, C.M., Reiss, D.J., Kornblith, S.J., Greenwald, D.P., Ulrich, R.F., and Carter, M. (1991). Family psychoeducation, social skills training, and maintenance chemotherapy in the aftercare of schizophrenia. *Archives of General Psychiatry, 48,* 340-347.

Johnson, E.D. (1998). The effect of family functioning and family sense of competence on people with mental illness. *Family Relations, 47,* 443-451.

Johnson, E.D. (2000) Differences among families coping with serious mental illness: A qualitative analysis. *American Journal of Orthopsychiatry, 70,* 126-134.

Johnson, E.D. (in submission). Can family functioning and appraisal buffer stress on a vulnerable family member? The mentally ill and their families.

Lefley, H.P. (1992). Expressed emotion: Conceptual, clinical, and social policy issues. *Hospital and Community Psychiatry, 43,* 591-598.

Lefley, H.P. (1996). *Family caregiving in mental illness.* Thousand Oaks, CA: Sage.

Lidz, T. and Fleck, S. (1960). Schizophrenia, human integration, and the role of the family. In D.D. Jackson (Ed.), *The etiology of schizophrenia* (pp. 323-345). New York: Basic Books.

McDaniel, S.H., Hepworth, J., and Doherty, W. (1992). *Medical family therapy: A biopsychosocial approach to families with health problems.* New York: Basic Books.

McFarlane, W.R. (1991). Family psychoeducational treatment. In A.S. Gurman and D.P. Kniskern (Eds.), *Handbook of family therapy,* Volume II (pp. 363-395). New York: Brunner/Mazel.

McFarlane, W.R., Link, B., Dushay, R., Marchal, J., and Crilly, J. (1995). Psychoeducational multiple family groups: Four-year relapse outcome in schizophrenia. *Family Process, 34,* 127-144.

Meissner, W.W. (1970). Thinking about the family—psychiatric aspects. In N.W. Ackerman (Ed.), *Family Process* (pp. 131-170). New York: Basic Books.

Miklowitz, D.J., Goldstein, M.J., Doane, J.A., Nuechterlein, K.H., Strachan, A.M., Snyder, K.S., and Magana-Amato, A. (1989). Is expressed emotion an index of a transactional process? I. Parents' affective style. *Family Process, 28,* 153-168.

Milkowitz, D.J. and Hooley, J.M. (1998). Developing family psychoeducational treatments for patients with bipolar and other severe psychiatric disorders. *Journal of Marital and Family Therapy, 24,* 419-435.

Minuchin, S. and Fishman, H.C. (1981). *Family therapy techniques.* Cambridge, MA: Harvard University Press.

Mishler, E.G. and Waxler, N.E. (1965). Family interaction processes and schizophrenia: A review of current theories. *Merrill-Palmer Quarterly, 11,* 269-315.

Rolland, J.S. (1994). *Families, illness, and disability: An integrative treatment model.* New York: Basic Books.

Torrey, E.F., Bowler, A.E., and Taylor, E.H. (1995). *Schizophrenia and manic-depressive disorder: The biological roots of mental illness as revealed by the landmark study of identical twins.* New York: Basic Books.

Vaughn, C.E. and Leff, J.P. (1976). The influence of family and social factors on the course of psychiatric illness. *British Journal of Psychiatry, 129,* 125-137.

Vaughn, C.E. and Leff, J.P. (1981). Patterns of emotional response in relatives of schizophrenic patients. *Schizophrenia Bulletin, 7,* 43-44.

Whybrow, P.C. (1997). *A mood apart: Depression, mania, and other afflictions of the self.* New York: HarperCollins.

Wing, J.K. (1978). Social influences on the course of schizophrenia. In L.C. Wynne, R.L. Cromwell, and S. Matthysse (Eds.), *The nature of schizophrenia: New approaches to research and treatment* (pp. 599-616). New York: John Wiley.

Wynne, L.C. and Singer, M.T. (1963). Thought disorder and family relations of schizophrenics. *Archives of General Psychiatry, 9,* 191-206.

Zubin, J. (1986). Models for the aetiology of schizophrenia. In G.D. Burrows, T.R. Norman, and G. Rubinstein (Eds.), *Handbook of studies on schizophrenia. Part I: Epidemiology, aetiology and clinical features* (pp. 97-104). New York: Elsevier Science Publishers.

PART II:
TRADITIONAL POPULATIONS

Chapter 3

Family Treatment of Schizophrenia and Bipolar Disorder

Kim T. Mueser

INTRODUCTION

Between 40 and 60 percent of persons with schizophrenia or bipolar disorder live at home (Brown and Birtwistle, 1998; Carpentier et al., 1992; Goldman, 1984), and many others maintain regular contact with their relatives. For many individuals with these illnesses, family ties are the most important social relationships in their lives, and family support is critical to their well-being. However, family relationships are often strained by the presence of a psychiatric illness, which can have important clinical implications for the management of the disorder. Several factors account for the difficulties families experience when coping with a severe mental illness in a member.

First, caring for and maintaining a close relationship with an individual with schizophrenia or bipolar disorder can be a difficult and emotionally draining task (Hatfield and Lefley, 1987, 1993). Caregiving often involves providing substantial amounts of time and money, and the unpredictable nature of severe psychiatric disorders can make managing the illness even more difficult. Second, the difficulties of helping a relative with a mental illness are compounded if family members are not informed about the causes, common symptoms, nature, and course of these disorders. Historically, mental health professionals have often viewed families with skepticism, with some theorists suggesting that major psychiatric disorders such as schizophrenia are actually caused by the family (Bateson et al., 1956; Fromm-Reichman, 1948; Sullivan, 1972). A result of the tension between mental health professionals and family members has been a tendency for professionals not to educate relatives about psychiatric illnesses and their treatment. This lack of understanding about mental illness can further hamper relationships between clients and their relatives as family members misperceive psychiatric symptoms as being under clients' control or as due to moral or character weaknesses (Barrowclough and Parle, 1997; Harrison, Dadds, and Smith, 1998; Lopez et al., 1999).

This lack of information about psychiatric illnesses provided to family members has given rise to demands by many relatives to be more informed and more involved in the treatment of their loved ones. Advocacy organizations of families, such as the National Alliance for the Mentally Ill, have lobbied the mental health profession to be more accountable to both clients and their relatives. Recently, extensive research has documented that high levels of stress in families caring for a person with schizophrenia or bipolar disorder substantially increase the risk of relapse and rehospitalization (Butzlaff and Hooley, 1998). High levels of tension in families can act as a chronic stressor on clients, which, according to stress-vulnerability models of severe mental illness, can overwhelm the client's coping skills, resulting in a more severe course of illness (Liberman et al., 1986; Zubin and Spring, 1977).

Family intervention for schizophrenia and bipolar disorder is aimed at reducing the burden of care on relatives and educating them about the psychiatric illness and the principles of treatment. By involving family members in treatment and working with them in a collaborative fashion, families are more able to monitor the course of illness, to alert mental health professionals when changes are noted, to reinforce adherence to treatment recommendations, and to encourage the client to take steps toward his or her personal recovery. Finally, collaboration with family members, which is the ultimate goal of family intervention, reduces stress and tension among clients and relatives, thereby improving the course of psychiatric illness.

Over the past two decades, with growing recognition of the importance of families of persons with severe mental illness, a variety of different models of family intervention have been developed and empirically validated (Anderson, Reiss, and Hogarty, 1986; Barrowclough and Tarrier, 1992; Falloon, Boyd, and McGill, 1984; Kuipers, Leff, and Lam, 1992; McFarlane, 1990; Miklowitz and Goldstein, 1997; Mueser and Glynn, 1999).

Models of family therapy for severe mental illness differ in their theoretical orientation (ranging from cognitive-behavioral to educational-supportive to modified family systems), format (single-family treatment sessions versus multiple-family group meetings), duration (time limited versus time unlimited), and locus of treatment (home based versus clinic based). Despite these differences, these effective models have much in common, including long-term intervention (more than six months); education about the psychiatric illness and its treatment; support and empathy; efforts to improve communication and decrease stress in the family; avoidance of blaming the family; a focus on the present and the future rather than the past; and an emphasis on improving the lives of everyone in the family, including the client. In addition, family treatment models that have been shown to improve the course of psychiatric illnesses have all been led by mental health professionals.

This chapter describes one family intervention model for schizophrenia and bipolar disorder, behavioral family therapy (BFT). BFT is the most extensively studied model of family intervention for severe mental illness, with multiple studies on both schizophrenia and bipolar disorder. BFT is also the only family intervention model that has been systematically examined in individuals with bipolar disorder; the other models have been evaluated only for schizophrenia. Several manuals for the BFT model exist, including Falloon and colleagues (1984) for schizophrenia, Miklowitz and Goldstein (1997) for bipolar disorder, and Mueser and Glynn (1999) for the range of severe mental illnesses, including schizophrenia, schizoaffective disorder, bipolar disorder, major depression, obsessive-compulsive disorder, and post-traumatic stress disorder.

SETTING

BFT is most commonly practiced on an outpatient basis by a mental health professional who functions as a member of the client's multi-interdisciplinary treatment team. Most individuals with schizophrenia or bipolar disorder require an array of professional services in addition to family intervention, including pharmacological treatment, case management, and access to other rehabilitation services such as supported employment (Drake et al., 1999). BFT is often practiced in the context of publicly funded mental health services, such as at local community mental health centers, although private applications of the model also occur.

BFT was originally developed as a home-based intervention (Falloon and Pederson, 1985), although clinic-based applications of the model have also proved successful (Randolph et al., 1994). In practice, a combination of home-based and clinic-based BFT is often optimal (Mueser and Glynn, 1999). Home-based sessions are helpful in engaging family members in treatment and provide valuable assessment information to clinicians about the environment in which family members reside. After families have been successfully engaged in treatment, the locus of sessions can often be shifted into the clinic in order to save valuable clinician time.

TREATMENT MODEL

Overview of the BFT Model

BFT is an intervention that combines education with social learning strategies designed to better equip families with the knowledge and skills necessary to manage psychiatric illness in a family member. To care for a person with schizophrenia or bipolar disorder, families need to understand basic information about these illnesses and the strategies used to treat them. Furthermore, to deal with the myriad problems that arise when managing a psychiatric illness, families need to have effective communication and problem-solving skills. The focus of BFT is on teaching family members the requisite information about psychiatric illnesses and the skills for effective communication and problem solving.

BFT is aimed at teaching information and skills to families, not on fostering insight. Therefore, sessions emphasize the importance of learning and routinely incorporate homework assignments for families to consolidate their understanding and competence. Family sessions are usually time limited, while the treatment team maintains ongoing contact with the family after formal sessions have ended. The ultimate goal of BFT is to enable family members to become effective collaborators with mental health professionals in the treatment of the psychiatric disorder.

Logistics

BFT is an intervention that is usually provided for at least six months and up to two years. With some families, such as those experiencing frequent crises or multiple stresses, ongoing maintenance family sessions can be conducted. Sessions typically last approximately one hour and are conducted on a declining contact basis (e.g., weekly for the first three months, biweekly for the next six months, then monthly until termination).

Family sessions involve the client and any relatives who have regular contact with a client (e.g., weekly contact) or who wish to increase their contact with a client. Children under the age of sixteen are usually not included in family sessions. Other people who are not relatives but who have a caring relationship with the client, such as a boyfriend, a girlfriend, or a member of the clergy, can be included in family sessions if they express a commitment to working with the client.

A quiet working environment is essential to conducting BFT in order to facilitate learning the requisite information and skills. If young children are present in the home, arrangements need to be made to ensure that they are taken care of and do not interrupt the family session. The early BFT sessions focus on teaching basic information and training in communication and problem-solving skills. These sessions follow a preplanned curriculum that is individualized based on the specific disorder, the history of its treatment, and the experiences of the family members. Educational handouts are used, as well as posters or other visual aids, and homework assignments are given to families to help them review the information or practice the skills they have learned in the session. Gradually, the family assumes the responsibility for structuring the session and using the therapist as a consultant in solving their problems or achieving desired goals.

Components of the BFT Model

The BFT model can be divided into six sequential components: engagement, assessment, education, communication skills training, problem-solving training, and special problems. The amount of time spent on each component varies from one family to the next, with teaching tailored to the individual family. We provide a brief description of each treatment component below.

Engagement

Engagement involves reaching out to both the client and the relatives to develop a personal connection and helping them understand how the BFT program is in the best interest of all parties involved. Engagement usually begins with the client. After the client has consented to be engaged, the relatives can be engaged. In some situations, especially in private practice, relatives seeking treatment for an ill family member may first contact and engage the clinician, who then reaches out to engage the client.

When engaging both clients and relatives, it is often crucial to emphasize that BFT is focused on helping families understand more about the psychiatric illness and its treatment and developing new skills for handling common problems. In order to engage some family members, BFT has to be distinguished from other approaches to family therapy that focus on understanding the past, delving into unconscious processes, or exploring psychodynamic formulations.

In helping family members understand the goals of BFT, emphasis is placed on avoiding psychiatric relapses and rehospitalizations, promoting greater client independence, and helping all members achieve personal and shared goals. Explaining the BFT model to family members, including its focus on education, communication skills, and problem-solving training, enables them to see that in many ways BFT is more similar to a class or a course on the management of psychiatric illness than to a traditional therapy experience. Family members, including both clients and relatives, are especially receptive to the message that they are important and that a fundamental goal of treatment is to make the family extended members of the client's treatment team.

Assessment

When family members have been engaged in treatment, assessments are conducted with each individual member and with the family as a unit. Individual assessments are aimed at solidifying the relationship between each member and the therapist, and understanding each person's perspective on family strengths, weaknesses, and desired changes. In the individual interviews the therapist probes family members' understanding of the psychiatric illness and its treatment, changes they would like to see as a result of the treatment, perceived obstacles to change, and perceived support from other family members.

Assessment of the family as a unit involves facilitating a discussion about desired changes, and using observational strategies to evaluate family problem-solving skills. Problem solving is evaluated by identifying one or two problems or goals for the family to work on while the clinician observes how the members attempt to reach a resolution. While families work on the task, the clinician sits back and observes the family or temporarily leaves the room and audiotapes the problem-solving discussion. The clinician then evaluates which steps of problem solving were observed and discusses with family members how they usually go about solving problems. During interactions with the family, the clinician also observes members' communication skills in order to determine the need for formal communication skills training.

Education

The goal of the educational sessions is to provide family members with basic information about the client's specific psychiatric disorder and its treatment. Between two and four educational sessions are usually provided, covering the topics of the psychiatric diagnosis, the effects of medication, the stress-vulnerability model of psychiatric disorders, and the role of the family. When comorbid substance abuse has been identified as a problem, or the client's substance use appears potentially problematic, an additional one or two educational sessions are devoted to discussing the effects of psychoactive substances on persons with a psychiatric disorder.

The session on the psychiatric diagnosis includes information about how a diagnosis is established, the characteristic symptoms, the prevalence and course of the disorder, and theories regarding its etiology. Education about medications includes the names and classes of specific medications used to treat the disorder, their effects on reducing acute symptoms and the likelihood of relapses, common side effects of the medications, and coping strategies for managing side effects. Education about the stress-vulnerability model is aimed at helping family members understand that psychiatric illnesses are caused by psychobiological vulnerabilities that can be brought on or made worse by stress. Improved coping skills and adherence to medication can reduce vulnerability to relapses, while substance abuse can increase such vulnerability. Education about the role of the family emphasizes that relatives can help the client by monitoring the symptoms of the illness, maintaining contact with the treatment team, lowering stress in the family, being supportive of the client, and encouraging him or her to follow treatment recommendations and take steps toward personal recovery. Clients with a dual diagnosis (psychiatric illness and a substance use disorder) also receive education about the nature of substance use disorders and its interactions with psychiatric illnesses.

Information reviewed in the educational sessions is summarized in handouts (see Mueser and Glynn, 1999). Education is done in an interactive style in which the therapist pauses frequently to help family members understand the relevance of information to their own personal experiences. The client is connoted as the "expert" in the psychiatric illness and is encouraged to describe his or her experiences with the illness and response to treatments. The therapist does not attempt to resolve disagreements between members about educational material but rather allows differences of opinion to stand to avoid confrontation and conflict. In order to evaluate comprehension of material, the therapist asks review questions and provides corrective information as needed.

Communication Skills Training

As previously noted, extensive research has demonstrated that the presence of a negative emotional climate in the family is related to a more severe course of psychiatric illness, including more frequent relapses and rehospitalizations (Butzlaff and Hooley, 1998). Families in which high levels of tension and conflict predominate benefit from communication skills training. For families who do not have high levels of negative affect, the principles of good communication can be briefly reviewed and the clinician can proceed to training in problem-solving skills.

Communication skills are taught using the principles of social skills training (Bellack et al., 1997). The steps of skills training include:

1. Establish a rationale for learning the skill.
2. Break the skill into component steps.
3. Demonstrate the skill in role-play.
4. Engage a family member in a role-play of the skill.

5. Provide positive feedback about what the member did well.
6. Provide corrective feedback about how the member could perform the skill better.
7. Engage the member in another role-play of the same situation, requesting that he or she make one or two changes.
8. Provide more positive and corrective feedback about the member's performance.
9. Engage each family member in two to four role-plays, each one followed by positive and corrective feedback.
10. Assign homework to family members to practice the skill on their own.

For families who need better communication skills, between three and six sessions are usually devoted to skills training. Up to six different communication skills are taught to families, including active listening, expressing positive feelings, making positive requests, expressing negative feelings, compromise and negotiation, and requesting a time out. Each skill is broken down into component steps, and skills training focuses on gradually shaping family members' ability to incorporate all the steps in a single cohesive skill. The steps of these skills are summarized in Table 3.1.

Homework assignments are designed to help family members practice skills they have learned in the session in their day-to-day interactions at home. Family members are given homework sheets and instructed to try to find at least one situation each day of the week in which they could use the communication skill taught in the previous session. After a skill has been introduced in a session, the next session begins with a review of homework, and role-plays based on actual situations that members experienced are used to evaluate their acquisition of the target skills and the need for additional training.

In addition to teaching good communication skills, clinicians are on the alert for pitfalls to good communication, such as speaking for another person and using blaming "you" statements, pejorative put-downs, and lacking specificity when expressing negative feelings. Sometimes communication problems can improve spontaneously by systematically teaching communication skills. Other times, however, families benefit from discussing rules of good communication and reviewing obstacles to effective communication.

TABLE 3.1. Communication Skills

Expressing Positive Feelings

- Look at the person
- Tell what he or she did that pleased you
- Tell how it made you feel

Making Positive Requests

- Look at the person
- Tell what you would like that person to do
- Tell how it would make you feel

Expressing Negative Feelings

- Look at the person with a serious facial expression
- Tell what that person did that upset you
- Tell how it made you feel
- Suggest how it could be prevented in the future

Active Listening

- Look at the speaker
- Nod your head
- Ask clarifying questions
- Paraphrase what you heard
- Wait until the speaker finishes before responding

Compromise and Negotiation

- Look at the person
- Explain your viewpoint
- Listen to the other person's viewpoint
- Repeat what you heard
- Suggest a compromise (more than one may be necessary)

Requesting a Time Out

- Indicate that the situation is stressful
- Tell the person that it is interfering with constructive communication
- Say that you must leave temporarily

Source: Adapted from Mueser and Glynn, 1999.

Problem-Solving Training

Training in problem-solving skills is aimed at helping family members solve problems and achieve goals through a cooperative effort. To avoid fostering dependence on the therapist, emphasis in problem-solving training is placed on helping family members learn the specific steps of problem solving, rather than on the resolution of the problem itself. When family members are successful in bolstering their problem-solving skills, they are prepared to handle problems they encounter in the future when the clinician is no longer available to help them.

Problem-solving training involves teaching a standard sequence of steps designed to involve all family members in solving the problem and achieving a suitable resolution. The steps of problem solving are as follows:

1. *Define the problem to everyone's satisfaction.* Everyone in the family gives his or her opinion about the nature of the problem and then a common definition is agreed upon by all members. It is important that everyone in the family agree on the definition of the problem to ensure that they will be invested in solving it.

2. *Brainstorm possible solutions.* Family members generate as many solutions to the problem as possible, with each person identifying at least one potential solution. No attempt is made to evaluate the solutions at this step of problem solving. By postponing the evaluation of solutions until the next step, a freewheeling brainstorming of possible solutions is encouraged, which can lead to unconventional but potentially useful solutions.

3. *Evaluate solutions.* Each solution is briefly discussed in terms of its advantages and disadvantages for solving the problem.

4. *Select the best solution or combination of solutions.* The family arrives at a consensus as to which solution is most likely to solve the problem. Sometimes more than one solution may be selected or several solutions can be combined to form a new solution that is deemed "best."

5. *Plan on how to implement the solution.* Implementation planning needs to take into account whether specific resources are needed to carry out the solution (e.g., information, money, transportation), who will do what, when different steps of the plan will be implemented, and what potential obstacles can be identified (and solutions to those obstacles) that could interfere with the plan.

6. *Set a time to follow up on the plan.* A time is set for family members to reconvene a meeting to review progress on implementing the plan and solving the problem. Some problems are solved after a single problem-solving meeting, but many others are not. During the review meeting, if the problem has not yet been solved (or goal

achieved), family members review the implementation plan and conduct additional problem solving as necessary to modify the plan or to identify new solutions and develop a new plan.

To facilitate learning the problem-solving method, families are encouraged to elect a chairperson who assumes the responsibility of keeping family members on track and following the steps of the skill. Problem-solving efforts are recorded on a standard form (see Mueser and Glynn, 1999), with either the chairperson or another family member (a "secretary") making the record. Families are encouraged to have weekly problem-solving meetings and to bring to the therapy session any difficulties in problem solving which they encounter. Toward the end of BFT, the therapist prompts families to work on solving problems without the guidance of the problem-solving sheet to facilitate the generalization of their problem-solving skills to typical day-to-day interactions.

Special Problems

The final component of BFT is aimed at addressing special problems that may persist in spite of problem solving. Therapists have a wide range of different strategies available for addressing specific problems. No definitive "list" of problems and techniques should be addressed. Mueser and Glynn (1999) describe strategies for addressing the following common problems: negative symptoms and/or secondary depression; suicidality; poor time management; disorganization; anger and violence; comorbid alcohol and drug use disorders in patients; substance use disorders in relatives; intoxication during the therapy session; persistent, psychotic symptoms; chronic anxiety; deficits in social functioning; problems in sexual intimacy and functioning; and parenting difficulties.

CASE EXAMPLE

Dave was the youngest of seven children and was raised by his father, a Baptist minister, and his mother, a homemaker, in a "protective" home environment. Dave began to develop his first psychiatric symptoms when he was sixteen years old, after starting his junior year at a new high school. He had difficulty adapting to the new school and was frequently teased by his classmates, who called him "dumb." Gradually, Dave began to spend more and more time by himself, remaining in his room for hours listening to music and interacting less with his family members and friends. Dave's parents' concern grew as his grades dropped from mediocre to poor, and he ceased playing the piano, which had formerly been his favorite activity. They attempted to talk to Dave about his problems at school, but he kept putting them off by saying that nothing was wrong; they did not press him further.

After several months of increasing social withdrawal, Dave's behavior became grossly disorganized and bizarre. He began staying up nights, pacing, and talking excitedly about the FBI and the Mafia following him and interfering with his thoughts. Later, he complained to his mother that voices were telling him to hurt himself and that he was receiving messages from the radio and television. After an especially difficult day in which Dave became extremely agitated, started to throw food around the house, and attempted to climb the walls, his parents realized that he would not "snap out of it" and needed immediate medical attention, so they took him to a mental health clinic.

Dave was admitted to a local psychiatric hospital, where he was treated unsuccessfully with antipsychotic medications for a month, and was then transferred to a state hospital for longer-term treatment. Throughout much of his inpatient stay, Dave's behavior alternated between aggressive, explosive outbursts, precipitated by delusions of having been raped or physically abused, to confusion in not being able to distinguish other patients from his family members, to apathy, depression, and social withdrawal. Eventually, he responded to electroconvulsive therapy (ECT) and was discharged after six months on maintenance chlorpromazine with a diagnosis of undifferentiated schizophrenia.

Dave returned home and completed high school. He did not have his second hospitalization until he was twenty-one years old and had begun attending music school. Although he was subsequently able to return to school and complete a two-year associate's degree in music, the following twelve years were characterized by multiple hospitalizations, declining vocational and social functioning, and marked negative symptoms. He attended day treatment programs sporadically, and several relapses were precipitated by his discontinuation of his medication.

When Dave was thirty-three years old and his parents were out of town for several weeks, he ran out of his antipsychotic medication and was not able to get his prescription refilled. He rapidly became psychotic and was involved in an altercation in which he was badly beaten by a security guard at a supermarket after leaving the store half naked with some food he had not paid for. Dave was charged with simple assault and placed in a detention center where he remained for two months, until his family was able to get the charges dropped and arranged a transfer to a psychiatric hospital. Dave was admitted to a psychiatric hospital, where he was enrolled in an outpatient treatment program that combined low-dose antipsychotic medication with BFT.

Following a six-week hospitalization, Dave's psychotic symptoms were well controlled, but he continued to have negative symptoms. His affect was flat, he had severe psychomotor retardation, he slept much of the time, and he interacted with few people other than his family. Dave began attending a day treatment program, he and his parents participated in monthly support groups, and they started BFT sessions, which were conducted by a therapist who came to their house.

Before the family sessions began, members were interviewed individually to identify specific goals for treatment and to assess their knowledge of schizophrenia. Despite more than ten years' experience with repeated hospitalizations, no one in the family knew even the most basic facts about the illness; they were unfamiliar with the symptoms, names, and side effects of medications, and they did not know about the effect of stress on the course of the illness. During the educational sessions, family members learned the early signs of a relapse of schizophrenia, which for Dave included suspiciousness, auditory hallucinations, and increased sleeping. On two occasions over the following two years, impending relapses were recognized and successfully avoided as Dave and his parents employed the family problem-solving skills that were taught in the family sessions.

In communication skills training, special attention was given to improving Dave's nonverbal communication (eye contact, voice volume, tone), which was muted owing to his pronounced negative symptoms. Over the course of more than twenty-five sessions, Dave engaged in numerous role-plays with his mother and father, rehearsing such skills as expressing positive and negative feelings. One skill that Dave found particularly difficult was making positive requests. In one family session, he engaged in several role-plays with his parents portraying co-workers or a supervisor at his part-time job, where he rehearsed requesting help on a job: "Chuck, could you show me how we're supposed to assemble this? I'd really appreciate it." Dave's parents focused on increasing their verbal reinforcement to shape desired changes in his behavior by expressing positive feelings to him for small improvements. In one meeting, Dave's father expressed his satisfaction with his involvement on the job: "Son, I'm really proud of you getting up so early every day to get to your job on time."

The family members learned quickly how to do cooperative problem solving following the steps of the skill. However, extensive prompting was necessary to get the family to meet on their own for weekly problem-solving sessions, which they finally began after ten months of treatment. A wide range of problems was addressed, including coping with auditory hallucinations, arriving late at the workshop, and feeling fatigued. One important goal for Dave was to begin practicing the piano again. After a period of four months and several problem-solving discussions, Dave moved from not practicing at all to practicing three to four times per week. Dave began to accept invitations to play the piano, which he had formerly rejected, such as for the church choir and at parties. Coupled with his increase in playing the piano, Dave began again to arrange and write his own music, something he had not done for several years.

Throughout the course of treatment Dave steadily improved. He gradually made the transition from a day hospital to a supported employment program. Although Dave continued to have negative symptoms, they were reduced in severity. By the end of the first year of combined drug and family therapy, Dave's Brief Psychiatric Rating Scale (Mueser, Curran, and McHugo, 1997; Overall and Gorham, 1962) scores declined from severe to mild for blunted affect, and from moderately severe to mild and very mild for psychomotor retardation and emotional withdrawal, respectively. Despite his residual symptoms, Dave's social adjustment continued to improve, enabling him to marry his girlfriend of several years. He was able to move out of his parents' home into an apartment with his wife, while continuing to attend his work program and remaining clinically stable. Much of the burden of care on his family was reduced as Dave assumed more responsibility for managing his illness, such as attending follow-up medication appointments and a vocational program. In addition, he was able to transfer skills learned in family therapy to his relationship with his wife. One example of this was the institution of regular marital problem-solving meetings.

Over the fourteen years since BFT was initiated with Dave and his family, he has continued to make steady gains toward greater independence and psychosocial functioning. Dave has not been hospitalized since he began the BFT program. On several occasions, early warning signs of a relapse were detected, medication dosage was temporarily increased, and full-blown relapses (and hospitalizations) were averted. Dave and his wife have had two children and their relationship continues to be strong. Dave has also continued to increase his involvement in music. In addition to doing some music composition, Dave plays the organ each week at his father's church, and he gives private piano lessons to students. Although Dave's psychosocial functioning is excellent, he continues to be significantly blunted, for which he compensates by using verbal feeling statements when appropriate. Dave also has some psychomotor retardation, and occasionally mild cognitive confusion. However, despite these symptoms, he continues to function well as a worker and a father and to enjoy the support of his family.

STRENGTHS AND LIMITATIONS

The major strength of BFT is that it is a flexible treatment model that can be tailored to meet the needs of families with a wide range of different problems associated with bipolar disorder and schizophrenia. The strong educational and behavioral focus of BFT is another strength. Families of clients with severe mental illness are often skeptical of family interventions that delve into historical analysis, fostering insight, and understanding "hidden motivations." Families appreciate the practical focus of BFT on solving immediately pressing problems and achieving valued goals. Furthermore, the emphasis of BFT on active collaboration with the treatment team is experienced by families as empowering.

Another major strength of the BFT model is the abundance of controlled research demonstrating its effectiveness. Several studies have demonstrated the effectiveness of BFT in reducing relapses and rehospitalizations over two years for clients with schizophrenia (Falloon and Pederson, 1985; Randolph et al., 1994; Randolph et al., 1995; Schooler et al., 1997; Tarrier et al., 1989; Xiong et al., 1994). Across multiple studies, BFT has been found to reduce the risk of relapse over two years from about 60 percent to about 30 percent in clients with schizophrenia. Controlled research has also shown similar benefits for clients with bipolar disorder (Clarkin et al., 1998; Miklowitz, 1998; Rea et al., 1998). Indeed, the research supporting the effectiveness of BFT for schizophrenia and bipolar disorder is more extensive than the research supporting any other model of family intervention for these disorders (Baucom et al., 1998).

BFT is well suited to educate families about psychiatric illness and help them develop better skills for its management. However, the model may be less helpful when the client and relatives have little ongoing contact with each other and when they share relatively few problems. For example, a client who sees his or her relatives only once every several weeks because they live far away is unlikely to experience much benefit from a course of BFT, although a limited course of just the educational sessions could be helpful.

Another limitation of BFT may be inherent to its emphasis on teaching information and skills. Although many families benefit from this learning-based approach, some families are in greater need of validation and social support for their experiences than learning specific information and skills. Alternative formats for family intervention, such as the multiple-family group approach (McFarlane, Link, et al., 1995; McFarlane, Lukens, et al., 1995), may be more helpful for such families.

INTEGRATION WITH PSYCHIATRIC SERVICES AND ROLE OF MEDICATION

BFT for schizophrenia and bipolar disorder is provided in the context of comprehensive psychiatric care, including pharmacological treatment, case management, and access to other rehabilitation services, such as supported employment (Drake et al., 1999). There is abundant evidence that antipsychotic medications for schizophrenia and mood-stabilizing medications for bipolar disorder are critical elements of effective treatment for these illnesses. One important goal of family intervention is to improve adherence to recommended medications by helping clients and their relatives understand the effects of medication, its role in treatment, and to identify and problem solve side effects related to medication.

CULTURAL AND GENDER ISSUES

To be effective, BFT must be practiced by a clinician who is culturally competent with the culture from which the family comes (McGoldrick, 1998; McGoldrick, Giordano, and Pearce, 1996). Cultural competence involves an appreciation and understanding of the central values held by a cultural group, especially as those values may relate to family life and mutual expectations among members. As with individual psychotherapy, a poor understanding of cultural values and beliefs may undermine the effectiveness of treatment and lead to inadvertently attempting to make changes that are not supported by the values of the culture.

There are several ways in which the BFT model may need to be adapted in order to make it consonant with different cultural norms. In communications skills training, BFT emphasizes the importance of behavioral specificity and, when appropriate, the expression of clear feeling statements, including expressing negative feelings. In some cultural groups, it may be considered inappropriate to directly express negative feelings or for one generation (e.g., younger) to express such feelings to another (older) generation. Naturally, the specific communication skills taught in BFT must be adapted to the norms of the cultural group to which the family belongs.

Another example of the need to adapt the BFT model may arise in the teaching of problem-solving skills. In some cultures, one family member has a designated role as the family leader, whereas in other cultures various members may act as the leader. If the family has a leader who is designated by the culture, training in problem-solving skills is most successful when that leader is given the role of chairing the family problem-solving efforts. On the other hand, when there is no culturally designated leader, the family can elect their own chairpersons to lead family problem solving.

Another area in the practice of BFT that requires cultural competence concerns educating family members about the nature of psychiatric illness. Some cultures have specific belief systems about mental illness, such as the phenomenon of *espiritismo* for understanding psychosis in Hispanic culture (Comos-Diaz, 1981; Morales-Dorta, 1976). In order to educate families about psychiatric illness and its treatment, therapists need to be familiar with cultural beliefs about mental illness and present alternative conceptualizations in a manner that demonstrates respect for other cultural interpretations. Whenever possible, working within the culture's belief system toward improved family management of the psychiatric disorder is most likely to prove beneficial.

Gender issues overlap with cultural issues in that cultural norms may dictate gender-specific behavior that the therapist must be familiar with to work effectively with the family. In addition to the interaction between gender and culture, several other gender issues are relevant to the practice of BFT. With respect to schizophrenia, women are more likely than men to marry and have children. Furthermore, because more women with children have parenting responsibilities than men, women with either schizophrenia or bipolar disorder frequently need help with issues of parenting and negotiating parenting responsibilities with their spouses. Indeed, the failure to address parenting and spousal issues may contribute to the dissolution of a marriage and the breakup of a family as the strain of coping with a serious mental illness without the collaboration of the treatment team becomes too great (Fox, 1999).

Although BFT can be used to treat any family constellation, with men the relatives most often involved are parents or siblings, whereas for women it is spouses or children. Different issues often arise when working with different family constellations. For example, when working with adult clients and their parents, common family issues involve improving the client's independence, including independent living. When working with spouses, important issues often revolve around the distribution and sharing of household and parenting responsibilities, intimacy and sexuality, and helping the spouse cope with feelings associated with unmet expectations stemming from a client's diminished capacity (e.g., as wage earner or homemaker).

Aside from gender differences related to different roles men and women may play in their families, gender may also be differentially related to other important comorbid disorders. Substance use disorders are common in persons with schizophrenia and depression, with about 50 percent of individuals with these psychiatric disorders having a lifetime diagnosis of substance abuse or dependence (Regier et al., 1990). Although substance abuse is common, men with schizophrenia or bipolar disorder are much more likely to have a substance use disorder than are women (Mueser et al., 1990; Mueser, Yarnold, and Bellack, 1992). Thus, the BFT therapist is more likely to encounter and need to address substance abuse when working with male clients and their families than female clients.

A second comorbid condition related to gender is trauma and posttraumatic stress disorder (PTSD). Although traumatic experiences are common in the lives of people with severe mental illness, women are more likely to be sexually abused and assaulted; they are also more likely to be physically injured in disputes with family members who are partners (Cascardi et al., 1996; Goodman et al., 1997; Mueser et al., 1998). The greater vulnerability of women to domestic violence means that BFT clinicians need to be alert to the signs of family violence, should screen for it routinely (e.g., using The Revised Conflicts Tactics Scale, Straus et al., 1995), and may need to take steps either to protect a client (or relative) from potential violence, to help the couple develop less aggressive methods for resolving conflicts, or to treat the aftermath of significant violence, such as PTSD.

FUTURE DIRECTIONS

Research has established that BFT is effective for improving the course of schizophrenia and bipolar disorder, but many questions remain. One unresolved issue concerns the optimal duration of treatment and the determination of when a family is prepared to end BFT sessions. In many families, BFT is provided on a time-limited basis, while a minority of families appear to require ongoing maintenance BFT sessions. However, reliable indicators of when BFT sessions may be stopped have not been identified, leaving the termination of sessions to clinical judgment. Examples of objective indicators might include the continued presence of strong levels of negative affect in the family, continued substance abuse, substantial psychosocial stressors on the family (e.g., extreme poverty, multiple impaired family members), or chronic psychotic symptoms.

Another issue requiring attention is the potential role of grief counseling for relatives of clients with a severe psychiatric illness. Clinicians have observed that some relatives experience substantial grief reactions in response to the emergence of a psychiatric illness in a close person and have advocated grief counseling as a treatment strategy (Miller et al., 1990). However, the benefits of grief counseling under such circumstances have not been established, and the timing and logistics of such counseling and BFT have not been determined.

Another question requiring elucidation is the role of multiple-family groups in addition to, or instead of, BFT. For some families, multiple-family groups may provide continued support after BFT has terminated. Other families may benefit from participating in both multiple-family groups and BFT, or from multiple-family groups alone. McFarlane, Link, and colleagues (1995) have conducted research suggesting that multiple-family groups may have advantages over single-family intervention, although this research did not examine the BFT model specifically. Schooler and colleagues (1997) compared the effects of multiple-family groups alone with BFT plus multiple-family groups. Although patients in both treatment groups (multiple-family groups alone and multiple-family groups plus BFT) had low rates of rehospitalization, with no differences between the groups (Schooler et al., 1997), the addition of BFT resulted in lower levels of family friction and rejecting attitudes toward the client on the part of relatives (Mueser et al., 2001). Further work is needed to determine the relative advantages of BFT compared to multiple-family groups, when and for which types of families each approach is most likely to be beneficial, and when a combination of the approaches is best.

On a final note, more attention needs to be given to the dissemination of the BFT model for schizophrenia and bipolar disorder and to understanding the obstacles to the implementation of BFT in typical community mental health center settings. Despite abundant evidence demonstrating that a variety of models of family intervention are effective for individuals with severe mental illness, only a minority of clients in contact with their family members actually receive family services (Dixon and Lehman, 1995). Clinical services research is needed to close the gap between state-of-the-art family intervention for schizophrenia and bipolar disorder and routine clinical practice.

REFERENCES

Anderson, C. M., Reiss, D. J., and Hogarty, G. E. (1986). *Schizophrenia and the family*. New York: Guilford Press.

Barrowclough, C. and Parle, M. (1997). Appraisal, psychological adjustment and expressed emotion in relatives of patients suffering from schizophrenia. *British Journal of Psychiatry, 171,* 26-30.

Barrowclough, C. and Tarrier, N. (1992). *Families of schizophrenic patients: Cognitive behavioural intervention.* London: Chapman and Hall.

Bateson, G., Jackson, D. D., Haley, J., and Weakland, J. (1956). Toward a theory of schizophrenia. *Behavioral Science, 1,* 251-264.

Baucom, D. H., Shoham, V., Mueser, K. T., Daiuto, A. D., and Stickle, T. R. (1998). Empirically supported couple and family interventions for adult mental health problems. *Journal of Consulting and Clinical Psychology, 66,* 53-88.

Bellack, A. S., Mueser, K. T., Gingerich, S., and Agresta, J. (1997). *Social skills training for schizophrenia: A step-by-step guide.* New York: Guilford.

Brown, S. and Birtwistle, J. (1998). People with schizophrenia and their families: Fifteen-year outcome. *British Journal of Psychiatry, 173,* 139-144.

Butzlaff, R. L. and Hooley, J. M. (1998). Expressed emotion and psychiatric relapse. *Archives of General Psychiatry, 55,* 547-552.

Carpentier, N., Lesage, A., Goulet, I., Lalonde, P., and Renaud, M. (1992). Burden of care of families not living with a young schizophrenic relative. *Hospital and Community Psychiatry, 43,* 38-43.

Cascardi, M., Mueser, K. T., DeGiralomo, J., and Murrin, M. (1996). Physical aggression against psychiatric inpatients by family members and partners: A descriptive study. *Psychiatric Services, 47*(5), 531-533.

Clarkin, J. F., Carpenter, D., Hull, J., Wilner, P., and Glick, I. (1998). Effects of psychoeducational intervention for married patients with bipolar disorder and their spouses. *Psychiatric Services, 49,* 531-533.

Comos-Diaz, L. (1981). Puerto Rican espiritismo and psychotherapy. *American Journal of Orthopsychiatry, 51,* 636-645.

Dixon, L. and Lehman, A. F. (1995). Family interventions for schizophrenia. *Schizophrenia Bulletin, 21,* 631-643.

Drake, R. E., Becker, D. R., Clark, R. E., and Mueser, K. T. (1999). Research on the individual placement and support model of supported employment. *Psychiatric Quarterly, 70,* 289-301.

Falloon, I. R. H., Boyd, J. L., and McGill, C. W. (1984). *Family care of schizophrenia: A problem-solving approach to the treatment of mental illness.* New York: Guilford.

Falloon, I. R. H. and Pederson, J. (1985). Family management in the prevention of morbidity of schizophrenia: The adjustment of the family unit. *British Journal of Psychiatry, 147,* 156-163.

Fox, L. (1999). Missing out on motherhood. *Psychiatric Services, 50*(2), 193-194.

Fromm-Reichman, F. (1948). Notes on the development of treatment of schizophrenics by psychoanalytic psychotherapy. *Psychiatry, 1,* 263-273.

Goldman, H. H. (1984). The chronically mentally ill: Who are they? Where are they? In M. Mirabi (Ed.), *The chronically mentally ill: Research and services* (pp. 33-44). New York: Spectrum Publications.

Goodman, L. A., Rosenberg, S. D., Mueser, K. T., and Drake, R. E. (1997). Physical and sexual assault history in women with serious mental illness: Prevalence, correlates, treatment, and future research directions. *Schizophrenia Bulletin, 23*(4), 685-696.

Harrison, C. A., Dadds, M. R., and Smith, G. (1998). Family caregivers' criticism of patients with schizophrenia. *Psychiatric Services, 49,* 918-924.

Hatfield, A. B. and Lefley, H. P. (1987). *Families of the mentally ill: Coping and adaptation.* New York: Guilford.

Hatfield, A. B. and Lefley, H. P. (1993). *Surviving mental illness: Stress, coping, and adaptation.* New York: Guilford.

Kuipers, L., Leff, J., and Lam, D. (1992). *Family work for schizophrenia: A practical guide.* London: Gaskell.

Liberman, R. P., Mueser, K. T., Wallace, C. J., Jacobs, H. E., Eckman, T., and Massel, H. K. (1986). Training skills in the psychiatrically disabled: Learning coping and competence. *Schizophrenia Bulletin, 12,* 631-647.

Lopez, S. R., Nelson, K. A., Snyder, K. S., and Mintz, J. (1999). Attributions and affective reactions of family members and course of schizophrenia. *Journal of Abnormal Psychology, 108,* 307-314.

McFarlane, W. R. (1990). Multiple family groups and the treatment of schizophrenia. In M. I. Herz, S. J. Keith, and J. P. Docherty (Eds.), *Handbook of schizophrenia. Volume 4: Psychosocial treatment of schizophrenia* (pp. 167-189). Amsterdam: Elsevier.

McFarlane, W. R., Link, B., Dushay, R., Marchal, J., and Crilly, J. (1995). Psychoeducational multiple family groups: Four-year relapse outcome in schizophrenia. *Family Process, 34,* 127-144.

McFarlane, W. R., Lukens, E., Link, B., Dushay, R., Deakins, S. A., Newmark, M., Dunne, E. J., Horen, B., and Toran, J. (1995). Multiple-family groups and psychoeducation in the treatment of schizophrenia. *Archives of General Psychiatry, 52,* 679-687.

McGoldrick, M. (Ed.) (1998). *Revisioning family therapy.* New York: Guilford.

McGoldrick, M., Giordano, J., and Pearce, J. (Eds.) (1996). *Ethnicity and family therapy* (Second edition). New York: Guilford.

Miklowitz, D. J. (1998). *Family-focused intervention for patients with bipolar disorders.* Paper presented at the VI World Congress, World Association of Psychosocial Rehabilitation, Hamburg, Germany.

Miklowitz, D. J. and Goldstein, M. J. (1997). *Bipolar disorder: A family-focused treatment approach.* New York: Guilford.

Miller, R., Dworkin, J., Ward, M., and Barone, D. (1990). A preliminary study of unresolved grief in families of seriously mentally ill patients. *Hospital and Community Psychiatry, 41,* 1321-1325.

Morales-Dorta, J. (1976). *Puerto Rican espiritismo: Religion and psychotherapy.* New York: Vantage.

Mueser, K. T., Curran, P. J., and McHugo, G. J. (1997). Factor structure of the Brief Psychiatric Rating Scale in schizophrenia. *Psychological Assessment, 9,* 196-204.

Mueser, K. T. and Glynn, S. M. (1999). *Behavioral family therapy for psychiatric disorders* (Second edition). Oakland, CA: New Harbinger.

Mueser, K. T., Goodman, L. B., Trumbetta, S. L., Rosenberg, S. D., Osher, F. C., Vidaver, R., Auciello, P., and Foy, D. W. (1998). Trauma and posttraumatic stress disorder in severe mental illness. *Journal of Consulting and Clinical Psychology, 66,* 493-499.

Mueser, K. T., Sengupta, A., Schooler, N. R., Bellack, A. S., Xie, H., Glick, I. D., and Keith, S. J. (2001). Family treatment and medication dosage reduction in schizophrenia: Effects on patient social functioning, family attitudes, and burden. *Journal of Consulting and Clinical Psychology, 69,* 3-12.

Mueser, K. T., Yarnold, P. R., and Bellack, A. S. (1992). Diagnostic and demographic correlates of substance abuse in schizophrenia and major affective disorder. *Acta Psychiatrica Scandinavica, 85,* 48-55.

Mueser, K. G., Yarnold, P. R., Levinson, D. F., Singh, H., Bellack, A. S., Kee, K., Morrison, R. L., and Yadalam, K. G. (1990). Prevalence of substance abuse in schizophrenia: Demographic and clinical correlates. *Schizophrenia Bulletin, 16,* 31-56.

Overall, J. E. and Gorham, D. R. (1962). The Brief Psychiatric Rating Scale. *Psychological Reports, 10,* 799-812.

Randolph, E. T., Eth, S., Glynn, S., Paz, G. B., Leong, G. B., Shaner, A. L., Strachan, A., Van Vort, W., Escobar, J., and Liberman, R. P. (1994). Behavioural family management in schizophrenia: Outcome from a clinic-based intervention. *British Journal of Psychiatry, 144,* 501-506.

Randolph, E. T., Glynn, S. M., Eth, S., Paz, G. G., Leong, G. B., and Shaner, A. L. (1995). *Family therapy for schizophrenia: Two year outcome.* Paper presented at the Annual Meeting of American Psychiatric Association, Miami, Florida, May.

Rea, M. M., Goldstein, M. J., Tompson, M. C., and Miklowitz, D. J. (1998). *Family and individual therapy in bipolar disorders: Outline and first results of the study.* Paper presented at the VI World Congress, World Association of Psychosocial Rehabilitation, Hamburg, Germany, May 4.

Regier, D. A., Farmer, M. E., Rae, D. S., Locke, B. Z., Keith, S. J., Judd, L. L., and Goodwin, F. K. (1990). Comorbidity of mental disorders with alcohol and other drug abuse: Results from the Epidemiologic Catchment Area (ECA) study. *Journal of the American Medical Association, 264,* 2511-2518.

Schooler, N. R., Keith, S. J., Severe, J. B., Matthews, S. M., Bellack, A. S., Glick, I. D., Hargreaves, W. A., Kane, J. M., Ninan, P. T., Frances, A., Jacobs, M., Lieberman, J. A., Mance, R., Simpson, G. M., and Woerner, M. G. (1997). Relapse and rehospitalization during maintenance treatment of schizophrenia: The effects of dose reduction and family treatment. *Archives of General Psychiatry, 54,* 453-463.

Straus, M. A., Hamby, S. L., Boney-McCoy, S., and Sugarman, D. B. (1995). *The Revised Conflict Tactics Scales (CTS2)*. Durham, NH: Family Research Laboratory.

Sullivan, H. S. (1972). The onset of schizophrenia. *American Journal of Psychiatry, 7,* 105-134.

Tarrier, N., Barrowclough, C., Vaughn, C., Bamrak, J. S., Porceddu, K., Watts, S., and Freeman, H. (1989). Community management of schizophrenia: A two-year follow-up of a behavioural intervention with families. *British Journal of Psychiatry, 154,* 625-628.

Xiong, W., Phillips, M. R., Hu, X., Ruiwen, W., Dai, Q., Kleinman, J., and Kleinman, A. (1994). Family-based intervention for schizophrenic patients in China: A randomised controlled trial. *British Journal of Psychiatry, 165,* 239-247.

Zubin, J. and Spring, B. (1977). Vulnerability: A new view of schizophrenia. *Journal of Abnormal Psychology, 86,* 103-126.

Chapter 4

Family Treatment of Depression and the McMaster Model of Family Functioning

Wilson McDermut
James W. Alves
Ivan W. Miller
Gabor I. Keitner

INTRODUCTION

A developing body of literature documents the important relationship between major depression and family functioning (Keitner and Miller, 1990). Families with a depressed member have significant levels of family dysfunction and/or marital discord (e.g., Miller et al., 1992; Rounsaville, Prusoff, and Weissman, 1980). Aspects of family functioning have also been found to be predictive of the course of major depression. For example, family dysfunction is associated with a slower rate of recovery from a depressive episode (Corney, 1987; Keitner et al., 1995; Keitner et al., 1992). In addition, high levels of expressed emotion (excessive criticism and/or emotional over-involvement) within the family increases the likelihood of relapse after hospital discharge for depressed patients (e.g., Hooley, Orley, and Teasdale, 1986).

Though a substantial body of research shows that the family is an important influence on depressed patients, few controlled studies have investigated the efficacy of family or marital treatment for depressed patients. Studies that have been conducted (e.g., Beach and O'Leary, 1986; Friedman, 1975; McLean, Ogtron, and Grauer, 1973) have generally found that marital or family therapies can be effective treatments for depression. Underscoring the significance of family functioning, some evidence has emerged (e.g., Jacobson et al., 1991) that a subset of depressed patients with high levels of family dysfunction may not respond to individual therapy alone.

It is against the backdrop of research underscoring the important association between depression and family functioning that we felt the importance of incorporating a strong family treatment and research component into our work with depressed patients. The particular family model we have adopted is the McMaster Model of Family Functioning (MMFF), which is described in further detail below.

SETTING

The Mood Disorders and Family Research Programs of Rhode Island Hospital espouse a biopsychosocial model of mental health functioning. The mission of the Mood Disorders Program is to serve adults with affective disorders (major depression and bipolar disorder), to conduct research, and to provide clinical care that addresses the needs of psychiatric patients at the biological, psychological, and family level. The mission of the Family Research Program is to develop methods for assessing family functioning and provide family treatment for psychiatric and medical populations. The program consists of researchers and clinicians from various backgrounds (psychology, psychiatry, sociology, education), psychiatry residents, psychology interns and fellows, and a number of experienced bachelor's and master's level research associates. The programs are housed together on the main campus of Rhode Island Hospital, a large general hospital in Providence, Rhode Island, that is affiliated with Brown University Medical School. The Mood Disorders and Family Research Programs are located near other branches of the psychiatry department which are also on, or very near, the main campus of the hospital. These include the inpatient psychiatry unit, an outpatient psychiatry clinic, acute psychiatric services, and the department of outpatient psychiatry. The hospital also has an active child and family psychiatry division with a number of clinical researchers who also have adopted the McMaster Model of Family Functioning approach, and with whom we have collaborated on projects of shared interest (e.g., Hayden et al., 1998).

TREATMENT MODEL

The McMaster Model of Family Functioning

The McMaster Model of Family Functioning has been in development for the past thirty years. The McMaster Model grew out of research and clinical work in the departments of psychiatry at McGill and McMaster Universities in Canada. The overall model encompasses a view of family functioning (both healthy and unhealthy), techniques for assessment, and an approach to treatment. The treatment component of the model is known as Problem-Centered Systems Therapy of the Family (PCSTF) (Epstein and Bishop, 1981; Epstein et al., 1990).

Research on the McMaster Model

Research on the MMFF has focused on establishing the reliability and validity of assessment instruments and testing the efficacy of PCSTF. The self-report Family Assessment Device (FAD) (Epstein, Baldwin, and Bishop, 1983; Kabacoff et al., 1990) has been found to have low correlations with social desirability and moderate correlations with global measures of marital functioning (Miller et al., 1985). Miller and colleagues (1994) have found that the FAD also correlates moderately with our observer rating of family functioning, the McMaster Clinical Rating Scale (MCRS). Concurrent validity of the MCRS was documented by studies demonstrating good correspondence between the MCRS scales and the self-report FAD (Fristad, 1989; Hayden et al., 1998; Miller et al., 1994). The MCRS has also been shown to correlate significantly with independently rated family behavior during mealtimes in the home (Hayden et al., 1998). In addition, Bishop and colleagues (1980) have developed a structured family interview, the McMaster Structured Interview of Family Functioning (McSIFF).

Although the number of treatment outcome studies based on the MMFF and PCSTF is relatively small, the results have been highly encouraging. In an early study, 279 families who entered treatment at an outpatient children's clinic for behavioral or academic problems were treated with PCSTF. The results provided strong support for the effectiveness of this treatment method, with over 65 percent of the families showing positive effects from the treatment (Woodward et al.,

1978). More recent federally funded studies have utilized PCSTF as part of a multimodal treatment program for inpatients with major depression (Miller, Keitner, et al., 1998) and patients with bipolar disorder (Miller et al., 1999). Finally, we have developed a telephone-administered intervention for stroke patients and their caregivers based on the MMFF (Bishop et al., 1997). This intervention has been tested in one study and found to produce significant improvements in family functioning following a stroke (Miller, Weiner, et al., 1998).

Dimensions of Family Functioning

The MMFF outlines a number of clinical dimensions that are important to address with families presenting for treatment. A family can be evaluated to determine the effectiveness of its functioning with respect to each dimension. To understand the family structure, organization, and transactional patterns associated with family difficulties, we focus on assessing six dimensions of family life: communication, problem solving, roles, affective responsiveness, affective involvement, and behavior control (Epstein, Bishop, and Levin, 1978); disturbances in these six dimensions often result in dysfunctional transactional patterns.

In our work with families with a depressed member, we have been impressed by the heterogeneity of the ways in which they behave, cope, and adapt. In our view, there is no prototypical presentation. Nevertheless, we have observed some common themes that we will describe when we discuss the dimensions of family functioning delineated by the McMaster model.

Communication

The MMFF defines communication as how information is verbally exchanged between family members. Communication is also subdivided into instrumental and affective areas. *Instrumental areas* refer to the mechanical problems of everyday life, such as money management. *Affective areas* refer to emotional experiences. In addition, family communication is evaluated along two dimensions: clarity and directness. *Clarity* refers to the extent to which a message is unambiguous versus vague. *Directness* relates to the degree to which a message is unequivocally addressed to the person for whom it is intended.

The communication style in families with a depressed member is often marked by hostility, which can be manifested as a pervasive low-grade tension and/or frequent bickering and arguing. This is seen clinically and has been remarked upon by numerous researchers (e.g., Hinchcliffe et al., 1975; Coyne, 1989). Communication between marital partners is often particularly acrimonious (Beach, Sandeen, and O'Leary, 1990; Kahn, Coyne, and Margolin, 1985; Rounsaville, Prusoff, and Weissman, 1980). It is also not uncommon to see stifled communication in which marital partners report a paucity of intimate exchanges or children of depressed parents are not informed that a parent is experiencing depression.

Problem Solving

The problem-solving dimension is defined as a family's ability to resolve problems in order to maintain effective family functioning. Problem solving in families with a depressed member is often impaired at the level of problem identification, such that family members cannot agree on the nature of the problem or even that a problem exists. Attempts at resolving problems often degenerate into arguments and then result in an impasse. Couples in which a family member is depressed, like distressed couples more generally, often report one or more issues that repeatedly result in unproductive arguing. This is a particularly difficult problem for the depressed family member whose sense of hopelessness about the possibility of an improved marriage is reinforced. In addition, the depressed family member may feel overwhelmed by problems that are perceived as "not such a big deal" to nondepressed family members.

Roles

Family roles are the recurrent patterns of behavior by which individuals fulfill their responsibilities. The provision of nurturance and support and adult sexual gratification fall under the rubric of roles. Normal family roles are often impaired at multiple levels in families with a depressed family member. The depressed individual may begin to fall behind in his or her household responsibilities. The backlog of chores is perceived as overwhelming and appears insurmountable. In addition, the framework provided by typical daily routines (what Beach et al., 1990, refer to as "scripted behavior") may begin to break down. Routines, such as eating meals together or a "good-bye kiss" in the morning, are not adhered to. This lack of structure may begin because the depressed family member withdraws. Other family members may withdraw or actively avoid in response. This lack of consistent routine is distressing to all family members—particularly to depressed individuals who may perceive the avoidance as evidence that they are unloved or unworthy. Sexual activity also tends to decrease in frequency because of depression-induced loss of libido or as a consequence of spouses spending less time together.

Affective Responsiveness

Affective responsiveness is defined as the ability of the family to respond to a range of stimuli with the appropriate quality and quantity of feelings. We attempt to ascertain if family members experience a full range of emotions, as well as the intensity and contextual appropriateness of their emotional experience. The affective milieu of a family with a depressed member is often characterized as angry or tense. Depressed individuals often report irritability; their family members, especially spouses of depressed individuals, may report feeling angry toward the depressed family member. The anger could spring from any number of sources, such as the perceived rejection by the depressed individual, resentment about having to "pick up the slack" and do more around the house, or anger that the depressed person "just can't snap out of it." Depressed family members often feel guilt above and beyond that which is symptomatic of depression. They often report feeling guilty about not keeping up with chores, about losing their temper so easily with their spouses and children, or about the very fact that they are depressed.

Affective Involvement

The dimension of affective involvement is defined as the degree to which the family as a whole shows interest in and values the activities and interests of individual family members. As a consequence of anhedonia (loss of pleasure in life), it is not surprising that depressed individuals report decreased interest in many things, including their family relationships. In cases in which the family members have withdrawn or actively avoid each other, they will present as lacking affective involvement.

Behavior Control

The behavior control dimension is defined as the pattern a family adopts for handling behavior in three domains: physically dangerous situations, situations that involve psychobiological drives (such as eating, drinking, sleeping, elimination, sex, and aggression), and situations involving intrafamily interactions and social behavior. In assessing behavior control in all families it is important to inquire about verbal and/or physical abuse. Physical abuse of a spouse is often associated with trauma-related symptoms and is thought to be sufficiently stressful to precipitate the onset of depression or hinder recovery. With regard to verbal abuse (e.g., excessive criticism, name-calling) in depressed families, it has been our experience that depressed individuals are the most likely to report being bothered by name-calling even if they engage in it to the same degree as other family members. Research indicates that depressed individuals with highly critical family members face increased vulnerability to relapse.

Dysfunctional Transactional Patterns

Dysfunctional transactional patterns refer to characteristic or common interactions between family members that are associated with impaired functioning in one or more of the dimensions of family functioning previously described. A common pattern we have seen is a depressed family member who seeks increased quality time or increased communication with his or her partner, who feels pressured and withdraws in response. The partner's withdrawal prompts stronger demands, which result in further withdrawal, and so on. Another form of this pattern is seen when a family member tries to draw out a depressed family member who withdraws even further, sometimes by overtly rejecting his or her help. These transactional patterns often spiral downward into very familiar arguments that are reenacted over and over again despite accomplishing nothing and leaving both family members frustrated, angry, and exasperated.

Problem-Centered Systems Therapy of the Family

The treatment model is founded upon several basic assumptions about family dynamics (Epstein and Bishop, 1981). It is predominantly a systems approach in which the family is viewed as an "open system" consisting of interwoven systems (individual, marital, dyadic) that are related to other systems (extended family, schools, industry, religion). The assumptions of the systems theory underlying the model are as follows:

1. All parts of the family are interrelated.
2. One part of the family cannot be understood in isolation from the remainder of the family system.
3. Family functioning cannot be understood fully by understanding discrete individuals or dyads.
4. The structure and organization of the family strongly impact and determine the behavior of family members.
5. Transactional patterns within the family strongly affect the behavior of family members.

Therapy for families in which a member suffers from a mental illness is aimed at changing systemic processes and thereby changing the behavior of the identified patient.

The treatment process is conceptualized as being composed of four macro stages (assessment, contracting, treatment, closure). Each macro stage begins with an orientation to the purpose of the stage and is composed of a sequence of substages. Therapists seek the permission of the family before moving to another step. In PCSTF, therapists repeatedly check to make sure families understand what the therapist is doing. Indirect or paradoxical interventions are incompatible with this principle and, thus, are not employed in PCSTF. Additionally, the model stresses that the family and therapist will be active collaborators.

Assessment

The first major stage, and in many ways the most important stage, is the assessment stage. The assessment stage consists of five steps: (1) orientation, (2) data gathering, (3) problem description, (4) clarifying and agreeing on a problem list, and (5) formulation. The family is oriented by clarifying what each member expects will happen during the initial session; why they think they are here; and what they hope will come out of it. The therapist summarizes the family's expectations, then outlines his or her understanding of why the family is there, what is already known about them in general, and what the therapist plans to do.

In the data-gathering stage, the therapist determines what the presenting problems are and assesses the functioning of the family across the six dimensions of family functioning (communication, problem solving, roles, affective responsiveness, affective involvement, behavior control) as well as the family's overall functioning and dysfunctional transactional patterns. The PCSTF approach stresses the importance of a thorough assessment; therapists are encouraged to complete a comprehensive assessment before starting treatment. A therapist using the MMFF approach and PCSTF has a number of assessment instruments with established psychometric properties at his or her disposal (e.g., FAD, MCRS, and McSIFF).

After gathering relevant data, the family, in conjunction with the therapist, summarizes and develops a formal list of problems to be addressed. The final step in the assessment process is to obtain agreement regarding the problem list. Before proceeding to the treatment phase, the therapist develops a formulation for the identified problems. The formulation ideally should take into account variables associated with each problem and include a detailed description of the problem, hypotheses regarding the variables associated with the problem's onset, and hypotheses regarding the variables that appear to maintain the problem.

Contracting

The second macro stage is contracting. The goal is for the therapist and family to prepare a written contract that delineates the mutual expectations, goals, and commitments regarding therapy. The steps in this stage are: (1) orientation, (2) outlining options, (3) negotiating expectations, and (4) contract signing.

After an orientation, the therapist determines whether the family plans to proceed with treatment. Therapists should make it clear that family members are ultimately responsible for most of the work in therapy and that therapy is designed to take place over the course of ten to fifteen sessions spanning weeks, months, or even years. The length of a typical session can range from two-and-a-half hours for an assessment session to twenty minutes for later task-setting sessions. If the family chooses not to enter treatment at this time, the decision is respected; the therapist should make it clear that the family is welcome to return at any time in the future to enter treatment.

If a family decides to proceed with treatment, the therapist proceeds to the negotiation phase, the goal of which is to formulate a set of expectations that each family member wants to see occur if treatment is successful. The technique for establishing these goals is to have each family member negotiate with every other family member how they want one another to change behaviorally. After negotiating expectations, a written contract is prepared that lists the problems and specifies desired outcomes. The therapist's expectations are included and the contract is signed by each family member and the therapist.

Treatment

The third macro stage is treatment. The goals of the treatment stage are to develop and implement problem-solving strategies to change the identified problems. The treatment stage consists of four steps: (1) orientation, (2) clarifying priorities, (3) setting tasks, and (4) task evaluation. After the orientation to the treatment stage, the next step is to prioritize the items on the problem list. We prefer to follow the order established by the family, reinforcing the idea that the family has much of the responsibility for the therapeutic work.

The therapist should help establish priorities if certain detrimental and/or dangerous situations exist in the depressed family but the family does not recognize that these issues need to be addressed immediately. Such issues include name-calling, threats of divorce or separation between spouses, and physically aggressive behavior. The therapist should stress that these behaviors are sufficiently disruptive as to hinder any progress. In addition, they are extremely stressful and may impede recovery from depression. Families with a history of ignoring urgent problems (i.e., suicidality of a family member) may also need direction from the therapist when setting priorities.

At the initiation of the task-setting stage, the therapist asks the family to negotiate and define a task, which, if carried out during the next week, would represent a move toward meeting the previously defined expectation. Typically one or more family members are assigned to monitor progress on the assigned task and report back to the therapist at the next session.

The PCSTF approach has a number of guidelines for task assignment. First, the therapist should be open and direct with the family regarding the purpose of any assigned tasks. Tasks should focus on current issues and be geared primarily toward increasing positive behaviors rather than decreasing negative ones. Tasks should be behavioral and concrete enough so they are easily understood and evaluated. The PCSTF therapist is encouraged to stress the importance of building on family strengths as therapy can sometimes focus too narrowly on the negative. In the treatment phase, the majority of each session is devoted to reviewing progress on assigned tasks and developing new tasks.

Finally, tasks should be feasible and have maximum potential for success. In working with families with a depressed member, it is especially important to start with setting tasks that are most likely to be attainable and to encourage the family to arrange the order of tasks from easy to hard. We encourage this approach because the depressed individual is limited by his or her symptoms (e.g., poor concentration, low energy) and will have less difficulty with tasks that are more likely to be accomplished. Accomplishing basic assignments will boost confidence and build momentum.

One of the tasks for the therapist is to educate the family about depression and its effects on family functioning. This can even be written into the contract. The process of educating the family about depression can have strong therapeutic effects. For example, family members sometimes attribute depressive behavior to personality factors or controllable factors. Family members may mistake the low energy and low motivation for laziness. Educating nondepressed family members may help them reattribute certain behaviors to illness factors. This in turn may allow them to be more understanding and patient with the depressed family member.

In the section below, we outline tasks used to address problems commonly encountered in family treatment of depression. Although we have not covered every dimension, and the following tasks are certainly not the only tasks used, their presentation illustrates the types of tasks used in PCSTF.

Communication. In some families the depressed family member may withdraw from and decrease communication with other family members. A family task might involve setting aside discrete amounts of time during which family members would come together to share their thoughts and feelings. In some families, the depressed member's style is to focus on and discuss primarily negative issues. Those families might agree to set aside discrete amounts of time in which they talk about positive topics. Sometimes when a depressed spouse shares depressive feelings and thoughts to the nondepressed spouse, the nondepressed spouse feels compelled to try to initiate problem solving when the depressed spouse simply wants to vent. In this case, couples can begin practicing new styles of communication; for example, the depressed spouse can begin by saying, "I wanted a chance to talk to you sometime today, but I want you to know ahead of time that I don't have any problems that need to be solved. I just want to share how I'm feeling with you." Families vary in their communication skills and may require more intensive communication skills training, such as that described by Gottman and colleagues (1976).

Problem Solving. Communication and problem solving are strongly linked in the sense that improvement in one domain can result in improvement in the other. If improvement in communication does not translate into improvement in problem solving, more in-depth problem-solving training (e.g., D'Zurilla and Goldfried, 1971) may be helpful.

Behavior Control. Sometimes family members may become angry or resentful toward the depressed family member and use hostile comments or engage in name-calling as a way to motivate the depressed individual. Family members first need to be educated that this approach is counterproductive. Tasks might involve self-monitoring, trying to curtail being critical or denigrating, and increasing positive verbalizations and caring/supportive gestures.

Affective Responsiveness. As discussed earlier, depressed individuals can be very irritable or short-tempered. Directing excessive amounts of anger at their loved ones often becomes a source of intense guilt. Again, family members need to be educated that irritability is often a symptom of depression. However, labeling irritability as a symptom is not an excuse for the depressed member to continue lashing out unchecked. The depressed family member can be assigned to take a time out when irritable. Also, the depressed family member can have the task of regularly giving positive, supportive comments to other family members.

Roles. It is not uncommon for a depressed member to experience low motivation and low energy, resulting in difficulty fulfilling their roles and responsibilities. The family can be assigned the tasks of prioritizing and reapportioning roles if the depressed family member is hospitalized or experiencing severe neurovegetative symptoms. However, the depressed family member should also be encouraged to develop a plan to gradually increase his or her involvement in household duties and responsibilities.

Task Evaluation. Task evaluation is a critical step in the PCSTF model. It is essential that the therapist review the success or failure of the family to accomplish assigned tasks. Information is obtained from the monitor and other appropriate family members. When the family is successful, the therapist provides positive reinforcement and discusses factors contributing to successful accomplishment of the task. However, if the family fails to complete the task, the therapist must initiate a discussion of why the task was not accomplished. Failure to accomplish a task may provide information about the family's difficulties that was not previously available. On the other hand, repeated failed task assignments may indicate that the family may not be ready to make a concerted effort to change

Closure

The final stage is closure, consisting of four steps: (1) orientation, (2) summary of treatment, (3) long-term goals, and (4) follow-up (optional). Orientation involves a discussion of progress and reaching a decision about when to terminate treatment. We generally encourage families that have made sufficient progress to try and resolve new problems on their own, but remind them that they can contact the therapist anytime. Families are asked to summarize what has happened during treatment and what they have learned. At this point, we ask them to identify potential future problems. In working with depressed patients and their families, it is again important to assess the family's need for education about the warning signs of relapse. An optional follow-up appointment may be scheduled to monitor progress.

CASE EXAMPLE

Background and Reason for Referral

The following case example is offered to illustrate several issues that occur when engaging in the assessment and treatment of families with a depressed member using PCSTF. The following description is of a Caucasian family, composed of a thirty-seven-year-old husband, thirty-three-year-old wife, and their son, fourteen, and daughter, eleven. The S family was referred for family assessment as one component of Mr. S's treatment plan following a ten-day inpatient psychiatric admission. Mr. S had been experiencing symptoms of depression for more than three months prior to his inpatient admission. Reluctant to seek treatment, it was only after nearly losing his job of sixteen years (due to disorganization, poor concentration, and irritability) that he sought a psychiatric evaluation. His depressive symptoms included depressed mood, psychomotor retardation, feelings of worthlessness, difficulty concentrating, and thoughts of suicide. There was no evidence of psychotic symptoms, and his devout religious beliefs deterred him from killing himself. He reported intense shame about his depression and perceived failures. Mr. S reported one prior episode of depression, seven years earlier, during which he took a three-month medical leave of absence from work. He was diagnosed with "Major Depressive Disorder, Recurrent, Severe."

Mr. and Mrs. S met through their church in their teens and were married at ages twenty-two and eighteen, respectively. They are devout members of their church, regularly participating in services and activities. Mr. S works long hours as an accountant and volunteers many hours to his church. Mrs. S is the principle homemaker. Both children are bright, capable students who are busy in a number of after-school activities. Mr. S's parents are divorced; his father reportedly abandoned the family when Mr. S was thirteen years old. Early on, Mr. S became the breadwinner and primary supporter of his mother and four siblings. Mrs. S grew up in a relatively stable, middle-class family with two siblings. Her parents strongly disapproved of her marrying "so young" but eventually developed a close relationship with the S family.

Assessment

During the initial interview, members of the S family were polite, attentive, and cooperative, but had a limited understanding of why they were referred for a family evaluation. They listened patiently to the customary orientation and provided brief responses to questions. Questions directed to the family in general were often met with long silences. Mr. or Mrs. S would eventually respond awkwardly and reluctantly. Following considerable efforts to engage the family in a fuller participation, Mrs. S indicated that her husband was not comfortable talking about problems and had intentionally withheld information about his condition, not wanting to burden his family. Mr. S concurred with his wife and, after further exploration of his concerns, agreed to keep an open mind and proceed with the assessment.

Presenting Problems

The following problems were identified:

1. The effect of Mr. S's depression on his functioning and its impact on the family
2. The family's "shock" and worry over Mr. S's hopelessness and thoughts of dying
3. Discord between Mr. and Mrs. S over the assistance (financial and other) that Mr. S gives to his family of origin, the church, and acquaintances
4. Dissatisfaction with lack of time spent in family activities
5. Dissatisfaction with limited amount of time spent on activities as a couple
6. Mrs. S's general medical health, poor nutrition, and poor physical conditioning
7. The family's pattern of not talking about affective issues
8. Limited nurturance and support and adult sexual gratification

An evaluation of the six dimensions revealed the following.

Problem Solving. The S family resolves instrumental problems effectively. This is largely due to their well-defined "traditional" roles and that Mr. S has final decision-making authority. The fact that he dictates the tone, however, also freezes efforts toward affective problem solving.

Communication. The family acknowledged that they do not spend adequate time together as a family, nor do Mr. and Mrs. S spend enough time talking with each other. When they do talk, instrumental communication is generally clear and direct. Affective communication is considerably masked and indirect.

Roles. The S family have established well-defined "traditional" roles that lend themselves to effectively accomplishing most necessary family functions. Mr. S is the breadwinning husband and father who has final say on all aspects of family life. Mrs. S is the primary homemaker who is quite ambivalent about her role. Her frequent disagreement with her husband's approaches and decisions places her in considerable conflict with her own religious beliefs and values of being "submissive" to her husband. This appears to have significantly strained their expression of nurturance and support as well as their sexual relationship. The children feel strongly connected to their mother but distant from their father. Mr. S's depression and resultant withdrawal from his family has intensified the family's feelings of alienation.

There is significant discord between Mr. and Mrs. S with regard to Mr. S's acknowledged excessive involvement with people outside of their family. Mr. S provides financial and personal support to his mother, siblings, and anyone in the church who asks him for assistance. Consequently, he has amassed considerable credit card debt.

Affective Involvement. Despite lack of open expression, the family genuinely cares about the welfare of one another. This lack of expression may be largely due to the impact of Mr. S's history of untreated depression coupled with the family's inability to effectively adapt to his decline in functioning.

Affective Responsiveness. Though generally uncomfortable with emotional expression, the S family is able to experience the full range of emotions. Mr. S has significant difficulty with the intensity of negative affect he experiences (shame, sadness, and anger), while Mrs. S feels "numbed."

Behavior Control. The S family's rules for behavior are clear and rigid. Most of the time, the family is satisfied with these rules and adheres to them. An exception is Mr. S's dealings with his extended family and others to whom he provides "handouts." He will promise his wife that he is not going to "give in" to family pressure, but will "help out anyway" behind her back.

Transactional Patterns. As Mr. S became increasingly overwhelmed by the impact of his depression, he withdrew. Worried and concerned, Mrs. S sought after her husband, only to be rejected. In her hurt and frustration, Mrs. S sought comfort in her children and by overeating. She gained weight and lost self-esteem. In turn, Mr. S blamed himself for his wife's unhappiness and withdrew further. The children, for the most part, remained on the sidelines. They were worried that "something was wrong with Dad" but kept their worry to themselves. This reinforced Mr. S's belief that he was protecting them from his problems. As this pattern progressed, Mr. S became significantly impaired and the family's functioning, particularly in affective areas, deteriorated.

Contracting

Orientation

Shifting and orienting the family to the contracting stage went rather smoothly as the family had become engaged during the three assessment sessions. Agreement on the formulation and outcome of the assessment was easily reached. The family opted to work with the therapist on their identified issues.

Negotiating Expectations

Negotiating expectations regarding affective problem areas was difficult at best. The S family's lack of experience addressing affective issues, coupled with Mr. S's severe depression, resulted in a setback in the therapeutic process. The family experienced an increase in anxiety and Mr. S's hopelessness intensified. In a consultation that included the S family, the family therapist, and Mr. S's psychiatrist (medication management was ongoing since Mr. S's inpatient admission), medication adjustments were made, and it was agreed Mr. S would begin individual psychotherapy. Gradually, through hard work (learning and practicing new skills) and with much support and encouragement from the therapist, the family was able to successfully negotiate their expectations of one another and their desired outcome for treatment.

The expectations which the family negotiated included:

1. Mr. and Mrs. S will spend quality time together on a regular basis.
2. The S family will plan for and participate in regular family activities.
3. The S family will have dinner together at least three nights per week.
4. Mr. S will participate fully in his treatment plan and keep his family informed of his progress.
5. Mrs. S will seek a full physical examination and begin a healthy eating/weight management program.

6. Mr. and Mrs. S will discuss and agree on any charitable donations contributed to Mr. S's family, their church, etc. If unable to agree, Mrs. S will have the final say (Mr. S was relieved by this agreement because he felt "out of control" in this area and trusted his wife's judgment).
7. The family will continue to address, rather than avoid, difficult emotional issues.

Therapist's Expectations

The therapist's expectations were that the S family:

1. Keep all scheduled appointments and work hard toward desired outcomes
2. Have fun and celebrate their successes
3. Be patient and open to learning from any slips or setbacks which may occur
4. Contact the therapist between sessions regarding urgent matters

Treatment

The S family readily accepted the customary orientation and was eager to start treatment.

Sessions 1 through 3. The S family progressed tentatively but consistently. They used sessions to further develop their affective communication and problem-solving skills and to negotiate between-session tasks designed to achieve their goals of spending more time together as a family and as a couple. Mr. S was feeling less depressed, and all were greatly relieved as he conveyed to his family that he was no longer feeling so hopeless. Mr. and Mrs. S were struggling but sticking to their arrangement of discussing and agreeing upon charitable contributions. On one occasion, this was seriously put to the test as Mr. S's mother, who lives out of state, wanted Mr. S to come to her immediately as she was upset about some legal problems of Mr. S's brother. With Mrs. S's approval, Mr. S was able to provide emotional support to his mother over the phone without losing his focus on himself and his immediate family.

Sessions 4 through 6. Between sessions 3 and 4, the therapist learned that Mrs. S's father had become gravely ill and died. Much of the focus of the subsequent sessions was on the family's response to this loss. The S family had enjoyed a close relationship with Mrs. S's parents, and her father's sudden death was a major stressor. The family used sessions to talk about how they felt and to provide support to each other. Assessment of family functioning after this significant life event revealed that all family members coped well and were proud of their progress. It was agreed to discuss terminating family treatment.

Closure

Sessions 7 and 8. Orientation with the S family involved discussion of typical concerns about ending treatment, such as fear of setbacks or being unable to resolve problems on their own. These sessions provided ample opportunity for the S family to reflect on their family therapy experiences, review their progress, and anticipate any potential obstacles to their continued progress. The S family acknowledged and was pleased by their significant progress. Mr. S noted several factors that he believed contributed to his own and his family's improved functioning. These included gaining an understanding of depression as an illness; learning of available treatments; overcoming his initial reluctance to participate in treatment; and "allowing those persons important to my well-being to participate in my treatment."

Concluding Remarks

A total of six sessions were conducted during the assessment (three sessions) and contracting (three sessions) stages. Treatment for the S family included eight additional family sessions spanning a total time period from assessment to closure of fourteen sessions over eleven months. Mr. S's medication management and individual psychotherapy continued after terminating family therapy. At the conclusion of treatment, assessment of general family functioning, utilizing the FAD and the MCRS, showed marked improvement and no significant disturbance in any of the six dimensions of family functioning.

Recognizing and showing proper respect for the S family's traditional role definitions proved critical to the establishment of trust in the therapeutic relationship. In addition, the discussion of Mr. S's thoughts about his wish to die revealed some important family strengths.

Specifically, the family was able to provide crucial emotional expressions of nurturance and support to Mr. S. The underlying cohesiveness of the family served as a foundation for further progress in treatment.

STRENGTHS AND LIMITATIONS

Problem-Centered Systems Therapy of the Family has several advantages for clinical use. PCSTF is desirable as a treatment approach for depression because it shares many of the same characteristics that are integral to psychotherapies (e.g., Beck et al., 1979; Klerman et al., 1984) that are known to be efficacious treatments for depression. Specifically, PCFTS is a brief, time-limited intervention that is problem oriented and focuses on the here and now. The time-limited nature of treatment makes it cost-effective, which is critical in today's mental health care environment. The PCSTF model is highly flexible, and allows the integration and coordination of a number of different treatment approaches, depending upon the specific clinical presentation or the theoretical propensities of the therapist.

In terms of problems with PCSTF, the model was developed as a generic treatment for family dysfunction without regard to the specific type of psychopathology that might be present in one or more family members. Thus, clinicians may need to modify their implementation in dealing with specific psychiatric disorders.

INTEGRATION WITH PSYCHIATRIC SERVICES AND ROLE OF MEDICATION

As seen in the case example, the integration and coordination of different treatment modalities is important in the treatment of depression. Generally speaking, the PCSTF approach is intended to complement pharmacotherapy or individual psychotherapy for depression. We have not advocated the use of PCSTF as a stand-alone or frontline treatment for depression for two reasons. First, our experience has been with inpatient populations who are often severely depressed and deemed to be in need of immediate somatic therapy. Second, not all families of depressed individuals have significant enough family dysfunction to warrant a referral for family therapy. In cases where family therapy is initiated before pharmacotherapy, we would recommend a referral to a physician for a psychiatric consultation under any of the following conditions: the depressed family member does not show substantial improvement after two to four sessions of therapy and/or when the depressed family member is moderately to severely depressed, exhibits melancholic or neurovegetative symptoms, or is suicidal. In general, experience suggests that PCSTF can be integrated with other modes of care quite easily.

Finally, PCSTF can be applied at the outpatient, day hospital, or inpatient setting. One of the authors routinely conducts family therapy with inpatients. However, with a shorter length of stay in the hospital, sometimes one session is all that is possible. Clearly this represents a highly compressed version of PCSTF, but experience so far suggests that patients and their families find it to be extremely helpful.

CULTURAL AND GENDER ISSUES

The developers of the model acknowledge that Western Judeo-Christian values have had a strong influence on the development of the model. The model is not alleged to be *the* best approach when dealing with families; it may not be appropriate at all when dealing with families who have dissimilar value systems. Nevertheless, the model seems to have cross-cultural appeal, evidenced by the fact that the FAD has been translated into fourteen languages, with empirical evidence of its utility in different cultures (Wenniger, Hageman, and Arrindell, 1993; Morris, 1990). In general, these studies support the validity of the FAD and its utility as a research instrument.

In the case of depression, women are about twice as likely as men to be affected. Thus, the typical family with a depressed member is comprised of a depressed wife and nondepressed husband, with or without children. As noted before, there is no prototypical pattern or profile of the depressed family. However, loosely speaking, clinical experience shows that families in which the wife is depressed do sometimes differ from families in which the husband is depressed with respect to which dimensions of family functioning are affected. With respect to the roles dimension, a very common complaint from depressed wives is that their spouses are not supportive or caring enough. Their husbands tend to be more vocal about identifying lack of sexual intimacy as a problem. In families where the husband is depressed, we often see a pattern similar to that described in the case study, in terms of affective responsiveness. That is, the husband may feel profound shame about being depressed. This shame gets translated into a pattern of communication in which discussion of depression is discouraged.

FUTURE DIRECTIONS

The MMFF and PCSTF are works in progress, and we continue to try to make modifications as needed. The PCSTF method was developed as a generic approach to the treatment of family dysfunction. As such, it was not developed with any specific form of psychopathology in mind. In conducting our treatment research on unipolar and bipolar depression, we have learned what modifications to the model are necessary in the treatment of affective disorders and stroke. This report is our first opportunity to disseminate information on how to apply the MMFF and PCSTF in the treatment of unipolar depression. It is our intention to eventually document how this model can be applied to the treatment of families with a member who has bipolar disorder. Empirical reports of the efficacy of the PCSTF in treating major affective disorders have been presented (Miller, Keitner, et al., 1998, 1999).

The applicability of the MMFF and PCSTF to families of diverse ethnic backgrounds remains an important goal. We recently had an opportunity to train mental health researchers and clinicians from India in the use of the model. Interestingly, it was they who approached us and requested training because they believed the approach would be useful in their work treating family dysfunction. However, future investigations into the usefulness of the MMFF and PCSTF in non-Western cultures, non-English speaking societies, and different ethnic groups within our own culture are still necessary.

REFERENCES

Beach, S.R.H. and O'Leary, K.D. (1986). The treatment of depression occurring in the context of marital discord. *Behavior Therapy, 17*, 43-49.

Beach, S.R.H., Sandeen, E.E., and O'Leary, K.D. (1990). *Depression in marriage.* New York: Guilford Press.

Beck, A.T., Rush, A.J., Shaw, B.F., and Emery, G. (1979). *Cognitive therapy of depression.* New York: Guilford Press.

Bishop, D., Epstein, N., Keitner, G., Miller, I., and Zlotnick, C. (1980). *The McMaster Structured Interview for Family Functioning*, Brown University Family Research Program. Providence, RI.

Bishop, D., Evans, R., Miller, I., Epstein, N., Keitner, G., Ryan, C., Weiner, D., and Johnson, B. (1997). *Family intervention: Telephone tracking: A treatment manual for acute stroke*. Brown University Family Research Program. Providence, RI.

Corney, R.H. (1987). Marital problems and treatment outcome in depressed women: A clinical trial of social work intervention. *British Journal of Psychiatry, 151,* 652-659.

Coyne, J.C. (1989). Interpersonal processes in depression. In G.I. Keitner (Ed.), *Depression and families: Impact and treatment,* pp. 33-53. Washington, DC: American Psychiatric Press.

D'Zurilla, T.J. and Goldfried, M.R. (1971). Problem solving and behavior modification. *Journal of Abnormal Psychology, 78,* 107-126.

Epstein, N., Baldwin, L., and Bishop, D. (1983). The McMaster Family Assessment Device. *Journal of Marital and Family Therapy, 9,* 171-180.

Epstein, N. and Bishop, D. (1981). Problem-Centered Systems Therapy of the Family. In A. Gurman and D. Kniskern (Eds.), *Handbook of family therapy,* pp. 444-482. New York: Brunner/Mazel.

Epstein, N., Bishop, D., Keitner, G., and Miller, I. (1990). A systems therapy: Problem-Centered Systems Therapy of the Family. In R. Wells and V. Giannetti (Eds.), *Handbook of brief psychotherapies,* pp. 405-436. New York: Plenum Publishing Corporation.

Epstein, N., Bishop, D., and Levin, S. (1978). The McMaster Model of Family Functioning. *Journal of Marriage and Family Counseling, 4,* 19-31.

Friedman, A.S. (1975). Interaction of drug therapy with marital therapy in depressive patients. *Archives of General Psychiatry, 32,* 619-637.

Fristad, M. (1989). A comparison of the McMaster and Circumplex family assessment instruments. *Journal of Marital and Family Therapy, 15,* 259-269.

Gottman, J., Notarius, C., Gonso, J., and Markman, H. (1976). *A couple's guide to communication.* Champaign, IL: Research Press.

Hayden, L., Schiller, M., Dickstein, S., Seifer, R., Sameroff, A., Miller, I., Keitner, G., and Rasmussen, S. (1998). Levels of family assessment. I: Family, marital and parent-child interaction. *Journal of Family Psychology, 12,* 7-22.

Hinchcliffe, M., Hooper, D., Roberts, F.J., and Vaughn, P.J. (1975). A study of the interaction between depressed patients and their spouses. *British Journal of Psychiatry, 126,* 164-172.

Hooley, J., Orley, J., and Teasdale, J.D. (1986). Levels of expressed emotion and relapse in depressed patients. *British Journal of Psychiatry, 148,* 642-647.

Jacobson, N.S., Dobson, K., Fruzzetti, A.E., Schmaling, K.B., and Salusky, S. (1991). Marital therapy as a treatment for depression. *Journal of Consulting and Clinical Psychology, 59,* 547-557.

Kabacoff, R., Miller, I., Bishop, D., Epstein, N., and Keitner, G. (1990). A psycho-metric study of the McMaster Family Assessment Device in psychiatric, medical and nonclinical samples. *Journal of Family Psychology, 3,* 431-439.

Kahn, J., Coyne, J.C., and Margolin, G. (1985). Depression and marital disagree-ment: The social construction of despair. *Journal of Social and Personal Rela-tionships, 2,* 447-461.

Keitner, G.I. and Miller, I.W. (1990). Family functioning and major depression: An overview. *American Journal of Psychiatry, 147,* 1128-1137.

Keitner, G.I., Ryan, C., Miller, I.W., Kohn, R., Bishop, D., and Epstein, N. (1995). Role of the family in recovery and major depression. *American Journal of Psy-chiatry, 152,* 1002-1008.

Keitner, G.I., Ryan, C., Miller, I.W., and Norman, W. (1992). Recovery and major depression: Factors associated with twelve-month outcome. *American Journal of Psychiatry, 149,* 93-99.

Klerman, G.L., Weissman, M.M., Rounsaville, B.J., and Chevron, E.S. (1984). *In-terpersonal psychotherapy of depression.* Basic Books.

McLean, P., Ogtron, K., and Grauer, L. (1973). A behavioral approach to the treat-ment of depression. *Journal of Behavioral Therapy and Experimental Psychia-try, 4,* 323-300.

Miller, I., Epstein, N., Bishop, D., and Keitner, G. (1985). The McMaster Family Assessment Device: Reliability and validity. *Journal of Marital and Family Therapy, 11,* 345-356.

Miller, I., Kabacoff, R., Bishop, D., Epstein, N., and Keitner, G. (1994). The devel-opment of the McMaster Clinical Rating Scale. *Family Process, 33,* 53-69.

Miller, I.W., Keitner, G.I., Ryan, C.E., and Solomon, D.A. (1998). *Matched versus mismatched treatment for depressed inpatients.* Presented at the meeting of the American Psychiatric Association, Toronto, Canada, May.

Miller, I.W., Keitner, G.I., Ryan, C.E., and Solomon, D.A. (1999). *Family treat-ment of bipolar disorder.* Presented at the meeting of the Society for Psychother-apy Research, Braaga, Portugal, June.

Miller, I., Keitner, G., Whisman, M., Ryan, C., Epstein, N., and Bishop, D. (1992). Dysfunctional families of depressed patients: Description and course of illness. *Journal of Abnormal Psychology, 101,* 637-646.

Miller, I.W., Weiner, D., Bishop, D., Johnson, B., and Albro, J. (1998). Telephone-administered family intervention following stroke. *Rehabilitation Psychology, 43,* 323-324.

Morris, T. (1990). Culturally sensitive family assessment: An evaluation of the Family Assessment Device with Hawaiian-American and Japanese-American families. *Family Process, 29,* 105-116.

Rounsaville, B., Prusoff, B., and Weissman, M. (1980). The course of marital dis-putes in depressed women: A 48-month follow-up. *Comprehensive Psychiatry, 21,* 111-118.

Wenniger, W., Hageman, W., and Arrindell, W. (1993). Cross-national validity of dimensions of family functioning: First experiences with the Dutch version of the McMaster Family Assessment Device. *Personality and Individual Differences, 14,* 769-781.

Woodward, C., Santa-Barbara, J., Levin, S., and Epstein, N. (1978). The role of goal attainment scaling in evaluating family therapy outcome. *American Journal of Orthopsychiatry, 48,* 464-476.

Chapter 5

Family Therapy for Panic Disorder: A Cognitive-Behavioral Interpersonal Approach to Treatment

Kristie L. Gore
Michele M. Carter

INTRODUCTION

The interpersonal aspects of panic disorder with agoraphobia deserve more clinical attention. Take, for example, the mother who experiences increased anxiety when her only child becomes school aged. The mother may develop anxiety attacks that subside in the child's presence, which may then create dependence on the child. The child might, in turn, feel important because of being depended upon. In this way, the family system is set up to both tolerate and enable the anxiety. A structural family therapist might intervene, using restructuring techniques to alter dysfunctional transactional patterns that maintain the symptomatic behavior. Using this example, the therapist might instruct the mother and child to schedule time away from each other, attempting to break the pattern of child as "safe person." Because change in any one part of the family system affects other parts of the system, one wonders how individual treatment of panic disorder with agoraphobia impacts the family system, and, further, what forces are in place to instigate a relapse.

Oppenheimer and Frey (1993) investigated the families of people with panic disorder. Based on self-report and clinical interview data from at least three family members, they found that the families of individuals with panic disorders tended to be enmeshed, overly involved in other family members' lives, used triangulation during family conflicts, and had less freedom to function independently of the family unit. They also found that panic-disordered families compared to nonclinical families tended to have more unresolved life-cycle issues, less warmth, and more current conflict.

Although the family system has been implicated in both the development and maintenance of panic, therapists and researchers currently disagree concerning whether marital or family therapy for panic disorder is warranted. Given the interpersonal nature of the disorder, one might expect that involving families in treatment could alter the interpersonal dynamics that may serve to create and/or sustain the disorder.

In this chapter, we will briefly review the literature on etiological theories of panic disorder. Next, we will review the theoretical relationship between family dynamics and agoraphobia. We will then discuss therapy techniques employing the spouse as partner and cotherapist, highlighting cognitive-behavioral techniques and communication skills training. Last, we will present a case example of cognitive-behavioral interpersonal therapy for a married woman suffering from panic disorder with agoraphobia.

Etiological Theories of Panic Disorder

The most widely held model for understanding the development of panic disorder is derived from cognitive-behavioral theory. At the core of this theory is the notion that irrational emotions are the result of misattributions or inappropriate appraisals. Barlow (1988) distinguishes between true alarms—fears that occur in the presence of an external stressor—and false alarms—fears that occur in the absence of external stressors. According to Barlow, true alarms trigger the "fight or flight" response and are considered the product of a biological mechanism that has persisted through natural selection. False alarms can become learned alarms if one's fear becomes associated with physiological changes. For instance, individuals may come to believe that a racing heart signifies imminent catastrophe; subsequently, when their hearts race, they experience fear, a process called *interoceptive conditioning.* When individuals mistakenly believe that something catastrophic will occur (e.g., "I will have a heart attack and die"), the mistaken belief intensifies the original fear caused by the physiological perturbation. As a consequence of this process, the individuals may become hypervigilant, scanning their bodies for signs of physiological change because they erroneously believe certain bodily sensations signify an impending catastrophe. Learned alarms may be triggered by physiological changes, negative thoughts, or both (Barlow, 1988; Carter and Barlow, 1995). In this way, the variables are in place to support recurrent panic attacks and fears.

An interpersonal model of panic disorder originated when Webster (1953) suggested that problematic interpersonal relationships could create and/or maintain one's agoraphobia. Similarly, Fry's (1962) early clinical observations led to what has been termed the "functionality hypothesis," or the notion that agoraphobia may serve the function of maintaining the marriage by satisfying both the spouse's need to be depended on and the agoraphobic patient's need to feel secure by depending on the spouse.

Goldstein and Chambless (1978) extended earlier interpersonal theories by suggesting an interplay between agoraphobia and the family. They hypothesized that the critical period for development of agoraphobia occurred during adolescence, and they believed that conflict between individuation and the desire to remain in a familiar environment can create physical symptoms of anxiety or early signs of panic. In support of an interpersonal model, Goldstein and Chambless (1978) observed benefits to exhibiting symptomatic behaviors in their sample of married women. Significant others and other family members socially reinforced the "sick" role by attending to the patient and accompanying her on excursions. When the symptoms lessened, family members frequently put pressure on the patient to be more dependent. In this model, panic disorder is considered to develop from repeated, problematic, interpersonal interactions in which passive, fearful behaviors are reinforced and thus perpetuated.

In some situations, it is plausible that the family system stresses the individual, thus creating panic. In others, one uncued panic attack is enough to create panic disorder, which may then exert pressure on family relations, as outlined above. Hence, causality appears to be circular, since faulty family dynamics can both create an individual's anxiety and be the consequence of panic symptoms. It is therefore necessary to examine causality on a case-by-case basis to determine how both cognitive-behavioral and interpersonal systems are affected by the panic syndrome.

Psychodynamic theory on the etiology of panic emphasizes the infant-mother relationship. The mother's ability to successfully calm the child during times of stress directly impacts the child's ability to

self-soothe later in life. The theory holds that normal child development involves the creation of an internalized object representation of
the mother, which may serve as a calming agent when the mother is
not present (Ballenger, 1989). In later years, the internalized representation is transferred to an external object. Ballenger stated that for
most adult panickers there is a safe person who can calm them down
in stressful situations and accompany them on difficult journeys.
More recently, this observation has found empirical support from
studies that have manipulated the concept of safety (Carter et al.,
1995; Rapee, Telfer, and Barlow, 1991). Carter and colleagues (1995),
for example, administered CO_2 to participants with panic disorder either in the presence or absence of their safe person and found that
panickers became more anxious during the biological challenge in
the absence of their safe person.

A neurobiological model of panic disorder comes from research
on neurotransmitters and autonomic and respiratory functioning.
Both noradrenergic and serotonin systems have been implicated as
predisposing factors for panic disorder, although data are currently
equivocal. Researchers suggested that alpha-2 hypersensitivity or peripheral beta-adrenoceptor sensitivity are related to the development
of panic disorder (Stein and Uhde, 1995). A postsynaptic serotonin
receptor sensitivity has also been implicated in the development of
panic (Kahn et al., 1988). Dysregulation of the hypothalamic-pitu-
itary-adrenal (HPA) axis, which is consistent with the previously implicated abnormalities, is thought to be central to panic disorder, and
autonomic hyperactivity is one indicator of HPA axis functioning.
Results from studies of autonomic arousal are mixed, and it remains
largely unknown whether these sensitive physiological subsystems
contribute to the development of panic disorder. Another hypothesis
of panic etiology comes from Klein (1993), who proposed the "false
suffocation alarm theory." This theory posits that some people are
more sensitive than others to levels of CO_2 in the brain. When CO_2
levels increase, an "alarm" is thought to go off, thus triggering a panic
attack. However, the false suffocation alarm theory is based solely on
indirect evidence from sodium lactate infusion and CO_2 inhalation
studies and requires further examination.

Research on Agoraphobia and Interpersonal Relationships

Surprisingly little research has been conducted on family therapy for panic and related disorders. As panic disorder with agoraphobia is most prevalent in women, research on family therapy for panic disorder has primarily focused on married women with agoraphobia, enlisting their husbands as cotherapists. Three specific research questions are addressed in this literature. The first is whether panic disorder with agoraphobia is associated, as predicted by early theories, with dysfunctional marriages. Second is whether individual treatment for panic disorder with agoraphobia affects marital adjustment. And third is whether incorporating family members in treatment increases treatment efficacy (Carter, Turovsky, and Barlow, 1994).

With respect to the first issue, investigations of whether agoraphobics have dysfunctional or dissatisfying marriages yielded mixed results. For example, Torpy and Measey (1974) found that 43 percent of their agoraphobic sample reported dissatisfaction in their marriage. On the basis of a median split from self-report data, they divided their female agoraphobic participants and their husbands into two groups: "good marriage" and "poor marriage." They found that wives in the "poor marriage" group failed to describe their husbands as the husbands described themselves. That is, agoraphobic wives tended to perceive their husbands at the extremes of stability and toughness, which was not the way the husbands described themselves.

On the other hand, Arrindell and Emmelkamp (1986) compared agoraphobic women and their husbands to three different samples: nonphobic psychiatric patients and their husbands, maritally distressed couples, and maritally nondistressed couples. They found that agoraphobics reported significantly more marital maladjustment than nondistressed couples but significantly less maladjustment than the nonphobic psychiatric controls and the maritally distressed couples. This suggests that marital conflict may not be a defining characteristic of agoraphobic women and/or that other psychiatric disorders might produce more marital conflict than agoraphobia does.

The second issue in the family therapy literature on agoraphobia is the impact of individual treatment on marital adjustment. At first glance, one might expect that relief from panic and agoraphobia would lead to a fuller individual life and, consequently, a happier marriage. However, if the spouse has become comfortable being depended upon, the loss of this role may be difficult, at least initially. The newfound mobility of the successfully treated agoraphobic may be interpreted by the spouse as a threat to existing homeostasis. If the spouse acts out these feelings, the dynamics may decrease the overall efficacy of treatment or increase the risk of relapse following treatment. In this way, working with the spouse to understand the interpersonal dynamics that sustain the agoraphobia could help prevent the above scenario from occurring.

Indeed, several investigations found that participants rated as having "better" marital adjustment prior to treatment improved more following treatment (Hafner, 1976, 1984; Milton and Hafner, 1979; Monteiro, Marks, and Ramm, 1985). An equal number of studies, however, found that marital satisfaction did not predict treatment outcome (Arrindell, Emmelkamp, and Sanderman, 1986; Craske, Burton, and Barlow, 1989; Emmelkamp, 1980). After their review of the literature, Steketee and Shapiro (1995) concluded that, "For agoraphobic clients, the quality of the marital/partner relationship seems unrelated to immediate therapy gains, but may be associated with more benefits at follow-up." Although never tested, they hypothesized that during individual treatment, the intense therapeutic relationship may shield the client from the stress marital discord creates but that the stress may negatively impact the client's progress over time when the therapeutic relationship is over.

Research addressing the potential benefits of family therapy over individual therapy has demonstrated that individual therapy is equivalent to family therapy immediately following the cessation of treatment, but that family therapy seems to be more effective during follow-up assessments (Barlow, Mavissakalian, and Hay, 1981; Barlow, O'Brien, and Last, 1984; Himadi et al., 1986; Cerny et al., 1987). Barlow, Mavissakalian, and Hay (1981), for example, found that after treating six agoraphobic women and their husbands with graduated exposure and cognitive restructuring in a group format using husbands as cotherapists, four couples reported increased marital satisfaction concurrently with increased therapeutic gains. Two couples, however, reported that as the agoraphobic symptoms improved, marital satisfaction decreased.

Using the same treatment protocol with a larger group of participants (fourteen women with agoraphobia accompanied by their husbands compared to fourteen women treated without their spouses present), Barlow, O'Brien, and Last (1984) found substantially larger symptom reduction favoring the spouse group at posttest. In the two-year follow-up investigation, Cerny and colleagues (1987) found that the agoraphobics treated with their spouses continued to improve after treatment while the agoraphobics treated without their husbands' participation evidenced deterioration at one-year follow-up. Although the tendency for the nonspouse treatment group to improve resumed at the two-year follow-up, differences in favor of spouse-aided treatment remained apparent. Overall, Cerny and colleagues (1987) found a correlation between improvement in phobic behavior and marital satisfaction. That benefits are most often found during long-term follow-up interviews suggests that changes in family dynamics produce lasting effects in individual family members with panic disorder and may also reduce risk for relapse.

Additionally, Himadi and colleagues (1986), using the same protocol as above with forty-two participants (twenty-eight patients were treated with their spouses and fourteen without), found that pretreatment levels of marital satisfaction were independent of treatment outcomes but that a nonsignificant trend toward greater positive change in marital adjustment appeared for the group treated with their spouses.

The picture is in fact more complicated than we have presented thus far. Goldstein and Chambless (1978) introduced an important distinction: that between *simple* and *complex* agoraphobia. They described simple agoraphobia as a relatively narrow syndrome consisting of panic attacks and subsequent fears often brought on by a physical disorder or drug experience. People with simple agoraphobia do not evidence the avoidant and/or dependent personality characteristics common among those with complex agoraphobia. People with complex agoraphobia are described as pervasively fearful and often have comorbid Axis I and Axis II diagnoses.

Research on comorbidity suggests the majority of agoraphobics have at least one additional psychiatric diagnosis or problem (Brown, Antony, and Barlow, 1995), yet in systematic treatment outcome research, rigid exclusion criteria often leads to the rejection of subjects with additional psychiatric diagnoses (Zitrin et al., 1983). Therefore, complex agoraphobics with a comorbid anxiety or other Axis I disorders may well be underrepresented in treatment outcome studies, which may, in turn, perpetuate faulty generalizations about complex agoraphobics from data on simple agoraphobics. Furthermore, treatment of complex agoraphobia may necessitate the use of additional methods beyond the most frequently used cognitive and behavioral techniques. Lange and de Beurs (1992) described their successful treatment of five people with complex agoraphobia using cognitive-behavioral, intrapsychic, and interpersonal interventions. They concluded that individual treatment may be effective for simple agoraphobia but that cognitive-behavioral family therapy may be a more effective treatment for complex agoraphobia.

SETTING

The case example described herein is an example of therapy conducted at the university clinic. The purposes of the research training clinic are to:

1. Provide clinical psychology PhD students with training in empirically supported treatments on a year-round basis
2. Generate a database for psychotherapy process-outcome research
3. Serve as a recruitment base and therapy site for prospectively designed therapy and assessment research projects
4. Develop teaching tools in the form of audiotapes of faculty/therapist sessions, for use in clinical practica
5. Provide low-fee psychotherapy to community residents

Licensed clinical psychologists on faculty at the university may serve as therapists in the clinic and/or supervisors to the graduate student clinicians.

TREATMENT MODEL

A cognitive-behavioral interpersonal treatment model, which includes components designed to address each of the major response dimensions (cognitive, physiological, behavioral, and interpersonal) associated with panic disorder, is described here. The cognitive component of therapy seeks to identify the irrational thoughts and erroneous core beliefs that trigger panic. Cognitive restructuring typically consists of decatastrophizing catastrophic thoughts, examining the realistic consequences of a perceived negative event, and examining the realistic probability of the feared negative event occurring (Barlow and Cerny, 1988). If it is a probable event, one must rationally examine how catastrophic it would be. Therapists teach clients to become their own cognitive therapist—to notice dysfunctional thoughts and apply restructuring methods to make the thoughts more rational.

The behavioral component of therapy for panic disorder with agoraphobia consists of exposure exercises (either imaginal, in vivo, or both) designed to reduce the avoidance behavior which is conceptualized as negatively reinforcing the fear. Gradual in vivo exposure, in which participants gradually move up a hierarchy of anxiety-producing stimuli, has been shown to be the most effective method of behavioral therapy (Emmelkamp, 1994). This aspect of therapy combats the damage done by having avoided activities for fear of panic attacks.

The third component of panic control treatment (PCT) targets the client's physiological sensations (Barlow and Cerny, 1988; Barlow and Craske, 1994). One technique is diaphragmatic breathing. Some people tend to overbreathe, taking in more oxygen than they can use. The increased alkalinity of the blood creates sensations of physiological arousal, similar to those experienced when anxious. Via interoceptive conditioning, the heightened arousal may trigger a panic attack. If the breathing is corrected, by teaching clients to breathe through their diaphragms, sensations may not occur as frequently and clients feel that they can control their breathing when anxiety does occur. A second technique designed to break the connection between the sensations and the experience of fear is interoceptive exposure (Carter and Barlow, 1993). This involves the repeated, deliberate evocation of the physical sensations that produce anxiety. Carter and Barlow (1993) recommend specific exercises to produce specific physical sensations. With repeated exposure, clients habituate to the sensations, thus providing data regarding the actual consequences of experiencing various physical sensations.

To address the interpersonal component of panic disorder, enlisting the spouse as a cotherapist enhances therapy in a variety of ways. Involving spouses allows them to better understand the panic syndrome. Their participation in treatment includes helping the patient conduct exposure and breathing exercises outside the scheduled therapy sessions. Their presence also enables relationship dynamics to enter therapeutic discussions and communication skills training to ensue. In this way, the spouses are involved and invested in the outcome of treatment while facilitating the couple's communication.

Arnow and colleagues (1985) examined the potential benefits of adding a communication training component to exposure therapy. Their communication training regimen sought to improve the patient's and spouse's listening abilities, self-statements, request making, delivering feedback, seeking clarification, and resolving conflict. In order to resolve conflicts, they taught subjects to begin problem-solving sessions with a positive statement about one's partner; to formulate complaints in specific behavioral terms; to admit one's role in the conflict; to brainstorm solutions; to offer to change one's behavior; and to make specific change agreements. Arnow and colleagues (1985) demonstrated that adding couples communication skills training to exposure therapy was more effective for treating female agoraphobics than adding couples relaxation training to the exposure therapy regimen. However, differences were not as great at eight-month follow-up. The relaxation group reported fewer panic attacks than the communication skills training group, although this might have been a function of their taking significantly fewer unaccompanied excursions.

In a dismantling study of behavior marital therapy, Jacobson (1984) compared the relative effectiveness of behavioral marital therapy to two of its components (behavior exchange and communication/problem-solving training), each used in isolation. Jacobson found that behavior exchange proved to be more effective initially, but at six-month follow-up, none of the behavior exchange subjects continued to improve and many had lost their original gains. On the other hand, the communication skills training group and those who received full behavioral marital therapy either maintained their treatment gains or continued to improve over the six-month follow-up period. This suggests that behavior exchange techniques might work initially to promote behavior change while the communication training works to maintain it; hence, the two techniques should be most effective when used together.

CASE EXAMPLE

Clear empirical evidence has supported the efficacy of cognitive-behavioral therapy in the treatment of panic disorder. However, since interpersonal dynamics in the evolution and maintenance of panic are at least theoretically important, the following is a case example using a combination of cognitive-behavioral and interpersonal psychotherapy techniques to treat a woman suffering from panic disorder with agoraphobia.

Samantha is a thirty-seven-year-old married Caucasian female. She presented at the clinic with complaints of unexpected rushes of anxiety consisting of heart palpitations, sweating, dizziness, and an intense fear of dying. She reported experiencing her first attack when she was twenty-two years old following graduation from college. At that time, she decided to move out of her mother's house and in with her boyfriend (who eventually became her husband). Since then, the attacks waxed and waned until five years ago, following the birth of their only child, Alice. At that time, Samantha was employed as a legal secretary but decided it was best for their child if she became a full-time housewife. For the first year following the birth of Alice, the attacks were more frequent, with numerous days of multiple attacks. In addition, Samantha noted that as a result of her intense fear of future attacks, she greatly restricted her lifestyle. She found it increasingly difficult to venture outside of the house unaccompanied. Following this difficult first year, the attacks began to subside, and Samantha regained some of her freedom.

Approximately one year ago, Samantha noted an increase in the anxiety and a return of occasional panic attacks. With each successive attack the symptoms worsened and within four to five months she was again experiencing frequent attacks and had greatly reduced her outside activities in the absence of her husband. On occasion, however, she noted that she could complete short errands in the company of her daughter. In the month prior to presenting at the clinic, she reported that she was virtually housebound when she was not in the company of her daughter or husband.

Following the initial interview, it became apparent that Samantha's panic and anxiety very much involved her family. They had clearly made changes to the way the family functioned to accommodate her symptoms. In recognition of the level of family involvement, Samantha was offered and agreed to couples treatment involving her husband, Brook. The basic treatment plan consisted of standard cognitive behavioral treatment with the goal of influencing the cognitive aspects of panic via cognitive restructuring. Through this component the client is taught to identify and challenge the catastrophic cognitions that occur during episodes of panic. In addition, Samantha and Brook were given instructions for diaphragmatic breathing in an effort to alleviate some of the physical sensations associated with anxiety, interoceptive exposure exercises (repeated exposure to the feared sensations), and in vivo exposure instructions to encourage Samantha to gradually and systematically enter feared and avoided situations.

In conjunction with standard cognitive-behavioral therapy, a variation of interpersonal psychotherapy focusing on marital and family issues was emphasized. Here the couple was taught to examine their relationship and to identify the sources of unhappiness in general and in relationship to the anxiety. A principle component of this phase of treatment was to identify the negative thoughts each held that contributed to their functioning as a couple. Each thought was then challenged for accuracy and restructured when appropriate. The underlying belief (consistent with interpersonal theories of panic disorder) was that both participants were contributing to the primary problem for treatment (Samantha's panic) and that improvement in Samantha's condition would be enhanced by simultaneously working on the relationship. From the outset of this approach, it is important to emphasize to the couple that changes in the primary patient's symptomatology will have an impact on the nature of the relationship.

Session 1

The first session is typically used to gather background information regarding the patient's panic (e.g., frequency, situations). As is typical of someone with frequent panic, Samantha's attacks appeared to occur in almost every situation and were associated with thoughts of impending doom. It is also during this session that a collaborative effort is established between identified patient, spouse, and therapist. This is the beginning of understanding how the identified patient's problem impacts the relationship and vice versa. The following interchange occurred between Samantha (the patient, P), Brook (the helper, H), and the therapist (T).

T: Brook, I was wondering what you make of all this. Are there any situations that Samantha may not have mentioned that you have seen as a problem?

H: Not really. I mean, it's basically everything. She won't go to the store or even to check the mail if I'm not with her. It seems to be getting worse lately, and now I am having to do everything for her. It's like she's not an adult anymore.

T: It sounds as though you feel that you've had to make a lot of changes in your life as a result of Samantha's concerns.

H: Yeah. It gets kind of frustrating. She's . . . Well, now I can't really do all the things I normally do because I've got to do everything else that she used to. I can't even hang out after work because she's got to have me at home right away. Either that or she's got to drag our daughter around, but that's going to end soon because she'll be starting school, and then what? I can't stay at home with her, and she doesn't feel safe by herself. Then it's really going to be a mess.

T: Let me stop you there for a moment. It sounds like Samantha's problem has been difficult for you as well. Were you aware of this, Samantha?

In this session, the therapist accomplished some of the major goals of treatment. The first goal is to get a description of the nature of the panic attacks from both partners' perspective. The second goal is to encourage the couple to discuss the impact of the problem on their relationship. Although the presence of interpersonal problems is typical, it is less typical for both partners to be aware of how the disorder has impacted the relationship. More typical is that one or both will deny the presence of such problems. This can be a tricky issue for the therapist because it is often difficult, if not impossible, to determine whether there are truly no relationship problems present, whether the couple simply does not recognize the impact of the disorder on them as a unit, or whether they are simply not comfortable enough with the therapeutic process to engage in an open discussion of such issues. In our experience, the first is relatively rare, while the second instance is relatively common. The last issue is also relatively common, particularly among ethnic minority populations (Carter, 1999; Carter, Sbrocco, and Carter, 1996).

It is also important for the therapist to consider the impact of a change in the patient's panic on the family relationship early in treatment, as that information will be used in future sessions when cognitive restructuring and in vivo exposure begins. By carefully exploring these issues in the context of the couple/family, the therapist sets the stage for a collaborative relationship while simultaneously indicating to the patient and her spouse that work on the relationship will continue throughout treatment.

Session 4

In the intervening sessions, the therapist continued to provide basic information regarding the nature of anxiety and panic and to openly discuss the impact of panic on the family. In addition, the couple was given instructions in diaphragmatic breathing. As part of the couple's treatment approach, both partners were given breathing instructions, and the husband was encouraged to help the patient in the completion of the exercises. In this session, the therapist used the interactions around the breathing exercises to discuss the family relationship in general.

T: How do you feel when Brook helps [with the breathing exercises]?

P: I think it makes me a little worse. I don't think he knows how hard it is, and he just tells me I'm not doing it right. It's not helpful at all. This is probably the one time I'm better off when he's not around.

T: It sounds as though you feel a little criticized.

P: I do.

T: Is that your intent, Brook?

H: Not really. But if she's not doing it right, what should I do, say nothing?

T: It sounds as though Brook's attempts at helping with the breathing are perceived as criticisms and that generates some negative feelings in you (P). It also sounds like you (H) are a little frustrated with Samantha not getting the exercises as quickly as you would like her to, but that you genuinely want her to get better. So it seems that there is some miscommunication and a little bit of upset around this issue. I wonder if this kind of interaction—

where one of you might be frustrated with the other's behavior—happens at other times in your relationship.

The therapist then discussed several situations in which Brook became frustrated and angry with Samantha in an attempt to gather additional information about the nature of their marital relationship and how the couple typically managed problematic situations. This process also encouraged open discussion about marital issues.

Session 5

In the fifth session, the couple was introduced to cognitive restructuring. One goal is to help the identified patient understand the relationship between catastrophic cognitions and the experience of anxiety and panic. In this regard, the couple was taught to identify maladaptive thoughts and to utilize specific restructuring techniques to combat such thoughts. A second goal is to identify the typical interactions between the couple that serve to exacerbate the patient's anxiety and problem solve more adaptive methods of interacting. The assumption here is that when one member of the dyad is experiencing panic, it often affects the other. There may also be issues of secondary gain for either the patient or her significant other.

P: My first thought was probably that I'm all alone. He's not calling because he's finally gotten tired of me and left.

T: For good?

P: Yes. So I'm stuck in the house by myself, and if I have a panic attack now it'll kill me because no one is here to help me.

T: Brook, were you aware that Samantha had thoughts like that from time to time?

H: Yes, but I try tell her that I'm not going to leave my family. But it doesn't seem to matter what I say. She still thinks that's a possibility.

T: What happens that you still have those kinds of thoughts?

P: Like last week. He says he's going to call and he doesn't. Then I think those thoughts because he's not around when he says he will be.

The focus of treatment now shifted to problem solving and communication training. Specifically, the couple was encouraged to be open in discussing their interpretations of each other's actions. It is clear in this case that Samantha often interpreted Brook's forgetfulness as an indicator that he wanted to leave the relationship, which then generated considerable anxiety in her. In part, this reflected a pattern of behavior for Samantha. Whenever she was faced with the possibility of separation from significant others in her life, she responded with an increase in anxiety and panic attacks. Sessions 5 and 6 also incorporated a discussion of the resentment that Brook felt toward Samantha as a consequence of her anxiety attacks. With encouragement, he was able to recognize that his unexpressed and unresolved anger at times influenced his behavior. This is important because it highlighted how the interaction between identified patient, symptoms, and significant other was complicated and often intertwined.

Session 8

In this session, the couple discussed in vivo exposure as a method for reducing the avoidance behavior Samantha exhibited. In vivo exposure is the process of gradually entering previously feared and avoided situations. Near the beginning of therapy, the therapist and patient construct a hierarchy of avoided situations ranging from least feared to most feared. Typically, in vivo exposure is accomplished in a graduated hierarchical fashion so that the least feared situations are attempted first. When these can be entered into with minimal anxiety, the patient proceeds to the next situation on the hierarchy. The purpose of in vivo exposure is to reduce avoidance, provide additional practices for the cognitive restructuring techniques discussed earlier, and to utilize the patient's reliance on safe persons as a method to probe further into the interpersonal issues that may underlie the maintenance of the disorder.

It should be noted that when conducting in vivo exposure it is important to make the exercises as specific as possible, including, for example, the length of time of the exposure, the particular situation, and the time of day. This not only provides necessary structure to the exercises but allows for systematic evaluation of progress made over the course of therapy. In addition, it is common for even minor variations in such variables to significantly affect the level of anxiety the patient will experience. That is, some situations may produce more anxiety when there are more people present; others may produce less.

H: It did go well. This is great. I don't have to do all of the shopping anymore. But she didn't tell you the rest.

T: The rest?

P: I took Alice with me. He (H) said it doesn't really count, but I think it does.

H: She has to be able to do it alone, right?

T: Before we address that, what would it mean if she couldn't do it alone?

H: That she's going to still be dependent of me to do stuff. So it hasn't really changed yet.

T: Samantha, when you hear Brook say that, what kind of images does that generate for you?

P: Well, I think he still thinks I'm not right.

T: And if he thinks that—not that he does—what does that mean to you?

P: That there is still a chance that he might leave me if I don't get over this pretty soon.

T: And what happens to your anxiety when you have those kinds of thoughts?

P: It goes up, and then it makes it harder for me to do the homework because I have something else making me anxious.

Therapy then turned toward challenging thoughts that Brook's comments indicated he might eventually leave her. It is important to encourage the patient to check the accuracy of her thoughts with her partner, and for the partner to recognize that any signal of disapproval may be interpreted as a sign of impending abandonment. This may further feed into some of the resentment the partner may be feeling due to increased responsibilities and the patient's apparent continued dependence.

This session then discussed the issues of abandonment that Samantha began to express. In this case, there was a connection between her feelings of anxiety and any interpretation of being alone, which for her indicated she would not be loved by anyone and, consequently, would not be able to survive. Although this type of exploration is typically an interpersonal psychotherapy approach, cognitive therapists will carefully subject those types of thoughts to cognitive restructuring as well. In addition to examining how this pattern of relating to others is expressed in the patient's current relationship, the therapist maintains a focus on traditional cognitive-behavioral techniques (e.g., exposure) to alleviate the outward manifestations of anxiety.

During subsequent sessions, the couple continued exploring interpersonal issues as they related to Samantha's panic. In addition, Samantha was encouraged to continue exposure exercises, utilizing them as a catalyst for the cognitive restructuring of both negative thoughts centered on the immediate experience of panic (i.e., fainting) and those regarding the implications of being alone. By the end of treatment (session 12), the patient's panic was significantly reduced and she was able to travel to many locations she had avoided for some time. Samantha, however, continued to exhibit some fear and avoidance of driving long distances and being in crowded places. Perhaps more important, she made tremendous strides in managing her feelings of abandonment and now felt that she could cope with life even if she were alone.

STRENGTHS AND LIMITATIONS

Cognitive-behavioral interpersonal family therapy is designed to affect psychological, physiological, and behavioral aspects of panic disorder as well as environmental variables. In this way, it is expected to produce longer-lasting improvements than cognitive-behavioral therapy alone since it targets the interpersonal dynamics thought to sustain or drive the panic symptoms. One advantage to this type of therapy is that it is fairly structured, which makes its dissemination easier. Therapists may be trained in its delivery with little difficulty, as it relies on techniques many therapists commonly use (e.g., cognitive restructuring, exposure). Another advantage is that cognitive-behavioral and interpersonal psychotherapy are readily combined. As was evident in the case example, cognitive therapy techniques are easily applied to interpersonal issues.

Currently, there is much more empirical support for cognitive-behavioral models of panic disorders than interpersonal ones, primarily because cognitive-behavioral theory is conducive to experimental investigation. On the other hand, support for interpersonal models of panic disorder first depends on the identification of family process and other relationship variables associated with panic, and these variables have not yet been clearly explicated. Additionally, research on the interpersonal aspects of anxiety disorders other than panic disorder is necessary, especially in people with generalized anxiety disorder. Therefore, the applicability of cognitive-behavioral interpersonal family therapy to the treatment of other anxiety disorders remains largely unknown.

INTEGRATION WITH PSYCHIATRIC SERVICES AND ROLE OF MEDICATION

More and more, selective serotonin reuptake inhibitors (SSRIs) are becoming the psychotropic treatment of choice for patients with panic disorder (Baldwin and Birtwistle, 1998; Wade, 1999), in part because evidence shows that Monoamine Oxidase Inhibitors (MAOIs) produce multiple side effects, many of which are intolerable to panic patients (Jefferson, 1997). Recently, the SSRI citalopram (20 to 30 mg) was found to be a more effective treatment for panic disorder than either the tricyclic antidepressant clomipramine (60 to 90 mg) or a placebo (Lepola et al., 1998; Leinonen et al., 2000; Wade et al., 1997). We found no research examining the combined effectiveness of interpersonal and psychotropic treatments for panic disorder. On the other hand, some research has been conducted on combination cognitive-behavioral and drug therapies. Mixed results were found when combining psychotropic medications with in vivo exposure therapy. Tricyclic antidepressants (e.g., imipramine) facilitated the effects of in vivo exposure therapy, but high-potency benzodiazepines (e.g., alprazolam) interfered with it (Marks et al., 1993), possibly due to its association with rebound panic when medicine is discontinued (Fyer et al., 1987; Noyes et al., 1991).

Unfortunately, the effectiveness of combination cognitive-behavioral and SSRI treatments is largely unknown. Two experiments recently examined the effects of using PCT (Barlow and Cerny, 1988; Barlow and Craske, 1994) to facilitate the discontinuation of benzodiazepine use (Otto et al., 1993; Spiegel et al., 1994). They found that while tapering very slowly (sometimes as little as .124 mg per week), patients given PCT were able to discontinue the drug without relapse more often than those who did not receive PCT. The two- to five-year follow-up investigation found that 75 percent of these patients discontinued the alprazolam therapy, maintained their treatment gains, and remained abstinent of any type of treatment (Bruce, Spiegel, and

Hegel, 1999). Despite the withdrawal symptoms and rebound panic attacks often associated with benzodiazepine use, they usually produce faster relief than SSRIs and other antidepressants and are, therefore, often prescribed for panic patients. For this reason, clinicians who treat panic and other anxiety disorders need to be aware of both the methods for their discontinuation and preferable alternative treatments. In addition, active consulting with the patient's psychiatrist will help the therapist to deliver the most effective treatment.

CULTURAL AND GENDER ISSUES

The case description we presented described the treatment process of a Caucasian couple in which one member of the dyad suffered from panic disorder with agoraphobia. When contemplating the potential utility of this approach in the treatment of minority populations, there are several things to consider. First is the rate at which psychological services are utilized. There is a concern and some empirical evidence which suggests that minorities will seek treatment less often than their nonminority counterparts (Sue and Sue, 1990). This most likely reflects a stronger tendency for minorities to seek treatment from family and religious organizations first, followed typically by visits to their physician, and then finally seeking a mental health professional. In all likelihood, the minority patient may present with more severe pathology.

Several theorists have suggested that cultural factors will impact the expression or form that symptoms of anxiety will take (Carter, Sbrocco, and Carter, 1996; Draguns, 2000). The impact of these differences on treatment response, however, has only recently been investigated. The results thus far are somewhat mixed. For example, Chambless and Williams (1995) provided individual behavioral treatment (primarily in vivo exposure) to African-American and white American patients with panic disorder and noted that even after controlling for socioeconomic status (SES), African-American patients were more severely phobic than the white American patients at the conclusion of treatment and at follow-up. Data generated at the American University Clinic from a small sample of African Americans who received treatment consistent with that described previously suggest that this approach is quite effective in alleviating panic and avoidance behavior. This may suggest that the combined model we describe may be more effective than traditional behavior therapy for African Americans. Although panic is a condition that is presumed to predominantly affect females, there have been no controlled trials examining the differential effectiveness of treatments between male and female patients. Clearly, this is an area in need of empirical investigation.

Additionally, research would gain ecological validity by examining relationships other than those of husbands and wives. Panic disorder is likely to occur in unmarried individuals, cohabitants, same-gender couples, etc., and these relationships have been neglected. Although panic disorder with agoraphobia is diagnosed three times more often in women than in men (*Diagnostic and Statistical Manual of Mental Disorders,* Fourth Edition [DSM-IV], American Psychiatric Association, 1994), little is known about men with panic disorders or about incorporating female spouses or male or female companions into treatment.

FUTURE DIRECTIONS

Interpersonal dynamics have been implicated in the development and maintenance of panic disorder, but we remain uncertain of what specific "faulty" processes contribute to psychopathology. Although some research on the topic exists, little is currently known about the marital and family environments of people with panic disorder. This may be due to the methods currently used to investigate. If, in fact, agoraphobic couples derive secondary gains from their symptoms, they may be inclined to underreport actual marital discord. In this way, self-report methods may underestimate levels of pathology and/or distress in relationships, and, thus, we are not currently aware of the degree to which agoraphobia is associated with dysfunctional marriages or family dynamics. Future research will have to find alternative methods to diagnose these problems (e.g., clinical interviews with more than one family member).

Furthermore, despite the research on interpersonal aspects of panic disorder, empirical evidence regarding the efficacy of treating this complex condition has largely been limited to cognitive-behavioral approaches. Cognitive-behavioral techniques utilize objective measures to assess therapeutic change and are, in this way, easier to study than interpersonal techniques are. Communication skills training, as outlined above, includes many components, not all of which are relevant for all cases. Family issues are largely idiosyncratic, and interpersonal therapy techniques require the therapist to be flexible. This can sacrifice methodological control. To facilitate interpersonal treatment outcome research on panic disorder, it would be useful to develop standardized objective measures to assess relevant interpersonal constructs.

After much research on the topic, it remains unclear whether marital distress interferes with the treatment of panic disorder and, therefore, whether including the spouse in therapy will increase treatment efficacy. One possible explanation for the ambiguity in this body of research is that without distinguishing between simple and complex agoraphobics, heterogeneous samples of subjects may have muddied the research waters. It may be, as Goldstein and Chambless (1978) reported, that complex agoraphobia is associated with interpersonal difficulties while simple agoraphobia is not. By collapsing the two groups, researchers may miss the opportunity to uncover important differences between them.

At present, we find no research examining the efficacy of family therapy for generalized anxiety disorder (GAD) or the role of interpersonal relationships in the context of GAD. One study (Torgersen, 1986) examined childhood experiences in a group of people diagnosed with panic disorder or GAD. Via examination of clinical interviews and psychiatric records, Torgersen (1986) concluded that people with GAD tended to have endured a significant loss before the age of sixteen, while people with panic disorder tended to have endured chronic stress throughout childhood. Given this difference, one possibility is that unresolved loss issues contribute to the development of GAD; such possibilities will have to be examined in future research. It may be that individual cognitive-behavioral treatment is the most efficacious therapy for GAD, but some exploration of interpersonal variables is warranted.

In summary, cognitive-behavioral therapy incorporating the spouse as cotherapist seems to be more effective than cognitive-behavioral treatment without involving the spouse. On the other hand, studies using exposure therapy alone did not find additional benefits of involving spouses in treatment. Although more research is needed, it appears that the addition of communication skills training to spouse-assisted cognitive-behavioral therapy may increase the effectiveness of psychotherapy for complex panic disorder.

REFERENCES

American Psychiatric Association (1994). *Diagnostic and statistical manual of mental disorders* (Fourth Edition). Washington, DC: Author.

Arnow, B. A., Taylor, C. B., Agras, W. S., and Telch, M. J. (1985), Enhancing agoraphobic treatment outcome by changing couple communication patterns. *Behavior Therapy, 16,* 452-467.

Arrindell, W. A. and Emmelkamp, P. M. G. (1986). Marital adjustment, intimacy and needs in female agoraphobics and their partners: A controlled study. *British Journal of Psychiatry, 149,* 592-602.

Arrindell, W. A., Emmelkamp, P. M. G., and Sanderman, R. (1986). Marital quality and general life adjustment in relation to treatment outcome in agoraphobia. *Advances in Behavior Research and Therapy, 8,* 139-185.

Baldwin, D. S. and Birtwistle, J. (1998). The side effect burden associated with drug treatment of panic disorder. *Journal of Clinical Psychiatry, 59* (Supplement 8), 39-44.

Ballenger, J. C. (1989). Toward an integrated model of panic disorder. *American Journal of Orthopsychiatry, 59,* 284-293.

Barlow, D. H. (1988). *Anxiety and its disorders: The nature and treatment of anxiety and panic.* New York: Guilford Press.

Barlow, D. H. and Cerny, J. A. (1988). *Psychological treatment of panic: Treatment manual for practioners.* New York: Guilford Press.

Barlow, D. H. and Craske, M. G., (1994). *Mastery of your anxiety and panic—II.* San Antonio, TX: Harcourt Brace.

Barlow, D. H., Mavissakalian, M., and Hay, L. R. (1981). Couples treatment of agoraphobia: Changes in marital satisfaction. *Behaviour Research and Therapy, 19,* 245-255.

Barlow, D. H., O'Brien, G. T., and Last, C. G. (1984). Couples treatment of agoraphobia. *Behavior Therapy, 15,* 41-58.

Brown, T. A., Antony, M. M. and Barlow, D. H. (1995). Diagnostic comorbidity in panic disorder. *Journal of Consulting and Clinical Psychology, 63,* 408-418.

Bruce, T. J., Spiegel, D. A., and Hegel, M. T. (1999). Cognitive-behavioral therapy helps prevent relapse and recurrence of panic disorder following alprazolam discontinuation: A long-term follow-up of the Peoria and Dartmouth studies. *Journal of Consulting and Clinical Psychology, 67(1),* 151-156.

Carter, M. M. (1999). Ethnic awareness in the cognitive behavioral treatment of a depressed African American female. *Cognitive and Behavioral Practice, 6,* 273-278.

Carter, M. M. and Barlow, D. H. (1993). Interoceptive exposure in the treatment of panic disorder. In L. VandeCreek and S. Knapp (Eds.), *Innovations in clinical practice: A source book,* Volume 12 (pp. 329 336). Sarasota, FL: Professional Resource Press/Professional Resource Exchange Inc.

Carter, M. M. and Barlow, D. H. (1995). Learned alarms: The origins of panic. In W. O'Donohue and L. Krasner (Eds.), *Theories in behavior therapy* (pp. 209-228). Washington, DC: American Psychological Association.

Carter, M. M., Hollon, S. D., Carson, R., and Shelton, R. C. (1995). Effects of a safe person on induced distress following a biological challenge in panic disorder with agoraphobia. *Journal of Abnormal Psychology, 104,* 156-163.

Carter, M. M., Sbrocco, T., and Carter, C. (1996). African Americans and anxiety disorders research: Development of a testable theoretical framework. *Psychotherapy: Theory, Research, and Practice, 33,* 449-463.

Carter, M. M., Turovsky, J., and Barlow, D. H. (1994). Interpersonal relationships in panic disorder with agoraphobia: A review of empirical evidence. *Clinical Psychology: Science and Practice, 1(1),* 25-34.

Cerny, J. A., Barlow, D. H., Craske, M. G., and Himadi, W. G. (1987). Couples treatment of agoraphobia: A two-year follow-up. *Behavior Therapy, 18,* 401-415.

Chambless, D. L. and Williams, K. E. (1995). A preliminary study of African Americans with agoraphobia: Symptoms severity and outcome of treatment with in vivo exposure. *Behavior Therapy, 26,* 501-515.

Craske, M. G., Burton, T., and Barlow, D. H. (1989). Relationships among measures of communication, marital satisfaction and exposure during couples treatment for agoraphobia. *Behaviour Research and Therapy, 27,* 131-140.

Draguns, J. G. (2000). Psychopathology and ethnicity. In J. F. Aponte and J. Wohl (Eds.), *Psychological intervention and cultural diversity* (pp. 40-58). Boston, MA: Allyn & Bacon.

Emmelkamp, P. M. G. (1980). Agoraphobics' interpersonal problems: Their role in the effects of exposure in vivo therapy. *Archives of General Psychiatry, 37,* 1303-1306.

Emmelkamp, P. M. G. (1994). Behavior therapy with adults. In A. E. Bergin and S. L. Garfield (Eds.), *Handbook of psychotherapy and behavior change* (Fourth Edition) (pp. 379-427). New York: Wiley and Sons, Inc.

Fry, W. F., Jr. (1962). The marital context of an anxiety syndrome. *Family Process, 2,* 225-232.

Fyer, A. J. Liebowitz, M., Gorman, J., Campeas, R., Levin, A., Davies, S., Goetz, D., and Klein, D. F. (1987). Discontinuation of alprazolam treatment in panic patients. *American Journal of Psychiatry, 144,* 303-308.

Goldstein, A. J. and Chambless, D. L. (1978). A reanalysis of agoraphobia. *Behavior Change, 9,* 47-59.

Hafner, R. J. (1976). Fresh symptom emergence after intensive behaviour therapy. *British Journal of Psychiatry, 129,* 378-383.

Hafner, R. J. (1984). The marital repercussions of behavior therapy for agoraphobia. *Psychotherapy, 21,* 530-542.

Himadi, W. G., Cerny, J. A., Barlow, D. H., Cohen, S., and O'Brien, G. T. (1986). The relationship of marital adjustment to agoraphobia treatment outcome. *Behavior Research and Therapy, 24,* 107-115.

Jacobson, N. S. (1984). A component analysis of behavioral marital therapy: The relative effectiveness of behavior exchange and communication/problem-solving training. *Journal of Consulting and Clinical Psychology, 52(2),* 295-305.

Jefferson, J. W. (1997). Antidepressants in panic disorder. *Journal of Clinical Psychiatry, 58* (Supplement 2), 20-24.

Kahn, R. S., Wetzler, S., Van Praag, H. M., Asnis, G. M., and Strauman, T. (1988). Behavioral indications for serotonin receptor hypersensitivity in panic disorder. *Psychiatry Research, 25(1),* 101-104.

Klein, D. F. (1993). False suffocation alarms, spontaneous panics, and related conditions: An integrative hypothesis. *Archives of General Psychiatry, 50(4),* 306-317.

Lange, A. and de Beurs, E. (1992). Multi-dimensional family treatment of agoraphobia. *Journal of Family Psychotherapy, 3(1),* 45-71.

Leinonen, E., Lepola, U., Koponen, H., Turtonen, J., Wade, A., and Lehto, H. (2000). Citalopram controls phobic symptoms in patients with panic disorder: Randomized controlled trial. *Journal of Psychiatry and Neuroscience, 25,* 24-32.

Lepola, U. M., Wade, A. G., Leinonen, E. V., Koponen, H. J., Frazer, J., Sjodin, I., Penttinent, J. T., Pedersen, T., and Lehto, H. J. (1998). A controlled, prospective, 1-year trial of citalopram in the treatment of panic disorder. *Journal of Clinical Psychiatry, 59,* 528-534.

Marks, I. M., Swinson, R. P., Basoglu, M., Kuch, K., Noshirvani, H., O'Sullivan, G., Leliott, P. T., Kirby, M., McNamee, G., Sengun, S., and Wickwire, K. (1993). Alprazolam and exposure alone and combined in panic disorder with agoraphobia: A controlled study in London and Toronto. *British Journal of Psychiatry, 162,* 776-787.

Milton, F. and Hafner, R. J. (1979). The outcome of behavior therapy for agoraphobia in relation to marital adjustment. *Archives of General Psychiatry, 36,* 807-811.

Monteiro, W., Marks, I. M., and Ramm, E. (1985). Marital adjustment and treatment outcome for agoraphobia. *British Journal of Psychiatry, 146,* 383-390.

Noyes, R., Garvey, M. J., Cook, B., and Suelzer, M. (1991). Controlled discontinuation of benzodiazepine treatment for patients with panic disorder. *American Journal of Psychiatry, 47,* 809-818.

Oppenheimer, K. and Frey, J. III (1993). Family transitions and developmental processes in panic-disordered patients. *Family Process, 32,* 341-352.

Otto, M. W., Pollack, M. H., Sachs, G. S., Reiter, S. R., Meltzer-Brody, S. and Rosenbaum, J. F. (1993). Discontinuation of benzodiazepine treatment: Efficacy of cognitive-behavioral therapy for patients with panic disorder. *American Journal of Psychiatry, 150,* 1485-1490.

Rapee, R., Telfer, L. A., and Barlow, D. H. (1991). The role of safety cues in mediating the response to inhalations of CO_2 in agoraphobics. *Behaviour Research and Therapy, 29,* 353-355.

Spiegel, D. A., Bruce, T. J., Gregg, S. F., and Nuzzarello, A. (1994). Does cognitive behavior therapy assist slow-taper alprazolam discontinuation in panic disorder? *American Journal of Psychiatry, 151,* 876-881.

Stein, M. B. and Uhde, T. W. (1995). Biology of anxiety disorders. In A. F. Schatzberg and C. B. Nemeroff (Eds.), *The American Psychiatric Press textbook of psychopharmacology* (pp. 501-521). Washington, DC: American Psychiatric Press.

Steketee, G. and Shapiro, L. J. (1995). Predicting behavioral treatment outcome for agoraphobia and obsessive compulsive disorder. *Clinical Psychology Review, 15,* 317-346.

Sue, D.W. and Sue, D. (1990). *Counseling the culturally different.* New York: John Wiley and Sons.

Torgersen, S. (1986). Childhood and family characteristics in panic and generalized anxiety disorders. *American Journal of Psychiatry, 143,* 630-632.

Torpy, D. M. and Measey, L. G. (1974). Marital interaction in agoraphobia. *Journal of Clinical Psychology, 28,* 270-276.

Wade, A. G. (1999). Antidepressants in panic disorder. *International Clinical Psychopharmacology, 14* (Supplement 2) (S13-S17).

Wade, A. G., Lepola, U., Koponen, H. J., Pedersen, V., and Pedersen, T. (1997). The effect of citalopram in panic disorder. *British Journal of Psychiatry, 170,* 549-553.

Webster, A. S. (1953). The development of phobias in married women. *Psychological Monographs, 67,* 1-18.

Zitrin, C. M., Klein, D. F., Woerner, M. G., and Ross, D. C. (1983). Treatment of phobias: 1. Comparison of imipramine hydrochloride and placebo. *Archives of General Psychiatry, 40,* 125-137.

Chapter 6

Family Treatment of Borderline Personality Disorder

Ira D. Glick
Emily L. Loraas

INTRODUCTION

Borderline personality disorder (BPD) is a disorder with a long clinical history. Despite extensive study, the etiology of this disorder remains unclear, and effective treatments are still in the developmental stage, with minimal or mixed research support. To date, most treatment approaches have focused on the patient with the disorder, with only secondary interest in the family or significant others. Only in the past decade or so has the disorder come to be viewed as a "family matter."

The most common clinical situation for the family therapist arises when a couple enters therapy with complaints about the relationship. As therapy evolves, it becomes apparent that the relationship difficulties are inextricably linked with one or both partners' basic character structure or personality. Often the relationship is initially functional, but difficulties emerge when one or both partners are unable to adjust to developmental changes in the family life cycle (e.g., birth of a child, death of a parent, etc.) or an acute crisis in the family, such as the loss of a job (see Carter and McGoldrick, 1988, for a description of family life-cycle stages and the impact of various stressors on the family system). The patient's ability to adapt is limited by his or her basic personality or character structure.

Effective treatment of BPD must address the complex interplay between relationship dynamics, character structure, and developmental crises and life stages. When BPD is viewed and treated with a relationship focus, it is often possible to help family members master life-cycle changes and tasks, adapt to the character styles of their partners, and move on to live happier and more satisfying lives.

Definition of Borderline Personality Disorder

The DSM-IV lists nine criteria for the diagnosis of BPD (American Psychiatric Association, 1994). Interestingly, seven of these nine criteria have obvious and important interpersonal implications; the first relates to the issue of unstable interpersonal relationships. The patient does not have a sense of permanence or consistency in his or her relationships with others (e.g., family members). The second criterion has to do with impulsivity, which results in impulsive, destructive behaviors that can cause destabilization of the family. The third deals with affective instability, which is related to the first criterion and directly undermines family emotional consistency. Fourth, and a related problem, is anger. The patient is a potential powder keg waiting to explode, and the family may serve to ignite the patient. The fifth criterion is suicidality—our sense is that this type of behavior stems not only from the emotional pain associated with the illness, but in part from conscious and unconscious attempts to control family behavior by use of the threat of suicide. The sixth criterion is identity disturbance—the patient experiences a shifting sense of who they are and, therefore, a lack of consistency and reliability within relationships. Finally, the eighth criterion deals with abandonment, which relates to situations in which family members are either perceived as or actually are unreliable or abandoning. Each of these criteria and their interpersonal implications will be elaborated on later.

Etiology

Data suggest that BPD may have, in part, a genetic etiology (Siever and Davis, 1991). There is a suggestion of familial transmission (Silverman et al., 1991). As we begin to know more about the life course, we see biological dysfunction and symptoms typically beginning early, perhaps in preadolescence, which reach their full expression during the individual's twenties and thirties, resulting in (at least) two decades of intense symptoms and problems for patients and their families. What is most fascinating is that the intensity of symptomatology levels off (i.e., lower levels with fewer peaks) in the forties and fifties, but there is evidence of a lower resultant functional level than prior to the illness. It should be noted that there are very few medical illnesses that fit this model (in psychiatry, one subset of patients with schizophrenia have this life course, and in internal medicine, there are some similarities to regional enteritis), again raising the perplexing question of BPD etiology.

Biological Data

For several decades, clinician-researchers, including Klein (1968) and others, have suggested that there may be a biological contribution to BPD. The evidence was mostly anecdotal and empirical, based on the use of antidepressants, mood stabilizers, and neuroleptics. Research into the biological correlates of behavioral and personality traits have provided data that there is a heritable biological component to some selected personality and behavioral traits (Siever and Davis, 1991). Specifically, as mentioned previously, there may be familial transmission of the hallmark borderline-related personality characteristics, an area recently reviewed by Coccaro and Siever (1995). These familial problems (i.e., the dysfunctional personality characteristics), in combination with cognitive impairments in perception and abstract thinking in BPD patients, present a situation with high potential for misunderstanding in both patients and their families (Burgess and Zarconi, 1992). More recently, in clinical psychopharmacologic trials, medication has been associated with global improvement in some patients with BPD (Coccaro, 1993). This empirical finding suggests (but does not prove) that a part of the cause of the disorder is "biological"—likewise, a medication alone cannot resolve the multiple intrapsychic and interpersonal issues.

Evidence of Family Pathology

As Clarkin, Marziali, and Munroe-Blum (1991) note, the data on family pathology have been mostly "correlational" (in contrast to causal), and relate to issues involving a complex interplay between innate vulnerability and traumatic experiences. Kagan and colleagues (1988) work demonstrates that a vulnerable individual in a severely dysfunctional family may produce the symptoms we associate with BPD. Similarly, Stone (1988) has proposed a "psycho-biological model of the borderline conditions that explores the role of a hyperirritability that may either antedate parent-child interaction or stand apart from traditional developmental stages" (p. 3). The model suggests that "one pathway towards this hyperirritability is the traumatic effect of abuse, which may alter the neuroregulatory response system."

Physical and Sexual Abuse

Many borderline patients have been found to have impulsive and chaotic family environments in which physical and sexual abuse occur (Marziali, 1992; Links and Blum, 1990). Physical and sexual abuse may be either a single traumatic event or chronic abuse, which has more adverse consequences. In one sample of twenty-one borderline patients, fourteen had been sexually abused (Herman, Perry, and van der Kolk, 1989). Numerous studies have found an association between sexual and physical child abuse and subsequent BPD (Herman, 1989; Stone, 1990). Bryer and colleagues (1987) found that subjects who had experienced both physical and sexual abuse had a higher mean borderline symptom score than those who had experienced more limited abuse or those who had not been abused. It has also been found that abuse and BPD are not gender specific. In a study of family relations in a mostly male sample (Snyder et al., 1984), the majority of patients experienced severe physical abuse and a moderate level of corporal punishment.

In a study examining childhood sexual abuse as a specific and distinct etiological agent in BPD, Links and colleagues (1990) found that sexually abused borderline patients reported more self-mutilation, substance abuse, recurrent illusions, depersonalization, derealization, and physically self-damaging acts than nonabused borderline patients. The results of this study are consistent with the clinical impression of Stone (1990), who noted that borderline patients, as well as patients with other personality disorders, often have a history of abuse. He concluded that severe abuse by a caregiver, when combined with an atmosphere of dislike and rejection, may be a causative factor of personality disorders characterized by impulsivity. Knowing that a patient has a history of family abusiveness is important in treatment planning, as traumatized patients need support, sanctuary, and specialized treatment.

Recently, Gladstone and colleagues (1999) have reported data collected from a series of 269 inpatients suggesting that "childhood sexual abuse appears to be associated with a greater chance of having experienced a broadly dysfunctional childhood home environment, a greater chance of having a borderline personality style, and in turn, a greater chance of experiencing depression in adulthood."

Neglect and Overprotection

Parental neglect and overprotection have also been examined in relation to BPD. In one study, borderline patients described their parents as less caring than other parents (Goldberg et al., 1985). Another study reported that patients viewed their fathers as less interested in and less approving of them (Frank and Paris, 1981). In another study, relationships with parents were seen as conflicted and negative, and mothers were seen as overinvolved (Soloff and Millward, 1983), while at the same time less caring or helpful.

Early separations from parental figures seem more prominent in samples of borderline patients. In one study, nearly half of the patients experienced a significant separation before age six, and a majority experienced a separation before age eighteen (Zanarini et al., 1989). In another sample, borderline patients experienced more separation from caretakers in childhood than did nonborderline patients in a control group. Moreover, this separation was more likely to be due to marital separation and death of a parent (Bryer et al., 1987).

When the parent is the identified patient, the child is often thought to be used as a target of projection and disturbed reality distortions. In other words, the parent plays out his or her internal conflicts on the child. Interestingly, most patients with borderline personality disorder are believed to not marry (although data on this are not solid), but if they do marry, such marriages are often fraught with conflict and sexual problems (McGlashan, 1987). Finally, most clinical reports have demonstrated that the emotional disruption of one member reverberates through the rest of the family (even more so than in nonborderline families) due to the intensity of the interactions. For example, mother nags father, who "beats the kids," who are oppositional to mother, and so on.

Therapy has been tailored to a patient's specific position in the family. If the identified patient is an adolescent (Berkowitz, 1981), then family dynamics tend to revolve around a marked impairment in individuation from parents. This impairment often involves hostile, overinvolved, rebellious, and chaotic interactions among the family. In addition, the family is often unable to provide the tools and the context to help the patient form a firm self-identity (Shapiro, 1978). It is also important to keep in mind that even if a patient is able to individuate, the family often overreacts (with regression) to the development of the identified patient. This is thought to occur because the family is unable to understand or cannot accept (because of their own needs) that the identified patient *has* the capacity to individuate.

Parental Pathology

When examining parental pathology in relation to BPD, it has been found that parents of borderline patients have a low incidence of schizophrenia and a high incidence of affective disorder (Soloff and Millward, 1983). In borderline patients with a comorbid history of major depression, the incidence of parental affective disorders is especially high (Pope et al., 1983). Families of borderline patients have a higher incidence of the same behaviors found in BPD patients (Loranger, Oldham, and Tulis, 1982), which includes alcoholism (Loranger and Tulis, 1985), antisocial personality disorder (Soloff and Millward, 1983), and other Cluster B personality disorders (Pope et al., 1983; Zanarini et al., 1990). Goldman, D'Angelo, and DeMaso (1993) recently reported higher rates of psychopathology among family members of patients with BPD compared to a control group with other psychiatric disorders. The nature and extent of parental pathology may be related to disruptive environmental events, such as increased risk of early loss or separation, physical and sexual abuse, and nonintact parental marriage (Links et al., 1990). In summary, "familial transmission" of various characteristics of borderline personality disorders seems likely; and such transmission may result from combinations of genetic, nongenetic biological, and epigenetic factors.

Borderline Couples

Although there is a substantial amount of literature on patients with BPD, this is not the case for "borderline couples." Up until recently, little was written on adults in a relationship or in a family with a borderline identified patient. There are two obvious reasons for this: First, most psychotherapy of patients with BPD has been psychoanalytically oriented, where the focus is on the individual. Second, family therapists usually are not interested in an individual family member's diagnosis, but rather on the effects of the illness on the family. In addition, much of what has been published is anecdotal.

BPD symptoms and personality characteristics often play an integral role in relationship dynamics and are a source of considerable stress. Partners often play a homeostatic or regulating role with respect to BPD interpersonal patterns. When one partner becomes angry, the other soothes; when one partner feels hurt and rejected, the other shows great affection. As a result, therapy with the "borderline couple" must include treatment of both the individual with the disorder and the partner in order to fully address these relationship dynamics (Koch, 1985). When both spouses in the marriage have a personality disorder, the therapist must provide an empathetic environment with delineated boundaries. This is often termed the "holding environment," and it allows the patient to develop trust and a sense of object constancy, which is often underdeveloped in borderline patients. Once the holding environment is established, the therapist becomes the "manager of the holding environment," allowing the couple to better focus on the sources of their distress (McCormack, 1989).

In summary, when examining the etiology of borderline personality disorder it can be said that *hard* data are accumulating that there *are* disturbed biological substrates in the patient (Siever and Davis, 1991) and probably in family members as well (Silverman et al., 1991). There is *suggestive* evidence that disturbed biology in combination with a disturbed "bad fit" family is etiologic in borderline disorder and that the issues of: (1) parental pathology, (2) physical and sexual abuse, and (3) neglect and overprotection are related in some way to the development of what we now label as BPD. No evidence exists that pathologic family relationships *alone* can cause borderline disorder. On the other hand, researchers agree that a family can cause a vulnerable identified patient great distress, and a very ill identified patient can certainly cause the family great burden.

SETTING

The Stanford University School of Medicine is a teaching institution affiliated with the Stanford University Hospital. The Stanford Department of Psychiatry and Behavioral Sciences offers comprehensive inpatient and outpatient psychiatric, psychological, and psychotherapeutic services for individuals, couples, and families experiencing problems ranging from addictions to serious mental illnesses, such as bipolar disorder and schizophrenia. The case example described later was drawn from this setting and was treated by the senior author in his private psychiatric practice affiliated with the School of Medicine.

TREATMENT MODEL

Our model is based on the belief that patients with borderline personality disorder are biologically derived from and psychosocially (i.e., interactionally) inseparable from the family. Our understanding of the literature dealing with the etiology of BPD suggests that in some cases, family psychopathology predates the birth of a vulnerable identified patient (IP), thus producing impaired relationships among family members in an already fragile family structure. In families where preexisting function is *within normal limits,* families can become dysfunctional with the addition of an impaired child, significant other, or parent. If these assumptions are correct, we believe a change from the current working family therapy models is indicated.

Evaluation and Family Assessment

Evaluation and treatment of the borderline patient and his or her family may occur in a number of settings. Depending on the needs of the patient, the therapy may be conducted on an inpatient or outpatient basis in private clinics or hospitals. Because of the explosive and crisis-like nature of borderline pathology, many therapists quickly jump from the initial interview directly into treatment. However, we strongly urge a careful evaluation of the borderline patient and the family *before* plunging into treatment (regardless of modality). A therapist should take the time to: (1) evaluate the strengths and weaknesses of the family system; (2) ask the question of whether (and how) the patient and family affect one another, especially in regard to family burden and "expressed emotion" (i.e., the coping mechanism of family members as they live with a chronic mental illness such as BPD), specifically high hostility and overinvolvement; and (3) evaluate the nature and severity of family members' psychopathology and their relationships to the patient's. Finally, when a patient with BPD is hospitalized (now rare in 2001), it is mandatory to identify both prehospital and (anticipated) posthospital family behavior that is associated with the patient's psychopathology (Clarkin, Marziali, and Munroe-Blum, 1999).

Treatment

When the family is available and motivated, we believe that the treatment of choice is family psychoeducation with family (systems or dynamic) intervention where possible in combination with pharmacotherapy and/or individual psychotherapy as needed. This prescription may put us at variance with many psychopharmacologists as well as psychotherapists of different schools, but, in our experience, this may lead to the best long-range function not only for the family but for the patient as well.

In our model, the focus of treatment is not either patient or family, but rather both. The goals of our treatment are as follows:

1. To educate the family unit on the nature of the disorder
2. To help the family assess and implement the degrees of both practical support (e.g., financial, shelter) and emotional support that might be planned and carried out
3. To reduce negative expressed emotion if present
4. To improve overall family and marital function (including sexual function), rather than focusing family life on patient psychopathology
5. To decrease enmeshment and, by extension, to decrease the rescue fantasies (of a spouse or parent)
6. To support patient compliance with other modalities (for example, hospitalization, medication, and/or individual psychotherapy)
7. To help the patient (regardless of age) individuate and, associated with that goal, respect the boundaries of the family

Enabling Factors

In order to accomplish treatment, we believe that certain enabling factors must be present. Central to these factors are motivated family members or significant others. For the treatment process to work, the family must have some ability to regulate affect, tolerate anxiety, control projection, and not denigrate treatment. In some situations, the presence of an active psychosis in one (or more) members may make family treatment impossible.

Strategies

We see family intervention as part of a treatment package. This includes medication when indicated for certain target symptoms, such as extreme depression or psychotic symptoms (Cornelius et al., 1993). Individual therapy may also be a part of the treatment if it is clinically judged that the patient has the capacity to do the cognitive work necessary to benefit from such an approach. In some cases, family therapy, marital therapy, and individual therapy are thought to be needed concomitantly.

If both family and individual therapy are deemed appropriate for a patient, we suggest that family therapy be used before individual therapy. Family therapy allows the therapist and the family to set the stage for and work together to achieve individuation (rather than the family fighting against the patient to prevent it). In other cases, however, it might be necessary to establish a therapeutic alliance with the patient before starting therapy. Although there is no evidence to indicate that one "school" of family therapy is more efficacious than another, we suggest a mixture of dynamic, psychoeducational, and systems models for family therapy, depending on the needs of the family members.

In our experience with large numbers of inpatients as well as very impaired outpatients, the family therapist preferably should do the individual therapy. The rationale is that there is more to be gained than lost by employing one instead of two therapists. Due to the severity of the illness and the impression that many patients and families of BPD have regarding therapy, patients often have difficulty trusting therapists. It is our belief that once a patient finds a therapist he or she can trust, it usually is too hard for the patient to transfer to another therapist (but hard data on this belief are lacking).

Family Techniques

One way to conceptualize family interventions is to divide them into psychoeducational, systems, and dynamic interventions. The role of the family therapist is to review with both the patient and family the symptoms, diagnosis, treatment, and prognosis of borderline personality disorder (Schultz et al., 1985). Especially "emotionally loaded" issues include individuation, blame, and sexual function. The list also includes suicidality and violence or the fear of emotional blackmail often manifested by suicidal threats on the part of the borderline patient. We always recommend a frank discussion of suicide risk with families in the presence of the patient. It is important for families to know patients may attempt suicide despite the "good intentions" of the family and despite good therapy. The family should understand that overprotection of an adult patient as a means to prevent suicide is often counterproductive. Often a core question is: "Who is guilty of causing the illness?" The answer, of course, is, "no one." As families increasingly understand the nature and origins of the illness, this helps moderate volatile family interactions and decrease expressed emotion. Finally, in this context, Linehan's cognitive behavior program may contain relevant material to include in a psychoeducation program for families (Linehan, 1987). It includes components of (1) psychoeducation, (2) balancing polarities between a couple (with the aim of a new synthesis, and flexibility arising out of opposing positions), (3) improving problem-solving strategies, (4) increasing communication, and (5) using case-management strategies for very impaired families (Linehan et al., 1991).

As to systemic family therapy, the first issue is to "join" with the family. This delicate operation involves issues of control and power. The next step is to "reframe." This involves positive connotation of the symptoms in light of the family's efforts to help. There are obviously different approaches if the patient is a spouse versus a young adult. The therapist must walk a fine line between siding with the younger versus older generation. The task of the therapist is to help the patient and the family to achieve maximum function. The usual problem in terms of boundaries is that the marital coalition is often undermined by mutual blaming related to the pathology of the young adult. Also, the young adult (as the identified patient) is sometimes in a "parental role" because of a weakened marital dyad.

Gunderson (1989, p. 2751) has described two patterns of family involvement and their management, which also speaks to the above issues:

> One pattern is characterized by overinvolvement. Borderline offspring of such families are often actively struggling with de-

pendency issues by denial or by anger at their parents. Whether denied or reviled, these needs for dependency are often being actively gratified by the family (Shapiro et al. 1975). Such a family requires active, ongoing family participation in treatment. To exclude the family from involvement in the index borderline person's treatment leads the parents to withhold support and, moreover, causes the patient to feel as if participation in therapy is disloyal to the parents and will lead to abandonment.

Borderline patients also come from families characterized by *abuse* (violent or incestuous) or neglect. In this pattern, the parents are likely to be angry at their offspring for having either solicited or been sent for treatment. These parents will be overtly resentful of treatment efforts that require their involvement in an examination of the family interactions. Meetings with the parents alone may be required in order to solicit their support for the borderline person's treatment. In such meetings, it is useful to be formally educative about the nature of the offspring's illness and to attempt to reassure the parents that the treatment is directed toward helping the patient develop more independence and, specifically, that it is not directed at blaming them.

In terms of dynamic family therapy, one of the central problems is the issue of transference. Transference is unusually intense and varied, ranging from "very idealized" to "devaluing," both of which often exist simultaneously. Countertransference problems are especially difficult and are often reflected in family myths. For example, a common problem is that the therapist "sides" with one group (or spouse) versus the other. Slipp (1981) has done an excellent job in outlining twelve guidelines for therapists working psychoanalytically with couples where one or both have borderline personality disorder. Unfortunately, space does not permit a detailed outline of these guidelines; however, readers are encouraged to examine this work in more detail.

It is important to emphasize that the techniques we are recommending are not unique to BPD. They can be found in contemporary family approaches to schizophrenia and mood disorders including bipolar illness. These techniques are also commonly and centrally utilized in the group therapy field. Namely, powerful reality testing is provided by the group (family) members, such that regression and intense transference distortions are minimized; group (family) members assume responsibility for their actions and for changing behaviors and come to expect the same of the identified patient; and the sessions can serve as a positive "holding environment" (Yalom, 1985).

Phases of Therapy

Early in therapy, the main issue to deal with is the anxiety and helplessness that the family feels with regard to the patient. Anger is strong on both sides and must be dealt with early on to lay the foundation of working into the more difficult issues of changing family structure and function. In the middle phases, issues of enmeshment and lack of conflict resolution come to the fore. In the late stages, the main issue is to try to reach the best possible functional compromise among all members and "close the wounds." We recommend continuous therapy, but intermittent therapy is common, as patient, family, and stressful life events interact with treatment interventions.

CASE EXAMPLE

The patient was a forty-five-year-old white married female with three children. She presented stating she had been "depressed" for about two years. History of present illness revealed that she was having recurrence of old symptoms—specifically, inappropriate anger, "cutoffs" from her parents, and anger at her husband for a "poor sex life." She reported that she had been treated about ten years earlier in individual psychoanalytically oriented psychotherapy and diagnosed as a "borderline." The therapy had been "of great help." It was useful in that she increasingly understood herself, controlled her anger, and felt more "hopeful." She presented now with a gradually increasing anger and frustration about (1) her inability to function as a writer, (2) difficulties with her "past," (3) complaints about her husband and their sex life, and (4) an inability to relate to her parents, who she reported had been "abusive" to her.

Her background revealed that she was one of three siblings with an emotionally distant father who was constantly critical of her. She described her mother as being "mentally ill," probably having bipolar mood disorder, most usually depressed. The major dynamic was that she felt angry at her father for not protecting her against an "angry, irritable, and depressed mother for all the years of her childhood." Adding insult to injury was the fact her father wanted *her* to take care of her mother now as the mother was medically ill.

Medical history was noncontributory. Neuropsychological assessment revealed that she had an above-average IQ with difficulties with working memory, plus lower than average verbal and perceptual/organizational abilities. Personality testing revealed low scores on the Millon Clinical Multiaxial Inventories in areas related to independence and that she tended to be overly sensitive and reactive. Her DSM-IV diagnosis was (1) borderline personality disorder and (2) chronic dysthymic disorder.

A decision was made to treat her with a combination of psychoeducation, individual therapy, and family therapy (in that order of implementation). She refused medication for her depression as she felt her symptoms were mild.

Treatment Focus

The patient's treatment began with psychoeducation. The therapist explained the nature of her illness, her symptoms, what the diagnosis meant, and the proposed treatment. The target symptoms were detailed for each treatment modality that was used. The therapist explained what "mood disorder" and "borderline disorder" meant. She did a lot of outside reading and gradually came to understand (and accept) the concept and what interventions needed to be done.

Following the psychoeducation, the therapist began individual therapy, doing twenty sessions over the next six months. The goal was to improve her moods and help her to begin to cope with the difficult areas in her life—that is, her current sexual relationship with her husband and her relationship with her parents. Following that, the therapist started to include family sessions on a monthly basis. The husband was also provided with psychoeducation regarding BPD. Then she and her husband began to talk about their intimacy and sexual relationship. The therapist introduced graduated sexual "exercises" with increased sexual intimacy (intimacy and intercourse had been almost nil in the past two years). As this progressed, the therapist encouraged her to make some contact with her parents (starting with phone calls and occasional visits of short duration).

The last stages of the therapy focused on vocational rehabilitation. Individual tutorials were used to work with her on her writing. At the same time, the marital therapy was continued to further work on the relationship. The husband was feeling a lot better about their relationship, which had been conflicted and high in hostility, and felt their intimacy level had improved. He now found he was more motivated (he previously had been somewhat reluctant to be "close" to his wife) and their intimacy had increased to a much more regular basis (i.e., sexual intercourse approximately once a week). Both he and the patient reported that not only did their own relationship improve, but so too did her relationship with her parents.

STRENGTHS AND LIMITATIONS

The major limitations of this model revolve around the fact that there have been no controlled trials of marital or family therapy intervention in BPD. As a result, all recommendations in the literature (as well as ours) are based on clinical experience. Moreover, limited correlations have been found between the family pathology literature and treatment recommendations. Despite these discrepancies, we believe family therapy to be an efficacious part of the treatment of borderline patients, especially in married couples who are committed to the relationship.

INTEGRATION WITH PSYCHIATRIC SERVICES AND ROLE OF MEDICATION

It is important to emphasize that when the treating mental health professional is a psychiatrist, he or she should also be attentive to the potential value of medications, and that when the treating mental health professional is not a psychiatrist, he or she should always work closely with a psychiatric cotherapist so that additional opportunities to help these patients with medication should not be missed. Situations where BPD requires medication include depressive and anxiety symptoms, psychotic symptoms, and breaks in reality testing. Obviously, the use of medication may impact family treatment in that a family member taking a "pill" suggests (to the family) that the individual is "sick" (which has negative connotations).

CULTURAL AND GENDER ISSUES

For years, researchers have thought that borderline personality disorder predominated in females. However, recent literature suggests that this is not the case; males are as likely to have borderline personality disorder as females (Carter, 1999). It is important, however, to consider gender in the treatment of borderline patients. The presentation of borderline personality disorder will often differ according to gender, due to the differences in parenting of males and females and differences in the social expectations of males and females (Simmons, 1992). There are important links to being female and having a greater risk of being abused—especially if an individual has borderline traits such as "histrionic" affect and behavior. Males may be underdiagnosed because "anger" is more acceptable, or they are more likely (than females) to show conduct disorder.

Culture is also an important variant that needs to be considered. Some cultures, usually traditional societies stressing "self-control," can provide protective factors that suppress the expression of borderline personality disorder (Miller, 1996). The therapist must recognize these factors and offer culturally acceptable reframing so that patients can understand their illnesses (Leetz, 1998).

FUTURE DIRECTIONS

This review of etiology, evaluation, and treatment has led us a to number of final points. We believe borderline personality disorder can be managed over time, but it is difficult. Along with data supporting the notion of crucial genetic-biological underpinnings, there are suggestions of family psychopathology, which may be related to etiology. As a result, the patient's behavior affects the family and vice versa. Therefore, successful treatment of borderline personality should involve a family therapy component.

Having mentioned that, it must be noted that prognosis for BPD families is unknown. Presumably the families, like their patient-members, get better (level out) after two decades of great difficulty, but information is lacking. In this context, the issue of "survival" for the family of the patient with BPD needs to be addressed. Families need to be educated about the illness of the patient—although it may have genetic roots, it is not their fault (i.e., they are not to blame).

Consumer support groups such as the National Alliance for the Mentally Ill (NAMI) are invaluable for providing support, psychoeducational material, and other help. Furthermore, the symptoms of BPD have the potential to cause great family distress and burden. Therefore, the family must be careful not to exacerbate a difficult situation by blaming the patient for symptoms of functional difficulties he or she is unable to control (a similar dilemma exists for families with bipolar disorder or schizophrenia). Finally, the family must be prepared for the fact that these conditions are often lifelong, and plan for the costs of therapy, estate planning, etc., accordingly.

Borderline personality disorder has high levels of morbidity and mortality, which involves both patients and their families. Our treatment model needs to be scientifically tested. Controlled studies of family treatment with concomitant drug and/or individual therapy need to be done.

REFERENCES

American Psychiatric Association (1994). *Diagnostic and statistical manual of mental disorders,* Fourth edition. Washington, DC: American Psychiatric Association.

Berkowitz, D. (1981). The borderline adolescent and the family. In M. Lansky (Ed.), *Family therapy and major psychopathology* (pp. 183-201). New York: Grune and Stratton.

Bryer, J. B., Nelson, B. A., Miller, J. B., and Krol, P. A. (1987). Childhood sexual and physical abuse as factors in adult psychiatric illness. *American Journal of Psychiatry, 144,* 1426-1430.

Burgess, J. and Zarconi, V. (1992). Cognitive impairment in dramatic personality disorders. *American Journal of Psychiatry, 149(1),* 136.

Carter, B. and McGoldrick, M. (1988), *The changing family life cycle: A framework for family therapy* (Second edition). New York: Gardner Press.

Carter, J. (1999). Gender differences in the frequency of personality disorders in depressed outpatients. *Journal of Personality Disorders, 13(1),* 67-74.

Clarkin, J., Marziali, E., and Munroe-Blum, H. (1991). Group and family treatments for borderline personality disorder. *Hospital and Community Psychiatry, 42,* (1038-1043).

Coccaro, E. (1993). Psychopharmacologic studies in patients with personality disorder: Review and perspective. *Journal of Personality Disorders* (spring supplement), 181-192.

Coccaro, E. and Siever, L. (1995). The neuropsychopharmacology of personality disorders. In F. Bloom and D. Kupfer (Eds.), *Psychopharmacology: The fourth generation of progress* (pp. 1567-1580). New York: Raven.

Cornelius, J., Soloff, P., Perel, J., and Ulrich, R. (1993). Continuation pharmacotherapy of borderline personality disorder with haloperidol and phenelzine. *American Journal of Psychiatry, 150(12),* 1843-1848.

Frank, H. and Paris, J. (1981). Recollections of family experience in borderline patients. *Archives of General Psychiatry, 38(9),* 1031-1034.

Gladstone, G., Parker, G., Wilhelm K., Mitchell, P., and Austin, M. (1999). Characteristics of depressed patients who report childhood sexual abuse. *American Journal of Psychiatry, 156(3),* 431-437.

Goldberg, R., Mann, L., Wise, T., and Segal, E. (1985). Parental qualities as perceived by patients with borderline personality disorder. *Hillside Journal of Clinical Psychiatry, 4,* 134-140.

Goldman, S., D'Angelo, E., and DeMaso, D. (1993). Psychopathology in the families of children and adolescents with borderline personality disorder. *American Journal of Psychiatry, 150(12),* 1832-1835.

Gunderson, J. (1989). Borderline personality disorder. In *American Psychiatric Association: Treatments of psychiatric disorders: A task force report of the American Psychiatric Association* (pp. 2749-2759). Washington, DC: American Psychiatric Association.

Herman, J., Perry, J., and van der Kolk, B. (1989). Childhood trauma in borderline personality disorder. *American Journal of Psychiatry, 146,* 490-495.

Kagan, J., Reznick, J., Snidman, N., and Gibbons, J. (1988). Childhood derivatives of inhibition and lack of inhibition to the unfamiliar. *Child Development, 59,* 1580-1589.

Klein, D. (1968). Psychiatric diagnosis and a typology of clinical drug effects. *Psychopharmacology, 13,* 359-386.

Koch, A. (1985). The treatment of borderline personality disorder within a distressed relationship. *Journal of Marital and Family Therapy, 11,* 373-380.

Leetz, K. (1998). Cultural interactions in the psychotherapy of borderline personality disorder. *American Journal of Psychotherapy, 52(2),* 176-190.

Linehan, M. (1987). Dialectical behavior therapy for borderline personality disorder: Theory and method. *Bulletin of the Menninger Clinic, 51,* 261-276.

Linehan, M., Armstrong, H., Suarez, A., and Allmon, D. (1991). Cognitive-behavioral treatment of chronically parasuicidal borderline patients. *Archives of General Psychiatry, 49,* 1060-1064.

Links, P. and Blum, H. (1990). Family environment and family psychopathology in the etiology of borderline personality disorder. In P. Links (Ed.), *Family environment and borderline personality disorder* (pp. 1-24). Washington, DC: American Psychiatric Press.

Links, P., Boigo, I., Huxley, G., Steiner, M., and Mitton, J. (1990). Sexual abuse and biparental failure as etiologic models in borderline personality disorder. In

P. Links (Ed.), *Family environment and borderline personality disorder* (pp. 105-120). Washington, DC: American Psychiatric Press.

Loranger, A., Oldham, J., and Tulis, E. (1982). Familial transmission DSM-III borderline personality disorder. *Archives of General Psychiatry, 39,* 795-799.

Loranger, A. and Tulis, E. (1985). Family history of alcoholism in borderline personality disorder. *Archives of General Psychiatry, 42,* 153-157.

Marziali, E. (1992). The etiology of borderline personality disorder. In J. Clarkin, E. Marziali, and H. Munroe-Blum (Eds.), *Developmental factors in borderline personality disorder: An empirical perspective* (pp. 27-44). New York: Guilford.

McCormack, C. (1989). The borderline/schizoid marriage: The holding environment as an essential treatment construct. *Journal of Marital and Family Therapy, 15,* 299-309.

McGlashan, T. (1987). Testing DSM-III symptom criteria for schizotypal and borderline personality disorders. *Archives of General Psychiatry, 44,* 143-148.

Miller, S. (1996). Borderline personality disorder in cultural context: Commentary on Paris. *Psychiatry: Interpersonal and Biological Processes, 59(2),* 193-195.

Pope, H., Jonas, J., Hudson, J., Cohen, B., and Gunderson, J. (1983). The validity of DSM-III borderline personality disorder. *Archives of General Psychiatry, 40,* 23-30.

Schultz, P., Schulz, S., Hamer, R., Resnick, R., Friedel, R., and Goldberg, S. (1985). The impact of borderline and schizotypal personality disorders on patients and their families. *Hospital and Community Psychiatry, 36,* 879-881.

Shapiro, E. (1978). Research on family dynamics: Clinical implications for the family of the borderline adolescent. *Adolescent Psychiatry, 6,* 360-376.

Siever, L. J. and Davis, K. L. (1991). A psychobiological perspective on the personality disorders. *Psychiatry, 148,* 1647-1658.

Silverman, J.M., Pinkham, L., Horvath, T.B., Coccaro, E.E., Klar, H., Schear, S., Apter, S., Davidson, M., Mohs, R.C., and Siever, L.J. (1991). Affective and impulsive personality disorder traits in the relatives of patients with borderline personality disorder. *American Journal of Psychiatry, 148,* 1378-1385.

Simmons, D. (1992). Gender issues and borderline personality disorder: Why do females dominate the diagnosis? *Archives of Psychiatric Nursing, 6(4),* 219-223.

Slipp, S. (1981). Marital therapy for borderline personality disorders. In A. Gurman (Ed.), *Questions and answers in the practice of family therapy* (pp. 258-259). New York: Brunner/Mazel.

Snyder, S., Pitts ,W., Goodpaster, W., and Gustin, Q. (1984). Family structure as recalled by borderline patients. *Psychopathology, 17,* 90-97.

Soloff, P. and Millward, J. (1983). Developmental histories of borderline patients. *Comprehensive Psychiatry, 24,* 547-588.

Stone, M. (1988). Towards a psychobiological theory of BPD: Is irritability the red thread that runs through borderline conditions? *Disassociation, 1(2),* 2-15.

Stone, M. (1990). Abuse and abusiveness in borderline personality disorder. In P. Links (Ed.), *Family environment and borderline personality disorder* (pp. 131-148). Washington, DC: American Psychiatric Press.

Yalom, I. (1985). *The theory and practice of group psychotherapy* (Third edition). New York: Basic Books.

Zanarini, M., Gunderson, J., Marino, M., Schwartz, E., and Frankenberg, F. R. (1989). Childhood experiences of borderline patients. *Comprehensive Psychiatry, 30,* 18-25.

Zanarini, M., Gunderson, J., Marino, M., Schwartz, E., and Frankenberg, F. R. (1990). Psychiatric disorders in the families of borderline outpatients. In P. Links (Ed.), *Family environment and borderline personality disorder* (pp. 67-84). Washington, DC: American Psychiatric Press.

Chapter 7

Systemic Treatment of Obsessive-Compulsive Disorder in a Rural Community Mental Health Center: An Integrative Approach

Malcolm M. MacFarlane

INTRODUCTION

Until recently, obsessive-compulsive disorder (OCD) could well be considered an invisible illness. The prevalence of OCD has historically been underestimated. Rudin (1953) estimated the lifetime prevalence of OCD to be 0.05 percent. Recent estimates based on the Epidemiological Catchment Area (ECA) Survey suggest a much higher lifetime prevalence of 2.5 percent (Robins et al., 1984), making it about twice as common as panic disorder and schizophrenia, and the fourth most common psychiatric disorder in the United States (Karno et al., 1988). Rasmussen and Eisen (1990) suggest a number of reasons for the failure to identify OCD symptoms. One of these reasons is that many clients are reluctant to talk about their symptoms for fear of seeming "crazy" or bizarre. Pollard and colleagues (1989) found that only 28 percent of individuals with OCD in the general population sought help for the illness. Another reason for the underreporting of OCD suggested by Rasmussen and Eisen (1990) is that many clinicians focus on underlying comorbid disorders, such as depression and anxiety, and fail to ask appropriate screening questions to identify OCD symptoms.

According to the DSM-IV (American Psychiatric Association, 1994), OCD is included with anxiety disorders. The hallmark of OCD is the presence of either obsessions or compulsions. Obsessions

155

are defined as recurrent and persistent ideas, thoughts, impulses, or images that are experienced as intrusive and inappropriate, and cause marked anxiety or distress. Compulsions, or "rituals" are defined as repetitive behaviors or mental acts that the person feels driven to perform in response to an obsession, or according to rules that must be applied rigidly. These compulsive or ritualistic behaviors are aimed at preventing or reducing distress and anxiety or preventing some dreaded event or situation, but the behaviors are either clearly excessive or are not connected in a realistic way with what they are designed to prevent.

Obsessions may include fears of contamination, personally unacceptable sexual thoughts, obsessions with a need for symmetry or exactness, hoarding or saving obsessions, obsessions with violent or aggressive images or behaviors, or a fear that harm will come to others. Typical rituals or compulsions which stem from these obsessions include ritual hand washing or cleaning to avoid contamination; ritual checking of locks, stove burners, and water faucets to avoid feared disasters such as fire, burglary, and floods; ritual hoarding or collecting of items to reduce a fear of items being needed and not available; and ritual ordering and arranging of items. Rituals involving repeated touching of objects, ritual avoidances such as not stepping on cracks, and ritual counting are also common (Steketee, 1993a).

Not surprisingly, these symptoms provoke considerable emotional distress and often interfere significantly with everyday functioning. Steketee (1997) outlines a variety of research findings regarding OCD and functional impairment, and notes that individuals with OCD have high mental health utilization rates. In one study (Leon, Portera, and Weissman, 1995), 22 percent of men and 13 percent of women with OCD were receiving disability payments. Often, routine activities such as sitting in chairs, using the telephone, and eating were disrupted because of contamination fears and elaborate cleaning rituals. It was also found that role impairment and social functioning in OCD individuals were substantially worse than population norms (Koran, Thienemann, and Davenport, 1996).

Given the disruptive nature of OCD symptoms, it would not be surprising to find that individuals with lowered quality of life due to OCD reported experiencing considerable depression. Indeed, Barlow, DiNardo, and Vermilyea (1986) report that a diagnosis of major depression has been found in 28 to 38 percent of OCD clients. These findings are supported by Rasmussen and Eisen (1994), who report that 67 percent of OCD patients will suffer from at least one episode of major depression over the course of their lives. Indeed, comorbidity seems to be more the rule than the exception with OCD, and Yaryura-Tobias and colleagues (1996) report finding that 42.2 percent of individuals in a large sample had at least one other DSM-III-R condition. Given that OCD is considered to be an anxiety disorder, it is also not surprising that other anxiety disorders such as social phobia and panic disorder are found with increased frequency among OCD clients (Rasmussen and Eisen, 1994). In a lifetime study of 108 patients with OCD, Crino and Andrews (1996) found that 50 percent met the DSM-III-R criteria for major depressive disorder, 42 percent for social phobia, 31 percent for generalized anxiety disorder, and 19 percent for dysthymia.

Family Impact

Individuals suffering from OCD are not the only ones who experience the disruption of this illness's symptoms; family members of OCD individuals also experience extreme stress. Steketee and Pruyn (1998) have found that many family members become involved in the OCD sufferer's avoidant behaviors and compulsions in an effort to relieve the sufferer's fear and anxiety. Often family members themselves become dysfunctional as a result of this involvement. Van Noppen, Steketee, and Pato (1997) outline a situation described by the sister of a twenty-three-year-old female OCD patient. The OCD family member barricaded herself in the living room and refused to allow other family members to enter out of a fear of contamination. The sister described a vile odor in the house from cans the OCD patient urinated in to avoid using the feared toilet, which was associated with germs and risk of contamination. The OCD sister was seen as controlling, had not let anyone in her room in four years, and there was major conflict between the patient and her mother.

In another case, Steketee and Pruyn (1998) describe the story of the wife of a man with severe hoarding rituals. The wife raised their children in a single room of their large home because the husband had filled it otherwise completely with papers, wood, and a variety of objects from the trash which he considered valuable. The husband became violent when she attempted to remove items or pressured him to do so. Items overflowed onto neighboring property, and eventually the city filed suit for removal of the items.

Although much information on the impact of OCD on families is anecdotal, Calvocoressi and colleagues (1995), in an interview of thirty-four family members of OCD patients, found that one-third of family members report frequently (three or more times per week) reassuring patients; one-third participated in behaviors related to patients' compulsions; family and leisure time routines were modified at least moderately to accommodate patients' distress in 35 percent to 40 percent of families; and 35 percent of families reported moderate distress, while 23 percent of families reported severe or extreme distress. These findings are consistent with studies by Emmelkamp, de Haan, and Hoogduin (1990) and Riggs, Hiss, and Foa (1992), who report that approximately 50 percent of partners of OCD patients experience marital distress.

Family Etiology

Although various authors have examined family-of-origin dynamics that may contribute to the development of OCD (Hoover and Insel, 1984; Steketee and Pruyn, 1998), there is little support for any specific precipitating family factors in the development of OCD (Steketee and Pruyn, 1998). Research does, however, suggest that family response to OCD symptoms can either aggravate symptoms or support treatment efforts. Steketee and Foa (1985) have found that impatience, protection, and accommodating behavior patterns on the part of family members are predictive of relapse. They have also found that negative family environments and stress exacerbate OCD symptoms. Emmelkamp, Kloek, and Blaauw (1992) have found that stress and high expressed emotion (EE) in families are predictive of relapse, and they recommend addressing significant family factors in treatment and involving spouses and family members in empathic listening skills and communication training. Hafner (1982) also describes a pattern of relapses in OCD patients after return to conflictual marriages. Steketee (1993b) found that poor family functioning predicted fewer gains on OCD symptoms at follow-up.

Family Treatment Research

Given these mentioned findings regarding the importance of family response to successful treatment outcomes for OCD, one would expect that considerable attention would have been paid to family treatment modalities, but this has not been the case. Some of the earliest writings regarding family treatment for OCD originate with Hafner and colleagues (1981) and Hafner (1982). Yet as Welfare (1993) points out, Hafner's writings have been largely ignored, and OCD has received little attention in the marriage and family therapy (MFT) literature. Much of the literature that does exist tends to be based on case studies rather than research. Hafner (1988) describes a spouse-aided treatment approach to OCD. He emphasizes that treatment needs to focus on OCD symptoms, not just on the marital relationship. He involves the spouse in behavioral interventions such as in vivo exposure and response prevention. Hafner also focuses on an exploration of gender issues in the expression of OCD symptoms (see section on Cultural and Gender Issues which follows later) and on the complicating influence of marital anger. Hafner suggests that some OCD symptoms may serve interpersonal functions in conflictual relationships and emphasizes that failure to deal with this aspect of OCD symptoms may result in the undermining of treatment progress. Hand (1988) also notes that symptoms may become a weapon in power struggles between couples and strongly advocates incorporating systems-oriented treatment approaches. In a more recent paper, Hafner (1992) reports clear improvement in small treatment samples with his approach of including spouses of OCD patients with conflictual marriages.

Although much of the literature on marital and family treatment of OCD tends to be case study, there is some relevant research literature. Thornicroft, Colson, and Marks (1991) report a 60 percent decrease in OCD symptoms at six-month follow-up in a study of spouse-assisted exposure/response prevention (EX/RP) behavioral therapy. Van Noppen and colleagues (1997) also report a significant decrease in OCD symptoms using a multiple-family behavioral treatment (MFBT) approach. A control group using a behavioral EX/RP approach without family involvement reported a similar decrease in OCD symptoms but without the same benefits on family functioning variables. Research on family involvement in behavioral exposure/response prevention treatment approaches remains mixed, with some researchers, such as Emmel-kamp, de Haan, and Hoogduin (1990), finding no significant differ-ences between individual versus marital EX/RP, and others, such as Mehta (1990), finding greater improvement for family-based EX/RP than individual-based approaches.

The current literature suggests that marital and family involvement in treatment for OCD may well be positive, but so far this involve-ment does not seem to make a big difference in reduction of OCD symptoms. Marital and family involvement does seem to result in im-proved marital and family functioning and helps to decrease relapses. Marital and family treatment alone without behavioral therapy does not appear to help reduce OCD symptoms. Steketee (1997) suggests that MFT may be especially useful for families with extensive partici-pation in OCD symptoms or in which marital and family relation-ships are severely impaired. Welfare (1993) notes that MFT may be crucial in shifting chronic situations in which OCD symptoms are rooted in interactional and relationship dynamics. Overall, it seems as though marriage and family therapists may have a great deal to of-fer in treating families with an OCD member, and that the most effec-tive therapeutic approach may well be a model which incorporates a combination of EX/RP behavioral therapy in combination with a family systems approach. This model will be outlined in more detail later.

SETTING

Ross Memorial Hospital (RMH) is a 200-bed community hospital situated in rural Southern Ontario. Community Counseling Services (CCS) is an off-site, community-based, mental health program serv-ing the population of Lindsay and surrounding Victoria County. The service is fully funded through the provincial Ontario Health Insur-ance Program (OHIP).

Counseling and psychiatric services are provided for individuals ages sixteen and over who are identified as experiencing mental health problems. Services provided include individual psychother-apy, psychiatric assessment, and psychoeducational and treatment groups, as well as marital and family therapy services when at least one family member has been identified as suffering from a mental health problem. The definition of a mental health problem utilized is a broad one and includes diagnoses of depression, anxiety, personality disorders, suicidal crises, and life transitions that result in significant impairment of social or occupational functioning. Serious mental illnesses such as schizophrenia and bipolar disorder are also included.

CCS programs cover a broad range and include a mental health program, psychiatric services, a clinical case management program, a crisis response program, and a child sexual abuse response program, which is funded separately through the Ministry of Community and Social Services. CCS employs a multidisciplinary team approach. Staff backgrounds include psychiatry, marriage and family therapy, social work, psychology, and psychiatric nursing. Although the treatment approach of individual therapists is influenced by their academic background and training, the Centre as a whole utilizes a broad-based systems approach. Individual treatment approaches are integrated into this systems framework, and every effort is made to ensure that treatment approaches for specific presenting problems reflect current research regarding best practices and therapeutic effectiveness. Although there may be individual differences in application, most Centre therapists would adhere fairly closely to the model outlined below when treating OCD clients.

It should be emphasized that CCS is a generic mental health program and does not specialize in the treatment of OCD. OCD would be diagnosed and treated in the course of a routine intake, assessment, and treatment process. When OCD symptoms are assessed, a treatment plan is established that addresses the OCD symptoms. The treatment model which follows presents an integrated treatment approach that is rooted in a family systems perspective and tailored to the individual based on current best practices research and the client's and client family's input regarding treatment needs and desires.

TREATMENT MODEL

In treating OCD, staff at Community Counseling Services draw on an integrative biopsychosocial model that incorporates elements of cognitive behavioral therapy (CBT) within the framework of a broader contextual systemic approach. We find this approach, which is solidly based on positive outcome research indicating the effectiveness of behavioral approaches in reducing OCD symptoms, to be quite effective. At the same time, the incorporation of a contextual and systemic approach allows clinicians to deal with the impact of OCD symptoms on the family and to assist family members to cope with the illness and avoid being drawn into dysfunctional interactions and accommodation to OCD symptoms.

A Behavioral Approach

Cognitive-behavioral therapy (CBT) is considered to be the most effective psychotherapeutic approach to the treatment of OCD (Franklin and Foa, 1998; Foa, Franklin, and Kozak, 1998; Foa and Franklin, 1998). The behavioral element that seems to be most effective is exposure/response prevention (EX/RP). In essence, this treatment procedure involves having clients expose themselves to the feared stimulus or situation (for example, leaving home without checking the locks, or sitting on a toilet, which they fear will contaminate them), while preventing the rituals or responses in which they normally engage as a way of reducing their anxiety (for instance, cleaning the toilet, washing themselves, or checking the door locks). Exposure to anxiety-producing thoughts or images seems to assist in reducing the intensity of obsessions by extinguishing associated fears. Foa and Franklin (1998:243) write that "repeated, prolonged exposure to feared thoughts and situations provides information that disconfirms mistaken associations and evaluations held by the patients, and thereby promotes habituation."

In vivo exposure and response prevention seems to be most effective. Imaginal exposure has been found to be helpful in some cases in programs that include in vivo exposure (Foa et al., 1980), although imaginal exposure alone or systematic desensitization has not been found to be particularly helpful (Foa, Steketee, and Ozarow, 1985); in vivo exposure appears to be needed. Relaxation training alone also does not seem to be helpful; however, some writers suggest that relaxation may be helpful in dealing with anxiety reactions during response prevention (Steketee, 1993a). Staff at CCS have found relaxation training to be very helpful for OCD clients in dealing with anxiety associated with response prevention, and we regularly employ progressive relaxation approaches through the use of relaxation tapes and in-session relaxation training. Exposure duration typically needs to be fairly long (approximately ninety minutes) in order for reduction of anxiety to take place (Foa and Chambless, 1978), and typically exposure tasks are assigned based on a hierarchy of gradually increasing levels of anxiety and difficulty.

The research on EX/RP is quite persuasive, and Foa and Kozak (1996) have found, in a review of twelve outcome studies, that an average of 83 percent of treatment completers show improvements short term, and 76 percent show improvement two years later. A variety of treatment manuals outline EX/RP in detail (Steketee, 1993a; Kozak and Foa, 1996; Kozak and Foa, 1997; Stanley and Averill, 1998), and readers are referred to these works for more complete descriptions of EX/RP procedures.

A Cognitive Approach

Many behaviorists argue that cognitive approaches may not really be necessary in treating OCD as EX/RP challenges and disconfirms erroneous associations and beliefs (Foa and Kozak, 1986). They also note that most OCD clients already regard their obsessions as irrational, so focusing on this adds little to the treatment. Research regarding the effectiveness of adding a cognitive component to OCD treatment suggests that cognitive therapy seems to add little to outcomes in terms of reduction of OCD symptoms when combined with EX/RP (Franklin and Foa, 1998; Foa and Franklin, 1998). Despite this, most therapists discuss dysfunctional thinking and erroneous beliefs as part of the rationale for EX/RP (Steketee, 1993a), and many find it does seem to help the client benefit from exposure treatment. Steketee (1993a) also suggests it may help with clients displaying fixed, unreasonable beliefs.

Staff at CCS have consistently found cognitive approaches useful in treating OCD. Although a variety of cognitive approaches may be utilized (i.e., Beck, 1976; Ellis, 1962), we have found the work of Padesky and Greenberger (1995), and Greenberger and Padesky (1995) to be particularly helpful. These authors have both a clinician's guide and a treatment manual/workbook for clients which many have found useful. We have also found cognitive approaches outlined in Bourne (1995) to be useful, especially the concept of coping scripts that incorporate "self talk," which reinforces clients' ability to cope with the anxiety they are experiencing during response prevention. Coping scripts or self talk for an OCD ritual such as checking locks may look something like this: "Relax. Breathe. It's OK. Nothing bad will happen. I have checked the lock once, and everything is OK. I can leave. I don't have to check it again. Breathe. Relax. The door is locked. I can cope with the anxiety. The anxiety will go away. I can get through this." Other cognitive techniques drawn from these approaches include use of distraction to interrupt escalating feelings of anxiety during response prevention and use of thought stopping to interrupt obsessive thought patterns.

Drawing on Padesky and Greenberger's approach, clinicians may encourage clients to develop a coping plan for disasters, so that disasters do not need to be "prevented" by compulsions. Alternatively, they may have clients "test" beliefs about OCD such as, "Thinking something means it will happen." As clients test these beliefs through behavioral experiments, they find that the feared disasters do not occur, and the obsessions become more manageable. We also find Padesky and Greenberger's description of three interconnected levels of thought to be useful. They describe these levels as: automatic thoughts, underlying assumptions, and schemas (or core beliefs). Core beliefs give rise to underlying assumptions, which, in turn, fuel automatic thoughts. In working with OCD clients, we may work on all levels, challenging and replacing automatic thoughts with more balanced thoughts that are incorporated into coping scripts, and couple this with relaxation to reduce anxiety. Underlying assumptions are challenged with behavioral experiments, and this integrates well with EX/RP exercises. Finally, we examine clients' core beliefs about themselves which fuel underlying assumptions. Often OCD clients display core beliefs about themselves such as beliefs that they are unlucky or beliefs that if they do not do everything perfectly, people will not love them. Steketee (1993a) notes the importance of dealing with such core beliefs and assumptions in therapy. Often these beliefs are tied into life stories or narratives that seem to confirm the beliefs. In working with these core beliefs, we often incorporate the systemic and narrative approaches described later, and this makes for a well-integrated treatment approach.

A Biological Approach

There is an increasing recognition that a biological basis exists for OCD. In part, evidence for a biological basis for OCD comes from findings that OCD tends to run in families. Pauls, Raymond, and Robertson (1991) have found that OCD is diagnosed in parents of clients with OCD in 20 to 25 percent of cases. Billett, Richter, and Kennedy (1998) also note that there is evidence from twin studies for a single major gene for OCD. There is also increasing evidence that OCD is linked to disturbances in brain chemistry and, in particular, to neurotransmitters associated with serotonin subsystems. For an excellent review of the serotonin hypothesis and the biological basis of OCD, see Gross and colleagues (1998). There is also evidence emerging from neuroimaging studies of structural differences in the brains of OCD subjects compared with control subjects (Pigott and Seay, 1998). The contribution of biology is an important element to incorporate into psychoeducational approaches with families with an OCD member. The recognition of a biological basis for OCD also leads to the recognition of the importance of medical and pharmacologic treatments for OCD, an issue which will be discussed later in this chapter.

A Systemic Approach

The behavioral, cognitive, and biological components of the model outlined previously are rooted in a systems approach that recognizes the family relationship and sociocultural context in which these other components are embedded. Many CCS clinicians have been drawn toward a postmodern perspective that integrates systemic, narrative, and social constructionist elements. This approach has been outlined in some depth by MacFarlane (1993). The approach stems from the work of the Milan team, and in particular the work of Boscolo and Cecchin as outlined by Tomm (1984a, b). Tomm (1987a, b, 1988) has subsequently expanded on this model, adding strategizing to the original three Milan team guidelines of hypothesizing, circularity, and neutrality (Selvini Palazzoli et al., 1980). Tomm has also moved toward an interventive interviewing approach that builds on the hallmark Milan approach of circular questioning (Penn, 1982; Tomm, 1985). Interventive interviewing moves away from major end-of-session interventions toward an approach where every question and action of the clinician is seen as an intervention with the potential for influencing clients' perceptions and creating change.

We find the systemic approach offers a great deal of flexibility. In hypothesizing, we can consider linear hypotheses about OCD (represented by biological and pharmacological approaches), as well as circular or interactional hypotheses that have implications for understanding the impact of OCD symptoms on family dynamics and the ways that OCD symptoms serve functional purposes in family roles and relationships. When strategizing about possible interventions, we are mindful that we are basing our intervention on our own constructions and beliefs about OCD and that these are not necessarily "truths." This awareness is especially critical when we are engaged in psychoeducational interventions or are discussing medication options or biological aspects of OCD. Our understanding in these areas is constantly changing, and it is important to convey this reality to our clients, rather than presenting our information as "fact." This more tentative presentation can give clients more permission for making their own informed treatment decisions, particularly in regard to pharmacological treatments, rather than believing that there is one "right" treatment approach that they must follow.

With the movement toward a postmodern, social constructionist, and narrative approach (Anderson and Goolishian, 1988; Hoffman, 1990), we are also tending to move away from a strict application of neutrality and more toward a second-order cybernetics or "observing system" perspective in which therapists are seen as part of the system, and are aware of their own position in larger cultural and treatment systems. Traditionally, the position of neutrality cautioned clinicians against imposing their own constructions of reality on clients. We believe that there may be useful information for clients in therapists' experiences and constructions of reality; however, therapists need to be aware of their own constructions and transparent about these constructions or biases in their interactions with clients. Therapists must recognize that clients' constructions have equal validity and offer information or interpretations in a tentative way that respects the client's right to reject the therapists' constructions if they do not seem to fit or are not found useful.

Our awareness of the broader social and cultural systems in which both clients and clinicians are embedded has encouraged a number of CCS therapists to incorporate the narrative approach outlined by White and Epston (1990) into our work. These authors emphasize the way in which dominant social discourses (such as the traditional medical model of mental illness) influence our constructions of reality, shaping both clinician and client views about mental illnesses and how to treat them. We endeavor to be conscious of these discourses, and avoid participating in dialogues with clients that perpetuate the stigmatizing impact of many of these discourses.

In treating OCD, we have also found White and Epston's technique of externalizing the problem to be particularly useful. The first step in applying this approach involves exploring how the problem of OCD has controlled or influenced the client's life and family interactions. Next, the times when clients and families were able to exert influence over OCD symptoms are explored and highlighted. Therapists then build on these previously ignored experiences of strength and competence, helping to weave them into a new narrative or story of family success in coping with OCD. We find this approach fits particularly well with both the cognitive and behavioral elements of this model, as behavioral successes in reducing OCD symptoms can be embedded in a new narrative of growing competence, and old core beliefs can be replaced with new and more satisfying stories that are based in health rather than illness.

CASE EXAMPLE

Sam Brown (age fifty-three) was referred to CCS for ongoing counseling by his psychiatrist. Sam's DSM diagnosis included an Axis I diagnosis of obsessive-compulsive disorder, and an Axis II diagnosis of obsessive-compulsive personality. A possible diagnosis of depression was also noted for Axis I but was not fully confirmed. A psychological assessment indicated the presence of post-traumatic stress disorder (PTSD) symptoms. Sam is married to Lynn (age forty-two); together the couple has three boys, ages twelve, nine, and seven (names and other identifying information have been altered to protect client confidentiality). Sam is retired from a major metropolitan police force, where he worked as a homicide detective.

Sam retired early from the police force as a result of job-related stress. He reported that during his last investigation, that of a suicide of a nineteen-year-old male, he had a vision of the body with the face of his eldest son. Sam also reported a variety of other PTSD symptoms, including being reminded of the morgue by large stainless steel freezer units in the grocery store, having flashbacks to autopsies triggered by seeing stainless steel cutlery in a stainless steel kitchen sink, and feeling as though he was standing in a grave while digging a trench in his backyard.

In his initial assessment, Sam was interviewed using the Yale-Brown Obsessive-Compulsive Scale (YBOCS) (Goodman et al., 1989).

He revealed a variety of obsessions, many of them centered on death and fears of harm coming to family members. He also revealed a variety of compulsions or rituals that were troublesome for him. Sam would often check the burners on the stove several times before finally being able to go to sleep at night. To do this, he would need to go up and down the stairs from the bedroom, getting out of bed each time. He also had a ritual of checking door locks four to five times before settling down for the night or leaving the house. At times, Sam would leave the home, drive some distance, then feel compelled to return to check the locks.

As we explored Sam's OCD symptoms, it seemed that many of these symptoms were related to his job and to PTSD sequalae. In the course of his employment, Sam investigated many fires that were related to stove burners being left on. He also attended many homicide scenes where entry was gained through unlocked doors. Sam's experiences in investigating these types of tragedies seemed to have left him with a high awareness of how vulnerable people can be, and this translated into a great deal of concern for the safety of his family and his loved ones. Sam was able to recognize that many of his compulsive rituals were fueled by a fear that if he did not do the ritual, something bad would happen to his family. As noted above, this type of presentation is characteristic of many individuals experiencing OCD, and, like Sam, their rituals are aimed at reducing the anxiety associated with these obsessions or worries.

Although there was a clear PTSD element underlying Sam's OCD symptoms, there were indications that his personality was fairly compulsive from childhood. Sam was likely drawn to police work in part because it fit well with his obsessive personality. Sam's personality was also influenced by family-of-origin factors. Sam indicated that his mother displayed OCD symptoms, suggesting the presence of a genetic component to his illness. Sam's father was an alcoholic, and Sam found him to be very unreliable. Sam decided very early in his life that he did not want to be like his father, and this seems to have been an influencing factor in his developing a very perfectionistic and, at times, controlling personality style. Sam's obsessive and perfectionistic personality also made it very difficult for him to accept his symptoms; he would often become angry at himself and depressed over his inability to "control" these symptoms. Sam would often attempt to conceal his rituals out of a sense of embarrassment.

Sam was able to identify that his OCD symptoms were worse when he was under stress. This intensification of symptoms during periods of high anxiety is typical of OCD. Sam found that his symptoms of checking increased dramatically during and after times he was required to testify in court regarding cases he was involved with prior to retirement. He also found that his OCD symptoms increased during a family camping vacation when he was worrying compulsively about whether they would be able to find campsites for the night. A significant part of Sam's treatment involved learning to manage his anxiety more effectively, thereby preventing the escalation of OCD symptoms.

The first two sessions of Sam's treatment were devoted to completing an initial assessment. Lynn was invited to attend the third session with Sam. Lynn was very supportive of Sam. She was aware of Sam's checking behavior, which he normally tried to conceal, but had been unsure how to help Sam with this, or whether to comment directly on his rituals. She did not identify a great deal of disruption to marital or family relationships as a result of Sam's OCD symptoms, but did admit to some minor inconvenience associated with his returning to check locks when leaving the home, and with his checking of burners and locks when going to bed.

Lynn's main concern was Sam's tendency to be unduly rigid regarding household routines, particularly regarding his expectations of the children. This rigidity is typical of many individuals with OCD. Like Sam, they become very perfectionistic and controlling in their attempts to structure family routines so as to minimize their anxiety and coerce accommodation to their rituals and obsessions. Lynn commented that Sam would often get angry at the children when they were disorganized or did not move quickly enough with chores. She felt Sam needed to moderate his expectations of the children and better control his anger and frustration.

Sam's treatment began with a psychoeducational component, and Lynn was included in this stage. Our current understanding of OCD was outlined, in particular noting that OCD appears to have a strong biological basis, and that there may well be a genetic component. This was particularly relevant since Sam's mother seemed to suffer from OCD symptoms. The tendency for the illness to be exacerbated by stress and conflict was explained. Treatment options involving EX/RP, cognitive therapy, relaxation training, and medication were outlined. The desirability of spousal and family participation in treatment was emphasized, and Lynn agreed to participate in Sam's treatment.

Sam had already been tried on fluoxetine by his psychiatrist prior to referral, but had discontinued this medication due to problems with side effects. Sam had also been prescribed alprazolam, a benzodiazepine often used to help reduce anxiety. During the course of his treatment, Sam consulted with two psychiatrists and was tried on a variety of medications including various antidepressants often useful in treating OCD (clomipramine, paroxetine, and fluvoxamine) and various benzodiazepines (lorazepam and clonazepam). Sam's symptoms seemed to respond best to a combination of fluvoxamine and clonazepam, but the side effect of reduced libido from the fluvoxamine created marital difficulties, and he ultimately decided to discontinue use of any SSRI antidepressant medications, and to rely only on clonazepam to assist him in dealing with his anxiety.

The EX/RP treatment approach was explained to Sam and Lynn, and exposure homework assignments were begun early in the treatment process. A number of ritual behaviors were targeted for EX/RP. Sam's checking locks and burners was a primary focus. Sam was instructed to perform these behaviors only once, then to continue on with other activities. He was reassured that his initial anxiety would gradually decrease as the time from his impulse to perform a ritual increased. Sam was coached in a number of techniques for coping while avoiding performing his normal rituals. These techniques included employing relaxation skills such as abdominal breathing, which were taught during the fifth session, and employing a number of cognitive techniques including distracting himself (i.e., reading a book, carrying on a conversation, listening to music, counting backward from one thousand by sevens) and reciting a "coping script," such as, "It's OK, breathe, relax, the anxiety will pass, nothing bad will happen if I don't do this, I am in control of my behavior, be calm, breathe, I don't need to do this, just keep going, everything will be all right."

A variety of other cognitive interventions was also used. One approach was that of "behavioral experiments" to challenge underlying assumptions that if certain rituals weren't performed, a disaster would occur. These behavioral experiments integrated well with the EX/RP approach and provided a rationale for response prevention assignments. Another cognitive technique utilized was one of assessing the probability of any feared event. One way of doing this was for Sam to ask himself, "What's the worst thing that will happen if I don't complete this ritual?" This question was followed by, "How likely is that to happen?" Sam found this type of intervention very helpful. Finally, cognitive interventions were used to challenge some of Sam's core beliefs, such as his fear that "if I don't take control, everything will fall apart." This type of core belief is very typical of adult children of alcoholics, who often have a strong need to control situations stemming from their chaotic family-of-origin experiences.

Lynn played a valuable role as an informal cotherapist. Lynn would draw attention to Sam's times when he was performing rituals. She would support and encourage him in "walking away" from situations where he was tempted to check locks or burners. She would remind him to breathe and to use his coping scripts and help distract him from his anxiety and his obsessions by engaging him in conversations. She would also remind him that the anxiety would not last forever, and that his symptoms would improve if he could just hang on and avoid performing his usual rituals. Sam found Lynn's assistance particularly helpful; by the tenth session, Sam was reporting that he was able to "breathe and walk on" in many situations, and he was finding his anxiety level during response prevention was decreasing. By the twentieth session, Sam's checking of burners had stopped and many other checking behaviors were greatly improved.

The systemic and narrative approaches were applied throughout the treatment process. Michael White's technique of externalizing the problem was helpful in allowing Sam to separate his OCD symptoms from his sense of self. This was beneficial for his self-esteem. Externalizing the problem also helped Sam to focus on the times when he was able to exercise control over his OCD symptoms. As Sam's symptoms improved, Lynn was able to provide positive feedback about how these changes affected their relationship and her feelings toward Sam. This feedback supported and reinforced a new developing story of success for this family in coping with OCD.

Another helpful aspect of the narrative approach was the shift from a narrative of Sam's OCD symptoms, which described a set of out-of-control and "crazy" behaviors that were embarrassing, to a new and healthier narrative in which these symptoms were understood as a natural outgrowth of the traumatic experiences Sam experienced in his employment as a homicide detective. Sam found the opportunity of telling stories of some of his work experiences very healing. Due to the upsetting nature of many of Sam's experiences, and his fear of upsetting Lynn, he had not talked about many of the traumatic events he had witnessed. As Sam came to understand the relationship between his OCD symptoms and his traumatic experiences in his work environment, he began to feel less "crazy;" his personal narrative shifted to one in which he could take pride in fulfilling a demanding and important social role and surviving a variety of painful and traumatic situations. Sam was able to take pride in his ability to heal his wounds and move forward with his new life in retirement.

Time was also spent focusing on Lynn's concerns regarding Sam's anger and his expectations regarding the children. In addition to discussing a number of parenting issues in couples sessions, Sam was encouraged to apply his relaxation skills to situations involving the children and to use a variety of cognitive techniques and "coping scripts" to moderate his obsessive personality traits and alter unrealistic or developmentally inappropriate expectations of the children. A number of sessions were also spent on developing and practicing improved communication and problem-solving skills. These interventions were reported to be helpful in improving family relationships.

Sam's treatment process was not always smooth. At times it was marked by severe anxiety attacks and periods of depression. Despite this, at two years' follow-up, Sam reported that on a scale from one to ten, he would now rate the disruptiveness of his symptoms as a five. At the time of his referral, these symptoms were rated as a ten. Sam indicated that his symptoms tend to flare up about twice per year usually in response to stress, but he feels he is much better at dealing with these symptoms when they arise. He currently has no problems with checking burners and locks. He still experiences some problems with counting things and some superstitiousness regarding numbers, such as the number six. In general, he feels his symptoms are much improved, and he has a sense of confidence in his own ability to cope and deal with his symptoms. His ability to relax and manage stress in his life helps prevent OCD symptoms from escalating and also helps to improve his family relationships.

STRENGTHS AND LIMITATIONS

One of the main strengths of this treatment model is that it is solidly based on behavioral interventions with documented research effectiveness. There is also considerable research support for the effectiveness of the pharmacological elements of this treatment approach described below. In combining a family systems approach with traditional CBT, we seem to get the best of both worlds: a solidly researched, effective behavioral treatment and an approach that recognizes the impact of OCD on the family. This approach not only has the ability to mobilize family supports for the treatment of OCD, but can also intervene in dysfunctional family participation in, or accommodation to, OCD symptoms. It can also address other elements of family pathology that may interfere with treatment or contribute to relapse. Research on family involvement in behavioral treatment of OCD strongly suggests that incorporating a family treatment component can enhance marital and family functioning, and this may be important in helping families to cope with residual OCD symptoms following the conclusion of behavioral treatment. Another advantage of this treatment model is that it is very respectful of client and family input and encourages extensive client involvement in selecting treatment options and making treatment decisions.

One disadvantage of this treatment approach is that not all clients are agreeable to a behavioral treatment approach, and even those who are willing to try this approach may have such difficulty dealing with the anxiety associated with EX/RP that they may tend to drop out of treatment. This is where the emphasis on relaxation and cognitive approaches to dealing with anxiety seems to help. Many clients who would have difficulty dealing with EX/RP treatment alone seem to be able to tolerate this treatment approach after being taught anxiety management skills. The difficulty in dealing with anxiety may also be addressed through incorporating the use of antianxiety medications as discussed later.

Overall, this treatment approach seems to offer many advantages, not the least of which is that it is cost-effective and can be conducted on an outpatient basis within a generic mental health program. It does require some knowledge and skills in applying behavioral treatment approaches, but the availability of the detailed treatment manuals for OCD mentioned previously can assist greatly in training therapists in implementing this approach. Finally, it is an approach that is flexible enough to allow clinicians to incorporate both linear and circular hypotheses and to integrate other models and interventions which research suggests have utility in treating OCD. These models and interventions are incorporated within a contextual observing systems framework, which encourages clinicians to remain mindful of their theoretical orientation and its influence on the entire treatment system.

INTEGRATION WITH PSYCHIATRIC SERVICES AND ROLE OF MEDICATION

Psychiatric services are an integral component of the mental health services offered by Community Counseling Services. In cases in which the treating therapist, rather than a psychiatrist, is the first to see a client, the therapist will routinely refer clients for psychiatric assessments if they feel medication may be a useful or necessary component of the treatment. This occurs frequently in treating OCD. In almost all cases where the psychiatrist is the initial contact, clients are referred for psychotherapy. In many respects, the model for psychiatric consultation is similar to that outlined by Griffith and colleagues (1991). CCS staff, including psychiatrists, believe that even with biologically based illnesses, such as OCD, involving the client and the client's family in the treatment process can help increase family members' understanding of the illness, increase compliance regarding pharmacological treatments, improve coping skills, and decrease the impact of the illness on family members, thus minimizing or avoiding the development of pathologizing interpersonal patterns centered on the illness.

As discussed previously, there is strong evidence for the presence of a biological basis for OCD. It is increasingly accepted that OCD has its roots in disturbances in brain chemistry, and in particular in the neurotransmitters associated with serotonin subsystems. This recognition of a biological basis for OCD leads naturally to the incorporation of biological and pharmacological treatments for OCD. In providing psychoeducational information to clients, the evidence for a biological basis for OCD is discussed with them, and they are routinely informed about medication options that may assist in their treatment. The choice rests with the clients as to whether to pursue medication options; if they choose to do so, they are either offered a referral to a psychiatrist at CCS, or their therapist will discuss the matter with their family physician.

The type of medications most typically used to treat OCD are those having serotonin effects, and in particular medications in the SSRI (selective serotonin reuptake inhibitor) class. Clomipramine is a tricyclic antidepressant with strong serotonin effects. It has been studied extensively and found to be effective in reducing OCD symptoms. Other SSRI medications that are typically used include fluvoxamine, fluoxetine, sertraline, and paroxetine (Pigott and Seay, 1998). Studies suggest that most of these medications have similar efficacies in treating OCD, and differences in tolerability and side effect profiles are the primary considerations in choice of medications (Pigott and Seay, 1998). SSRI medications are occasionally augmented by anxiolytic medications such as buspirone and benzodiazepines such as clonazepam. Research regarding the effectiveness of these medications is very preliminary, but there have been some promising results, especially with clonazepam (Pigott and Seay, 1998; Steketee, 1993a).

Research regarding combining pharmacotherapy and CBT yields mixed results. Patients treated with a combination of antidepressants and CBT tend to improve more quickly but after four months, differences between groups disappear (van Balkom and van Dyck, 1998). A combination of pharmacotherapy and CBT is as effective as CBT alone and more effective than antidepressants alone. The research does not clearly indicate that combination therapy with CBT and pharmacotherapy is superior to CBT alone. Treatment with antidepressants alone tends to give higher relapse rates than CBT after discontinuation of medication. The main advantage of medication is that it can provide more rapid relief of symptoms. Van Balkom and van Dyck (1998) recommend a three-phase treatment process. In phase one, treatment is started with medication; in phase two, CBT is added; in phase three, medications are reduced, ultimately leading to discontinuation once clients have achieved symptom reduction through CBT. Van Balkom and van Dyck acknowledge that patient preference will be a determinant in choice of CBT or pharmacotherapy. They recommend going with the patient's wishes, but emphasize the importance of a psychoeducational component to ensure that clients are making informed choices. Greist (1992) also supports such combination treatment, noting that it can be readily provided on an outpatient basis.

CULTURAL AND GENDER ISSUES

Research findings regarding OCD and gender, ethnicity, and religion tend to support the view of OCD as a biological illness rather than a psychosocial illness, although there are some indications that the expression of specific OCD symptoms tends to be influenced by sociocultural factors. Religious background of those individuals and families with an OCD member does not differ significantly from that of the general population (Raphael et al., 1996; Rasmussen and Eisen, 1992). OCD does seem to be somewhat more predominant among Caucasians (2.1 percent) than nonwhite populations (.5 percent) (Nestadt et al., 1994); however, few studies have explored these differences and relatively little is known. OCD certainly does occur in other cultures, and findings regarding family burden and family involvement in treatment appear to be fairly consistent with North American findings (Mehta, 1990).

In terms of gender, White, Steketee, and Julian (1992) have found that the ratio of males to females experiencing OCD is almost equal (1.0 to 1.1), although actual ratios varied widely across studies. There are some gender differences in the expression of OCD symptoms, with men tending to show more sexual obsessions and obsessions about symmetry and exactness, and women tending to display more aggressive obsessions and cleaning rituals (Lensi et al., 1996). Hafner (1988) also describes gender differences in symptoms consistent with those described by Lensi and colleagues, and he suggests that in some cases OCD symptoms may serve the purpose of reaction formation and diffusion of anger, particularly women's anger regarding unrealistic demands of partners or cultural role expectations. Hafner notes the importance of addressing sociocultural messages and gender roles when treating OCD and the importance of exploring any functional purposes OCD symptoms may play in family dynamics.

It is in exploring such issues that this treatment model may be particularly effective. The treatment approaches of White and Epston (1990) are particularly sensitive to power imbalances and the social discourses in which gender roles and expectations are often situated.

The narrative approach recognizes the unique nature of each individual's story and explores the contribution of each individual's perceptions and constructions of reality to the formation and resolution of problems. The systemic process of circular questioning and interventive interviewing can be an excellent tool for drawing out and highlighting gender differences and exploring alternative ways of relating. The key is for clinicians working with OCD patients to be conscious of these issues and to be prepared to explore them as fully as possible as part of the treatment process.

FUTURE DIRECTIONS

This treatment approach certainly has many strengths; however, a number of areas exist where the model could be developed further. Most notably, there is relatively little research on the use of marital and family therapy approaches with OCD; there is a major need for more research in this area. We need to determine how and when MFT approaches should be integrated with CBT. There is also a need to determine whether dysfunctional family dynamics play a role in those cases which do not respond to CBT or pharmacotherapy, and, if so, determining whether MFT approaches can assist in resolving symptoms in these cases. More research on the role and efficacy of cognitive approaches in general in treating OCD and on the usefulness of Padesky and Greenberger (1995), and Greenberger and Padesky (1995) approach in particular is also needed. The findings of the staff at CCS suggest that such cognitive approaches coupled with relaxation training are useful adjuncts to EX/RP treatment of OCD, but these findings are very preliminary and based on clinical impressions rather than research.

In terms of the program at CCS, clients with OCD would likely benefit from participation in a support group for OCD. Stanley and Averill (1998) note that such groups are experienced as helpful by OCD patients, but caution that there is limited empirical research on the usefulness of support groups in treating OCD. They suggest that such support groups are likely most effective if they are homogeneous and if clients participating in them have already had treatment through EX/RP. CCS has run a support group for anxiety and panic disorder; the client discussed in the case example did attend this group. He found it quite helpful, but, in keeping with Stanley and

Averill's observation, he indicated that he would have found it more helpful if there had been more individuals with OCD in the group (he was the only one). Unfortunately, the number of individuals in treatment for OCD at any one time has not been sufficient to make a support group for OCD practical.

Finally, there appears to be a need within mental health programs in general to more systematically involve family members early in the process. There is a tendency when working within individually focused mental health programs to move toward an individual focus in providing treatment. This is an outgrowth of diagnostic and compensation systems that are tied to individuals rather than to families and which invite an individual focus. Clinicians must constantly guard against the tendency to see clients in isolation from their family and social context, particularly with illnesses such as OCD that have a strong biological basis. Even though the origins of OCD symptoms may be rooted in disturbances in neurobiology and brain chemistry, these symptoms have a profound effect on family dynamics, and families are a valuable treatment resource. It is crucial for family members and significant others to be as fully involved as possible in the process of treating OCD.

REFERENCES

American Psychiatric Association (1994). *Diagnostic and statistical manual of mental disorders* (Fourth edition). Washington, DC: American Psychiatric Association.

Anderson, H. and Goolishian, H. A. (1988). Human systems as linguistic systems: Preliminary and evolving ideas about the implications for clinical theory. *Family Process, 27,* 371-393.

Barlow, D. H., DiNardo, P. A., and Vermilyea, B. B. (1986). Comorbidity and depression among the anxiety disorders. *Journal of Nervous and Mental Disease, 174,* 63-72.

Beck, A. T. (1976). *Cognitive therapy and the emotional disorders.* New York: International Universities Press.

Billett, E. A., Richter, M. A., and Kennedy, J. L. (1998). Genetics of obsessive-compulsive disorder. In R. P. Swinson, M. M. Antony, S. Rachman, and M. A. Richter (Eds.), *Obsessive-compulsive disorder: Theory, research, and treatment* (pp. 181-206). New York: Guilford Press.

Bourne, E. J. (1995). *The anxiety and phobia workbook* (Second edition). Oakland, CA: New Harbinger Publications.

Calvocoressi, L., Lewis, B., Harris, M., Trufan, S. J., Goodman, W. K., McDougle, C. J., and Price, L. H. (1995). Family accommodation in obsessive-compulsive disorder. *American Journal of Psychiatry, 152*(3), 441-443.

Crino, R. D. and Andrews, G. (1996). Obsessive-compulsive disorder and Axis I comorbidity. *Journal of Anxiety Disorders, 10,* 37-46.

Ellis, A. (1962). *Reason and emotion in psychotherapy.* New York: Lyle Stuart.

Emmelkamp, P. M. G., de Haan, E., and Hoogduin, C. A. L. (1990). Marital adjustment and obsessive-compulsive disorder. *British Journal of Psychiatry, 156,* 55-60.

Emmelkamp, P. M. G., Kloek, J., and Blaauw, E. (1992). Obsessive-compulsive disorders in principles and practice of relapse prevention. In P. H. Wilson (Ed.), *Principles and practice of relapse prevention* (pp. 213-234). New York: Guilford Press.

Foa, E. B. and Chambless, D. L. (1978). Habituation of subjective anxiety during flooding in imagery. *Behaviour Research and Therapy, 16,* 391 399.

Foa, E. B. and Franklin, M. E. (1998). Cognitive-behavioral treatment of obsessive-compulsive disorder. In D. K. Routh and R. J. DeRubeis (Eds.), *The science of clinical psychology* (pp. 235-263). Washington, DC: American Psychological Association.

Foa, E. B., Franklin, M. E., and Kozak, M. J. (1998). Psychosocial treatments for obsessive-compulsive disorder. In R. P. Swinson, M. M. Antony, S. Rachman, and M. A. Richter (Eds.), *Obsessive-compulsive disorder: Theory, research, and treatment* (pp. 258-276). New York: Guilford Press.

Foa, E. B. and Kozak, M. J. (1986). Emotional processing of fear: Exposure to corrective information. *Psychological Bulletin, 99,* 20-35.

Foa, E. B. and Kozak, J. J. (1996). Psychological treatment for obsessive-compulsive disorder. In M. R. Mavissakalian and R. F. Prien (Eds.), *Long-term treatments of anxiety disorders* (pp. 285-309). Washington, DC: American Psychiatric Association Press.

Foa, E. B., Steketee, G., and Ozarow, B. J. (1985). Behavior therapy with obsessive-compulsives: From theory to treatment. In M. Mavissakalian (Ed.), *Obsessive-compulsive disorders: Psychological and pharmacological treatments* (pp. 49-129). New York: Plenum.

Foa, E. B., Steketee, G., Turner, R. M., and Fischer, S. C. (1980). Effects of imaginal exposure to feared disasters in obsessive-compulsive checkers. *Behaviour Research and Therapy, 18,* 449-455.

Franklin, M. E. and Foa, E. B. (1998). Cognitive-behavioral treatments for obsessive-compulsive disorder. In P. E. Nathan and J. M. Gorman (Eds.), *A guide to treatments that work* (pp. 339-357). New York: Oxford University Press.

Goodman, W. K., Price, L. H., Rasmussen, S. A., Mazure, D., Fleischmann, R. L., Hill, C. L., Heninger, G. R., and Charney, D. S. (1989). The Yale-Brown obsessive-compulsive scale: Part I. Development, use and reliability. *Archives of General Psychiatry, 46,* 1006-1011.

Greenberger, D. and Padesky, C.A. (1995). *Mind over mood: A cognitive therapy treatment manual for clients.* New York: The Guilford Press.

Greist, J. H. (1992). An integrated approach to the treatment of obsessive-compulsive disorder. *Journal of Clinical Psychiatry, 53*(4), (Supplement), 38-41.

Griffith, J. L., Griffith, M. E., Meydrech, E., Grantham, D., and Bearden, S. (1991). A model for psychiatric consultation in systemic therapy. *Journal of Marital and Family Therapy, 17,* 291-294.

Gross, R., Sasson, Y., Chopra, M., and Zohar, J. (1998). Biological models of obsessive-compulsive disorder: The serotonin hypothesis. In R. P. Swinson, M. M. Antony, S. Rachman, and M. A. Richter (Eds.), *Obsessive-compulsive disorder: Theory, research, and treatment* (pp. 141-153). New York: Guilford Press.

Hafner, R. J. (1982). Marital interaction in persisting obsessive-compulsive disorders. *Australian and New Zealand Journal of Psychiatry, 16,* 171-178.

Hafner, R. J. (1988). Anxiety disorders. In I. R. H. Falloon (Ed.), *Handbook of behavioral family therapy* (pp. 203-230). New York: Guilford Press.

Hafner, R. J. (1992). Anxiety disorders and family therapy. *Australian and New Zealand Journal of Family Therapy, 13*(2), 99-104.

Hafner, R. J., Gilchrist, P., Bowling, J., and Kalucy, R. (1981). The treatment of obsessional neurosis in a family setting. *Australian and New Zealand Journal of Family Therapy, 15,* 145-151.

Hand, I. (1988). Obsessive-compulsive patients and their families. In I. R. H. Falloon (Ed.), *Handbook of behavioral family therapy* (pp. 231-256). New York: Guilford Press.

Hoffman, L. (1990). Constructing realities: An art of lenses. *Family Process, 29,* 1-12.

Hoover, C. F. and Insel, T. (1984). Families of origin in obsessive-compulsive disorder. *Journal of Nervous and Mental Disease, 172,* 223-228.

Karno, M., Golding, J. M., Sorenson, S. B., and Burnham, A. (1988). The epidemiology of obsessive-compulsive disorder in five US communities. *Archives of General Psychiatry, 45,* 1094-1099.

Koran, L. M., Thienemann, M. L., and Davenport, R. (1996). Quality of life for patients with obsessive-compulsive disorder. *American Journal of Psychiatry, 153,* 783-788.

Kozak, M. J. and Foa, E. B. (1996). Behavior therapy for obsessive-compulsive disorder. In V. B. Van Hasselt and M. Hersen (Eds.), *Sourcebook of psychological treatment manuals for adult disorders* (pp. 65-122). New York: Plenum Press.

Kozak, M. J. and Foa, E. B. (1997). *Mastery of obsessive-compulsive disorder: A cognitive behavioral approach.* San Antonio, TX: Psychological Corporation.

Lensi, P., Cassano, G. B., Correddu, G., Ravagli, S., Kunovac, J. L., and Akiskal, H. S. (1996). Familial-developmental history, symptomatology, comorbidity, and course with special reference to gender-related differences. *British Journal of Psychiatry, 169,* 101-107.

Leon, A. C., Portera, L., and Weissman, M. M. (1995). The social costs of anxiety disorders. *British Journal of Psychiatry, 166* (Supplement 27), 19-22.

MacFarlane, M. M. (1993). Empowering the client: Toward a systemic, constructivist, and narrative treatment approach in Ontario's community mental health centres. In G. Duplessis, M. McCrea, C. Viscoff, and S. Doupe (Eds.), *What works: Innovation in community mental health and addiction treatment programs* (pp. 179-193). Toronto: Canadian Scholars Press.

Mehta, M. (1990). A comparative study of family-based and patient-based behavioural management in obsessive-compulsive disorder. *British Journal of Psychiatry, 157,* 133-135.

Nestadt, G., Samuels, J. F., Romanoski, A. J., Folstein, M. F., and McHugh, P.R. (1994). Obsessions and compulsions in the community. *Acta Psychiatra Scandinavica, 89,* 219-224.

Padesky, C. A. and Greenberger, D. (1995). *Clinician's guide to mind over mood.* New York: Guilford Press.

Pauls, D. L., Raymond, C. L., and Robertson, M. (1991). The genetics of obsessive-compulsive disorder: A review. In J. Zohar, T. Insel, and S. Rasmussen (Eds.), *The psychobiology of obsessive-compulsive disorder* (pp. 89-100). New York: Springer.

Penn, P. (1982). Circular questioning. *Family Process, 21,* 267-280.

Pigott, T. A. and Seay, S. (1998). Biological treatments for obsessive-compulsive disorder: Literature review. In R. P. Swinson, M. M. Antony, S. Rachman, and M. A. Richter (Eds.), *Obsessive-compulsive disorder: Theory, research, and treatment* (pp. 298-326). New York: Guilford Press.

Pollard, C. A., Henderson, J. G., Frank, M., and Margolis, R. B. (1989). Help-seeking patterns of anxiety-disordered individuals in the general population. *Journal of Anxiety Disorders, 3,* 131-138.

Raphael, F. J., Rani, S., Bale, R., and Drummond, L. M. (1996). Religion, ethnicity, and obsessive-compulsive disorder. *International Journal of Social Psychiatry, 42,* 38-44.

Rasmussen, S. A. and Eisen, J. L. (1990). Epidemiology of obsessive-compulsive disorder. *Journal of Clinical Psychiatry, 51* (Supplement), 10-13.

Rasmussen, S. A. and Eisen, J. L. (1992). The epidemiology and clinical features of obsessive-compulsive disorder. *Psychiatric Clinics of North America, 15,* 743-758.

Rasmussen, S. A. and Eisen, J. L. (1994). The epidemiology and differential diagnosis of obsessive-compulsive disorder. *Journal of Clinical Psychiatry, 55,* 5-10.

Riggs, D. S., Hiss, H., and Foa, E. B. (1992). Marital distress and the treatment of obsessive-compulsive disorder. *Behavior Therapy, 23,* 585-597.

Robins, L. N., Helzer, J. E., Weissman, M. M., Orvaschel, H., Gruenberg, E., Burke, J. D., and Regier, D. A. (1984). Lifetime prevalence of specific psychiatric disorders in three sites. *Archives of General Psychiatry, 41,* 949-958.

Rudin, E. (1953). Ein beitrag zur frage der zwangskrankheit insebesonder ihrere hereditaren beziehungen. *Archiv fur Psychiatrie und Nervenkrankheiten, 191,* 14-54.

Selvini Palazzoli, M., Boscolo, L., Cecchin, G., and Prata, G. (1980). Hypothesizing—circularity—neutrality: Three guidelines for the conductor of the session. *Family Process, 19,* 3-12.

Stanley, M. A. and Averill, P. M. (1998). Psychosocial treatments for obsessive-compulsive disorder: Clinical applications. In R. P. Swinson, M. M. Antony, S. Rachman, and M. A. Richter (Eds.), *Obsessive-compulsive disorder: Theory, research, and treatment* (pp. 277-297). New York: Guilford Press.

Steketee, G. (1993a). *Treatment of obsessive-compulsive disorder.* New York: Guilford Press.

Steketee, G. (1993b). Social support and treatment outcome of obsessive compulsive disorder at 9-month follow-up. *Behavioural Psychotherapy, 21,* 81-95.

Steketee, G. (1997). Disability and family burden in obsessive-compulsive disorder. *Canadian Journal of Psychiatry, 42*(9), 919-928.

Steketee, G. and Foa, E. B. (1985). Obsessive-compulsive disorder. In D. H. Barlow (Ed.), *Clinical handbook of psychological disorders: A step-by-step treatment manual* (pp. 69-144). New York: Guilford Press.

Steketee, G. and Pruyn, N. A. (1998). Families of individuals with obsessive-compulsive disorder. In R. P. Swinson, M. M. Antony, S. Rachman, and M. A. Richter (Eds.), *Obsessive-compulsive disorder: Theory, research and treatment* (pp. 120-140). New York: Guilford Press.

Thornicroft, G., Colson, L., and Marks, I. M. (1991). An inpatient behavioural psychotherapy unit description and audit. *British Journal of Psychiatry, 158,* 362-367.

Tomm, K. (1984a). One perspective on the Milan systemic approach: Part I. Overview of development, theory and practice. *Journal of Marital and Family Therapy, 10,* 113-125.

Tomm, K. (1984b). One perspective on the Milan systemic approach: Part II. Description of session format, interviewing style and interventions. *Journal of Marital and Family Therapy, 10,* 253-271.

Tomm, K. (1985). Circular interviewing: A multifaceted clinical tool. In D. Campbell and R. Draper (Eds.), *Applications of systemic family therapy: The Milan method* (pp. 33-45). New York: Grune and Stratton.

Tomm, K. (1987a). Interventive interviewing: Part I. Strategizing as a fourth guideline for the therapist. *Family Process, 26,* 3-13.

Tomm, K. (1987b). Interventive interviewing: Part II. Reflexive questioning as a means to enable self-healing. *Family Process, 26,* 167-183.

Tomm, K. (1988). Interventive interviewing: Part III. Intending to ask circular, strategic, or reflexive questions? *Family Process, 27,* 1-15.

van Balkom, A. J. L. M. and van Dyck, R. (1998). Combination treatments for obsessive-compulsive disorder: Clinical applications. In R. P. Swinson, M. M. Antony, S. Rachman, and M. A. Richter (Eds.), *Obsessive-compulsive disorder: Theory, research, and treatment* (pp. 349-366). New York: Guilford Press.

Van Noppen, B., Steketee, G., McCorkle, B. H., and Pato, M. (1997). Group and multi-family behavioral treatment for obsessive compulsive disorder: A pilot study. *Journal of Anxiety Disorders, 11,* 431-446.

Van Noppen, B., Steketee, G., and Pato, M. (1997). Group and multifamily behavioral treatments for OCD. In E. Hollander and D. J. Stein (Eds.), *Obsessive-*

compulsive disorder: Diagnosis, etiology and treatment (pp. 331-336). New York: Marcel Dekker.

Welfare, A. (1993). Systemic approaches in the treatment of obsessive-compulsive disorder. *Australian and New Zealand Journal of Family Therapy, 14*(3), 137-144.

White, M. and Epston, D. (1990). *Narrative means to therapeutic ends.* New York: Norton.

White, K., Steketee, G. S., and Julian, J. (1992). *Course and comorbidity in OCD.* Unpublished manuscript.

Yaryura-Tobias, J., Todaro, J., Grunes, M. S., McKay, D., Stockman, R., and Neziroglu, F. A. (1996). *Comorbidity versus continuum of Axis I disorders in OCD.* Paper presented at the meeting of the Association for Advancement of Behavior Therapy, New York, NY, November.

Chapter 8

The Psychoeducational Model and Case Management: The Role of Marital and Family Therapy in the Treatment of the Chronically Mentally Ill

Joan Keefler

INTRODUCTION

Since the discovery of the efficacy of neuroleptic medication and the deinstitutionalization movement of the 1960s, case management has been adopted as the most effective method, both clinically and economically, of delivering service to individuals who suffer from severe and chronic mental illness. Schizophrenia, the major illness afflicting the severely and chronically mentally ill, is multidetermined. The stress-diathesis model, a combination of genetic, biological, and environmental factors, is generally accepted as a basis for treatment (Zubin and Spring, 1977). Such a complex illness requires the cooperation of many professionals and a combination of many therapeutic approaches, both psychopharmacological and psychosocial.

In the field of marital and family therapy (MFT), the psychoeducational model is the major intervention model that has been developed for working with the families of individuals who suffer from severe and chronic illness. Marital and family therapists have been slow to develop this model and elaborate the MFT role within the context of case management. The mental health literature usually lists case management and family interventions as separate modalities (Mueser, Drake, and Bond, 1997). It is time that the two intervention models were integrated and that family intervention, in particular the psychoeducational model, was considered an integral part of the case management service system. Marital and family therapists must be a part of this integration process, define the importance of their role as a case manager within a psychiatric interdisciplinary team, and make the links between case management and family intervention in the field of mental health.

This chapter will discuss the evolution of the psychoeducational model within a psychiatric setting treating chronic mental illness using the case management system of service delivery. It will discuss and illustrate the strengths and limitations of the psychoeducational model, the integration of that model into a case management system using a case example, the role of the family and marital therapist within an interdisciplinary team, and it will make suggestions for improving the integration of the two models.

The Family and Chronic Mental Illness

Research from a variety of mental health disciplines and countries on the psychosocial aspects of treatment illustrates the core role of the family in planning treatment for the patient with a chronic mental illness. Family interventions have a very positive effect on reducing relapse rate and hospital admissions, encouraging compliance with medication, improving outcome, and reducing family burden and the cost of outpatient treatment (Azrin and Teichner, 1998; Droogan and Bannigan, 1997; Goldstein and Miklowitz, 1995; Penn and Mueser, 1996). Family involvement continues to have a positive outcome on the patient's progress whether or not the patient is living at home (Brekke and Mathiesen, 1995).

The research on burden of care experienced by families with a relative who is mentally ill is extensive and spans many countries (Grad and Sainsbury, 1968; Fadden, Bebbington, and Kuipers, 1987; Loukissa, 1995; Karanci, 1995; Magliano et al., 1998). Caregivers who live with a mentally ill relative report that caring for the relative is a burden. The family support network can diminish with the age and duration of illness of the sick relative (Ohaeri, 1998). As well, negative effects have been reported on the physical and psychological health of these caregivers (Gallagher and Mechanic, 1996; Song, Beigel, and Milligan, 1997). The coping abilities of families, however, improve with the quality and quantity of social support both from professionals and their own social support system (Jutras and Veilleux, 1991; Solomon and Draine, 1995b).

Despite the results from this research, a significant number of families continue to be dissatisfied with the level of professional contact with mental health professionals (Biegel, Song, and Milligan, 1995). The Schizophrenia Patient Outcomes Research Team analyzed a very large sample from national Medicare data (N = 15,425) and one state's Medicaid data (N = 5,393) for patients with schizophrenia in the United States. Only 0.7 percent of persons in the Medicare sample and 7.1 percent in the Medicaid sample had claim for outpatient family therapy. In addition, only 30 percent reported that their families had received information about the illness, and only 8 percent of the families attended an educational or support program (Dixon et al., 1999). These data alone would indicate that families, despite the lip service paid to the role of families by most mental health professionals, are still not receiving the help and support necessary to aid them in their task of caring for a mentally ill relative.

The Contribution of Marital and Family Therapy to Chronic Mental Illness

Until very recently, the relationship between family therapists and other mental health professionals has been distant, despite the fact that family therapy has deep roots in the field of mental health. Family therapy was born out of a desire to understand the etiology of schizophrenia. Early family therapy literature postulated that the origins of psychosis lay within poor family communication. After Murray Bowen concluded in 1975 that conventional family therapy based on improving communications and problem solving between family members was not effective in preventing relapses in the psychotic members, the family therapy movement in general lost interest in developing theory and techniques to work with these families (McFarlane, 1983). Family therapists moved into other domains of practice in which their theories and techniques were more effective. Medication worked; family therapy did not. Concurrently, families felt blamed by family therapists for the illness of their relative, yet families were expected to assume more and more of the care for their sick relative who was being discharged after increasingly short hospitalizations.

Fortunately, some family therapists and researchers continued to work to understand and help families with a psychotic member. Once family therapists stopped considering the family as a cause of the illness and started to view the family as the major support system for the sick relative, they began to work with modes of intervention that were actually helpful to families and to the individuals in their care. Many of these clinicians were instrumental in the development of the psychoeducational model of service delivery to families of the mentally ill.

The Psychoeducational Model

The psychoeducational model is the major model of intervention with families of the chronically mentally ill and has now been universally accepted as an essential part of any treatment program. In this approach, the professional elicits the cooperation and collaboration of the patient and family by teaching them to understand the illness better and to respond to its manifestations more appropriately. It was developed from the work of four seminal studies—one in England (Vaughn and Leff, 1976), two in California (Falloon et al., 1982; Goldstein et al., 1978), and one in Pittsburgh (Hogarty et al., 1986). From the field of marital and family therapy, the clinical work of Carol Anderson in Pittsburgh and the careful research of Michael Goldstein have influenced the development of the model and the work of clinicians from many professional backgrounds. It is the one model of family therapy for schizophrenia that research has proved effective in treatment (Goldstein and Miklowitz, 1995).

It was Anderson who first published a paper recommending that the family of a psychotic patient be seen separately from the patient until the patient's psychosis had resolved. This was a revolutionary idea in the 1980s when current marital and family orthodoxy dictated that the family was always to be seen as a unit (Anderson, 1977). Anderson was the first MFT clinician to advocate immediate help for the family during a first psychotic break, and she pointed out the gaps in the psychiatric service delivery system based on the medical model that provided for the patient but excluded the family (Anderson, Reiss, and Hogarty, 1986). The case management system for the chronically mentally ill had not yet become general practice, but Anderson's notion of a family ombudsman to advocate and integrate services for the family into the treatment plan for the patient foreshadowed the case management system.

Goldstein has reviewed the research from those programs that have published data attesting to their effectiveness in preventing relapse and has very usefully isolated their common ingredients and critical treatment issues (Goldstein and Miklowitz, 1995). Common ingredients include engagement of the family early in the process, education about the illness, recommendations for coping, communication and problem-solving training for the family, and intervention in times of crisis. Critical issues include the integration of the psychotic experience, the acceptance of vulnerability to future episodes, the importance of psychotropic medication, the significance of stressful life events for relapse, and distinguishing personality traits from symptoms of the disorder. The elements of a psychoeducational program have been developed and adapted to various health settings (Anderson, 1983; Goldstein and Miklowitz, 1995; Keefler and Koritar, 1994; Marsh, 1998).

The Case Management System of Service Delivery

Individuals who suffer from a complex and chronic mental illness will have diverse and varied needs for service over many years. Providing continuity of care for them has long been a preoccupation of mental health professionals (Bachrach, 1981), and research clearly demonstrates that this care is a major factor in improving their psychosocial functioning (Brekke et al., 1999). The case management system grew out of a desire to improve continuity of care and to avoid bureaucratic gaps in service. Evidence from research all over the world and from a variety of mental health professions attests to the beneficial effects of using case management as the basic model to coordinate services (Albers, 1998; Kent and Yellowlees, 1994; Lehman and Steinwachs, 1998; Macias et al., 1994).

Practitioners in the field of social work were the first to develop a theory and model of case management, but other professionals soon adopted its principles in the long-term treatment of mental illness (Karls and Wandrei, 1992). A useful definition of case management has been proposed by Joel Kanter (1988).

Clinical case management can be defined as a modality of mental health practice that, in co-ordination with the traditional psychiatric focus on biological and psychological functioning, addresses the overall maintenance of the mentally ill person's environment with the goals of facilitating his or her physical survival, personal growth, community participation, and recovery from or adaptation to mental illness. (p. 361)

Ideally, the case manager integrates all the therapeutic services needed by the individual to achieve and maintain well-being, given the limitations imposed by mental illness. Understanding the history of the individual is valuable in making the most advantageous clinical decisions on his or her behalf. The system is based on the individual and his or her clinical progress. Work with families is considered desirable but is not specifically built into the case management structure. Case managers may choose to see the family or not, depending on the plan established by the interdisciplinary team.

Case management tends to be practiced differently depending on the service delivery system in which it is practiced. A single professional may work as a case manager coordinating services for his or her client. More typically, the case management model as practiced in the mental health field is integrated into a comprehensive biopsychosocial treatment based on an interdisciplinary team.

The Need for Integration

The integration of the psychoeducational model into the case management model is long overdue. Family intervention should be treated as a part of case management rather than a separate treatment modality. Long-term funding is an assumption of the case management model, whereas this has not always been true of the psychoeducational programs that are sometimes dropped when research money was used up. Goldstein and Miklowitz (1995) have pointed out that administrators often limit family intervention programs to time-limited teaching programs to reduce costs.

Research even indicates that case management itself might interfere with the relationship of the sick relative and his or her family. Greater client face-to-face contact with case managers was related to less satisfaction with family relations after one year of service (Solomon and Draine, 1995a). Solomon and Draine suggested that case managers might have tried to replace rather than support the family, with a less than satisfactory result for family relationships.

Other elements of the family psychoeducational model may be ignored that could expand the clinical effectiveness of the traditional case management approach focused on the individual alone. In developing a relationship with the family, the psychoeducational model pays careful attention to the emotional reactions of the family, especially the feelings of grief, guilt, and blame. Before an effective treatment plan can be established, both the individual and the family must come to terms with shattered hopes and dreams and accept the severe limitations engendered by the illness (Miller, 1996; Solomon and Draine, 1996). For the family, the loss of a child to mental illness can lead to a pattern of chronic grief, unlike the loss of a child by death, in which there is a decrease in the intensity of the grieving over a period of five years (Atkinson, 1994). Grieving is an essential first step in the adjustment to the illness.

The grieving process is complicated by denial. Acceptance of the illness by the sick individual can often take a very long time and prevents the case manager from establishing a realistic treatment plan. McFarlane even argues that self-awareness in the patient is actually physically difficult to achieve due to a neurophysiological disorder of the prefrontal cerebral cortex (McFarlane and Lukens, 1998). In some cases, initial denial may be helpful to prevent overwhelming the individual and family, but eventually it will be detrimental to both if the afflicted individual refuses treatment. It is often the family who will take the first steps to acknowledge the mental illness and start the grieving process. The treating team and family are thus able to establish a realistic treatment plan that can accommodate the problem of the patient's denial.

Families often feel guilty for having provided either a defective genetic or environmental background for their sick relative. As Carol Anderson has pointed out, "the despair of the family . . . is complicated by fears that they may have contributed to the patient's problem; fears that may be reinforced and exacerbated by the very professionals who are supposed to offer help and support" (Anderson, Reiss, and Hogarty, 1986, p. 26). The clinician who attributes either the etiology or the exacerbation of the mental illness to the family will find it difficult to elicit the family's cooperation. This is not to say that clinicians ignore the detrimental effect of a highly charged emotional environment on the sick relative but that, instead, they avoid a blaming stance with the family when discussing the issue. Referring a family to family therapy can be construed as a subtle form of blame. In the psychoeducational model, clinicians do not offer their services as family therapists. They establish themselves in a role that is more analogous to that of a case manager.

The integration of the psychoeducational model into a case management system permits the full exploitation of the family's resources in assessing the patient, both initially and throughout the course of the illness. They are the most important and reliable people in the patient's social network (Monking, Staroste, and Buiker-Brinker, 1996). Family ratings of the patient's problems have been found to be more reliable than standardized psychiatric measures (Perlick et al., 1992). Patients who suffer from schizophrenia are not reliable in their self-report of functioning (Glynn et al., 1990). Negative symptoms of the illness are subtle and easily attributed to other causes, especially personality or adjustment problems. Families are often the only source of information about negative symptoms. The family can also be helpful in detecting active symptoms of psychosis. Many psychotic individuals can pull themselves together to mask psychotic symptoms in front of a psychiatrist or other mental health professional, but cannot contain these symptoms when only a family member is present. Close collaboration between family members and the family clinician, therefore, can often prevent hospitalization and further deterioration in the patient's mental health status.

Clinicians trained to work with a focus on the family are sensitive to life-cycle issues. The diagnosis of mental illness during late adolescence or young adulthood interferes with the process of establishing autonomous functioning, the important life-cycle task of the period. Deficits in both cognitive and social functioning resulting from the illness force the patient to become more dependent on the family rather than less. The family has a major problem in assessing the capabilities of the sick individual to find the balance between making excessive demands for autonomy, thereby stimulating a psychotic break, or fostering dependency. Clinicians who work within an individual case management model tend to focus on autonomy issues and disregard the family side of the equation in achieving this balance between appropriate autonomy and dependence.

Family clinicians understand the family as a system. They are, therefore, more likely to pay attention to the needs of the siblings and children of the sick individual. Although not immediate caregivers, both siblings and children need information and support necessary to process the impact of psychosis. They are the support system of the future as well as the present.

Confidentiality Barriers

Members of a mental health team often debate issues of confidentiality involving the patient and the family, especially when a psychotic patient refuses to allow the mental health professional to contact the family. Reconciling the needs of the family while respecting patient confidentiality is a persistent and thorny problem (Furlong and Leggatt, 1996; Petrila and Sadoff, 1992; Zipple et al., 1990). Family clinicians are familiar with the ambiguities of confidentiality issues. The AAMFT Code of Ethics recognizes that marriage and family therapists have unique confidentiality problems because the "client" in the therapeutic relationship may be more than one person. It states that marriage and family therapists "respect and guard confidences of each individual client" (American Association for Marriage and Family Therapy, 1998).

Families often complain that the medical team, based on the principle of patient-physician confidentiality, will use them as sources of information about the patient but refuse to give them the information necessary to support and succor their sick relative. As they are often the patient's prime social support, they must be involved in the treatment plan. The family clinician negotiates this delicate issue by establishing a relationship with each member of the family. Even if the sick individual initially refuses contact with his or her family, this resistance usually disappears gradually as he or she improves with medication. Family clinicians often act in a mediating role between family members, helping them to clarify and share information that is in the best interests of all parties. It is not too difficult to find areas of mutual benefit, especially related to problems of money and housing. Other strategies to maintain the confidentiality of the ill individual while helping the family will depend on the particular characteristics of the family and on the relationship it has with the treating team.

The psychoeducational model is particularly helpful to an individual clinician or psychiatric team when the patient flatly refuses to allow any information to be shared with the family. The treating clinician or team can still provide general didactic information to the family about psychiatric illness. This can be done through provision of written pamphlets, and referrals to psychoeducational workshops and support groups in hospital or in the community. Groups such as the Alliance for the Mentally Ill provide valuable help and support to families outside the hospital setting.

The model is based on cooperation with the family. This is a two-way street and should not be hampered by an overemphasis on confidentiality. As Joel Kanter (1988) has pointed out, "unlike other mental health interventions based on privacy and confidentiality, the majority of case management relationships have a significant public dimension, as case managers interact directly with clients' families, social networks, and formal caregivers" (p.17). The principle of confidentiality is appropriate to individual psychotherapy but is impractical and detrimental to the patient when applied to the multidimensional problems caused by mental illness. A strict adherence to the principle of confidentiality reduces treatment options for the case manager or treating team that could be beneficial to the patient (Petrila and Sadoff, 1992). It should not be used to avoid building the support systems and finding the resources necessary for the patient to achieve and maintain well-being.

SETTING

The setting is the Department of Psychiatry at Montreal General Hospital. Montreal General is an acute care hospital in a major Canadian city that provides inpatient and outpatient care to a large downtown catchment area. Patient demographics encompass a wide variety of racial and cultural groups and various economic circumstances. All services are offered in the two official languages of the province. The department provides a comprehensive range of inpatient and outpatient services to individuals with serious mental illnesses and their families. Outpatient services include a transitional day program, a continuing care team, a community link team, a rehabilitation day centre, and a variety of other services.

Transitional Day Program. On discharge, the patient is referred to the transitional day program (TDP). TDP is a six-week program designed to ease the transition of the patient from the inpatient ward into the community. The team is interdisciplinary and staff:patient ratio is 1:4. This team refers patients to long-term care depending on clinical needs.

Continuing Care Team. Patients with a diagnosis of schizophrenia are referred to a continuing care team. Each continuing care team is interdisciplinary and responsible for the continuing biopsychosocial treatment of the patient. The team consists of a psychiatrist, a psychiatric nurse, a social worker, and an occupational therapist. From these professionals, a case manager is assigned to each patient. The assignment depends on the particular primary need of the patient. One of the teams has been given special responsibility for patients with a dual diagnosis. Frequency of contact is every two weeks or longer. Staff:client ratio ranges from 1:10 to 1:25.

Community Link Team. The most difficult and complicated patients are referred to another interdisciplinary team, the community link team. Its philosophy is to establish and maintain contact with reluctant and noncompliant patients and is especially designed to visit the patient in his or her home environment and to be immediately available for crisis situations in the community. Staff:client ratio is 1:10. Frequency of contact ranges from daily to every two weeks.

Rehabilitation Day Centre. This service, based on an interdisciplinary team, was established to meet the long-term rehabilitation needs of chronic psychiatric patients and to improve their social functioning and acquisition of skills in daily living. Patients attend three times a week and may stay for as long as a year. Patient:staff ratio is 1:5.

Other Services. The department provides other services for its chronic population, especially different types of chronic care groups that focus on specific issues such as self-esteem and sexuality. Patients with a diagnosis of bipolar illness are referred to the affective disorders team, which does not have a formal case management system.

TREATMENT MODEL

The Department of Psychiatry adopted the psychoeducational model at Montreal General Hospital in 1984. It was previously described in the work of Keefler and Koritar (1994). It has evolved over the past fifteen years to meet changes in service delivery patterns, in particular the emphasis on outpatient treatment and the discharge of more fragile patients to family and community due to economic constraints resulting in the closure of inpatient beds.

To meet the needs of the severely mentally ill, its most vulnerable patients, the department recently reorganized the structures of its outpatient department and adopted the case management model as the most effective method of service delivery. A permanent case manager is assigned to each patient when he or she is assigned to a continuing care team after discharge. The patient, however, has access to a variety of resources depending on his or her clinical needs after inpatient treatment.

Inpatient Treatment

The inpatient treatment team takes advantage of the high emotionality during the crisis of the admission of a psychotic member to establish a working relationship with the family. The interdisciplinary team sees the family as soon as possible after admission. The patient is usually not included in this meeting as he or she is generally too psychotic for the meeting to have a positive clinical effect. The family is immediately referred to the Relatives Group for Family and Friends. The family may also be seen individually by any member of the interdisciplinary team depending on clinical needs and resources. Families are encouraged to telephone the nurses on the inpatient ward and freely make use of this service. Over the years, nurses have been encouraged to work with families of patients and have been given extra training in family work.

The clinical focus is on the reduction of anxiety, distress, and feelings of guilt in the family. The staff gives the family as much information as the family requests, as a cognitive grasp of the situation helps reduce the family's anxiety. Clinicians do not assume, however, that information is retained during this period of crisis. They assume, because of the high emotionality, the information is usually either imperfectly retained or not retained at all. The family is seen before discharge to consolidate discharge plans.

Relatives Group for Family and Friends

The Relatives Group for Family and Friends was originally designed to meet the needs of the family during the crisis period of admission. The clinical work followed the traditional crisis intervention model, exploring the events preceding and following the admission, with special attention paid to the family's emotional reactions. The group has developed into a long-term support group to which a family may return during periods of crisis or difficulties. For the new family, the group provides a sensitive holding environment while the family adjusts to the impact of the admission. The clinical focus has expanded to include the whole range of problems a family must cope with when caring for a member with a severe mental illness. These may include problems with diagnosis, medication changes, the negative symptoms of the illness, service delivery, and, as a constant, the continuous process of grieving. An MFT or a clinician under the supervision of an MFT has animated the group. The group performs, albeit informally, the role of the family ombudsman as developed by Carol Anderson. The MFT often advocates for and helps the family through the intricacies of the psychiatric system.

Psychoeducational Workshop

This workshop is based on the all-day model developed by Carol Anderson (1983). The workshop provides structured information for relatives about psychotic illnesses, about medication, and about community resources. The workshops are held every two months on a Tuesday and are organized and animated by an MFT. Average attendance is ten participants. Families usually attend when their relative has been discharged and the high emotionality of the admission has subsided.

The program is comprehensive and intensive with ample time left for discussion between each segment. The morning is roughly divided between teaching about the symptoms of the illness and the importance of medication in treating those symptoms. Families are, by now, well aware of medication as the principle medical treatment. They are taught about the full range of medications available and their side effects. The afternoon is devoted to giving them information about rehabilitation, resources, and coping and management strategies. Families are usually particularly interested in discussing the impact of deficits in cognition and motivation for the social functioning of their relative.

The content of the program has been altered during the past few years as the length of stay in the hospital has diminished. If the admission has been due to the first psychosis of a family member, a firm diagnosis of schizophrenia may be premature. The content now includes information for the families on all the major psychotic disorders: schizophrenia, schizoaffective disorders, and bipolar illness. This information can help families as the illness of their relative begins to manifest itself in the months following discharge. They are more aware of possibilities and better prepared for appropriate action.

A medical certificate is given to relatives who must leave their work to attend. All members of the family or significant caregivers are invited and encouraged to attend, including parents, siblings ages twelve and above, children, grandparents, etc. Both professionals and families who participate in this workshop attest to its powerful impact.

Postdischarge

After discharge, the patient is referred to the transitional day program and a continuing care team or the affective disorders clinic. A very difficult, hostile, or reluctant patient with multiple needs is referred to the community link service. The family meetings now include the sick relative if the latter is well enough to be present. This requires the judgment of the clinician. The patient may become more psychotic only when controversial material is discussed or may be too psychotic for the meetings to have any relevance for him or her. The patient does need to be included as soon as possible in treatment planning to promote his or her socially responsible behavior and motivation to participate in an appropriate plan. The first task is to clarify expectations: of the patient by the family, of the patient of the family, of the patient of himself or herself, and of the family of itself. This is the process that usually evokes a period of mourning in the family members and occasionally in the patient. Another task is to identify those stressful events that stimulate disorganized thinking in the patient. This is a long and torturous process as the family and the patient work to metabolize the illness.

CASE EXAMPLE

Robert and His Family

The following case example will illustrate the progress of a family through psychiatric services, the application of the model's philosophy, and some difficulties with its implementation within a case management system. Robert was a nineteen-year-old single man and a student at a junior college living with his mother, a secretary. Robert's mother was divorced from his father, who was from the Caribbean. Robert had a successful brother, one year older, who attended college in another part of the country on a football scholarship and whom Robert had always sought to emulate. Robert was admitted to the inpatient ward of the hospital, psychotic and secretive. For the past year he had performed poorly at college, at football at which he had previously exceled, and at an undemanding part-time job as an unskilled worker.

The treating interdisciplinary team saw his mother on admission and before discharge. She was seen individually by the social workers and by the inpatient nurses as needed for supportive work. She was referred to and started to attend the relatives' group. A pleasant and cooperative woman, she participated well in group, started to accept the seriousness of the illness, and was appropriately upset and tearful. The staff attempted to involve Robert's father in family meetings but was not successful, although the father did visit Robert and took him out from time to time.

On discharge, Robert returned home to live with his mother; he agreed to attend the transitional day program. A psychiatric nurse became his primary resource person (PRP). She also worked as co-therapist with the MFT animating the relatives' group, which Robert's mother continued to attend. Robert stayed in the program the full six weeks. He attended dutifully every day, was compliant with medication, and participated minimally in the groups, although he was more expressive in individual sessions with his PRP. He became marginally less secretive, but his difficulties in social functioning became more apparent, especially his lack of motivation. His PRP saw Robert together with his mother on several occasions. They talked about expectations of Robert, discussed the symptoms of psychosis, and made plans for his rehabilitation.

After some discussion, Robert and his mother agreed to make an application for medical welfare payments for Robert. This was certainly tangible evidence that both of them were beginning to accept his problems as an illness. Both Robert and his mother agreed to a referral to long-term rehabilitation after discharge from the short-term program. Robert remained more unrealistic about his future than did his mother. She used the relatives' group to mourn her hopes and dreams for her son and was thus able to be calm and understanding in the family sessions. She was also quite aware, through discussion with other members of the group, that a diagnosis of schizophrenia was possible. She attended the psychoeducational workshop at which she was given a great deal of information about the psychotic illnesses.

The PRP also managed to engage Robert's father in two conjoint sessions with his son. Robert's father was much more demanding of his son than Robert's mother was. In the short time the father was willing to participate in sessions, the PRP taught the father as much as she could about the symptoms of a psychotic illness and implications for Robert's functioning. The father found Robert's negative symptoms difficult to tolerate and, despite teaching, was not reconciled to them as symptoms of the illness. The treating team felt that the father's denial was a potential problem for the management of Robert's treatment. He was not invited to the same psychoedcational workshop as his ex-wife, as it is hospital policy to invite divorced parents together only if they have been previously working cooperatively on behalf of their child. He was invited to but did not attend the next workshop.

Robert was referred to the rehabilitation day centre to improve his social functioning. His mother met the treating team and continued to attend the relatives' group. A professional with no training in family therapy became Robert's mentor. It was at this juncture in his treatment that the philosophy of the psychoeducational model began to unravel. As his symptoms became less of a problem to him, Robert was less willing to accept psychiatric treatment, and his old dreams for himself at a university and on a football scholarship like his brother resurfaced. Robert stayed only two months in rehabilitation, and his attendance during those two months was mainly due to the efforts of his mother and the treating team. They did not, however, coordinate their efforts in planning strategies to work with his denial of the illness and increase his motivation. While attending the relatives' group, his mother expressed her disappointment with Robert's decision but felt she had made every effort she could to have him continue in rehabilitation. No attempt was made to engage either Robert's father or his brother during the latter's return home from school during vacations. Robert was referred to a continuing care team for long term follow-up.

Robert was assigned a case manager, a member of the continuing care team, who had no specific training in family therapy. Robert and his mother met with the treating team and a treatment plan was made based on Robert's desires for himself. Robert moved into his own apartment, enrolled in a college, and agreed to take his medication. Robert's mother had reservations about Robert's ability to function so autonomously, which she expressed to members of the relatives' group but which she was reluctant to express to the case manager. Part of her, of course, wanted this plan to succeed as it reflected the normal progression of a young man of Robert's age. No formal family meetings were held to monitor this plan, so this ambivalence was never explored. The treating team felt it was important to support Robert's autonomy and that involving Robert's mother more closely would jeopardize that autonomy. Neither did the case manager make any attempt to involve either Robert's father or brother in the treatment plan. Robert's mother stopped attending the relatives' group.

Robert started two courses at college and did well at midterm, but unilaterally stopped his medication. Because of her positive relationship with the psychiatric staff, the knowledge she acquired from the relatives' group and from the psychoeducational workshop, Robert's mother was able to detect the signs of impending psychosis quickly and knew exactly how to proceed. She cooperated with the case manager to arrange an admission.

Robert recovered from his overt psychotic symptoms very rapidly. On this admission, he was diagnosed as suffering from schizophrenia. His mother returned to the relatives' group to work further on her sadness. On discharge, Robert returned to live with her once more; this time, Robert's mother advocated successfully for a more realistic treatment plan for her son. She and the case manager started to work on strategies to promote Robert's compliance with medication. He returned to college with a very reduced workload.

When interdisciplinary teams were following Robert on the inpatient unit and in the transitional day program, the psychoeducational model worked well for him and his family. MFTs are members of both these teams. When Robert was transferred to outpatient teams with no MFT presence, the influence of the model began to diminish.

A treatment philosophy based on the individual and the development of autonomy apart from the family was the main influence on treatment plans. Although these teams did establish a relationship with Robert's mother, they did not make full use of the family relationships in devising treatment plans. Family intervention became separate from case management, to the detriment of collaborative work in promoting Robert's progress. The full richness and clinical usefulness of the psychoeducational model was never fully realized.

There were some gains for Robert and his family. Robert's mother developed a good relationship with all the teams treating her son; understood Robert's symptoms as part of a chronic illness; was comfortable in returning for help during a crisis; and started the long process of mourning her hopes and dreams for her son. While Robert and his mother were both involved in conjoint counseling, he was compliant with treatment, albeit quite reluctantly. He had the experience of improvement on medication that might help his compliance in the future. He developed a relationship with his case manager and was not lost to follow-up. This may indicate some partial acceptance of his illness. Robert's father had, at least, been marginally engaged in a relationship with a member of his son's treatment team.

On the negative side, Robert's mother had, at first, been easily persuaded of the validity of an ambitious treatment strategy focused on Robert's autonomy, especially since it was appropriate to Robert's age and position in the life cycle. Conjoint sessions might have encouraged her to state her ambivalence about Robert's capacity to function autonomously so early in his recuperation and might also have helped the case manager to assess Robert's capacity for autonomy more realistically. More work might have been done with Robert's father and brother to elicit their cooperation in the establishment and implementation of a treatment plan with a focus on compliance with treatment. A closer relationship with all the members of Robert's family may well have averted the second hospitalization.

STRENGTHS AND LIMITATIONS

Strengths of the Psychoeducational Model

Collaboration with the Family

The strength of the model lies in its basic philosophy of collaboration with the family of the individual who suffers from a chronic psychotic illness. Since the advent of neuroleptic medication has stabilized the patient sufficiently to allow him or her to return to the community and to the family, the family has become the principle caregiver. The model advocates supporting the family in this task to assure the patient of a stable and constant environment.

The Therapeutic Relationship

The model is based on establishing a working relationship with.all members of the family. Therapeutic work is limited and ineffective unless the clinician truly tunes into the emotional life of the patient and the family, understands the impact of the illness, and conveys this understanding to the patient and family. The model pays careful attention to this process of grief and mourning both in the family and in the patient.

The early establishment of a therapeutic relationship with the family is often the only way to help an individual who denies an illness. Mental illness, when denied by the afflicted individual, is in many cases a cause of his or her alienation from the family and may ultimately lead to homelessness. These are undesirable psychosocial consequences that can be prevented only by engaging the family early in the treatment process.

Continuity of Care

It is a basic premise of the model that families know the patients best and, if given the proper support, will continue to work and advocate for their sick relative. In fact, families have been acting as assessors, monitors, crisis managers, and advocates for their sick member since the deinstitutionalization movement of the 1970s (Saunders, 1997; Kanter, 1989). Last, but probably most important, is that families love and have a future with the individual. Case managers come and go. The family is the one true constant in the life of the individual who suffers from mental illness.

Limitations of the Model

Diagnosis

As the model is now elaborated, work with the family cannot begin until a physician has made a diagnosis. The diagnosis of schizophrenia and the related psychoses is a long and difficult procedure and, throughout the world, there is great latitude of diagnostic criteria (Gottesman, 1991). The onset of schizophrenia is often insidious, taking place during adolescence, which is a period of adjustment and turmoil for the entire family. The individual is often either unaware of what is happening or will not reveal psychotic symptoms. It is not unusual during the initial phases of schizophrenia that the individual will turn to street drugs to relieve psychotic anxiety and mask positive symptoms of the illness. Families attribute difficult or strange behavior of their relative to adolescence or use of street drugs and are usually quite bewildered and unsure of how to react.

A problem for families lies within the referral process to case management. During the course of the illness, it is not unusual for a psychotic illness to be first diagnosed as bipolar. In the setting described in this chapter, for example, a patient with a diagnosis of manic-depressive illness is referred to the affective disorders clinic, which does not have a case management structure. Even when the symptoms of a young person meet the criteria for a DSM-IV diagnosis of schizophrenia, psychiatrists are often loath to make a definitive diagnosis at the time of a first psychotic break, preferring a more conservative "wait and see" approach. Without a diagnosis of schizophrenia, it is rare that the individual and family are referred to a classic long-term case management system. In a survey of one family support organization for the mentally ill, of 186 respondents, 47 percent experienced a delay of over two years before being referred to a support group (Looper et al., 1998). This conservative approach to diagnosis has often left families floundering, trying to cope with symptoms they do not understand.

Lack of Commitment to a Family Treatment Approach

If the philosophy of collaboration with the family is not consistently and persistently brought to the attention of members of an interdisciplinary team, team members will revert to individual models of treatment, to the detriment of family intervention. The traditional professions—psychiatry, nursing, psychology, and social work—tend to be influenced by medical or casework models based on the individual. In contrast, MFTs are specifically trained in those elements of clinical work that promote and encourage collaboration with the family.

INTEGRATION WITH PSYCHIATRIC SERVICES AND ROLE OF MEDICATION

Case Management and the Interdisciplinary Team

MFTs are not yet considered essential members of interdisciplinary teams in the practical world of treating the mentally ill. One problem of the interdisciplinary approach is that family research in mental health is usually published in separate journals, and the insights into effective family interventions developed by each discipline remain isolated from one another (Kellam, 1987). The fields of psychiatry, nursing, social work, and occupational therapy have extensive literature on the role of the case manager. The role of a marital and family therapist is neither discussed nor delineated. On the other hand, in MFT journals, there is an important body of writing about working with families of the mentally ill and a dearth of literature about case management (Anderson, Reiss, and Hogarty, 1986; Marsh, 1998; McFarlane, 1983).

There is no clear agreement among mental health professionals about the essential elements of good case management. Each mental health professional—psychiatrist, psychologist, occupational therapist, nurse, and social worker—tends to approach case management with the ideas and practice principles based on previous professional training (Slade, 1996). These diverse points of view are discussed, re-examined, and a unified treatment plan negotiated within the context of the interdisciplinary team. The patient is theoretically the beneficiary. The MFT can bring very important expertise and perspectives to case management, and the clinical richness of the psychoeducational model can be fully exploited to the benefit of the patient and family.

MFTs can be helpful to the functioning of an interdisciplinary team. Ideally, professionals cooperate with one another to develop a joint treatment plan, each contributing his or her special expertise to the plan. In practice, however, many barriers to the effective functioning of interdisciplinary health care teams are in place. Over twenty years ago, Given and Simmons (1977) described these barriers as educational preparation, role ambiguity and incongruent expectations, authority, power, status, autonomy, and personal characteristics of members. As teams form and reform in response to changes in personnel and health care delivery systems, such barriers still exist. MFTs can be very valuable members of interdisciplinary teams in helping forge the bonds between professionals and in contributing to the team effectiveness. Being systems thinkers, they can easily integrate themselves into complex treatment systems with multiple orientations, and even facilitate the discussion between team members with different philosophies, training, and orientations.

Medication

The psychoeducational model became popular with physicians when they recognized that working with family members helped promote the patient's compliance with medication. The patient's denial of the illness—especially its chronicity—still remains a problem in promoting medication compliance. Once families accept the reality of the illness, they become immediate allies of the staff in encouraging medication compliance. Strategies to achieve compliance are a constant theme of meetings with families.

CULTURAL AND GENDER ISSUES

Cultural Issues

Schizophrenia is universal. It is found in every culture and all over the world (Gottesman, 1991). The variation in its incidence across cultures is modest. Clinicians, however, must take cultural differences into account in both assessing symptoms and in treatment. The course of the illness has been shown to be more benign in a cohesive village structure of nonindustrialized cultures (McFarlane, 1997). This is possibly due to the stability of social structures and fewer changes in the daily life of a nonindustrialized village. Less stimulation and adaptation to change in the course of daily life makes life less stressful and easier for an individual with a thinking disorder. The faster pace and shifting social relationships in an industrialized urban setting are more difficult. An urban environment makes the connection with family especially important for someone with a chronic mental illness.

In the multicultural and multiracial setting described in this chapter, cultural issues are ever present. The diagnosis and treatment of a mental illness must take into consideration cultural issues. Language of service is an especially sensitive issue. Every effort is made to have the patient served in his or her mother tongue and to adapt treatment plans to cultural differences. All services are bilingual, in French and English. In addition, the department of psychiatry makes full use of translation services. The staff of the hospital is also multicultural and multiracial, is sensitive to cultural issues, and many of them donate their time and knowledge to help patients. Not surprisingly, families are the most important source of help and cultural knowledge. We know, for example, that Italian families will usually refuse to place a sick relative in a psychiatric boarding home, as their culture dictates that families care for ill family members in the home.

The most striking cultural variation in the setting pertains to the stigma of the illness. The staff is very careful to assess the reaction of the patient's culture to psychosis and mental illness. In our setting, it is Chinese families (especially if the parents were born in China) and Hasidic Jewish families who suffer the most stigma from their cultural communities. Cultural stigma, however, appears in a variety of cultures and, because of their perception of stigma, many families remain isolated from their community support networks. The psychoeducational model, which frames the psychotic symptoms as a legitimate illness, is helpful for these families. These families respond well to a biological explanation of the illness. In addition, they are encouraged to have close relatives or friends attend the psychoeducational workshop in order to enlarge their support network.

Gender Issues

Most studies indicate that men and women are affected by schizophrenia in equal numbers (American Psychiatric Association, 1994). Gender differences occur in the age of onset and course of the illness. The age of onset for a first psychotic episode is earlier in men than in women. Men tend to have their first episode in their midtwenties, women in their late twenties. The prognosis is better for women possibly because of better premorbid functioning. Women have had more time to establish their social skills. For families, this has meant that women are marginally more compliant with treatment and rehabilitation. In the setting at the Montreal General Hospital, it is our clinical impression that young men are more prone to deny the illness and be noncompliant with treatment.

More women than men tend to be caregivers for the dependent members of the family. In the setting described in this chapter, this was true. More women attend the relatives' groups and the psychoeducational workshops, in a ratio of approximately 4:1. We have noticed no differences between men and women in their response to the psychoeducational program. As with cultural differences, education seems to be the differentiating factor in responding to psychoeducation. With more education, both sexes tend to take the most advantage of psychoeducational services.

FUTURE DIRECTIONS

Diagnosis Problems

A growing body of literature from all over the world advocates early detection and treatment of schizophrenia and related psychotic illnesses, noting that this treatment should combine medication and psychosocial interventions (Falloon et al., 1998; Linzen et al., 1998; Kopelowicz and Liberman, 1995; McGlashan and Johannessen, 1996; Waring et al., 1988). General agreement exists that early detection and treatment must be coupled with long-term case management to maintain the initial benefits of psychopharmacotherapy.

Early appropriate referrals to the psychiatric system are of invaluable help for the family and its ill member. Working either outside the psychiatric system or as a member of a psychiatric team, the MFT who suspects a member of the family might have a mental illness can advocate for the family and help it obtain appropriate services from the psychiatric system for its relative during the difficult diagnosis period. The MFT may have to assume an unofficial case management role, helping the family through the psychiatric system. This intervention is the beginning of the family ombudsman role as described by Carol Anderson (Anderson, Reiss, and Hogarty, 1986).

There has been some movement lately from mental health professionals to establish first psychosis clinics to institute closer follow-up after a first psychotic episode. These clinics should also be organized to incorporate case management principles and a treating team that includes a family clinician. The content of psychoeducational workshops should be revised to contain information about all the psychotic illnesses when the diagnosis is not clear. This information will better prepare families as they move through the psychiatric system. It would seem logical for the individual who has suffered a psychotic break to be referred with the family to a case management system as soon as possible. Such a treatment philosophy would spare the family much hardship and grief.

MFT Internships in Psychiatric Settings

Internships in psychiatric settings should be offered routinely to trainees in marital and family therapy. The purpose is twofold; first, the MFT trainee learns to work with these families under an MFT supervisor and second, the interdisciplinary team learns the value of a clinician trained to work with families. At present, these internships are being negotiated in the psychiatric setting described in this chapter. Both the department of psychiatry and the trainees in marital and family therapy are convinced of the benefits of such a relationship.

Conclusion

Although mental health professionals do not always agree on the elements that constitute good case management, all agree that some form of enhancement of the individual's support system is essential, and that the support system starts with the family. It is this field of practice in mental health for which the marital and family therapist is uniquely trained and in which research has clearly demonstrated that family intervention has been effective. The marital and family therapist should be considered as an essential member of any interdisciplinary team that treats the chronically mentally ill.

REFERENCES

Albers, M. (1998). [Long-term treatment of chronic schizophrenia]. *Nervenarzt, 69(9)*, 737-751.

American Association for Marriage and Family Therapy (1998). AAMFT Codes of Ethics. [Brochure]. Washington, DC: Author.

American Psychiatric Association (1994). *Diagnostic and statistical manual of mental disorders* (Fourth edition). Washington, DC: American Psychiatric Association.

Anderson, C. M. (1977). Family Intervention with severely disturbed inpatients. *Archives of General Psychiatry, 34*, 697-702.

Anderson, C. (1983). A psychoeducational program for families of patients with schizophrenia. In W. R. McFarlane (Ed.), *Family therapy in schizophrenia* (pp. 99-116). New York: Guilford Press.

Anderson, C. M., Reiss, D. J., and Hogarty, G. E. (1986). *Schizophrenia and the family*. New York: Guilford Press.

Atkinson, S. D. (1994). Grieving and loss in parents with a schizophrenic child. *American Journal of Psychiatry, 151(8),* 1137-1139.

Azrin, N. H. and Teichner, G. (1998). Evaluation of an instructional program for improving medication compliance for chronically mentally ill outpatients. *Behaviour Research and Therapy, 36(9),* 849-861.

Bachrach, L. (1981). Continuity of care for chronic mental patients: A conceptual analysis. *American Journal of Psychiatry, 138,* 1449-1456.

Biegel, D. E., Song, L., and Milligan, S. E. (1995). A comparative analysis of family caregivers: Perceived relationships with mental health professionals. *Psychiatric Services, 46(5),* 477-482.

Brekke, J. S., Ansel, M., Long, J., Slade, E., and Weinstein, M. (1999). Intensity and continuity of services and functional outcomes in the rehabilitation of persons with schizophrenia. *Psychiatric Services, 50(2),* 248-256.

Brekke, J. S. and Mathiesen, S. G. (1995). Effects of parental involvement on the functioning of noninstitutionalized adults with schizophrenia. *Psychiatric Services, 46(11),* 1149-1155.

Dixon, L., Lyles, A., Scott, J., Lehman, S., Postrado, L., Goldman, H., and McGlynn, E. (1999). Services to families of adults with schizophrenia: From treatment recommendations to dissemination. *Psychiatric Services, 50(2),* 233-238.

Droogan, J. and Bannigan, K. (1997). A review of psychosocial family interventions for schizophrenia. *Nursing Times, 93(26),* 46-47.

Fadden, G., Bebbington, P., and Kuipers, L. (1987). The burden of care: The impact of functional psychiatric illness on the patient's family. *British Journal of Psychiatry, 150,* 285-292.

Falloon, I. R. H., Boyd, J. L., McGill, C. W., Williamson, M., Razani, J., Moss, H. B., and Gilderman, A. M. (1982). Family management in the prevention of exacerbations of schizophrenia. *New England Journal of Medicine, 306,* 1437-1440.

Falloon, I. R., Coverdale, J. H., Laidlaw, T. M., Merry, S., Kydd, R. R., and Morosini, P. (1998). Early intervention for schizophrenic disorders. Implementing optimal treatment strategies in routine clinical services. OTP Collaborative Group. *British Journal of Psychiatry* (Supplement), *172(33),* 33-38.

Furlong, M. and Leggatt, M. (1996). Reconciling the patient's right to confidentiality and the family's need to know. *Australian and New Zealand Journal of Psychiatry, 30(5),* 614-622.

Gallagher, S. K. and Mechanic, D. (1996). Living with the mentally ill: Effects on the health and functioning of other household members. *Social Science and Medicine, 42(12),* 1691-1701.

Given, B. and Simmons, S. (1977). The interdisciplinary health-care team: Fact or fiction? *Nursing Forum, 16(2),* 165-184.

Glynn, S. M., Randolph, E. T., Eth, S., Paz, G. G., Leong, G. B., Shaner, A. L., and Strachan, A. (1990). Patient pychopathology and expressed emotion in schizophrenia. *British Journal of Psychiatry, 157,* 877-880.

Goldstein, M. J. and Miklowitz, D. J. (1995). The effectiveness of psychoeducational family therapy in the treatment of schizophrenic disorders. *Journal of Marital and Family Therapy, 21,* 361-376.

Goldstein, M. J., Rodnick, E. H., Evans, J. R., May, P. R. A., and Steinberg, M. R. (1978). Drug and family therapy in the aftercare of acute schizophrenics. *Archives of General Psychiatry, 35,* 1169-1177.

Gottesman, I. (1991). *Schizophrenia genesis: The origins of madness.* New York: Freeman.

Grad, J. and Sainsbury, P. (1968). The effects that patients have on their families in a community care and control psychiatric service: A two-year follow-up. *British Journal of Psychiatry, 114,* 265-278.

Hogarty, G. E., Anderson, C. M., Reiss, D. J., Kornbluth, S. J., Greenwald, D. P., Javna, C. D., and Madonia, M. J. (1986). Family psychoeducation, social skills training, and maintenance chemotherapy in the aftercare treatment of schizophrenia. *Archives of General Psychiatry, 43,* 633-642.

Jutras, S. and Veilleux, F. (1991). Informal caregiving: Correlates of perceived burden. *Canadian Journal of Aging, 10,* 40-55.

Kanter, J. S. (1988). Clinical issues in the case management relationship. In M. Harris and L. Bachrach (Eds.), *Clinical case management* (pp. 15-27). San Francisco: Jossey-Bass.

Kanter, J. (1989). Clinical case management: definition, principles, components. *Hospital and Community Psychiatry, 40(4),* 361-368.

Karanci, A. N. (1995). Caregivers of Turkish schizophrenic patients: Causal attributions, burdens and attitudes to help from the health professionals. *Social Psychiatry and Psychiatric Epidemiology, 30(6),* 261-268.

Karls, J. M. and Wandrei, K. E. (1992). The person-in-environment system for classifying client problems: A new tool for more effective case management. *Journal of Case Management, 1(3),* 90-95.

Keefler, J. and Koritar, E. (1994). Essential elements of a family psychoeducation program in the aftercare of schizophrenia. *Journal of Marital and Family Therapy, 20,* 369-380.

Kellam, S. (1987). Families and mental illness: Current interpersonal and biological approaches (Part 1). Contributions by the Society for Life History Research on Psychopathology: Epidemiology life course development, and family research. *Psychiatry, 50(4),* 303-307.

Kent, S. and Yellowlees, P. (1994). Psychiatric and social reasons for frequent rehospitalization. *Hospital and Community Psychiatry, 45(4),* 347-350.

Kopelowicz, A. and Liberman, R. P. (1995). Biobehavioral treatment and rehabilitation of schizophrenia. *Harvard Review of Psychiatry, 3(2),* 55-64.

Lehman, A. F. and Steinwachs, D. M. (1998). Translating research into practice: The schizophrenia patient outcomes research team (PORT) treatment recommendations. *Schizophrenia Bulletin, 24(1),* 1-10.

Linzen, D., Lenior, M., de Haan, L., Dingemans, P., and Gersons, B. (1998). Early intervention, untreated psychosis and the course of early schizophrenia. *British Journal of Psychiatry* (Supplement), *172(33)*, 84-89.

Looper, K., Fielding, A., Latimer, E., and Amir, E. (1998). Improving access to family support organizations: A member survey of the AMI-Quebec Alliance for the Mentally Ill. *Psychiatric Services, 49(11)*, 1491-1492.

Loukissa, D. A. (1995). Family burden in chronic mental illness: A review of research studies. *Journal of Advanced Nursing, 21*, 248-255.

Macias, C., Kinney, R., Farley, O. W., Jackson, R., and Vos, B. (1994). The role of case management within a community support system: Partnership with psychosocial rehabiitation. *Community Mental Health Journal, 30(4)*, 323-339.

Magliano, L., Fiorillo, A., Malangone, C., Aletti, A., Belotti, G., Bevilacqua, P., Delle Femine, A. L., Fontana, G., Maucioni, F., Travi, M., Zanus, P., Rossi, A., and Maj, M. (1998). [Family burden in schizophrenia: Effects of socio-environmental and clinical variables and family intervention]. *Epidemiologia E Psichiatria Sociale, 7(3)*, 178-187.

Marsh, D. T. (1998). *Serious mental illness and the family*. New York: John Wiley and Sons.

McFarlane, W. R. (Ed.) (1983). Introduction. In W. R. McFarlane (Ed.), *Family therapy in schizophrenia* (pp. 1-13). New York: Guilford Press.

McFarlane, W. R. (1997). Fact: Integrating family psychoeducation and assertive community treatment. *Administration and Policy in Mental Health, 25*, 191-198.

McFarlane, W. R. and Lukens, E. P. (1998). Insight, families, and education: An exploration of the role of attribution in clinical outcome. In X. F. Amador and A.S. David (Eds.), *Insight and psychosis* (Vol xviii, pp. 317-331). New York: Oxford University Press.

McGlashan, T. H. and Johannessen, J. O. (1996). Early detection and intervention with schizophrenia: Rationale. *Schizophrenia Bulletin, 22(2)*, 201-222.

Miller, F. E. (1996). Grief therapy for relatives of persons with serious mental illness. *Psychiatric Services, 47(6)*, 633-637.

Monking, H. S., Staroste, A., and Buiker-Brinker, M. (1996). [The social status of schizophrenic patients during the course of 8 years catamnesis and significance of relatives for psychosocial integration]. *Psychiatrische Praxis, 23(6)*, 282-284.

Mueser, K. T., Drake, R. E., and Bond, G. R. (1997). Recent advances in psychiatric rehabilitation for patients with severe mental illness. *Harvard Review of Psychiatry, 5(3)*, 123-137.

Ohaeri, J. U. (1998). Perception of the social support role of the extended family network by some Nigerians with schizophrenia and affective disorders. *Social Science and Medicine, 47(10)*, 1463-1472.

Penn, D. L. and Mueser, K. T. (1996). Research update on the psychosocial treatment of schizophrenia. *American Journal of Psychiatry, 153(5)*, 607-617.

Perlick, D., Stastny, P., Mattis, S., and Teresi, J. (1992). Contribution of family, cognitive and clinical dimensions to long-term outcome in schizophrenia. *Schizophrenia Research, 6(3)*, 257-265.

Petrila, J. P. and Sadoff, R. L. (1992). Confidentiality and the family as caregiver. *Hospital and Community Psychiatry, 43(2),* 136-139.

Saunders, J. (1997). Walking a mile in their shoes . . . Symbolic interactionism for families living with severe mental illness. *Journal of Psychosocial Nursing and Mental Health Services, 35(6),* 8-13.

Slade, M. (1996). Assessing the needs of the severely mentally ill: Cultural and professional differences. *International Journal of Social Psychiatry, 42(1),* 1-9.

Solomon, P. and Draine, J. (1995a). Adaptive coping among family members of persons with serious mental illness. *Psychiatric Services, 46(11),* 1156-1160.

Solomon, P. and Draine, J. (1995b). Consumer case management and attitudes concerning family relations among persons with mental illness. *Psychiatric Quarterly, 66(3),* 249-261.

Solomon, P. and Draine, J. (1996). Examination of grief among family members of individuals with serious and persistent mental illness. *Psychiatric Quarterly, 67(3),* 221-234.

Song, L. Y., Beigel, D. E., and Milligan, S. E. (1997). Predictors of depressive symptomatology among lower social class caregivers of persons with chronic mental illness. *Community Mental Health, 33(4),* 269-286.

Vaughn, C. and Leff, J. (1976). The influence of family and social factors on the course of psychiatric illness: A comparison of schizophrenic and depressed neurotic patients. *British Journal of Psychiatry, 129,* 125-137.

Waring, E. M., Lefcoe, D., Carver, C., Barnes, S., Fry, R., and Abraham, B. (1988). The course and outcome of early schizophrenia. *Psychiatric Journal of the University of Ottawa, 13(4),* 194-197.

Zipple, A. M., Langle, S., Spaniol, L., and Fisher, H. (1990). Client confidentiality and the family's need to know: Strategies for resolving the conflict. *Community Mental Health Journal, 26(6),* 533-545.

Zubin, J. and Spring, B. (1977). Vulnerability: A new view of schizophrenia. *Journal of Abnormal Psychology, 86,* 103-126.

Chapter 9

Family Treatment of Borderline Personality Disorder Through Relationship Enhancement Therapy

Marsha J. Harman
Michael Waldo

INTRODUCTION

The American Psychiatric Association's (1994) *Diagnostic and Statistical Manual,* Fourth Edition (DSM-IV) defines borderline personality disorder (BPD) as a pervasive pattern of instability in self-image, interpersonal relationships, and mood. The pattern is usually evident by early adulthood and marked by frequent mood shifts, persistent identity disturbance, fluctuating extremes of overidealization and devaluation, fear of abandonment, and many narcissistic features.

Most therapists would agree that borderline personality disorders are pervasive and difficult to treat. Indeed, Herkov and Blashfield (1995) found to it be the most frequently diagnosed personality disorder. Meyer (1989) described individuals with BPD as emotionally unstable personalities because they exhibited considerable emotional instability, impulsiveness, and unpredictability, as well as irritability and anxiousness. Snyder (1986) alleged that pathological lying could also be a basic characteristic of BPD. When such characteristics are exhibited by individuals in a marital or family relationship, dysfunctional interaction may result, which negatively impacts the quality of the relationship.

No doubt exists that borderline dynamics can take a severe toll on a marriage and on a marital partner. Because the dynamics of BPD are largely expressed in interpersonal relations, and because they so profoundly affect marriage, marital therapy is seen as a uniquely appropriate approach to treatment (Waldo and Harman, 1993, 1998). However, relatively few treatises have addressed couples therapy in which one of the mates has been diagnosed with BPD.

Both Solomon (1998) and Lachkar (1998) have addressed narcissistic and borderline couples. Lachkar (1992, 1998) maintains that an individual with narcissistic personality disorder (NPD) seeks to couple with an individual with BPD and then commence to "dance" in such a fashion that the partner with BPD attacks and the partner with NPD withdraws. The ability to address this type of repetitive circular interaction is one of the strengths of marital and family therapy, which employs a systems perspective to intervene in dysfunctional interactional patterns. A treatment approach that focuses on relationship dynamics and dysfunctional interactional patterns and communication may be very useful in treating individuals with BPD and their families.

This chapter briefly outlines the evolution of the diagnosis of borderline personality disorder, then summarizes various treatment approaches that have been used with BPD. The setting in which the authors practice will be described. A specific treatment model, relationship enhancement therapy, which may be helpful to some couples in which one partner has been diagnosed with BPD, will then be presented. A case study and example of a couple's interaction during therapy are also included.

History of Borderline Personality Disorder

Becker (1997) was taught during her graduate program that persons with BPD were on the border between neurosis and psychosis—the border between sanity and insanity. Earlier labels for BPD were dependent personality disorder and self-defeating personality disorder, and BPD was associated with object-relations disturbance. For example, Kernberg (1975, 1976) hypothesized that borderline patients had difficulty with the rapprochement stage (Mahler, Pine, and Bergman, 1975) and, therefore, were unable to move beyond the use of primitive splitting (Klein, 1996).

Zanarini (1997) indicates that the etiology of BPD continues to be examined. She summarizes three psychodynamic theories related to BPD: (1) Kernberg's (1975) explanation that excessive early aggression, inborn or caused by actual frustration, causes the young child to split positive and negative images of self and mother; (2) Adler and Buie's (1979) suggestion that early mothering failures result in a lack of stable object constancy; and (3) Masterson's (1972) belief that fear of abandonment is the central factor. Zanarini further examines environmental factors of etiological significance for BPD. These factors include parental separation and loss, disturbed parental involvement, and the relatively common incidence of both physical and sexual abuse, with sexual abuse consistently reported significantly more often than in patients with depression or other personality disorders.

Zanarini's biosocial perspective proposes that an invalidating environment—one that communicates that the child's thoughts and feelings are disregarded, trivialized, or punishable—can be harmful. The biosocial theory asserts that the invalidating environment disrupts the normal learning of emotional meaning, discrimination, and modulation. The child, therefore, distrusts personal reactions and relies on the environment to provide information regarding how to feel, think, and act. Several ways in which the experience of sexual abuse can be invalidating include:

1. The invasion of the body is against the child's will and despite the child's efforts to avoid the abuse.
2. Confusing messages are relayed about the meaning of the abuse, such as the child being told that the act is wrong, but it results in special attention for the child.
3. The abuse is frequently perpetrated by a person upon whom the child is dependent and trusts.
4. The abuse must be kept a secret.
5. If the abuse is disclosed, significant others commonly minimize or rationalize the abuse, especially if it was perpetrated by a family member.

Becker (1997) believes that the borderline diagnosis is the most misused and abused of all psychiatric labels. She also believes it is used to blame the patient who makes life difficult for the therapist or who fails to make therapeutic progress. She refers to Reiser and Levenson (1984), who catalogued abuses of the borderline label including (1) an expression of countertransference that explains the loss of empathy between therapist and patient; (2) a mask for imprecise diagnosis; (3) a rationalization for treatment mistakes or failure;

and (4) a legitimation of inappropriate countertransference behavior. Reiser and Levenson criticized the practice of calling these patients "borderlines" rather than "patients with borderline qualities" because such language failed to perceive their individual characteristics and could create an unwarranted sense of cynicism and the tendency to overlook treatable parts of conditions.

Strong indications of gender bias occur in the diagnosis of BPD. Swartz and colleagues (1990) suggested that men with BPD are frequently treated for conditions such as substance abuse rather than diagnosed with BPD. Dohrenwend and Dohrenwend (1976) found the overall prevalence of personality disorders among men to be significantly higher than among women, yet Becker (1997) found women with BPD symptoms to be overrepresented, generally, in treatment settings (Swartz et al., 1990). These findings offer support for Chesler's (1972) suggestion that women's "madness" is often societal invention.

Treatment for BPD has included classical psychoanalysis, modified psychoanalytic psychotherapy, and low-frequency, low-intensity supportive treatment (Horwitz, 1985; Waldinger, 1987). Horwitz and his colleagues (1996) delineated the supportive versus expressive controversy regarding treatment. Expressive treatment included exploring the unconscious fears, conflicts, defenses, and wishes of the patient as well as underlying difficulties in relationships, which included transference with the therapist. Supportive treatment included activities to promote the patient's adaptive functioning within and outside the therapeutic setting. The therapist provides emotional support and affirms adaptive behavior. The patient is also encouraged to identify with the therapist, who helps the patient analyze reality testing, judgment, consequences, emotional stability, and appropriate behavior. Horwitz and his colleagues favored tailoring the psychotherapy to the patient rather than trying to have the patient adapt to the psychotherapy model.

Marziali and Munroe-Blum (1994) believe that interpersonal group psychotherapy is the treatment of choice for patients with borderline personality disorder because they perceived that every group transaction carries a message about a current relationship issue between the patient(s) and therapist. That is, each patient communication, be it verbal, nonverbal, direct, or indirect, was meant to transact some patient expectation with an anticipated therapist response. They maintain that patients with BPD long for care, comfort, and love but expect abuse, rejection, and abandonment. In their study of interpersonal group psychotherapy, four themes emerged:

1. A search for boundaries that included engagement, testing group parameters, developing connections, and forming some commitment to group membership
2. A pattern of attack and despair that manifested itself in intense complaining that the therapy was inadequate, nothing in the patients' lives would ever change, and a blaming of the therapist for not doing something about it
3. Mourning and repair that helped patients process the meanings of their unattainable wishes and expectations to the extent that they realized that the past cannot be relived in the present and the wounded, abandoned, despairing representations of the past are replaced with experiences of greater control over self-motivation and positive self-esteem
4. Integration of self-control that allows the patient to affirm the self while processing the limitations of self and others

Silk (1994) reviewed biological and neurobehavioral studies of BPD and decided that there were no clear biological answers but that everything could not be viewed as developmental, since psychotherapy to correct developmental issues had not proved to be greatly successful in patients with BPD (Waldinger and Gunderson, 1984). Silk asserts that psychotherapy may be assisted with pharmacological interventions so that psychotherapeutic work can proceed more calmly and more constructively.

To summarize, the controversial BPD diagnosis has evolved to describe those patients whose behaviors and interactions in families as well as other relationships are often viewed as self-destructive. BPD is frequently treated with expressive and supportive individual and group therapy models as well as biological approaches.

SETTING

Relationship enhancement (RE) has been used and studied in hospital settings (Waldo and Harman, 1999) and university settings (Waldo, 1989). Although both authors are employed in university settings as full-time trainers of teachers, counselors, and master's and doctoral level psychologists, they also maintain private practices that are not affiliated with their respective universities. The case example described later was drawn from the authors' private practice setting.

In this setting, most clients are referred to us either by word of mouth from previous satisfied clients or through the telephone book. Although the authors sometimes have the luxury of working with other cotherapists or graduate students, this is generally not the case, and clients are normally seen by only one therapist. Clients are typically seen in the evenings or on weekends. We work with both individuals and couples; when approached by an individual for counseling on relationship issues, we normally make every effort to involve the partner.

Working with BPD in this setting can present some challenges. As our clients are seen on a fee-for-service basis, financial considerations are often a factor influencing length of service and involvement of other family members. Although, as our model indicates, we believe that marital and family therapy interventions are often critical, many health maintenance organizations (HMOs) do not cover family therapy, as a service must be medically necessary to use insurance benefits. Many HMOs also do not provide coverage for treatment of personality disorders, as preference is given to Axis I disorders. These restrictions often make it difficult for clients to involve partners and to receive the full benefit from the relationship enhancement approach, although RE treatment can often be effective even when presented in a brief therapy format.

In many instances, individuals with BPD may also have comorbid Axis I disorders, such as adjustment disorders, depression, anxiety disorders, or other somatic or biologically-based complaints. These disorders may both affect and be affected by marital and family relationship dynamics. When Axis I disorders (usually mood or anxiety disorders) indicate a need for medical or pharmacological intervention, we routinely discuss the issue with clients and refer them to their primary care physician, collaborating with the physician as necessary to ensure a coordinated treatment approach.

TREATMENT MODEL

Relationship Enhancement Therapy

When couples talk, particularly about problems they are having, the skill that is frequently used least is empathic listening. As proposed by Carl Rogers (1961), empathic listening includes one partner paraphrasing what the other partner is saying to ensure not only that communication is clear but also to understand the communication from the sender's point of view. Instead of using empathic listening, most partners think about what they are going to say in response rather than check for understanding of what is being communicated. In addition, when partners are presenting their points of view, they may neglect to express themselves in such a way that it is clear that they are relating their perceptions as opposed to declaring shared reality. Declarative statements which do not convey recognition that they represent the speaker's subjective point of view can arouse defensiveness in listeners. For example, "You are lazy!" is more likely to arouse defensiveness in the person hearing it than would, "I think you could do more around the house." Helping couples use subjective self-expression can increase the degree to which they demonstrate ownership of their thoughts and feelings and decrease the defensiveness they provoke in their partners.

Relationship enhancement, developed by Bernard Guerney (1977), is an experiential model similar in some respects to Virginia Satir's work with having couples talk to each other, but without the posturing that she sometimes advocated. RE coaches both listening and expressive skills. It combines psychodynamic, humanistic, behavioral, and interpersonal perspectives to create a set of skills to be acquired by the couple. The skills, then, provide a structure inside and outside of therapy for the couple to discuss significant issues without resorting to previously ineffective interaction patterns. Research has demonstrated the effectiveness of RE with premarital couples (Ridley et al., 1982) and married couples (Brock and Joanning, 1983; Granvold, 1983; Jessee and Guerney, 1981). It has also been effective with couples in which one partner experienced sexual dysfunction (Harman, Waldo, and Johnson, 1994, 1998).

Waldo and Harman (1993) have previously described the successful use of RE in couples counseling in which the wife suffered from BPD. We believe that RE has a great deal to offer in addressing the many ways in which BPD symptoms are expressed in relationships. As Lachkar (1992, 1998) has noted, many relationships with a BPD partner are characterized by a pattern of attack and withdrawal. RE, with its emphasis on empathic communication skills and avoidance of generalized statements about another's character, can help interrupt dysfunctional attack and withdrawal interactions. The structured role changes in RE from expresser to listener and the need to attend carefully to the partner's feelings prior to paraphrasing them may also assist in overcoming narcissistic qualities, which are typical of many BPD clients and their relationships.

The RE approach also represents an effective blend of both the expressive and supportive treatment approaches recommended by Horwitz and his colleagues (1996). The strong communication focus of RE can assist BPD clients in expressing their fears, wishes, and conflict in a supportive environment, so that they can feel heard and understood by their partner. At the same time, the highly structured approach and modeling of appropriate communication skills (and correcting of narcissistic or attacking interactions) can provide the support needed for BPD clients to develop more healthy and adaptive communication, relationship, and problem-solving skills. Therapist interventions and feedback can also help BPD clients understand their partner's feelings and views more accurately, thereby interrupting negative interpretations and reducing tendencies toward idealization and devaluation (splitting) and feelings of abandonment.

The decision to use RE with couples depends on the characteristics of the individual partners. In the initial couples counseling sessions, it is useful to gain information about what made the couple decide to come for therapy at this time and to get some sense of the current communication patterns. The couples with whom the authors usually work are verbal and have average to above-average intelligence. A prerequisite for suggesting the use of skills training is the commitment of both individuals to make the communication between them better.

There are two major roles in RE therapy: (1) expresser and (2) listener. The partners alternate between the roles. Expressers are responsible for including five features when presenting issues about which they are concerned, as follows:

1. State the problem from a subjective stance, such as, "It seems to me," or "From my point of view."
2. Disclose the feelings or emotions associated with the situations.
3. Offer specific examples of events or behaviors related to the problem while avoiding making generalized statements, particularly generalized statements about the listener's character (i.e., "I thought you would get here at five o'clock and you did not come until six" instead of "You are inconsiderate and irresponsible").
4. Tell the listener why what the expresser is describing matters to the expresser, what the issues raised say or mean about the positive qualities preferred in the relationship.
5. Make requests of the listener, informing the listener about behavioral changes that could move the relationship in the direction the expresser desires.

The listener puts aside whatever thoughts and emotions this issue brings to mind and concentrates solely on what the expresser says, realizing that the listener will soon be the expresser and be able to explain an alternative view of the issue. The listener attempts to be empathic, to understand the situation from the expresser's point of view by sharing brief paraphrases of what the expresser says. The paraphrasing is to make certain that the listener understands clearly what the expresser is verbalizing, and the expresser confirms the listener's understanding or corrects mistaken impressions. Once the expresser has included the five characteristics in the communication and indicates being heard and understood, roles are switched. Then, the listener becomes the expresser, and the former expresser becomes the listener.

The therapist's tasks include explaining, demonstrating, coaching expression and listening, and negotiating role changes. It is important in the initial interactions to suggest that the listener have a chance to show understanding after short explanations by the expresser. This helps the listener practice paraphrasing with shorter bits of information before attempting to paraphrase longer strings of information. It is also encouraging to the listener, who is reinforced for accurately paraphrasing the expresser's explanation. Thus, it is important for the therapist/coach to reinforce appropriate progress. Positive phrases, such as "Good work," "You're doing well," and "Beautiful," give positive feedback so that individuals are aware of their progress. It is also necessary to address inappropriate body language, such as arms crossed over the chest, or sarcastic tone of voice. Usually these inappropriate behaviors are emitted by the listener, who is having a difficult time putting aside personal thoughts and feelings in order to empathically listen to the partner. In those cases, it is important to: (1) either switch roles so that the listener can become the expresser, or (2) gain the cooperation of the listener through the therapist's empathic response to the listener.

The most frequent issue the therapist/coach must address is helping the listener respond in second person when paraphrasing. When the therapist says to the listener, "OK, can you show understanding to that much?" The listener will frequently say to the therapist, "She said . . . " at which point the therapist must direct the listener to speak to the partner in the second person, using a phrase such as, "You feel . . . ." Occasionally, the listener will paraphrase and then continue in the first person, saying, for example, "You feel hurt when you perceive that I ignore you. I'm just trying to . . . ." Again, the therapist must stop the first-person expression and ask the listener to paraphrase only what the expresser has said.

Because direct communication between couples is a major objective of RE, an office setup that facilitates this communication is important. Furniture should be arranged so that the individuals can sit directly across from one another. The therapist should sit in a position so that each partner can easily be seen and heard. This focus on direct couple interaction is not always preferred in family therapy. For instance, Bowen's (1978) primary technique of having the individuals talk to the therapist rather than to each other is very effective and is particularly helpful in the initial sessions before the RE skills training is implemented. However, the primary RE goal is to assist the couple to communicate more effectively with each other. With RE, the couple begins to negotiate their own relationship at an early stage of therapy and usually fairly soon are able to communicate effectively without a therapist, which is the ultimate goal of therapy. The couple may still need assistance when major upheavals arise but do not usually need ongoing marital therapy. Although the primary goal of RE, improved communication, differs from Bowen's primary goal of differentiation, there is evidence that RE can also effect increases in differentiation and adjustment in marital couples (Griffin and Apostal, 1993).

After RE therapy has been explained, but before the first skills-training session begins, there are two important tasks we ask each partner to accomplish: (a) determining what the individual loves about the mate; and (b) making a list of problems for the couple, ranked from low level to highly volatile. We have found that it is helpful for partners to determine what they love about the other partner before they arrive for the first skills-training session because it can be antitherapeutic if one partner is perceived as having to struggle to think of what is positively viewed about the other.

CASE EXAMPLE

Amy originally came to therapy without her husband Ron's knowledge. She seemed obsessed with the fact that her husband had written a letter to a friend in the past indicating his preference for certain women's body parts over others and that Amy did not meet the qualifications. She had many depressive symptoms including suicidal ideation. She had attempted suicide as an adolescent and had been hospitalized in a psychiatric facility. Although she had recently sought therapy, she had not connected with the most recent therapist she had visited. Amy's present symptoms clearly indicated diagnoses of adjustment disorder with mixed depressive and anxious symptoms on Axis I, and she had previously been diagnosed with BPD on Axis II. She was referred to her primary care physician, who prescribed antidepressant medication because of suicidal ideation and her obsessive thoughts regarding her suspicions that her husband was having or thinking about having an affair. Within several weeks, Amy was responding to the medication, had established a therapeutic relationship with the current therapist, and had accepted the suggestion that her husband had not anticipated her reaction to the letter even if he had intended for her to find it, as she suspected.

After Amy began responding to the medication and exploring personal issues related to herself and her marriage, she was willing to ask Ron to join her in therapy. He also appeared to establish a therapeutic relationship with the therapist. It was obvious from their interaction during the initial joint session that Amy took a parental role with Ron when discussing his behavior. She would alternately tell him that she could never trust him again, tell him that he was responsible for her feeling devastated and suicidal, and express fear that he would leave her for another woman. Ron, on the other hand, tried not to upset her further and was reticent to share his feelings with Amy present for fear that she would become upset. His fears were confirmed several times during the initial joint session when Amy burst into tears and/or responded with angry verbiage to his explanations. If he appeared hesitant to share, she would accuse him of not wanting to work on the relationship. Ron seemed to be in a lose-lose situation during this initial session.

Amy's presentation and her interactions with Ron reflected a number of characteristic BPD qualities. Her initial suicidal feelings were typical of individuals with BPD, who often display impulsive self-destructive behaviors. Her emotional instability was also typical. Amy displayed a characteristic BPD fear of abandonment in her fear that Ron was thinking about or having an affair. She also displayed a characteristic pattern of splitting or alternating idealization and devaluation in her interaction with Ron, which was expressed in her verbal attacks on Ron, holding him responsible for her feeling devastated and suicidal. These verbal attacks, which led to Ron's withdrawal, reflected her lack of differentiation, her ambivalence about her dependence on Ron, and her anger at his perceived inability to respond fully to her emotional needs.

As many of these dynamics surfaced in the couple's communication pattern, and as the couple seemed sufficiently verbal and intelligent to benefit, a decision was made to use RE to treat them. The RE skills and procedures were explained to both individuals, and they agreed that they would give the process a try. At the next session, they expressed what they found lovable about each other and worked on some low-level problems to practice the skills. In the excerpt of a session that follows, Amy is performing the expresser role and Ron has agreed to be the listener.

AMY: It seemed to me that you were more distant than usual. So I went through your study and found the letter to Larry. You had left it on a shelf out in the open, so maybe you wanted me to find it. Anyway, you wrote that you now realized that you had married someone with a great ass but that you were really a tits man. That really hurt my feelings because I told you before we were married that I would probably always look the way I did then. You chose to marry me anyway. I just feel devastated.

THERAPIST: Try to be more specific in the feeling—maybe hurt or humiliated?

AMY: Yes, I feel very hurt, crushed, and very humiliated that you would think about me that way.

THERAPIST: Let's have him show understanding to that much. OK? Ron, just briefly paraphrase what you heard.

RON: She found . . .

THERAPIST: Look at her. Talk to her.

RON: You found my letter and read that I was attracted to . . . er . . . breasts more than . . . er . . . hips.

THERAPIST: And you felt . . .

RON: And you felt hurt.

THERAPIST: Amy, does he have it?

AMY: It was more than just hurt. It didn't just hurt my feelings. It changed the way I thought about myself, about him, about our whole relationship.

THERAPIST: Ron, can you perhaps summarize the magnitude of her hurt?

RON: She—I mean you felt more than hurt. You felt crushed, devastated, and humiliated.

THERAPIST: Beautiful. Does he have it now, Amy?

AMY: (nods)

THERAPIST: You are both working very hard at this. OK. Let's continue. Amy, talk about the situation more if you need to, but let's move to how you would like it to be.

AMY: I'd like for you to care about me for more than just my body. I'd like for you to love me for who I am, not the packaging that I am in.

THERAPIST: And if he could do that, what would that say about your relationship?

AMY: It would say he—you value me in the relationship and that the relationship is more important to you than my breasts or my ass.

THERAPIST: Good job. Ron, can you summarize that last part?

RON: You'd like for me to love you for yourself and not how you look, and if I could do that it would mean that I care more about you and our relationship and not so much how you look.

THERAPIST: Super work, both of you. Are we ready to switch? OK. Ron, you'll be the expresser and talk about this specific situation and how it seems to you. You'll talk about your feelings and about how you'd like it to be and what that would mean about your relationship. And Amy, you'll put aside anything you are thinking about this and simply listen and try to understand it from his point of view. OK? Go ahead, Ron.

RON: Well, first of all, you . . .

THERAPIST: It seems to me . . .

RON: It seems to me that you had no business reading my letter, and I did not leave it where you could find it. I never wanted you to see what I had written. I was just writing down my thoughts. I never mailed it because I never meant for anyone to read it but me. I wrote that back when we were having some trouble. I hadn't read it for a while, and I haven't written anything recently.

THERAPIST: Your feelings?

RON: I feel violated, blamed for hurting you when I never meant for you to read it. If you hadn't read it, you wouldn't be hurt.

THERAPIST: And maybe angry?

RON: Well, I am angry.

THERAPIST: Let's have her show understanding to this point.

AMY: You don't think I should have read your letter because you didn't intend for me to read it and it makes you mad that you got caught.

THERAPIST: Ron, is that what you're saying?

RON: Not that I got caught; that you read my private things.

THERAPIST: Amy, can you clarify that for him?

AMY: You're angry because I read your letter.

THERAPIST: Is that it, Ron? Does she have it? OK, good job, both of you. Go on.

RON: I went to talk to my priest and told him what has happened and that I might not be as attracted to you as I once was and that I might want to leave. He said it didn't matter what I felt or wanted, that I had to honor my vows and commitment and do what was best for the relationship.

AMY: I don't want you to stay with me like that.

THERAPIST: Whoa! Amy, you're out of role. As the listener you are trying to understand Ron's point of view. You will have a chance to respond with your thoughts when we switch roles. OK?

RON: Anyway, I think he is probably right and I am willing to try. But I think all of this is all about you and how you feel, and you don't listen to what I say. I told you I was sorry that I wrote it and that you found it and that you read it, but I can't do anything about that now.

THERAPIST: Good. How would you like it to be? What's your request of Amy?

RON: I want to work on our relationship, but I don't want to constantly rehash what was in the letter. I want us to get past that.

THERAPIST: What specifically would you like from Amy?

RON: I want you to realize that I want to do what is right because I am still here. I haven't left and I don't want to leave. Well, when you start all of this all over again, I do want to leave. But I am not going to leave right now.

THERAPIST: And if she could realize that you do want to work on this, what would that mean about your relationship?

RON: It would mean that we could start making the relationship better so we could both be satisfied and happy.

THERAPIST: Beautiful. Amy, can you briefly summarize?

AMY: You don't want me to keep bringing up the letter. You want to work on our relationship because it is the right thing to do, and you think both of us can be satisfied in the relationship again.

RON: Right.

THERAPIST: Super work, both of you.

STRENGTHS AND LIMITATIONS

As can be seen in this example, RE therapy can frequently help the partner with BPD to individuate between self and others and develop more boundaries for self. In RE therapy, the partner with BPD is able to express personal perspective without being interrupted and attacked and may find the other partner listening rather than protesting. The familiar interaction pattern is interrupted, and each partner is validated even though the two may not agree. Thus, RE therapy may assist partners with BPD to gain ego strength and develop a more stable identity that does not need to overidealize or devalue their partners. Less frequent fear-of-abandonment episodes may decrease mood swings, which in turn would curb some impulsivity. Increased ego strength may also diminish narcissistic tendencies that alienate others. Of course, all these benefits would not emerge from one session of RE therapy. Similar intense but productive sessions would be necessary to solidify cognitive shifts for both partners but particularly for the partner with BPD.

Relationship enhancement therapy may be useful to therapists who operate from both systemic and humanistic perspectives. The skills training involves both explanation and practice of the skills so that retention and continued use are more likely. Although the couple may not use the exact structure when they communicate outside therapy, the use of subjective expression, specific examples, underlying meaning, and empathic listening frequently continues. Thus, couples develop confidence in their ability to negotiate and sustain their relationships and become less dependent on the therapist to mediate their interaction. Additionally, the skills developed will enhance interpersonal communication in other relationships and arenas such as work and leisure.

RE therapy alone may be limited if the partner with BPD has biologically based symptoms that require medication, as will be addressed subsequently. RE therapy for the couple may need to work in conjunction with individual therapy for the partner with BPD. Limitations may also arise when couples have waited to seek help until destructive interactions have made each individual so defensive that vengeance and/or escape are the primary objectives for one or both partners. Recall that RE therapy is of benefit to those who want the relationship to be better and are willing to work to that end.

INTEGRATION WITH PSYCHIATRIC SERVICES AND ROLE OF MEDICATION

As was true in the previous case example, psychotropic medication may be necessary if there appears to be a biological need for it. For example, depression is frequently a biological condition as well as a psychological condition at this point in our understanding of mental health. Research has shown that the most promising intervention may be psychotropic medication combined with psychotherapy (Beck, 1985; Frank, Karp, and Rush, 1993). Certainly, psychotic individuals would be inappropriate for RE therapy until they are stable. In addition, if an individual is severely depressed and contemplating suicide, a situation that some physicians would interpret as psychotic, RE would only be appropriate after stabilization. However, once an individual is feeling less depressed and is able to focus on issues other than escaping the intense emotional difficulties, RE therapy is definitely appropriate. There is also some speculation and evidence that medication can assist individuals with personality disorders toward increased adjustment (Kellner, 1986; Klein, 1989). Thus, RE therapy combined with psychotropic medication may result in better physical and psychological adjustment for the partner with BPD.

CULTURAL AND GENDER ISSUES

Communication is a basic skill across all cultures. In our experience, RE therapy is appropriate for most cultures. Some cultures, particularly those which are more patriarchal, are characterized by very defined and rigid gender roles, such that the feelings or thoughts of the female partner may be considered insignificant. This can present a challenge in applying RE; however, a therapist can often make a case for listening and empathy. For example, even a very fundamentalist Christian perspective may allow a husband whose wife is required to submit to his authority to listen and attempt to understand dissatisfaction from her point of view. Then, because he wants to care about her needs, he would be open to her requests. The application of the RE approach in this situation may contribute to the development of a more egalitarian and less hierarchical relationship that better meets the needs of both partners.

As previously noted, research indicates that many BPD clients, particularly female BPD clients, have experienced abuse. Many of these clients have had little opportunity to have their thoughts, feelings, and experiences validated. Women in our society, and even more so in some traditional cultures, tend to have their views minimized or discounted by men who are more privileged or empowered. Unfortunately, many women who have experienced abuse also find themselves in abusive marital relationships or relationships where their feelings, thoughts, and perceptions are not respected.

RE, with its emphasis on respectful listening and validation of others' communications, can be a very positive therapeutic experience for individuals who have experienced abuse or been disempowered. The structured nature of RE encourages both partners to fully express their viewpoints and allows both genders to speak and be heard. If gender inequalities are communicated, the therapist may assist the couple to explore the feelings and thoughts associated with such inequalities but remain nonjudgmental in the coaching role. The emphasis is placed on the couple exploring their issues and being heard and understood by each other. If one partner remains rigid and makes demands rather than requests, then RE is inappropriate at that time. Individual sessions or other approaches may be necessary until both partners are able to hear and respond to the expressions and requests of the other. Typically, however, a negotiated middle ground that uses characteristics of solution-focused therapy may break an impasse.

FUTURE DIRECTIONS

Although RE shows promise as a modality for couple and family treatment of BPD, the model remains very much in the developmental stage. Case studies indicate RE can be effective for couples in which one partner suffers from BPD, but to date there are no controlled studies of RE as a treatment for BPD couples and families.

Whether partners suffer from personality disorders or not, additional investigation of RE therapy with various cultures and families of homogeneous as well as heterogeneous ethnic origins is a continuing need. Sexual orientation is also an important variant in present society as increased numbers of couples in committed homosexual relationships are seeking family counseling to improve interaction and communication. RE therapy should certainly be appropriate in these cases, but little has been published to support the use of the RE model in alternative committed relationships. The same need is evident in therapy with various parent-child combinations and sibling relationships that emerge in original nuclear families as well as step-and blended families. Finally, current investigators believe that the differentiation and increased communication skills individuals develop in RE family therapy tend eventually to encourage more successful interpersonal relationship interaction outside the family. However, the generalizability of the skills has yet to be documented through research.

REFERENCES

Adler, G. and Buie, D. (1979). Aloneness and borderline psychopathology: The possible relevance of child developmental issues. *International Journal of Psychoanalysis, 60,* 83-96.

American Psychiatric Association (1994). *Diagnostic and statistical manual of mental disorders* (Fourth edition). Washington, DC: Author.

Beck, A. T. (1985). Is behavior therapy on course? *Behavioural Psychotherapy, 13,* 83-84.

Becker, D. (1997). *Through the looking glass: Women and borderline personality disorder.* Boulder, CO: Westview Press.

Bowen, M. (1978). *Family therapy in clinical practice.* New York: Jason Aronson.

Brock, G. W. and Joanning, H. (1983). A comparison of the relationship enhancement program and the Minnesota couple communication program. *Journal of Marital and Family Therapy, 9,* 413-421.

Chesler, P. (1972). *Women and madness.* New York: Avon Books.

Dohrenwend, B. P. and Dohrenwend, B. S. (1976). Sex differences and psychiatric disorders. *American Journal of Sociology, 81,* 1447-1454.

Frank, E., Karp, J. F., and Rush, A. J. (1993). Efficacy of treatments for major depression. *Psychopharmacology Bulletin, 29,* 457-475.

Granvold, D. K. (1983). Structured separation for marital treatment and decision-making. *Journal of Marital and Family Therapy, 9,* 403-412.

Griffin, J. M. and Apostal, R. A. (1993). The influence of relationship enhancement training on differentiation of self. *Journal of Marital and Family Therapy, 19,* 267-272.

Guerney, B. G. Jr. (1977). *Relationship enhancement: Skill-training programs for therapy, problem prevention, and enrichment.* San Francisco, CA: IDEALS.

Harman, M. J., Waldo., M., and Johnson, J. A. (1994). Relationship enhancement therapy: A case study for treatment of vaginismus. *The Family Journal, 2,* 122-128.

Harman, M. J., Waldo., M., and Johnson, J. A. (1998). The sexually dysfunctional couple: Vaginismus and relationship enhancement therapy. In J. Carlson and L. Sperry (Eds.), *The disordered couple* (pp. 83-95). Bristol, PA: Brunner/Mazel.

Herkov, M. J. and Blashfield, R. K. (1995). Clinician diagnoses of personality disorders: Evidence of a hierarchical structure. *Journal of Personality Assessment, 65,* 313-321.

Horwitz, L. (1985). Divergent views on the treatment of borderline patients. *Bulletin of the Menninger Clinic, 49,* 525-545.

Horwitz, L., Gabbard, G. O., Allen, J. G., Frieswyk, S. H., Colson, D. B., Newsom, G. E., and Coyne, L. (1996). *Borderline personality disorder: Tailoring the psychotherapy to the patient.* Washington, DC: American Psychiatric Press.

Jessee, R. E. and Guerney, B. G. Jr. (1981). A comparison of gestalt and relationship enhancement treatments with married couples. *American Journal of Family Therapy, 9,* 31-41.

Kellner, R. (1986). Personality disorders. *Psychotherapy and Psychosomatics, 46,* 58-66.

Kernberg, O. F. (1975). *Borderline conditions and pathological narcissism.* New York: Jason Aronson.

Kernberg, O. F. (1976). Technical considerations in the treatment of borderline personality organization. *Journal of American Psychoanalytic Association, 24,* 795-829.

Klein, M. (1996). Notes on some schizoid mechanisms. *Journal of Psychotherapy Practice and Research, 5,* 164-179.

Klein, R. (1989). Pharmacotherapy of the borderline personality disorder. In J. F. Masterson, and R. Klein (Eds.), *Psychotherapy of the disorders of the self: The Masterson approach* (pp. 365-394). New York: Brunner/Mazel.

Lachkar, J. (1992). *The narcissistic/borderline couple: A psychoanalytic perspective to marital conflict.* New York: Brunner/Mazel.

Lachkar, J. (1998). Narcissistic/borderline couples: A psychodynamic approach to conjoint treatment. In J. Carlson and L. Sperry (Eds.), *The disordered couple* (pp. 259-284). Bristol, PA: Brunner/Mazel.

Mahler, M. S., Pine, F., and Bergman, A. (1975). *The psychological birth of the human infant: Symbiosis and individuation.* New York: Basic Books.

Marziali, E. and Munroe-Blum, H. (1994). *Interpersonal group psychotherapy for borderline personality disorder.* New York: Basic Books.

Masterson, J. (1972). *Treatment of the borderline adolescent: A developmental approach.* New York: Wiley.

Meyer, R. G. (1989). *The clinician's handbook: The psychopathology of adulthood and adolescence* (Second edition). Boston: Allyn & Bacon.

Reiser, D. E. and Levenson, H. (1984). Abuses of the borderline diagnosis: A clinical problem with teaching opportunities. *American Journal of Psychiatry, 141,* 1528-1532.

Ridley, C. A., Jorgensen, S. R., Morgan, A. C., and Avery A. W. (1982). Relationship enhancement with premarital couples: An enhancement of effects on relationship quality. *American Journal of Family Therapy, 10,* 41-48.

Rogers, C. R. (1961). *On becoming a person: A therapist's view of psychotherapy.* Boston: Houghton Mifflin.

Silk, K. R. (1994). *Biological and neurobehavioral studies of borderline personality disorder.* Washington, DC: American Psychiatric Press.

Snyder, S. (1986). Pseudologia fantastica in the borderline patient. *American Journal of Psychiatry, 143,* 1287-1289.

Solomon, M. F. (1998). Treating narcissistic and borderline couples. In J. Carlson and L. Sperry (Eds.), *The disordered couple* (pp. 239-258). Bristol, PA: Brunner/Mazel.

Swartz, M., Blazer, D., George, L., and Winfield, I. (1990). Estimating the prevalence of borderline personality disorder in the community. *Journal of Personality Disorders, 4,* 257-272.

Waldinger, R. J. (1987). Intensive psychodynamic therapy with borderline patients: An overview. *American Journal of Psychiatry, 144,* 267-274.

Waldinger, R. J. and Gunderson, J. G. (1984). Completed psychotherapies with borderline patients. *American Journal of Psychotherapy, 39,* 190-202.

Waldo, M. (1989). Primary prevention in university residence halls: Para-professional-led relationship enhancement groups for college roommates. *Journal of Counseling and Development, 67,* 465-471.

Waldo, M. and Harman, M. J. (1993). Relationship enhancement therapy with borderline personality. *The Family Journal, 1,* 25-30.

Waldo, M. and Harman, M. J. (1998). Borderline personality disorder and relationship enhancement marital therapy. In J. Carlson and L. Sperry (Eds.), *The disordered couple* (pp. 285-297). Bristol, PA: Brunner/Mazel.

Waldo, M. and Harman, M. J. (1999). Relationship enhancement groups with state hospital patients and staff. *Journal for Specialists in Group Work, 24,* 27-36.

Zanarini, M. C. (1997). *Role of sexual abuse in the etiology of borderline personality disorder.* Washington, DC: American Psychiatric Press.

Chapter 10

Treatment of Suicidal Clients and Their Families

Peter D. McLean
Lynn Miller

INTRODUCTION

Few forces within a family are as disturbing as the threat of suicide. This is universal across cultures, social class, and family configuration. Suicidality in a family member usually drives families to seek help, and this provides therapists with unique challenges as well as opportunities. One quickly learns that suicidal intent is seldom spontaneous and isolated. Instead, it normally betrays an evolution of failed expectations, perceived rejection, loneliness, and loss of hope. The antecedents to suicidal intent are normally either invisible to family members or misinterpreted by them. However, once the acute risk of suicide is identified and under control, the issues that induced suicidal intent in the first place need to be addressed, and family members are critical resources in the reversal of depression. This chapter underscores the complementary role mental health workers and family counselors can play in the treatment of suicidal clients and their families. The theoretical model we work from blends brief solution-focused techniques and cognitive-behavioral therapies, although the therapeutic techniques will be familiar to many practitioners of other therapies within the family systems framework. For safety purposes, immediate attention is often on the suicidal client, but soon, and inevitably, the therapeutic focus shifts to the family in order to bring about change and to promote prevention. The recommendations herein represent a relatively structured approach to family therapy and stem from experience in a multidisciplinary community out-patient clinic, which is part of a university training clinic.

Suicide Demographics and Depression

Suicide is the ninth leading cause of death in the United States, the third leading cause of death among fifteen to twenty-four-year-olds (Canada and the United States), the fifth leading cause of death for children ages five to fourteen, and the fifth leading cause of death for adults aged twenty-five to forty-four (National Center for Health Statistics, 1998). Death rates increase dramatically during adolescence, at a rate of 11.3 deaths per 100,000 for ages fifteen to twenty-four years. These rates, however, do not reveal the anguish of others who unsuccessfully attempt suicide. It is estimated that for every completed suicide, fifty to two hundred attempts are made. Hafen and Frandsen (1986) estimate that one teenager attempts suicide every ninety seconds and one completes the act of suicide every ninety minutes.

Suicidal risk most commonly occurs in the context of clinical depression. Approximately 70 percent of psychiatric hospitalizations and 60 percent of suicides are associated with mood disorders (U.S. Department of Health and Human Services [USDHHS], 1993). In this chapter, we refer to clinical depression as nonpsychotic, reactive depression, or major depression. This is by far the most common form of depression and, in our experience, approximately 50 percent of clients at the moderate level of clinical depression routinely experience suicidal ideation. There is broad agreement that in Western industrialized nations the lifetime prevalence for major depression is 7 to 12 percent for men and 20 to 25 percent for women (USDHHS, 1993). Less appreciated is the poor functioning and quality of life associated with depression. For example, Wells and his colleagues (1989) found that those with either clinical depression or subclinical symptoms of depression were comparable or worse, in terms of functioning, relative to eight major chronic medical conditions (e.g., gastrointestinal disorder, advanced coronary artery disease).

There are multiple contributors to the expression of depression in particular cases. At the individual level, poor self-esteem as the result of abuse, academic underachievement, or poor social skill development can result in an enduring vulnerability to depression. Independently, family influences, such as marital conflict, economic stress, and reduction in role importance can foster depression. Broader ecological influences, including poverty, community violence, and modeling of suicide, further contribute to the risk of depression and suicide potential within families.

Model of Depression

In conceptualizing the development and reversal of clinical depression, we suggest a psychosocial, four-step model to account for the development and maintenance of depression. It is assumed that those who succumb to depression have vulnerabilities that may not otherwise be noticeable. The psychosocial model of depression as outlined in Figure 10.1 is useful in accounting for the formation and maintenance of depression and suggests means by which depression can be overcome with therapeutic support.

The four progressive steps in the development of depression occur over a period of at least two weeks and typically take longer. In the first step, the idea is that important individual goals are thwarted in a number of key life areas on a continuous (i.e., cumulative) basis. A fire at one's summer cabin or the unexpected pregnancy of one's unmarried teenage daughter would not qualify. Instead, imagine a man whose work performance in recent months had plummeted, whose wife appeared indifferent and increasingly busy with friends, whose best friend recently left town, who experienced a sudden loss in his investment portfolio, and who is becoming noticeably overweight. It is important to note that it is the perception and not necessarily the reality of these events that is salient for the generation of depression.

If these unfulfilled expectations are significant, comprehensive, and enduring, they give rise to a generalized feeling of loss of control (see Figure 10.1, Step 2). If one's attempts to reestablish control are unproductive in the face of sustained goal frustration, individuals appear to become disengaged from incentives, as if responding would make no difference (see Figure 10.1, Step 3). At this point, individuals give the appearance of not caring about most things, including not only daily routines but also lifelong plans and aspirations. It is as if they have acquired a belief that whatever they do will be insufficient and irrelevant in rectifying what has gone so terribly wrong in their lives. In the clinical literature, this is commonly described as withdrawal, which is accompanied by rumination in place of normal problem-solving activities. The development of depressive symp-

FIGURE 10.1. Psychosocial Model of the Development of Depression

---

Step 1.   Perception of sustained goal frustration

Step 2.   Feeling of loss of control in important areas

Step 3.   Disengagement from incentives and corresponding belief that
               responding will not make a difference

Step 4.   Appearance of depression symptoms, starting with withdrawal,
               rumination, and progressing to physical symptoms

---

tomatology (see Figure 10.1, Step 4) now becomes more evident to close observers. Family members will have noticed a growing lack of interest, pervasive glumness, and possibly changes in sleep and appetite patterns.

Some individuals by virtue of inheritance (e.g., personality factors such as high neuroticism) and poor adaptive modeling will have a relatively low coping capacity and hence will be vulnerable to reacting sooner and more negatively than will individuals who enjoy protective factors. Basically, this model suggests that in order to sustain a positive mood, the perception of current, or anticipated, positive events must be greater than current, or anticipated, negative events. The job of therapy is to ensure that a positive ratio of rewarding, as opposed to negative, events is achieved (see Figure 10.2).

To elaborate somewhat on this model, clinical depression is maintained by behavioral passivity (e.g., procrastination), social avoidance, and worry-based cognitions about oneself, the world, and the future. Such activities have predictable consequences. They tend to evoke criticism from family members who become frustrated by the sufferer's "attitude" and unwillingness to cooperate or engage in role-related expectations. Further, the sufferer is relatively cut off

FIGURE 10.2. The Job of Therapy

The job of therapy is to increase the ratio of positive events and recognition, relative to negative events and recognition (e.g., criticism) in the lives of depressed individuals.

i.e., $\dfrac{+\,+}{-\,-}$ $+\,+\,+$ self-esteem   hope and adaptive performance

from the rewards of successful task performance in goal-related activities as well as from positive social recognition by virtue of withdrawal. Depressed individuals are, of course, sensitive to their relative personal failures and negative perception on the part of others. The tendency is to engage in a high rate of negative cognitions (i.e., ruminations), involving self-recrimination, guilt, and a variety of cognitive distortions.

As is suggested by the model, there are two important principles that are highly relevant to positive treatment outcomes. The first is that successful performance is a powerful antidepressant. The second principle is that self-esteem flows from positive social recognition. These two principles are related from a practical point of view, inasmuch as successful performance is also valued by members of the depressed person's social network, which results in relatively more social recognition and hence, self-esteem.

Why Family Therapy?

The family can be a dramatic, valuable ally, and treatment can be enhanced significantly by using a family systems therapeutic approach (Brown, 1996). First, the family is very often deeply troubled by another family member's potential death. Sometimes the family inadvertently contributes to the suicidal client's stresses, although in their distress their efforts seem well intentioned. Often the family is the first to see signs of depression or of impending suicide (i.e., traditional behavior markers such as changes in sleep patterns, changes in weight, changed affect, giving away prized possessions, etc.) but are not informed or are confused by the suicidal member's actions and intentions. Finally, for any family in crisis, especially in cases of adolescent depression or suicide threat, the parents are in the best position to help children develop healthy psychological mechanisms to deal with stress and to encourage and reinforce resilient behavior. Similarly, failing marriages are a potent source of depression, particularly for women, which raises their risk for suicidal intent. Again, family members (in this case, the spouse) are in a strong position to resolve this conflict in cooperation with the depressed party.

Furthermore, a significant body of research suggests that depression (and suicide) "runs in families." Bucy (1994) reports that 26 to 42 percent of children with depressed parents will receive the same DSM diagnosis. Research suggests that parent-child interaction exerts a potent influence on the maintenance of child psychopathology in the case of depression and anxiety (Rapee, 1997). Specifically, the research is consistent in identifying rejection and control by parents as being precursors to later anxiety and depression in children and adolescents. Some evidence in these studies suggests that rejection may be more salient for depression.

In contemplating family therapy for depression and the reduction of suicidal potential, one might well ask, "What is the relative role played by genetic influences, family upbringing, and unique life experiences?" This is important in family therapy, as attributions to other causes, such as genetics (e.g., "You're just like your mother") or brain chemistry (e.g., "chemical imbalance") serve to absolve families from the responsibility of developing good communication and problem-solving systems within the family. Gatz and colleagues (1992) investigated this question in a large study of identical and fraternal twins reared apart or together in order to understand the relative genetic and environmental contributions to individual differences in self-reported depressive symptoms. They found that genetic influences accounted for no more than 16 percent of the variance in depression scores in 481 twin pairs. By far the largest factors in determining depression were the family rearing context and unique life experiences. These data strongly support the value of a family systems approach to the treatment of depression and suicidal risk. Such information can help family therapists offer an objective and realistic viewpoint to families who are struggling with confusing and sometimes misleading information.

Families often understand depression from a unidirectional, biological view and may look to pharmaceuticals for relief of their symptoms. Virtually all clients family therapists will see who are suicidal and/or substantially depressed will already be on some form of antidepressant medication, typically prescribed by their primary care physician. Most families will want to get all the therapeutic help they can, regardless of the source. Cognitive-behavioral therapy and pharmacotherapy are relatively equal in therapeutic effect during the acute phase of depression treatment (McLean and Taylor, 1992), and some studies show a mild therapeutic additive effect for combining pharmaceutical and cognitive-behavioral therapy interventions. As family therapists, we want to underscore the advantages of both approaches. Pharmaceutical interventions can be very helpful in stabilizing emotional flooding and sleep loss, while family therapy techniques can be most useful in establishing productive decision making, communication practices, and conflict resolution skills, for example. Families need to be encouraged to view these as complementary forms of treatment and not to rely on antidepressant medication alone to restore optimal functioning in all areas.

As family therapists, we need to keep in mind that families have changed radically in structure and composition over the past few decades. The term "family" struggles for definition in the literature, in political circles, and even in our everyday language. New relationship combinations and nontraditional roles and ways of thinking and problem solving are the rule rather than the exception. Common-law households, homosexual couples, multigenerational families, commuter marriages, blended/stepfamilies, female-headed households, and other family systems supplant the notion of a "traditional" family where the male is the main breadwinner and the woman stays at home with the children (which account for less than 10 percent of all homes in the United States).

Almost all family theorists, whatever the composition of the "family," view the family from an interactive and systemic perspective, which sees the individual dysfunctional behavior (e.g., suicide attempt) as a manifestation of dysfunctional behavior within the system or, at a minimum, as affecting the system negatively. Family therapy is a diverse field, comprising various theories of how change occurs within the family and includes an equally diverse set of intervention strategies. Theories of family therapy share a common philosophy of the importance of dealing with all parts of the system if change is to take place and be maintained. Therefore, a family therapist would (a) view a suicide attempt as a systems problem that affects the entire family, (b) involve the entire family in treatment to whatever extent possible, and (c) expect that the family would hold the solution to this critical problem. Additionally, obtaining multiple descriptions of family history and describing problems has the advantage of describing the symptom bearer (i.e., suicidal client) in a more holistic way, as well as strengthening the therapeutic alliance that in turn heightens family dedication and adherence to treatment planning.

Finally, the potency of family therapy has been demonstrated. Family-based interventions have a robust body of process and outcome research, including data with specific disorders, specific populations, treatment adherence, specific interventions, and cost-effectiveness. However, given the rates of prevalence of mood disorders in children, there is a stunning lack of empirical evidence on what is classically defined as family therapy in regard to childhood disorders. Nonetheless, what research is available offers initial support for the integration of parents into the treatment of childhood disorders that are often a precursor to suicide (Estrada and Pinsof, 1995).

SETTING

We think the treatment model recommended herein is applicable to most outpatient settings, such as private practice configurations, agencies, and clinics associated with hospitals or universities. As mentioned earlier, our setting is an outpatient service that is part of a teaching clinic. Although we accept referrals from any professional source, most of our referrals come from family physicians. In this particular setting, there is no cost to clients or their families, as the service is covered by the government's health plan. Our setting is multidisciplinary in nature and although families are seen by a single therapist, cases are reviewed weekly in the context of a peer case review meeting. Our treatment time frame is relatively short term (three to four months, plus follow-up), and treatment blends brief solution-focused therapy with cognitive-behavioral therapy techniques. In cases in which a family member has been hospitalized, we do not recommend this treatment as an adjunctive treatment to inpatient care, due to the complexity and lack of privacy associated with inpatient treatment. However, it is important to start family therapy immediately upon discharge from an inpatient setting.

TREATMENT MODEL

Treatment goals are to establish safety, personal competence, and successful performance on the part of the suicidal family member, as well as healthy family functioning. Suicidal intent is viewed as a painful fall into helplessness on the part of the depressed family member, and the family is viewed as key in restoring hope and functioning in both the suicidal member and the whole family. The focus of treatment is on the present and the future rather than the past. It is recognized that although there are likely many conflictual issues upon which family members disagree, these are best understood from a position of strength once normal family functioning is restored. This is a strategic position, designed to instill confidence, interpersonal control, and personal effectiveness quickly. The intent is to provide family members with tools—a process—with which they can constructively influence one another. Solution-focused therapies work from the premise that (1) therapy should be brief, (2) people are not pathological, and (3) clients can change rapidly. Techniques draw heavily upon solution-focused counseling approaches as well as the techniques of Beck and colleagues (1979) and Lewinsohn and colleagues (1984) in their approaches to conceptualizing and managing clinical levels of depression.

Key to the proposed treatment is the "reciprocity hypothesis" (Silverstein and Auerbach, 1999; Stuart, 1980). The reciprocity hypothesis predicts that in social environments where members of a family have few benefits to exchange, interpersonal influence between family members will be low. The treatment model employs reciprocity training to help individuals within the family bargain effectively and fairly for personal benefits while requiring personal accountability. We appreciate that not all families with a suicidal member are dysfunctional or that they are necessarily contributing to the suicidal member's depression. Nonetheless, they are in a position to help structure the depressed family member's activities, and by participating themselves they reduce the illness stigma associated with the identified client.

Assessment

It is useful to distinguish between acute stage assessment, in which the risk of suicide is high, and regular assessment of a family with a suicidal member for purposes of family therapy. In the acute stage, much of the focus is on stabilization and crisis intervention, and the assessment focuses on safety issues. In the regular or comprehensive assessment stage, the suicidal family member is more stable, and the assessment focuses on broader personal and family issues.

Acute Stage Assessment

There are four important objectives to accomplish during the acute stage assessment:

- Opening communication—listening to gain understanding
- Evaluation of suicidal risk and previous attempts
- Safety evaluation
  — Means
  — Need for one-to-one monitoring
  — Destabilizing influences
- Assess possible referral networks

The first objective in acute stage evaluation is to open communication with the suicidal person by listening to gain understanding of his or her self-perception and expectations. The evaluation of suicidal risk involves determining where a client is on the continuum between (1) suicidal ideation but no intent, (2) intent but no plan, (3) the presence of a plan for suicide, and (4) the presence of a plan and the available means. Acute stage assessment also involves the evaluation of safety. This includes a thorough review of means, such as the presence (and removal) of firearms, poisons, toxic medications, and other means of suicide. Relevant information for the determination of means of suicide will come from a review of previous attempts (if any) and a review of any recent or current suicide plans. The second component of safety evaluation involves ensuring that the suicidal member is closely monitored. This may involve one-to-one coverage on the part of family members, relatives, or close friends if the family member continues to have suicidal ideation and a plan is present. The need for monitoring will become relaxed as communication becomes open, intent declines, and confidence and safety are restored. Finally, it is useful to evaluate for the presence of destabilizing influences available to the suicidal person. These could include alcohol and nonprescription drugs, exploitive friends/acquaintances, and the pursuit of written or Internet material on how to commit suicide. It is important that the clinician also inquire whether the family physician or any specialists (e.g., other mental health workers or agency, psychiatrist, etc.) are familiar with the primary client's suicide history, recent attempt, or depression history. If not, it is appropriate (with primary client's permission) to contact the family physician. Doing so will help mobilize a team approach to care.

Comprehensive Assessment Stage

Having evaluated the primary client during the acute phase of suicidal risk, the therapist will need to turn to the task of comprehensive and ongoing assessment. Comprehensive assessment encompasses the following areas:

- Suicide risk (ongoing monitoring)
- Psychometric assessment of level of depression (monitor)
- Within-family communication patterns
- Family members' respective views of key issues affecting primary client
- Primary client's perception of personal problems
- Level of functioning on part of primary client
- Faulty beliefs of primary client
- Personal goals of primary client

We recommend the use of a psychometric instrument such as the Beck Depression Inventory (Beck and Steer, 1987) in addition to the ongoing periodic assessment of suicide risk. This assessment should be repeated every two to four weeks in order to document change in level of depression symptomatology. In determining the family members' view of key issues affecting the primary client, as well as family communication patterns, it is necessary to talk to all family members. This can best be done in a group and should include the primary client. We try to avoid "pathologizing" the primary client by seeking information salient to the primary client from other family members while making it clear that the focus on family interactions is critical both for the recovery of the primary client and the health of the family unit. Often the suicidal family member has private concerns he or she does not wish to share with their family members (e.g., the occurrence of a sexual affair). If the therapist determines a secret to be a primary source of the suicidality, the therapist will have to decide whether individual or family intervention would be most appropriate for this limited time.

As practitioners, we need to take close account of the details of daily functioning of the primary client. This provides a picture of the primary client's level of personal organization and efficiency, which is useful for targeting treatment suggestions. In many cases, depression is due to a relative lack of social and personal organizational skills, such as a lack of assertiveness, disorganization due to poor problem-solving skills, or shyness. It is helpful for the therapist to have an idea of skill levels in these areas so that suggestions to remedy them can be made by the therapist, regardless of whether they are brought up by the primary client or other family members. As mentioned earlier, depressed individuals often harbor faulty beliefs or dysfunctional cognitions that serve to misinterpret relatively benign situations. Beliefs that a person should be liked by everyone or that the world should be fair are examples of the sort of faulty beliefs that need to be documented as they become apparent, so that the primary client can be encouraged to challenge these beliefs during the course of treatment. Finally, it is important to document a range of important, although perhaps dormant, goals held by the primary client. It is interesting to note that depressed people have often given up on reaching goals to the point that they are not even aware of them. Practitioners might prompt the primary client by asking, "If you weren't depressed, what are some of the important goals you would like to pursue?" The "miracle question" technique of solution-focused therapy ("Suppose one night, while you were asleep, there was a miracle and this problem was solved. What would be different?") can help activate problem-solving skills and allow the client to begin envisioning life without the obstruction of the problem.

Intervention

Educational

Role of Unconditional Family Support. Family members can often be perceived as judgmental or indifferent. We ask all family members to consciously and consistently provide an atmosphere of unconditional support. We ask them first if they are able to do so and then how they might accomplish this. If family members are unsure, we ask, "Would you like some suggestions to consider?"

Mood-Driven Performance and Cognitive Biases. All family members are often of the opinion that once the family member's depression lifts, the member will then be able to resume normal productivity. In other words, the depressed person will be ready to do things only when the depression starts to improve. We explain that self-esteem is a product of successful performance and that depressed persons may need to force themselves to do things even though they do not feel like it at the time. In this way, they increase the probability of feeling better about themselves because they have accomplished something. Family members are educated about cognitive biases that accompany depression. Specifically, attention and memory recall tend to be negatively biased (e.g., "Come to think of it, I've screwed up all my life"). It is explained that these cognitive biases will remit as depression improves. Depression is presented as a time-limited dysfunction caused by a combination of misperception of one's current and future prospects, the amount of control available, and withdrawal (i.e., nonperformance).

Reciprocal Behavioral Agreements. In an effort to make interpersonal influence constructive and to allow all family members to exert some control over others within the family sphere, reciprocal behavioral agreements are negotiated between family members, practiced, and both reviewed and updated on a weekly basis. This process is designed to enhance interpersonal influence in a positive manner to replace ineffectual means of interpersonal influence that often result in hostilities, withdrawal, and resentments. This is based on the premise that all members of a family have an age-appropriate right to have other family members do what they have committed themselves to. Of course, this works well only if it is reciprocal ("You do *this* for me and I'll agree to do *that* for you").

Action Steps

Ground Rules for Family Meetings. We suggest to family members that family meetings designed to negotiate behavioral agreements require everyone's presence. The meeting should be limited to an hour, and members are asked to be on their best behavior. That is to say, lengthy monologues, anger, criticism, and methods of unwanted influence are not allowed. In a bargaining table format, each family member is asked to request a specific and positive action from another family member and in return will entertain a reciprocal request for personal change on his or her part from the family member to whom he or she made the original request. Family members and therapists should not get weighted down with the equality of such requests. The idea is to mobilize the process with the assumption that the nature and value of requests will end up being relatively equal over time. Not every family member has to make a request of each remaining family member. Instead, any one member may have up to three requests (to keep things manageable) of any one member. Normally, any one family member will negotiate approximately five requests from other family members taken together. This is not a coercive system, and no family member needs to agree to a request if he or she does not wish to. However, that family member should encourage the requesting member to make a replacement request, in the spirit of good bargaining, should he or she decline. The parents may have a side agreement between themselves for purposes of privacy (assuming the primary client is one of the two parents), in which case they would feel more comfortable negotiating such matters as intimacy and finance.

Translating Complaints into Requests. Family dynamics are often characterized by complaints and blaming interactions in families in which there is a depressed or suicidal member, and it is likely that family interactions as a whole have been unrewarding. Family members, however, find it difficult to contribute in a positive and supportive manner when they feel ignored or "ripped off" by another family member. In keeping with the focus on the present and the future, we ask family members to translate their complaints into positive specific requests for purposes of bargaining in the context of family meetings. For example, "You are never on time!" may become "I would appreciate it if you would be ready to leave when you say you will." Similarly, family members are asked to be very specific about their requests. Accordingly, appeals for someone to change their personality, be mature, or have a better attitude are inappropriate. Instead, the practitioner might ask, "If John were to be more 'mature,' in your view, what would he do in this case?"

Reciprocal Behavioral Agreements. These agreements are negotiated among all family members, first during therapy and then during a weekly family meeting, the time for which is relatively convenient to all. An effort is made to have the meeting chaired by someone other than the most powerful figure within the family. The chairperson can rotate on a weekly basis. In keeping with the "best behavior" directive, all members should try and stay positive, focused, and supportive of one another.

Once there appears to be reasonable and reciprocal agreement among family members in the exchange of things requested of one another, family members are asked to commit to these undertakings for a one-week trial period, subject to review at the next family meeting. Further, all members are asked to commit to doing what they said they would do regardless of whether the other party complies with their request. All members are asked to keep track of how often they got what they asked for. In subsequent family meetings, clarifications and adjustments can be made and new requests can be added. Frequently, once a request is being performed routinely it is often dropped from the list as another request is added. In this way, the list becomes dynamic. It is expected that families will continue with this process for approximately five to eight meetings. Thereafter, as members become more skilled at this means of interpersonal influence within the family, the meeting is shortened and eventually replaced by more spontaneous requests between family members, without a formal meeting. Some families prefer to keep a brief family meeting on a weekly basis for purposes of anticipating issues and preparing for how they might be handled. In summary, this is a type of democratic governance that is initially formalized. This process is faded out as family members become adept in the art of positive influence.

Reversing the Direction of Aversive Interactions. Family members, like everyone, have a long memory for slights and perceived transgressions. Such "evidence" provides the basis for many aversive interchanges. We ask each family member to take personal responsibility for using positive methods of influence in the family. The definition of criticism is expanded to include being laughed at, being ignored, being taunted, or giving nonverbal signs of boredom, etc. We recommend a therapist ask all family members to refrain from all negative means of influence within the family. Instead, when they have a complaint, they are encouraged to translate it into a positive, specific request for the next family meeting. One of the most powerful means of interpersonal influence is to give positive recognition. Each family member is asked to find two credible and positive things to say about each member in the family every day. Again, they are asked to commit to this as part of their weekly behavioral agreement. We advise clients that compliments can be justified both on humanitarian and selfish grounds. Generally, everybody aims to please, and if given some encouragement in the form of a compliment it increases the probability that they will do so again. Compliments can include comments on personal appearance, observations of competence about events in or outside of the home, and the other person's thoughtfulness on virtually any manner. The idea is to bring to someone's attention something he or she did right and to underscore the responsibility of all family members for participating in this covenant.

Daily Structure for Primary Client. By definition, a suicidal or depressed person has given up. Accordingly, they need to be reintroduced into the advantages of daily structure. Structures are not meant to be unnecessarily confining or rigid. Instead, they are meant to pace sleeping and food intake and to create predictable efficiencies in performing the tasks that one wishes to engage in. However, the primary client within the family is likely to be somewhat fragile, undermotivated, and subject to negative mood and cognitive biases, and is not necessarily acting in his or her own best interest. The content of daily structure is usually determined the day or evening before and slotted into morning, afternoon, or evening time blocks as "things to be done." The primary client is encouraged to refer to this frequently and to cross off those things that are accomplished. This activity record helps good intentions become reality and serves to focus the primary client on performance. There is an obvious need to start slow and to graduate the demands of daily structure. We recommend that practitioners encourage the primary client to balance the daily activity to include social functions, activities outside the home, and leisure (e.g., group television, a leisurely bath). A common error is that the primary client is too ambitious, tending to cram too many difficult and/or unrealistic goals into a day. We find that just mobilizing the primary client in terms of minor activities, such as errands, small household tasks, paying a few small bills, etc., is helpful.

Pleasant Event Schedule for Primary Client. Depressed or suicidal clients tend to be hard on themselves. As a result, they usually have not, in recent times, accorded themselves pleasurable activities, as they view themselves as undeserving. Consequently, the normal pleasant activities we would all partake in have been discontinued. The problem with this is that the pleasure derived from participating in such activities is also discontinued by such avoidance. We encourage the primary client, with the help of other family members, to identify a wide range of pleasant activities that in the past he or she has either participated in or thought about participating in. These activities can be of a solitary nature or social. The intent is to have the primary client experiment with such activities to see if he or she enjoys them or not and to distribute them within the client's planned activities list (e.g., going out to movies with someone, eating favorite foods, fitness activities). Participating in such activities not only normalizes one's life and permits an opportunity for enjoyment, it also affords relief from rumination.

CASE EXAMPLE

Allison S. is a forty-three-year-old married mother who lives with her husband Dean and two teenage children. Although she claims a history of being "moody," she first became clinically depressed three months ago and has been unresponsive to several antidepressants. Recent stressors include a family move to an unfamiliar city (Dean had been transferred through his work); a suspicion that Dean was "burnt out" on their marriage and interested in other women; high rates of family conflict, especially with their daughter; unsatisfactory reentry into the job market after being a full-time mother for eighteen years; and weight gain. Being "a private person," Allison had not disclosed her growing dismay to Dean, anticipating he would gloss it over ("He has an answer for everything"). She overdosed with medication and was taken to the emergency room by Dean after an incoherent phone call she made to him at work.

This case illustration has been selected because it is so typical. In spite of the progress that women have made toward gender equality, men continue to have more power than women in traditional relationships largely because mothers are at a disadvantage in terms of earning power by virtue of having stepped out of the job market for child-rearing purposes. Given that no biological evidence exists to support gender differences in prevalence of depression, we, along with many others, assume that such gender differences reflect role strain. Yet the impact of these gender differences and role strain is often not recognized by the client. Allison's perception of the problem was, "I've failed. I'm redundant. I'm a problem to my family. It's too late." Her perceptions of the problems are not analytical and content-focused but rather pejorative and personal.

By the end of the comprehensive assessment stage, Allison had identified the following goals: to have friends, to have a meaningful job, to have more "happy times at home," to trust Dean, to be more physically active, to plan the future together, and to share the household workload. These goals are organized along a task continuum from easy to difficult. Allison is asked to select activities reflecting her goals at a level she can tolerate and routinely include them in her daily plans. In this manner, she is bringing important goals forward into her daily routine. For example, the goal of making new friends might involve initiating conversations with neighbors, volunteering for some neighborhood activity (e.g., community center), or taking noncredit evening classes for fun.

In family meetings, Allison's husband and her two children negotiated a variety of reciprocal agreements. Many of these agreements tied into Allison's personal goals. A partial list of the negotiated behavioral agreements includes:

Dean:
1. Cook three nights per week; responsible for vacuuming
2. Restrict work to forty-five hours per week and fully plan his spare time with Allison
3. Take Allison out one to two times per week and go for daily walks together
4. Listen to Allison's concerns/opinions without judgment

Allison:
1. Promise to tell Dean of serious mood swings so they deal with them together
2. Share her thoughts and opinions with Dean routinely
3. Allow their daughter to adopt her own dress code
4. Not to "screen" her son's phone calls

Daughter:
1. Leave name and phone numbers of where she will be when going out
2. Clean dinner dishes on weeknights

Son:
1. Allow sister equal choice in television channel selection
2. Be in bed by 11 p.m. on weeknights

Everyone:
1. Avoid all criticism of other family members
2. Give each other family member two sincere compliments per day

This list provides a flavor of the types of items frequently requested. It is worth reminding family members that they can all benefit from communicating clearly and positively in the form of making requests of other family members as well as being responsible in fulfilling agreed-upon requests made to them.

This family was seen for nine sessions and complied quite well with their planned assignments. The primary client, Allison, reported a reduction in depression symptoms (Beck Depression Inventory score of 12 [i.e., mild range]), no suicidal ideation, and a general sense of increased control and "forward thinking" in her life. Allison and Dean instituted a date night once a week and undertook to continue counseling. Dean began to spend family time on Sundays exploring the new city. Allison had submitted a job application to a community college. After two more sessions of family therapy, Allison and Dean requested couple therapy and focused on communication and sharing affection. Upon one-year telephone follow-up, these gains had endured and Allison had experienced no further episodes of depression.

In managing the suicidal client, the first tasks are to ensure safety and open communication. Another important therapeutic task is to offer hope. Suicidal clients may be confused and thinking unclearly, but they have decided to give up and need a coherent counterplan to inspire giving life another chance. We ask suicidal clients if they will agree to postpone that decision while they give therapy a try. Typically, we ask them to postpone consideration of suicide for three months, but have accepted a period as short as two days, upon the client's insistence. On each occasion, we diary date the review and bring it up with the primary client again, at that time. The basis of our request for postponement of suicidal consideration is that suicide is ultimately an irreversible civil right that requires more careful consideration than they have given the matter so far. Clients seem to respect this approach as long as therapeutic support is available and once they understand the episodic nature of depression and its biases as explained by the therapist.

STRENGTHS AND LIMITATIONS

Strengths

Our experiences with this approach to the management of suicidal individuals within a family have allowed us to identify a number of strengths for the general application of this approach. First of all, many therapists are familiar with family systems approaches and increasingly familiar with cognitive-behavioral approaches as well. The efficacy of cognitive-behavioral approaches for the treatment of depression has been well established in numerous clinical trials. The approach is structured and relatively easy to follow. We have found that families relate well to the "hands on" approach of these combined methods. Finally, although the prospect of suicide is highly disturbing, it is relatively rare. This approach might best be described as a preventive measure inasmuch as it focuses on many events that determine mood on a routine basis. From this point of view, it is very practical and easy to perform by family members.

Limitations

A structural limitation with this form of treatment is that it requires family involvement, which is logistically more difficult than is working only with the "identified client." A second limitation of this form of intervention is that not all members of the family may be available (e.g., shift work), willing, or able to participate. In these cases, the practitioner must adapt the therapeutic program and may end up treating the client alone.

INTEGRATION WITH PSYCHIATRIC SERVICES AND ROLE OF MEDICATION

When moderate to serious suicide risk is present, it is always advisable to pursue a psychiatric consultation. Usually, this is done prior to referral to a family therapist, but since the course of depression is variable, the therapist should be prepared for the possibility that the client's severity could increase over the treatment period. Warning signs include sleep deprivation, physical agitation (e.g., muscle tremors in legs), suicidal preoccupation, advanced avoidance (e.g., inability to get out of bed for daily activities), and loss of sufficient concentration and attention to participate in verbal therapy. In this case, a psychiatric consultation is warranted. The therapist may have a working relationship with a psychiatrist, which would facilitate a rapid consultation. Otherwise, the client's family physician may have a similar relationship with a psychiatrist. If the situation is urgent, or if none of these options are available, a visit to the local hospital's emergency room by the primary client may be necessary to access a crisis psychiatric consultation.

If one or more of the above conditions is present, an antidepressant medication should be tried. The current SSRI class of antidepressants are safe, well studied, and produce minimal side effects. Properly presented, clients will view antidepressant medication as complementary to family therapy and necessary to produce stability. The normal short course for antidepressants is three to six months; therapeutic effects can be expected in two to three weeks. When psychiatric or other service providers are involved, a plan is required involving clear communication and agreement in order to avoid the predictable problems of working in isolation. In the worst case, service providers inadvertently end up working at cross-purposes with one another, and the primary client and family are often caught in the middle.

CULTURAL AND GENDER ISSUES

As a field, family therapy has become increasingly aware of and sensitive to ethnic legacies of families, including gender, age, race, socioeconomic privileges and barriers, physical abilities and handicapping conditions, spiritual dimensions, and so forth. When life-threatening issues such as suicide are introduced, therapists are reminded to encourage the family to educate the therapist on critical differences and strengths so that the therapy can maximize family resources. Of course, although therapists typically are very careful not to impose personal values on families and strive to be culturally sensitive, there is the very real position that some values are universally destructive (i.e., cult group suicide, wife or child beating, etc.). Feminist family therapists, however, do not advocate therapist neutrality, as they recognize that North American culture, and hence the family, continues to be steeped in patriarchal values. Simply asking couples whether they both believe in and practice gender equity in terms of role division and workload expectations may not be sufficient. As differential power in terms of role and workload expectations continues to favor men, and women continue with their "second shift" in managing the household after work, such imbalances can contribute to depression in women. This imbalance can be usefully addressed in terms of the negotiated behavioral agreements, which feature prominently in this treatment model.

In the event of physical abuse within the family, therapists must consider the immediate safety and well-being of the victim, as well as the legal constraints of working conjointly with abusive couples (prohibited in several U.S. states). This may involve assistance in relocating a family member. Similarly, in cases of sustained and severe verbal abuse, the therapist must work closely with the victim in order to consider alternatives in living arrangements. These are difficult ethical issues that cannot be avoided when dealing with this population, but these are issues with which all experienced clinicians are familiar.

FUTURE DIRECTIONS

Due to obvious ethical considerations concerning the treatment of suicidal individuals, they cannot be randomly assigned to clinical trials. As a result, it is more difficult to examine issues such as treatment efficacy. However, much is known about the effectiveness of cognitive-behavioral therapy in the treatment of depression and family therapy in general. It is our strong belief that the future course of this, or any, intervention model is best informed by a well-rounded assessment program. In the proposed model, there are daily (e.g., planned "things to do" lists of the primary client), weekly (e.g., performance reports on negotiated behavioral agreements), and periodic symptom-status measures (e.g., rate of suicidal ideation, psychometric test results on the presence of depression symptoms and family functionality scale), all of which offer opportunities to guide treatment and compare across cases. Sharing of such information in various formats will allow conclusions about its application across different populations to be evaluated. The Internet now offers a promising new way of comparing cases among interested practitioners, regardless of distance.

REFERENCES

Beck, A. T., Rush, A. J., Shaw, B. F., and Emery, G. (1979). *Cognitive therapy of depression*. New York: Guilford.

Beck, A. T. and Steer, R. A. (1987). *Manual for the revised Beck Depression Inventory*. San Antonio, TX: Psychological Corporation.

Brown, J. C. (1996). Adolescent suicide. *Child and adolescent therapy*. New York: The Hatherleigh Guide (Volume 5), pp. 251-274.

Bucy, J. E. (1994). Internalizing affective disorders. In R. J. Simeonsson (Ed.), *Risk, resilience and prevention: Promoting the well-being of all children* (pp. 219-238). Paul Brookes Publisher.

Estrada, A. U. and Pinsof, W. M. (1995). The effectiveness of family therapies for selected behavioral disorders of childhood. *Journal of Marital and Family Therapy, 21*, 403-440.

Gatz, M., Pedersen, N. L., Plomin, R., Nesselroade, J. R., and McClearn, G. E. (1992). Importance of shared genes and shared environments for symptoms of depression in older adults. *Journal of Abnormal Psychology, 101*, 701-708.

Hafen, B. Q. and Frandsen, K. J. (1986). *Youth suicide: Depression and loneliness*. Provo, UT: Behavioral Health Associates.

Lewinsohn, P. M., Antonuccio, D. O., Steinmetz, J. L., and Teri, L. (1984). *The coping with depression course: A psychoeducational intervention for unipolar depression*. Eugene, OR: Castalia.

McLean, P. D. and Taylor, S. (1992). Severity of unipolar depression and choice of treatment. *Behaviour Research and Therapy, 30*, 443-451.

National Center for Health Statistics (1998). Fast Stats A to Z <http://www. cdc.gov/nchswww/fastats/suicide/htm>, May 28.

Rapee, R. M. (1997). Potential role of childrearing practices in the development of anxiety and depression. *Clinical Psychology Review, 17*(1), 47-67.

Silverstein, L. B. and Auerbach, C. F. (1999). Deconstructing the essential father. *American Psychologist, 54*(6), 397-407.

Stuart, R. B. (1980). *Helping couples change.* New York: Guilford Press.

Wells, K. B., Stewart, A., Hays, R. D., Burnam, M. A., Rogers, W., Daniels, M., Berry, S., Greenfield, S., and Ware, J. (1989). The functioning and well-being of depressed patients: Results from the Medical Outcome Study. *Journal of American Medical Association, 262*(7), 914-919.

U.S. Department of Health and Human Services (USDHHS), (1993). *Depression in primary care: Volume 1. Detection and diagnosis.* AHCPR Pub. No. 93-0550. Rockville, MD: Author.

Chapter 11

Family Therapy in Walk-In Mental Health Centers: The Eastside Family Centre

Arnold Slive
Nancy McElhcran
Ann Lawson

We once assumed that long term therapy was the base from which all therapy was to be judged. Now it appears that therapy of a single interview could become the standard for estimating how long or how successful therapy should be. (Haley, 1993)

INTRODUCTION

This chapter describes a walk-in counseling service in which clients are afforded immediate family therapy for a wide range of mental health concerns. The service is provided at the Eastside Family Centre, a community-based mental health resource that is strategically located in a busy shopping mall in a high-needs area of Calgary, Alberta, Canada, a rapidly growing city of 900,000 people. Wood's Homes, an agency that focuses on treatment services for adolescents and their families, conceived the Centre in 1990. A task force of concerned community representatives, funders, and service providers, guided its development. The Centre offers a one-stop, multifaceted, multipartnered resource that is linked to existing services on the east side of Calgary and overseen by a community advisory council. The walk-in counseling service is the centerpiece and the core from which other services are created.

SETTING

Demographic and Political Context

The east side of Calgary is an area of high ethnic diversity, high density, and low socioeconomic status. Single-parent-headed families are in the majority; the remainder are primarily two-parent working families. A large number of first- or second-generation immigrant families live in this area. At the time of the Centre's inception in 1990, this area was identified as both in high need and under serviced. There was a shortage of schools, health centers, and mental health services. Seventy percent of the city's child protection referrals came from this quadrant of the city. Compounding these factors, governments in Canada were in a phase of cutbacks to medical, educational, and social services. Citizens were concerned about the inaccessibility of services, long waiting lists, and fees. New approaches to service delivery were needed. A set of consumer-oriented principles was developed to guide the responses to these consumer issues.

Philosophical Principles

The service is accessible. The hours are convenient for families (afternoon and evening during the week; Saturdays during the day), and anyone can come for a walk-in session. There are no restrictions and no red tape. An individual family member will be seen or a whole family or community group.

The service is affordable. A combination of government contracts, partnerships, fund-raising, and volunteering of time by community professionals makes it possible for community members to access the service at *no fee.*

The service provides an immediate response to community needs. Clients can come when *they decide* they are most in need. This principle contrasts with more traditional forms of service delivery in which clients are screened, "intaked," then given a future appointment or placed on a waiting list. Community-based referral sources have described the walk-in service as their "savior," because now they know that they can recommend a resource that is immediately available.

The service is designed to be a safety net for the community. Schools, hospitals, crisis lines, community agencies, primary care physicians, and others send people to the walk-in service because they have confidence that their clients will be served immediately and in a manner that respects and works in harmony with other community resources. The service has become a primary resource for persons who have experienced very recent traumatic events.

The walk-in counseling service is committed to working in close collaboration with other existing community resources. New components of the Eastside Family Centre are developed only when there is an identified community need and an existing service does not fully address that need. Formal partnerships with other organizations are in place so that resources can be shared; some organizations have satellite offices at the Centre. An example of this community cooperation and trust is the utilization of the walk-in service by other counseling agencies for clients who are on their waiting list.

The walk-in counseling service is "owned" by the community. A community advisory council, consisting of both community and service agency representatives, guides the Centre in directions that fit the community. The council reviews new ideas for services, and community approval is sought before implementation takes place.

The walk-in counseling service provides a session of family therapy. It is not a screening service; it is not an assessment and triage service. The focus of the therapist is to learn what the clients want and to endeavor to give it to them. It is a context that supports pragmatics, utilization of client resources, and responsiveness to immediate need.

The service utilizes an egalitarian approach to family therapy. The clients are viewed as equals, and the therapy process is a form of consultation in which the consultee is the client family. Paralleling the therapy process is a synergy that develops among clients, therapists, advisory council, and community which supports an evolution of services to fit client need and the mandate of the Centre.

Community Therapist Program

Most of the service is delivered by what we call "community therapists." This therapist group is a combination of experienced master's and doctoral level professionals who volunteer their time; practicum students from graduate programs in psychology, social work, and nursing; family physicians; and recent graduates accumulating supervised hours for their credentialing. The supervision of the community therapists is built into the service delivery model; that is, therapists work in a team format with the availability of one-way mirrors and supervision. One highly experienced professional, designated as the shift coordinator, is responsible for the quality of the work during that shift.

Our research indicates that the community therapists get involved at the Centre for a variety of reasons (Whitford, 1994). They appreciate the quality of the professional collegiality and the experience that they can gain with a very wide variety of presenting concerns in a short amount of time. They have an opportunity to network with a large number of professional colleagues (presently there are about fifty community therapists). Students and credentialing therapists appreciate the quality and quantity of live supervision. These individuals find the clinical work rewarding, despite the fact that many of the clients who access the walk-in service have serious mental health issues and are labeled as "hard to serve" or "resistant." These clients access the service at a moment of need when they have decided that they want to talk. A synergy is created, and, in most instances, the clients express gratitude to the therapist for their assistance.

In addition to the community therapists, the walk-in service is also delivered by staff who are seconded from a variety of partner organizations. This arrangement augments the opportunity to direct clients back to the community resources that best fit the clients needs.

Structure of the Service

The Centre operates under the umbrella of Wood's Homes, a private, nonprofit mental health center serving adolescents and their families through a wide variety of residential, day treatment, outreach, and community programs. A twenty-four-hour mobile crisis team, in-home counseling, and a focused five-session brief counseling service are supported by Wood's Homes and delivered through the Centre.

The walk-in counseling service is open during convenient afternoon, evening, and weekend hours. It operates in four-hour "shifts" with three to five therapists working as a team during each shift. When clients walk through the door of the Centre they are greeted with respect, openness, and dignity. They are invited to sit in a comfortable waiting room with play activities for children. The clients are requested to complete two forms. These forms are designed, with the help of the advisory council, to be user-friendly and provide the client with the opportunity to guide the therapy team in developing useful solutions to the particular problem. Filling out these forms is always optional. Included on the forms is a written explanation of the therapy process.

The therapy process is explained again at the beginning of the session. The client is offered information about the team/consultation process that will be part of the session. They are asked whether they elect to have a team behind a one-way mirror, participating directly in their session, or whether they choose a traditional office setting. Clients who give permission for a team behind a mirror receive the maximum benefit from the process. The opportunity that arises to "put heads together" over the course of the client interview enhances the generation of ideas and supports the creativity, learning, and "community spirit" of the volunteer therapists in relation to the clients needs. Even when clients choose not to use the mirror, the therapist always consults with the team at the intersession break. Thus, all walk-in sessions have a team consultation.

The format for the clinical work at the Centre is guided by the Milan systemic approach (Boscolo et al., 1987) and consists of five parts: presession, interview, intersession, delivery of intervention, and postsession. The senior therapist designated as shift coordinator is available for consultation throughout the shift. At the end of the session, clients are thanked for coming and invited to return at their discretion. Approximately 20 percent of clients return for another walk-in session within a year, sometimes with the same issue or, just as often, to talk about something else. Due to the numbers of therapists who work at the Centre, clients are advised that it is likely that they will see a different therapist if they should return. They are also informed that a brief and confidential note of their visit is documented.

Formal Training Programs

A certificate training program in single-session therapy involving formal course work and supervised clinical practice has been in place since 1994. The Centre has gained a reputation as a graduate and postgraduate training venue for psychologists, nurses, social workers, and physicians. The Centre's two consulting psychiatrists find it a rich training ground for their residents to learn about psychiatric disorders. Medical students comment on the depth of their experiences, particularly in relation to the variety of critical mental health issues they face in the therapy room (Slive et al., 1995; Lawson, McElheran, and Slive, 1997).

TREATMENT MODEL

From its inception, no single model of therapy has been utilized at the walk-in counseling service. Those therapists who developed the service lean toward family systems orientations that emphasize brief forms of interventions, which take a keen interest in utilizing already-existing client resources. The therapists have always worked to discover those approaches to family therapy that would be most effective in this unusual therapy context. The overall aim of the service is to provide consumers with an outcome that they can "point to" by the end of their single session; the outcomes are not limited to assessment and referral. Regardless of orientation, the very nature of a single, fifty-minute session dictates an attention to pragmatism (Amundson, 1996) and a very clear understanding of how to organize the session. Over the course of eleven years of experience with this work, the therapists have developed a number of practice guidelines.

Relationship Building

Despite the extraordinarily brief nature of the service, the intent is to develop long-term relationships with community members. We want to be perceived as always there, always available. This is accomplished in several ways. First, no one is turned away from the service. Anyone can come, and the consumer can decide on the most appropriate time for the session. Second, clients are received in a friendly, inviting, dignified manner and wait in a comfortable space with an open play area for children. Third, clients are asked to fill out a user-friendly form that does not pry about personal information and is designed to give clients an opportunity to guide the therapist and begin to think about solutions.

For approximately 50 percent of our clients, this is their first experience with professional counseling of any kind (Miller, Slive, and Protinsky, 1997). The therapists feel a responsibility to make this an experience that increases the likelihood that clients will utilize professionals in the future. The fact that clients now identify a major referral source as word of mouth suggests that the Centre has had some success at developing long-term relationships with the community.

Setting the Parameters

When the client enters the therapy room, the therapist carefully explains the nature of the service. The intent is to set the context for the client in a respectful and informative manner. This is important, because therapy is an unusual context for most people; walk-in therapy is especially unusual. The therapist might say:

> My name is Jane Doe. I'm a clinical psychologist by profession, and I volunteer some of my services to the Eastside Family Centre. Let me explain how we work. As you know, this is a walk-in counseling service; you can come as you have, without an appointment; there is no fee. We'll meet for about fifty minutes. After we've talked for a half hour or so, I'll take a break to consult with my colleagues about our conversation. Then I'll come back and share our feedback and ideas about the questions that you have presented to us today. After our meeting, I'll write a summary of our session; that way, if you decide to come back at some time in the future you will not have to start over again at the beginning.
>
> The information you share with us today is confidential and will not be shared outside of this Centre without your written consent. The exceptions to our rules about confidentiality are in situations in which a person is at risk (e.g., child abuse, harm to self or others) or if our records are legally subpoenaed. In those situations we are required to share information outside of the Centre. Do you have any questions either about my qualifications or about the Centre?

The First Question

When a therapist has fifty minutes, every minute counts. The therapist is continually reflecting on what to ask and what not to ask. We have been experimenting with first questions that do not even ask about the problem; instead, we focus attention upon the following:

- "How will you and I know at the end of our meeting that this has been useful to you?"
- "What will work for you today?"
- "How will you and I know that things are on the road to getting better?"

Often, when asked these kinds of questions, clients will initially respond with "problem talk." It is accepted that this is where the client prefers to start. Nevertheless, a seed has been planted that the purpose of the meeting is a pragmatic and useful outcome.

The Rules of the Salesperson

Addressing what the client wants from the session is more important than addressing the presenting concern. The fact that a client's presenting concern is that "thoughts in my head are racing out of control" does not orient the therapist to potential outcomes. More helpful is learning that the client wants to know "if I am crazy" or that "I am afraid to tell my psychiatrist that I do not want to be on medication." This is a "consumer-driven" service that borrows from the vocabulary of the salesperson:

Rule 1: Find out what the customers want.
Rule 2: Give it to them.

Clients do not always express what they want in a straightforward manner. Sometimes the therapist must read between the lines. Therapists who are new to single sessions often become more engrossed with "the problem" or "the solution" and forget to explore the question of what the client wants. For example, some clients are not looking for a solution. They just want to talk. We accept that. The Centre is so committed to the idea that the therapist must, first and foremost, address what the client wants that it has added a third rule to the previous two:

Rule 3: Give it to them some more!

There are limitations to these rules. The Centre is, after all, serving the community as well as individual clients. Thus, when children are at risk, the appropriate authorities are informed. When a woman is being assaulted by her partner, she is provided information about the abuse cycle and its impacts, patriarchal social structures, and resources that will provide for her safety, whether she asks for this information or not.

Competency-Based Resource Model

In this consumer-driven approach, the client is always in charge. For example, when clients present more than one concern, they are asked to tell us which is the most important one to address today, or the therapist seeks to aggregate concerns under incorporating "themes" or unifying descriptions.

Of paramount interest in all sessions is to search for already existing client resources. During the session, clients will be asked to describe what is currently working well, what kinds of things they have done to keep the problem "at bay" for even brief periods of time, or the strengths they have used to keep the problem from overtaking every aspect of their life. The answers to these questions provide ideas for end-of-session interventions.

All Sessions Are Family Therapy Sessions

Before a walk-in session ever begins, the client/family has already decided which family members will attend. Many sessions involve a single family member; others include various combinations of members. Irrespective of who attends a session, the therapists view every session as a family therapy session. Family therapy is more a way of thinking than a head count of clients in the room. Our understanding of "the problem" and our ideas for interventions are based on how the problem fits into a larger social context. Questions asked of the clients are intended to flesh out this understanding (for both therapist and client). We are at least as interested in who is *not* present in the session as who is present. A common end-of-session intervention is to ask the family to return with absent family members.

Useful Questions

Two questions that facilitate the therapist's quest for direction in the fifty-minute session are:

- "Why now?"
- "What makes this a problem?"

The "Why now?" question addresses the immediate factors that led to a decision to seek therapy now. The "What makes this a problem?" question helps a therapist appreciate a client's idiosyncratic basis for defining something as problematic.

Other frequently used questions include solution-focused scaling questions and miracle questions (de Shazer, 1985), empty-chair questions ("If your husband were present today, what would he suggest doing about your daughter's poor school attendance?"), or "externalizing the problem" questions. Questions about beliefs are also useful. For example: "Do you believe that I understand enough of your story?" (Wright, 1989).

Prior to the intersession break, most clients are asked: "Are there any questions you wish I would have asked that I didn't get to?" As well, we often return to the very first question: "What do you want today?"

Pragmatic Interventions

Interventions utilized in the walk-in counseling service are derived from a number of models that are favored by the therapists who work there. As stated previously, the approach is not based on any single model but rather subscribes to the philosophical principle of pragmatism. The therapists strive to utilize that which is likely to be effective in this therapeutic context at this point in time (Amundson, 1996). This does not mean that the therapists who work in the walk-in service do not favor certain models of family therapy over others. Most therapists utilize ideas taken from solution-focused, narrative, strategic, and Ericksonian models of practice (e.g., de Shazer, 1985; Haley, 1987; Madanes, 1981; O'Hanlon and Weiner-Davis, 1989; White, 1986). The primary intention, nevertheless, is to make a best guess at what interventions fit at a certain moment in time for a certain client, irrespective of therapeutic model.

Interventions

In keeping with a pragmatic approach, our intervention strategies are limited only by therapist creativity. We always begin the intervention section of the interview with commendations: highlights of client/family strengths (McElheran and Harper-Jaques, 1994). Families almost always respond favorably to these comments and often become more receptive to what follows. The commendations are usually followed by the therapist's feedback of the family's story, often framed in a manner that will enhance receptivity to the intervention. The frame may be based on developmental, narrative, or solution-focused ideas. This retelling of the family story is then followed with ideas for addressing the "wants" of the family. Usually, more than one idea is presented—a menu of options that may include ideas to think about or experiments to try on for size. Centre staff aim to think small in the use of interventions, adhering to the systemic belief that one perturbation in a system can promote significant change. Interventions are always based on strengths and resources (both internal and external) that family members have presented in earlier parts of the session. At times, interventions are presented by utilizing the format of a reflecting team (Andersen, 1991).

Client-Therapist Relationship

The position of the clients in relation to therapy (i.e., how close or available they are for therapy proper) (e.g., Watzlawick, Weakland, and Fisch, 1974) needs to be addressed in single-session work. Frameworks such as the solution-focused approach's visitor-complainant-customer dimension (Berg and Miller, 1992) are useful to keep in mind for the ideas they provide about the relationship between client and therapist and how to address the differing positions of the clients. The Centre revised these terms to visitor-surveyor-customer to ensure a respectful attitude toward all clients. Many trainees report that attending to this dimension can restrain the beginning therapist from providing more help than the clients want in their fifty minutes. Eastside Family Centre research (Miller, Slive, and Protinsky, 1997) suggests that the single aspect of the service that is most appreciated by clients is the opportunity to be heard. Often, being heard is the most that clients want from their session.

Therapy As Consultation

Therapists are encouraged to conceptualize the service as a form of consultation in which the consultee is the client/family. Ideas emerge during the course of the therapeutic conversation that clients can take with them to try out. This framework is respectful of clients and reminds the therapist that the client is in charge of the therapy.

Follow-Up

We usually do not arrange follow-up meetings; clients return of their own volition. However, strategies for follow-up are employed when a situation is assessed to be high risk. These strategies might include utilization of the Centre's twenty-four-hour crisis service, a return visit (by appointment) with a consulting psychiatrist, or accessing either a hospital emergency service or child protection services.

CASE EXAMPLES

An Opportunity to Listen and Understand

This case example illustrates the provision of client-centered crisis diffusion using a single-session framework. A serious disagreement is resolved in a family in which immigrant and second-generation family members clashed over a decision-making process that was wracked with powerful negative emotions.

It is 1 p.m. at the walk-in center; the doors are just opening. A worried, middle-aged couple comes in with their young adult son, requesting to talk to a doctor. They explain that their son has just been discharged from the hospital after a three-day stay in the psychiatric ward. The hospital staff has recommended that they come here for further help. The therapist explains that she is not a medical doctor, but there is a psychiatrist working with her today who can observe the session behind the one-way mirror.

The parents take turns describing the fear and dread they have encountered over the past few weeks. At first, their son says very little, although he offers corrections and explanations when his parents attempt to explain their story in a language they have learned only since coming to Canada nineteen years ago. He admits that he has discharged himself against medical advice and expresses his own fear about what the medications he received might be doing to his mind. He also expresses frustration and anger when his parents speak about the anxiety and shame that have enveloped them as they struggle to deal with their only son's sudden onset of mental illness.

In order to validate the parents' concerns while still leaving space for the young man to enter the conversation more wholeheartedly, the therapist reviews the conversation highlights, seeking frequent confirmations but using more neutral language. At the request of the team behind the mirror, the therapist asks the young man what his younger sister would say about his situation if she were here today. The young man becomes tearful and relates almost word-for-word his mother's fears and worries, attributing them to his beloved sister, and concedes that his current bizarre thoughts and behavior may be worrisome for himself as well as others.

At the intersession, the team members hypothesize that the young man may have experienced a psychotic break that was terrifying both for himself and his family members. The family's culture seems to support a shame-based model of mental illness, and the young man's desire to leave the hospital quickly can be viewed as an attempt to protect his parents from further embarrassment. The team chooses to focus on the entire family's request to assist with alleviating their intense sense of fear, shame, and dread, rather than the parents' initial request to make their son listen to reason and do what the doctors say. The psychiatric consultant wonders about a possible sudden-onset neurological event because of the description of a few unique and unusual symptoms.

The therapist returns to find a noticeable change in the atmosphere of the room. The parents are speaking in a respectful and kindly way to their son. He is attentive to the therapist and comments positively on her observations and feedback. They respond appreciatively to the recommendations offered by the team. They appear relieved by the team's description of the behavior resulting in hospitalization as a possible physical illness rather than a flaw in character or parenting style. The son agrees to readmit himself to hospital in order to complete a neurological assessment. On a client satisfaction survey form given to all clients after the session, the father writes "Thanks go to the team and the doctor who made my son listen to us," while the son writes on his form, "The session helped my parents understand me better."

Traumatic Loss: A Journey from Remorse to Recovery

This case illustrates the notion that clients can become attached to a place where they feel comfortable and believe they will be well served versus becoming attached to a particular therapist. It also illustrates that the walk-in counseling service is not, in actuality, a single-session service; rather, it is a walk-in service where clients receive therapy one session at a time.

It is Monday evening. A pair of troubled and exhausted parents has arrived at the walk-in counseling service accompanied by their angry and resentful sixteen-year-old son, Jason. Jason sits as far away from his parents as possible. The parents choose one of the couches in the Centre reception area and huddle together filling out the forms they were offered as they came in the door. This is not the first time they have experienced exhaustion or worry. It is, however, the first time they have come for counseling. It was recommended by a friend as an "effective service, one that has good therapists who are respectful and offer good ideas in one session. You don't have to go back unless you want to."

As their story unfolds, we learn that Jason has had a year of turmoil; trouble has been at the center of his life for most of that time. Jason entered high school at a time when his father, Bob, lost his job. While his mother, Cheryl, and Bob were focused on finding new employment opportunities for Bob, Jason was seeking new adventures with a peer group of which his parents did not approve. Jason became increasingly noncompliant with house rules and routines, was using language the parents found unacceptable, and as recently as this past weekend was arrested for shoplifting in a mall. His school grades were dropping from a solid grade average to failing marks. Today, Jason's basketball coach threatened to remove Jason from the team if his school attendance did not improve. Jason also reported he had a medical condition and was refusing to take the required medication. Bob and Cheryl are most concerned about Jason's peer group, believing his change in habits and behavior is a direct result of peer influence. They do not know how to bring Jason back into the family unit.

The family members are asked what they want for themselves and the family that evening. All members have arrived at a point where they want change. No one is prepared to go on living together with this level of tension and disharmony in the home. Jason is tired of having his parents yell at him, and the parents are tired of yelling. Jason misses his old peer group and wants to reconnect with them even though he is not sure how to go about this. His parents miss them too. Jason wants to do better in school and, in particular, he does not want to leave the basketball team, a sport in which he excels. The parents are supportive of his desire for success. When does Jason think all this will happen? "Soon," he believes. The parents wonder what is getting in the way of making it happen now. Jason is not sure, but says he is interested in continuing to talk to his parents and work out their relationship at home while he figures out how to reconnect with old friends at school. The family leaves this session with a sense they are on the road to a different connection with one another. The therapy team offers ideas for them to take with them in relation to their communication as well as suggestions for staying on the track they have chosen. They say they will return if they want other ideas or if they want to tell us how they are doing on this new journey.

Unfortunately, trauma is around the corner. That night, Jason has a fatal accident. While swimming with friends, he accepts a challenge to swim to the middle of the lake and cannot get back. Why him? "My fault," says Bob. "Fate," says Cheryl. The parents begin the struggle to make sense of their loss at a time when new hope was beginning to emerge.

The parents return to the Eastside Family Centre, the place where they last connected with their son and where they felt they were heard and understood. They meet with a new therapist. In response to the question about their most pressing concern this time, Cheryl writes that for this single session she and Bob need the therapist to help them with their pain and help them to make sense of their loss. Cheryl also writes that Bob has previously undergone psychiatric care for depression. She is currently worried for his safety. What she mainly wants from this single session is assurance that Bob will not attempt suicide out of a sense of guilt over Jason's death.

A walk-in counseling service, such as the Eastside Family Centre, that offers single-session therapy where each session is viewed as its own whole, also offers connections to other counseling and mental health resources. The Centre, with its continuum of services, becomes a pathway for clients to receive consistent and qualified care (Slive et al., 1995). For Bob and Cheryl, the path they traveled included ongoing counseling at the Centre's five-session brief counseling service and then in the community. Included in the process of therapy was psychiatric consultation and ongoing psychiatric services for Bob, who struggled with thoughts of ending his life in order to join Jason. Support was also available for Cheryl, who worried about Bob while grieving the loss of her son. For the couple, the path also led to community-based bereavement counseling and a new supportive peer group. All of these therapeutic resources came about as a result of the family's initial decision to access a service they had heard about from a friend. Their experience led them to return again and again for walk-in sessions and connection to community resources until their need for closure and peace of mind was met.

The availability and accessibility of the walk-in service at moments of client need and at a time of intense pain is highlighted by Bob and Cheryl's situation. They became their own consultants as to what would best fit for them in grieving the loss of their son and moving on with their lives. At the end of a year, Bob and Cheryl "walked back in" to the Centre to tell the therapy team of that particular day that they were doing alright. The weekend past had brought them to a place where they could spread their son's ashes and find peace in the ritual. They thanked the team and were thanked in return for sharing this part of their lives.

STRENGTHS AND LIMITATIONS

Strengths of the Model

The Centre advertises itself as "immediate, accessible, affordable." Clients are not frustrated by the cost, waiting lists, or screening and intake interviews. For the therapists, there is no downtime as a result of no-shows or cancellations. There is minimal paperwork (a brief computer template to complete at the end of each session) and rarely any follow-up phone calls. The service is open evenings and Saturdays. The location, close to a busy rapid-transit station and in a building providing a variety of professional services, is both convenient and anonymous. The resource-based model of treatment supports clients in finding appropriate community services, both formal and informal, and allows clients to choose the level and intensity of further assistance. There is no cost to the client for the single session. The primary funder views the service as solidly cost-effective.

The single-session model is pragmatic and appealing to clients who are taking their first step toward problem relief. Drawing on research that indicates that the modal number of psychotherapy sessions is a single interaction (Talmon, 1990), the Centre's method of service delivery accommodates the research findings in a planned way. If therapy has the potential to do harm to clients, single sessions provide less of an opportunity for harm to occur. A single session sets the client in a position to be in charge of each stage of the process of uncovering solutions to the presenting dilemma.

A team of therapists who collaborate in a learning/teaching model delivers the service. Therapists have the opportunity to teach and to learn with their colleagues. Students have the opportunity to work with a particular supervisor to explore and consolidate a therapeutic model, while learning from other experienced therapists who have already done so. Therapists see a wide range of presenting concerns and are kept on their creative toes by the need to respond effectively to clients in one hour. The community therapists who donate professional time at the Eastside Family Centre appreciate the opportunity to contribute to their community in ways that lead to immediate problem relief and improved family and individual functioning.

This climate of support and respect that encompasses both the therapist-client relationship and professional colleague relationship contributes to community well-being like ripples in a pond. The Centre is always one of the first social service organizations to see the fallout from significant cultural and economic changes. The close connection of the Centre with the local community provides firsthand information about the "pulse" of the community. The members of the advisory council bring information and ideas to the Centre from a wide variety of sources. New and problematic personal issues that arise in the community, such as gambling addiction, Internet infidelity, or family homelessness, are dealt with at the Centre in sufficient volume to develop and refine useful therapeutic strategies. The Centre is at the forefront of coordinated community responses to larger social issues, such as community violence, hospital closures, or social service cutbacks. The Centre is regularly invited to join both community-based and agency-based partnerships to address particular issues in a coordinated way and is often in a position to initiate the formation of such partnerships.

Research Findings

Since 1990, the Eastside Family Centre has grown in depth and breadth. The centre served 260 clients in the year of its opening. In 1999, 2,022 walk-in sessions occurred; in 2000, there were 2,016 walk-in sessions. The walk-in, resource-based, single-session counseling model remains the core service. It continues to be unique in concept and service delivery. While other partner agencies and community resources offer essential services to the community and augent the work of the Centre, the Eastside Family Centre has become an increasingly important and supportive resource to other systems such as schools, police, hospitals, and to other mental health counseling agencies. Client satisfaction with the walk-in service is consistently between 83 and 90 percent. A study by Miller, Slive, and Protinsky (1997) also reports satisfaction with the reception (85.4 percent), clarity of forms (83.8 percent), first impressions of the Centre (77.6 percent), team approach (80.1 percent), and therapist explanation of confidentiality (95 percent). This study compares favorably with others of its kind (Talmon, 1990; Talmon, Hoyt, and Rosenbaum, 1990). Preliminary results of an outcome study (Miller, in process) suggest that approximately two-thirds of clients contacted two to six months after their single walk-in session report improvement in their presenting concern. This compares favorably with research into psychotherapy outcomes that focus on multisession therapy and raises the question of whether single sessions should be the standard by which longer-term psychotherapy is judged.

Limitations of the Model

The single-session model does not fit all client situations. A client who is looking for an ongoing therapist/client relationship to meet multiple needs or who is looking for friendship or a relationship to fill a void in life will not have those needs met with this model. Some clients come expecting to begin a multisession process that will unfold over a considerable length of time. When they learn that they may return at any time to continue a conversation about their issue, some are disappointed that the same therapist may not be available to them. The Centre has addressed this obstacle to client satisfaction by developing a brief counseling service that provides up to five sessions with one therapist. Referrals are made to this service for clients who have a very specific issue that they wish to continue to address and who, for some apparent reason, do not want to use the services of other longer-term counseling agencies in the city. A typical referral would be a couple who has been very reluctant to seek outside assistance for serious trouble and is disturbed about being required to go to yet another agency and tell the story again to another stranger. If an outside referral is perceived as a barrier to optimal client service, a referral to the brief counseling service can be initiated.

A criticism that has been leveled about the walk-in model is that the therapist typically does not know what happens to clients after the session. Two outcome studies that carried out postsession interviews and data collection obtained a sampling of outcomes with positive and encouraging results (Hoffart and Hoffart, 1994; Miller, in process). However, for the majority of therapeutic interactions, the therapist never learns how the intervention unfolded. Some community therapists struggle with this lack of feedback and eventually decide that they cannot embrace the model. Their contribution of doubt and uncertainty assists the Centre to continue to devise innovative ways of determining the effectiveness of the service.

Some community therapists who work in private practice find themselves questioning their contribution to the walk-in counseling service. The perceived conflict between the goals of earning a living by providing ongoing therapy to paying clients during the week and providing no-cost single-session therapy once or twice a month is more than an examination of pro bono work. They wonder if, by not charging a fee, we are supporting a societal tendency to devalue the worth of therapy.

INTEGRATION WITH PSYCHIATRIC SERVICES AND ROLE OF MEDICATION

For as long as it has been open, Eastside Family Centre has benefited from the support of psychiatrists who have embraced the single-session model. Rather than see clients directly, psychiatrists as a rule support the Centre by providing timely consultation to therapists whose clients have mental health-related questions about themselves or family members. Psychiatric consultation is particularly valuable when larger systems issues are present and a client is perplexed about how to access appropriate and timely mental health support.

Psychiatric consultants use the Eastside Family Centre as a training setting for psychiatric residents and family practice interns. This is a particularly beneficial mutual arrangement; psychiatrists and family physicians entering the field have an elementary understanding of the nature of single-session therapy, as well as the array of supports available to patients at the Centre. Residents and interns receive exposure to a wide variety of mental health situations and have the opportunity to work with a therapy team in novel and creative ways. An orientation to the Centre during their training has led several community-based physicians to participate in the single-session certificate training program offered by the Centre and to continue to donate professional time as therapists, enhancing the continuum of disciplines available to clients at the Centre.

Psychiatrists in settings such as mental health clinics and hospitals refer patients who require effective, supportive crisis diffusion assistance, particularly those who are waiting to enter a service or who are about to be discharged. Patients who are discharged from emergency room settings because of a mental health crisis are often referred to walk-in service upon discharge, and frequently come directly from the hospital. The Centre assists the client to devise a plan that pays attention to personal safety and community supports, while respecting client choice.

Clients who are deemed by the walk-in therapy team to be at significant risk are sent directly to the closest hospital emergency department, with a phone call made to the psychiatric service. The two systems are able to make a plan that protects the client and ensures that any other systems that can contribute to the client's well-being are activated.

The Centre views the family physician (primary care physician) as the case coordinator and works with the client to make effective use of the relationship. Clients are asked, before the start of the session, if a session report can be sent to their family physician. Telephone consultation can also occur with the client's permission. Clients are referred back to the physician for any questions about medication. The physician is updated before the client's appointment to assist in the provision of effective treatment. The psychiatric consultant may also speak with the physician if warranted.

CULTURAL AND GENDER ISSUES

Cultural Issues

Eastside Family Centre is located in a culturally diverse community, housing significant populations who have come to Canada from India, Africa, Southeast Asia, Eastern Europe, the Balkans, and Latin America, among other locales. However, the population seen at the walk-in service does not reflect the diversity of the community (a disproportionate number are from the dominant culture), and the therapists who provide service are overwhelmingly from the dominant culture.

The Centre has undertaken some innovative projects and partnerships in order to position itself to better recognize and meet the mental health needs of the entire city and region. For example, therapists from another counseling agency who speak Vietnamese and Spanish are on loan to the Centre one half-day per week. The Centre manager speaks Mandarin, and another staff member offers counseling in Serbo-Croatian. However, offering therapy in a variety of languages does not completely address the problem of making the Centre user-friendly to diverse cultures (Aponte, 1994). In the process of this work, the Eastside Family Centre is participating in a subtle process of connecting with people, respecting their experiences and their values, and helping them to locate strengths and resources both within themselves and within the community. The Centre hopes to assist these clients to make changes in their interaction patterns that will restore well-being not only to individual families, but will also enhance their larger cultural community.

The idea of talking to a stranger about personal problems is unfamiliar and alien to many new Canadians. The Centre has discovered that therapists who speak the language but are less involved in the cultural community are more valued, primarily because of privacy issues. The Centre has experienced the most success with second-generation clients, especially when issues such as child-rearing dilemmas, privacy, and marital conflict are the focus. These clients report that first-generation practices in many areas of family life are often directly at odds with the sanctions and permissions of the mainstream culture. Second-generation clients often come with the experience of "doors closing before them" and are looking for assistance in opening doors to a new and significantly different way of interacting with family members, their own cultural community, and the community at large (DiNicola, 1997).

Partnerships with minority-serving agencies designed to provide services other than individual and family therapy have also increased the Centre's ability to serve all Calgarians. The Centre has been involved in a breast cancer screening project for East Asian women, a weekly support group for immigrant women who are dealing with violence in the home, and a preschool program for children of immigrant families. Although these projects are significantly outside of the mandate of the Centre, each has identified a particular need that the Centre was able to fill, as well as having exposed a large number of minority-culture family members to the location and services of the Centre.

Gender Issues

The Eastside Family Centre was developed with basic philosophical premises that are feminist, egalitarian, and collaborative. Paying attention to issues of gender is an overarching process in the therapeutic work. Recognizing the influence of preconceptions and prior experience is an ongoing challenge taken up by all of the therapists who contribute to the work at the Centre. The importance of power differentials is not ignored or discounted (Burck and Speed, 1995).

The Centre has a large number of clients who come to address issues of family violence. More than in most counseling centers, many of these clients are male (Miller, in process). Its first partnership was with a local women's emergency shelter that now houses two programs at Eastside Family Centre. The shelter established a crisis service for men offering ongoing therapy and groups for partners of women who have used the shelter's services. It then developed a group program for adolescents who have witnessed violence in their family homes. These services continue to educate walk-in counseling service therapists about the needs of both women and men in therapy and alert them to the pitfalls of gender stereotyping in single-session work.

The utilization of therapy teams assists in reducing gender bias and promoting a gender-sensitive perspective. Safety is regarded as a top priority for both men and women. Safety plans are always developed when the issue of violence is revealed, and agents of social control, such as the police, are asked to assist when necessary.

The Centre also serves many couples who are experiencing marital disharmony. A partner's voice, which may have been subdued over a period of time, is given room to speak, while the therapist and team continue to respect the needs and emotions of the other person in the dyad (Walters et al., 1992). A focus in the single-session work is to open up space for change in family relationships without sacrificing the well-being of any one family member.

The gradual shift in the therapy profession over the past twenty years to a female-dominated workforce also prompts the Centre to look at gender bias in service provision. All-women therapy teams risk minimizing a male perspective, in spite of inservice training and professional experience. A gender-balanced group of contributors to the work of the Centre is highly valued and sought after as the Centre develops in new directions.

FUTURE DIRECTIONS

Community needs change over time. The east side of Calgary is not the same community in 1999 as it was in 1990. The infrastructure of social services and agencies that was absent in 1990 is now more developed. Schools, health clinics, a twenty-four-hour hospital emergency room, and neighborhood-based mental health and social service systems have emerged or been enhanced. At the same time, consumer expectations for convenience, immediacy, and variety of service delivery have increased, as has the population to be served. A major restructuring of health and social services at the provincial government level and changes to government policy in the past five years have resulted in shifts to traditional funding patterns and funding opportunities. The net result is that agencies such as the Eastside Family Centre continue to be highly relevant but are faced with the challenge of offering services in new and creative ways.

In the beginning, the Eastside Family Centre offered a mental health service that was unlike any other. It was "fast-food" service delivery—a selection of quality services with immediate access. In a way, the notion of walk-in, resource-based therapy could be likened to the comic strip *Peanuts,* with the approach of putting up a booth that says, "The therapist is in" and waiting to see how clients respond. An evaluation of the walk-in model (Hoffart and Hoffart, 1994) indicated that community response was highly favorable, and a replication of the Eastside Family Centre was developed on the west side of Calgary.

A recent review of the Centre's services and model of service delivery suggests a need to change to a "both/and" approach. The Eastside Family Centre's "one-stop shopping" concept of walk-in counseling supported by partnerships with other service providers will continue. In addition, "walk-out" services, in which Centre staff and volunteers walk out and deliver services closer to the neighborhoods where clients reside, will also be developed. These services will include the twenty-four-hour mobile crisis team, in-home family counseling, and small counseling kiosks, located in neighborhood community centers and shopping malls. Therapists at the kiosks will be linked to the Eastside Family Centre via computer and telephone. The aim of this shift toward walk-out services is to provide still greater therapist accessibility to the community. *Peanuts* is alive and well and living in Calgary.

REFERENCES

Amundson, J. (1996). Why pragmatics is probably enough for now. *Family Process, 35,* 473-486.

Andersen, T. (1991). Guidelines for practice. In T. Andersen (Ed.), *The reflecting team: Dialogues and dialogues about the dialogue* (pp. 42-68). New York: Norton.

Aponte, H.J. (1994). *Bread and spirit: Therapy with the new poor: Diversity of race, culture, and values.* New York: Norton.

Berg, I.K. and Miller, S.D. (1992). *Working with the problem drinker: A solution focused approach.* New York: Norton.

Boscolo, L., Cecchin, G., Hoffman, L., and Penn, P. (1987). *Milan systemic family therapy.* New York: Basic Books.

Burck, C. and Speed, B. (1995). *Gender, power, and relationships: New developments in family therapy.* New York: Norton.

de Shazer, S. (1985). *Keys to solution in brief therapy.* New York: Norton.

DiNicola, V. (1997). *A stranger in the family: Culture, families and therapy.* New York: Norton.

Haley, J. (1987). *Problem-solving therapy: New strategies for effective family therapy* (Second edition). San Francisco: Jossey-Bass.

Haley, J. (1993). Dust jacket quote, in Talmon, M. *Single session solutions.* New York: Addison-Wesley.

Hoffart, B. and Hoffart, I. (1994). *Program evaluation of Eastside Family Centre.* Synergy Research Group. Unpublished manuscript.

Lawson, A., McElheran, N., and Slive, A. (1997). Single session walk-in therapy: A model for the 21st century. *Family Therapy News, 30(4),* 15-25.

Madanes, C. (1981). *Strategic family therapy.* San Francisco: Jossey-Bass.

McElheran, N. and Harper-Jaques, S. (1994). Commendations: A resource intervention for clinical practice. *Clinical Nurse Specialist, 8(1),* 7-10.

Miller, J. (in process). *Client outcomes in walk-in single sessions*

Miller, J., Slive, A., and Protinsky, H. (1997). *Investigating new clinical delivery system: Walk-in single session therapy and client satisfaction.* Unpublished manuscript.

O'Hanlon, W. and Weiner-Davis, M. (1989). *In search of solutions: A new direction in psychotherapy.* New York: Norton.

Slive, A., MacLaurin, B., Oakander, M., and Amundson, J. (1995). Walk-in single sessions: A new paradigm in clinical service delivery. *Journal of Systemic Therapies, 14(1),* 3-11.

Talmon, M. (1990). *Single-session therapy.* San Francisco: Jossey-Bass.

Talmon, M., Hoyt, M., and Rosenbaum, R. (1990). Effective single session therapy: Step by step guidelines. In M. Talmon (Ed.), *Single-session therapy.* San Francisco: Jossey-Bass.

Walters, M., Carter, B., Papp, P., and Silverstein, O. (1992). *The invisible web: Gender patterns in family relationships.* New York: Guilford.

Watzlawick, P., Weakland, J., and Fisch, R. (1974). *Change: Principles of problem formation and problem resolution.* New York: Norton.

White, M. (1986). Negative explanation, restraint and double description: A template for family therapy. *Family Process, 25(2),* 169-184.

Whitford, D. (1994). *Survey of volunteer retention.* Unpublished master's thesis.

Wright, L.M. (1989). Our obsession with "therapist questions." What about "client questions"? *The Family Therapy Networker, 13(6),* 15-16.

PART III:
SPECIAL POPULATIONS

Chapter 12

Behavioral Couples Therapy for Comorbid Substance Abuse and Psychiatric Problems

Rob J. Rotunda
Jane G. Alter
Timothy J. O'Farrell

INTRODUCTION

A substantial proportion of all clients presenting for help in mental health settings have misused alcohol or other drugs, and many struggle with concurrent psychological and substance use disorders. The lifetime prevalence of substance use disorders in the general population exceeds that of any mental disorder, with estimates ranging from 16 to 27 percent (Kessler et al., 1994; Regier et al., 1990). Regier and colleagues (1990) report that comorbidity rates between substance use disorders and common psychological afflictions such as affective and anxiety disorders are substantial (32 percent and 14.6 percent, respectively). Comorbid substance abuse is also common among the seriously mentally ill. Regier and colleagues report that 47 percent of those with schizophrenia meet the lifetime criteria for at least one drug/alcohol disorder, and 32 percent of those with affective disorders also meet these criteria. Perhaps more important, lifetime prevalence of substance use disorders among those in psychiatric inpatient settings is approximately 39 percent (Regier et al., 1990).

Given these findings, clients presenting in traditional mental health settings may be at greater risk of having concomitant substance abuse problems. Therapeutic pragmatics dictate that practitioners in these clinics will inevitably assess and treat many clients who meet criteria for both psychological and substance use disorders. Many cannot and should not be referred to specialized addiction settings due to their psychiatric disorders, so it is incumbent upon mental health professionals to receive proper training in treating the dual-diagnosed patient. Once the decision to treat the multi-issue client has been made, an array of individual and family therapy approaches are available. Because a client's substance abuse and mental disorders affect family members, who in turn may help or hinder recovery efforts, it is often efficient and therapeutically indicated to include them in treatment (Rotunda, Scherer, and Imm, 1995).

Marital and family therapy (MFT) approaches for alcohol use disorders have been the subject of increasing clinical and empirical attention. The clinical applications of MFT have increased in the past two decades, and the scope of these applications includes various marital and family therapy interventions that can be used effectively at different stages of the alcoholism recovery process to initiate change when the alcoholic is unwilling to seek help, to stabilize sobriety and relationships once the alcoholic has sought help, and to prevent relapse and maintain long-term recovery (O'Farrell, 1993). Effective methods range from brief family participation in treatment and discharge planning to intensive family therapy that supports recovery and helps repair damaged relationships. One example of such a program is the Harvard Counseling for Alcoholics' Marriages (CALM) Project, which utilizes a behavioral couples therapy (BCT) approach.

SETTING

Project CALM, an outpatient clinical research program operating at sites in the greater Boston area, focuses on treating substance use disorders and understanding related dysfunctional family processes. Clinic teams are interdisciplinary and typically include psychologists, social workers, doctoral level psychology interns, addictions specialists, and psychiatrists. Research psychologists and research assistants conduct pretreatment assessments working in conjunction with the treatment team and are primarily responsible for obtaining posttreatment and follow-up data from couples. CALM outpatient clinics are affiliated with inpatient addictions and psychiatric treatment units of hospitals and medical centers.

The overall purpose of Project CALM is to increase relationship factors conducive to sobriety. Couples are encouraged to reward abstinence and refrain from punishing sobriety, increase positive feelings and activities, and learn better communication skills. This reduces high levels of negative emotions, family stress, and the risk of relapse. To meet basic program eligibility criteria, CALM clients must be diagnosed with a substance use disorder and (1) be married or in a stable common-law relationship, (2) reside with their partner or attempt reconciliation for the program, and (3) not currently suffer from a psychotic disorder. If both members of a couple are substance abusers, one of them must be at least ninety days abstinent. About two-thirds of CALM clients start the program after discharge from an inpatient detoxification or rehabilitation program, and one-third are direct outpatient referrals from the community.

TREATMENT MODEL

CALM has four distinct phases including initial engagement of the identified patient (IP) and his or her partner, ten to twelve weekly couples sessions, ten weekly couples group sessions, and quarterly follow-up visits for the final twenty-four months. Portions of the following summary appear in more detail elsewhere (O'Farrell, 1993; O'Farrell and Rotunda, 1997).

Alcoholics who come to CALM referred by community sources or in response to advertisements and outreach efforts are often still drinking. The task becomes one of helping the couple appreciate the significance of the drinking problem and prompting the alcoholic into an inpatient or outpatient detoxification or rehabilitation program. Engaging and joining with couples who are ambivalent about stopping drinking or entering treatment usually precludes the clinician from making immediate demands for sobriety, although the program's goal of abstinence is made explicit. Supporting the struggle of both partners and processing the problem drinker's typical ambivalence about abstinence are general methods used to facilitate treatment acceptance. Empathizing with the painful consequences of drinking for the family and highlighting the more subtle effects of the addiction, such as how it prevents them from attaining personal and family aspirations (e.g., spending quality time with children, growing old peacefully and enjoying the "golden" years), can instill a feeling of urgency to begin treatment. In sum, the central themes that are conveyed to clients in different ways throughout the engagement process include how the IP's addiction and psychological dysfunction affects family members, the benefits of including the spouse in therapy, the necessity to act soon before things worsen, and the acknowledgment that the patient deserves the chance to have a more satisfying relationship, which first requires abstinence.

Initial Couple Sessions

About ten to twelve weekly conjoint couples sessions occur after the couple has committed themselves to the CALM program. These initial sessions have four important parts, which include (1) making specific Project CALM promises or commitments, (2) establishing a sobriety contract, (3) strengthening the therapeutic relationship and managing immediate problems, and (4) providing feedback of assessment results and preparing couples for the group phase of the program.

The CALM Promises

The couple is asked to make three commitments that provide a framework for the therapy and help shape treatment expectations. First, they agree not to threaten divorce or separation during the course of the therapy, even when in a heated argument. This discourages the use of threats as ammunition during conflict or out of frustration and reinforces the idea that both partners can work to repair the relationship without fear of abrupt decisions to separate.

Second, the couple agrees to focus on the present and future, and not the past drinking or negative events. This commitment is usually kept by the IP because there is natural motivation to avoid the guilt and shame aroused by processing unsuccessful efforts to stay sober and the painful consequences caused by the drinking. However, the burden of this agreement falls on spouses who struggle to contain their anger and frustration with the IP's past behavior. In this case, it is suggested that the couple discuss the drinking-related past only in the safer context of sessions where the therapist can help them discuss these issues with a minimum of destructiveness. Thus, while critical incidents and reminders of the past may demand clarification and ongoing management, the message made explicit to the couple emphasizes their current responsibilities and potential to make their relationship better rather than become mired in mutual blaming, criticism, and hostility. For couples with a history of domestic violence, a non-violence contract is explained and closely monitored.

Third, the couple is asked to dedicate themselves to completing whatever weekly homework assignments they agree to in session. The rationale given is that doing something always produces better results in maintaining sobriety and improving relationships than simply talking about it, and that CALM may expect more than other types of counseling as it is action oriented and focused on behavior change. Emphasis is placed on getting couples to renew their relationship in a more positive way by changing their behavior first and then assessing changes in feelings, rather than waiting to feel more positively toward each other before initiating changes in their own behavior. At each couples session, the therapist reviews the extent to which each spouse has kept these promises in order to promote compliance and utilizes a problem-solving approach when noncompliance occurs while being careful not to take a punishing stance.

The Sobriety Contract

The goal of the sobriety contract is to reward abstinence, to reduce distrust and conflict, and to refrain from punishing sobriety. The sobriety contract includes either an Antabuse contract or sobriety-trust discussion, attendance at twelve step meetings or other self-help group involvement, and weekly drug urine screens for those with current drug problems.

In the Antabuse contract, each day at a specified time the alcoholic asks the spouse to witness the taking of Antabuse and thanks the spouse for doing so (O'Farrell and Bayog, 1986). The spouse, in turn, thanks the alcoholic for taking the Antabuse and records the observation on a calendar provided by the therapist. Both partners agree not to discuss past drinking or fears about future drinking at home, but to reserve these discussions for the therapy sessions. In addition, both spouses agree to contact the therapist if the taking of Antabuse is not observed for two consecutive days. It is extremely important that each spouse view the agreement as a cooperative method for rebuilding lost trust and a symbolic ritual of recovery and not as a coercive checking-up operation by an overinvolved, embattled (nonalcoholic) partner. Expressing appreciation and gratefulness for sobriety often softens or ameliorates alcoholics' defensiveness when confronted with the need to remain sober, and avoids the not uncommon refrain of the alcoholic who says, "Why shouldn't I drink if my spouse continues to live in the past, nag me, and worry so much about me relapsing in the future?"

For those who are not medically cleared to take Antabuse, a daily sobriety-trust discussion is used instead of the Antabuse contract. Each day at a specified time, the alcoholic initiates a brief discussion reiterating his or her commitment not to drink that day. The spouse expresses thanks for the IP's sobriety and statement of commitment; then the alcoholic asks if the spouse has any questions or fears about possible drinking that day. The alcoholic answers the questions and attempts to reassure the spouse. The couple does not discuss past drinking or any future possible drinking beyond that day. The couple agree not to discuss drinking at other times, to keep the daily trust discussion very brief, and to end it with a positive statement of appreciation to each other.

At the start of each session, the therapist reviews the sobriety contract calendar, which provides an ongoing record of progress, to see how well each spouse has done his or her part. Each session also examines any urges to drink or use drugs that may have occurred since the last therapy session. For many couples, the sobriety contract also includes weekly goals for twelve-step or other self-help involvement by the alcoholic and spouse and weekly drug urine screens for those with current drug problems. The sobriety contract is a crucial foundation of the CALM program. The contract helps the alcoholic refrain from drinking even when the desire exists, and it gives concrete assurances to spouses that drinking will not occur, which builds trust over time and decreases anxiety and conflict about alcohol. The contract also focuses the couple on present matters, promotes teamwork and the exchange of mutual appreciation, and serves as an initial exercise in positive and direct communication. These contract behaviors appear to be helpful, in part, because they are antithetical to the high hostility and criticism levels often manifested by nonalcoholic partners, and thus interrupt negative cycles of blaming and criticism, which often lead to relapse.

Problem Solving and Stabilization

After the initial foundations of the program are set (commitments, sobriety contract), we seek to establish a strong therapeutic relationship and provide couples with a positive, protective structure to help them cope with the tensions of the early recovery period. We help them actively cope with or find solutions to immediate problems such as financial strains, parenting problems, medical concerns, and legal difficulties. Moreover, assessment and treatment of dual-diagnosed clients (e.g., major affective disorders, PTSD, personality disorders) is undertaken in the context of conjoint therapy as the situation permits; referral to concurrent individual therapy is not uncommon. We stress the need for the IP to achieve sobriety before working on relationship issues or individual psychopathology.

Feedback of Assessment Material

In a feedback session held just before the couples group begins, the therapist shares impressions from the assessment of the nature and severity of the psychological and substance use disorders and relationship problems and invites the couple to respond to these impressions. The feedback is based on information obtained from the conjoint sessions, a brief interview with each partner conducted separately, and questionnaires that are completed soon after the couple enrolls in CALM. Finally, the therapist prepares the couple for entering the ten-week couples group (which ideally is co-led by the therapist who has seen the couple since they started the program) by letting them know what to expect and discussing any apprehensions about the group experience.

The Couples Group: Purpose and Goals

The objectives of Project CALM couples groups are to promote sobriety, increase positive couple/family activities, teach communication skills, negotiate desired behavior changes, and plan for maintenance of change. The CALM couples group consists of four to five couples, a male and female cotherapist team, and ten weekly two-hour sessions.

Abstinence is promoted by reinforcing compliance with the sobriety contract, reviewing urges to drink or use drugs, and facilitating group discussion of effective coping strategies. Crisis intervention for any drinking or drug use that occurs is also very important. In this case, therapists meet with the couple as soon as possible to explore antecedents for the relapse, suggest coping alternatives to drinking, and reframe the incident as a learning experience. Group support and feedback to those who are struggling in this regard is especially powerful.

Increasing positive couple and family activities is accomplished through three homework exercises. The "Catch Your Partner Doing Something Nice" exercise has each spouse record one caring behavior performed by the other spouse each day. This exercise is adapted from Richard Stuart's (1980) behavioral couples therapy approach. This procedure is designed to compete with the tendency to ignore positive aspects of the relationship or person and focus on negative behavior. At the next group meeting each spouse practices acknowledging caring behaviors from his or her daily list for the previous week ("I liked it when you . . . It made me feel . . . "). Then therapists assign for homework a two-to-five-minute daily communication session in which each partner acknowledges one pleasing behavior noticed that day. In the "Caring Day" assignment, each person plans ahead to surprise his or her spouse with a day when he or she does something special for the spouse to show caring. Reluctant partners are encouraged to take risks and act lovingly toward their spouses rather than making their actions contingent on what their partners do for them.

Planning and engaging in "Shared Rewarding Activities" (SRA) is an important assignment because it seeks to reverse the past tendency for the alcoholic to participate only in activities involving alcohol apart from the family. Each recreational activity must involve both spouses, either by themselves or with their children or other adults, and can be at or away from home. It is necessary for the couple to agree that time spent doing an SRA is for enjoyment and not for discussing problems or arguing. Lists of possible activities are generated by each partner, and group leaders model an SRA planning session illustrating solutions to common obstacles.

Communication Skills Training

Teaching communication skills can help the alcoholic and spouse deal with stressors in their relationship and in their lives, which can reduce the risk of relapse. Therapists use instructions, modeling, and behavioral rehearsal with coaching and feedback to teach couples how to communicate more effectively. Core communication skills that are taught include structured listening techniques (e.g., "What I hear you saying is . . . Is that right?") and direct expression of positive and negative feelings. Listening skills help each spouse to feel understood and supported and slow down couple interactions to prevent quick escalation of negative exchanges. Although it is often new to couples, the concept that they can understand each other's position without agreeing with it is stressed repeatedly. Learning how to clearly express one's thoughts and feelings, especially in regard to emotion-laden issues, is taught in the group as an alternative to the blaming, hostile, and indirect responsibility-avoiding communication behaviors that characterize many alcoholics' relationships. Speakers take responsibility for their own feelings by using statements beginning with "I" rather than "you," thereby reducing listener defensiveness and making it easier for their partner to receive the intended message. Training starts with positive or neutral topics and moves to problem areas and charged issues only after each skill has been practiced on less problematic topics.

Using Communication Sessions and Negotiating Behavior Changes

Communication sessions are planned, structured discussions in which partners talk privately, face-to-face, without distractions and with each person taking turns expressing his or her point of view without interruptions. Starting with session five, much of each group meeting consists of supervised practice of communication sessions about couples' problems and conflicts. The group is split into two subgroups, and each therapist works with couples to find a specific resolution to a problem or conflict. Similar sessions, ten to fifteen minutes each, three to four times weekly are assigned for homework. Negotiating desired changes is an important part of this intensive phase of the group. Couples learn to make specific requests and to negotiate and compromise to resolve their differences, or at least begin to address them in a nondestructive manner before the group ends and the follow-up period begins.

Planning for Maintenance of Change

Discussion of relapse prevention principles and efforts to maintain relationship gains is a critical final activity of the CALM couples group. Each couple completes a continuing recovery plan that specifies what parts of their sobriety contract and other behavior changes accomplished during the group the couples would like to continue after the group ends. In general, couples are encouraged to continue what has already worked for them up until this point in the early recovery period, namely, a combination of the sobriety contract, individual treatment for the substance abuser or further marital therapy, self-help group involvement, and use of communication skills.

Quarterly Follow-Up Contacts for Twenty-Four Months

Project CALM clients have in-clinic or at-home quarterly follow-up visits for two years after the group ends. Initially used for data collection in our research, we became impressed with the important continuing care and maintenance functions served by these follow-up contacts. The follow-up counselor schedules and reminds the couple of these contacts. The couple can call for unscheduled meetings as needed; thus there exists an ongoing bridge between couples who have enrolled in the program and their previous therapists. Regular and long-term contact is a very useful method to assess compliance with the continuing recovery plan, to monitor progress, and to evaluate the need for additional treatment.

Outcome Data on Project CALM

Outcome studies on Project CALM have shown that behavioral marital therapy (BMT) combined with individual counseling for the alcoholic produced marital outcomes that were superior to individual conseling alone during, and in the six months after, treatment (O'Farrell, Cutter, and Floyd, 1985). In the two years after treatment, couples who received BMT in addition to the alcoholic's individual counseling showed significant improvements in both drinking and marital adjustment and better marital outcomes than couples in which the alcoholic received individual treatment only, although these positive effects diminished as time after treatment increased (O'Farrell et al., 1992). However, when a relapse prevention (RP) component was added in the year following completion of the BMT couples group, it produced better sobriety and relationship outcomes compared to those who received BMT alone, with the superiority of BMT plus RP over BMT alone particularly apparent for alcoholics who had more severe alcohol and marital problems (O'Farrell, Choquette, and Cutter, 1998).

CASE EXAMPLE

Couples Therapy for Comorbid Alcohol Dependence and Major Depression

Elaine was a fifty-two-year-old woman diagnosed with recurrent major depressive disorder and alcohol dependence. She was married to a man for whom drinking was not a central feature of his life. He drank occasionally at family gatherings, or maybe had a beer with dinner once a week. This was the first marriage for both of them. Elaine worked as an administrative assistant in a medical clinic; her husband was a firefighter. They had two grown children who lived in the area and whom they saw about once a month. Elaine had been in alcoholism treatment twice before and had maintained six months of sobriety since the last treatment. Before this time of sobriety she had several undiagnosed and untreated bouts of depression, which she identified as a problem since her late twenties. By the time Elaine and her husband, Tom, came into our program, she had already been on antidepressant medication under psychiatric supervision and in therapy with a licensed social worker for six months, excluding the three weeks of heavy drinking that preceded her entering treatment again. She had tried different medications but was now doing well on a combination of Paxil and Wellbutrin. We were glad that she was so well supported in dealing with her depression, and obtained her permission to speak with both the psychiatrist and the social worker. If she had not been in treatment, we would have referred her for this kind of medical and psychological support.

Although she had been drinking regularly for years, according to Elaine and her husband she did not develop a problem with drinking until her early forties. At this time, she began drinking when she came home from work and continued until the time she went to bed. Her first treatment occurred when she realized that she was doing this every evening and more so on weekends, and that she was beginning to miss work because of it. Her husband had tried to get her to seek treatment sooner, but they only ended up fighting about it, with Elaine denying that her drinking was a problem. Elaine claimed her drinking "helped her relax and unwind" and took the edge off her feeling blue. This blue feeling had begun to get worse around the time she first began noticing premenopausal changes. This most recent relapse, which brought her to Project CALM after a short inpatient stay, was precipitated by her discovery that her husband had had a brief affair about ten years earlier. The inpatient staff had referred them to CALM to address her continuing recovery, the strain of her alcoholism and depression on the marital relationship, and the impact of his affair and his general emotional unavailability.

Although most of our clients take Antabuse unless unable to for medical reasons, Elaine was adamant about not taking Antabuse because of her fear of the potential side effects and "not wanting to put something else" into her body. The team psychiatrist supported her position. An agreement was negotiated with Elaine and her husband to do the sobriety trust discussion daily and to reintroduce the requirement for Antabuse only if she were to drink again. We were also encouraged by the fact that Elaine had gone to AA meetings in the past and was willing to do so again. Tom had never been to Al-Anon, and, unlike Elaine, was not willing to go at first. Like many partners, he considered his participation in the project to be sufficient. As part of each weekly session, even though she had an individual therapist, the CALM therapist assessed Elaine's mood and helped her monitor her tendency toward depression. This aspect of the therapy also served to increase Tom's awareness about her depressive symptoms and the impact the disorder had on her functioning and on the couple's relationship.

Helping Elaine and Tom get started in Project CALM meant helping them each agree to the behaviors that would start to restore trust and good will in the relationship, since each of them considered that they had been betrayed. Tom felt blindsided by Elaine's return to drinking, and Elaine was deeply hurt by Tom's past affair, especially the secrecy of it. With the help of their therapist, they developed a daily sobriety trust discussion and contract that included the following:

1. A statement of intention by Elaine that she planned to stay sober that day
2. Tom's acknowledgment and appreciation of her plan and her efforts in sobriety thus far
3. Elaine's appreciation of Tom's support for her sobriety
4. Tom's statement of his intention to work on strengthening and repairing their relationship
5. Elaine's appreciation of his efforts to repair the relationship
6. Tom's appreciation of Elaine's willingness to work on healing the pain
7. The couple's agreement to the CALM promises, with strong emphasis for both on not bringing up past negative events or fear of future ones, especially Elaine's drinking and Tom's infidelity, unless they were to do so in the context of the therapy session
8. Elaine's agreement to attend two to three AA meetings per week

Although both were hurt and fearful, and sometimes angry at each other, they had twenty-five years of a solid and loving relationship on which to base their attempts at healing. Watching them practice their sobriety trust discussion each week in the session turned out to be a moving experience that was very tender and which gradually helped restore hope and trust. They faithfully enacted the contract at home, recorded it on their sobriety calendar, and reviewed it with the therapist during each session. Tom suggested that to support Elaine's efforts, he would not store or drink any alcohol in the house, and he was able to fulfill this agreement throughout the treatment. Elaine was clear that she did not mind if he had a drink when they were out, but he was not interested in doing so. They both agreed to go out together for an enjoyable activity once a week, which was something they had grown out of the habit of doing over the years. They found this really helped their growing closeness, as did the daily trust discussion.

Elaine complained that Tom was not a good listener and that he would try to cheer her up or come up with a solution any time she began to express dissatisfaction or sadness. To address this problem, their therapist began teaching them the basic listening skills of good communication even before they entered the group. The skills not only helped Tom learn how to be more emotionally supportive to Elaine, but were also employed in helping the couple discuss the affair in session. Initially, Elaine found that it was difficult for her to comply with the CALM promise of not bringing up Tom's affair, but she was able to make progress once the couple began using these communication skills in session.

As the therapy continued, both Tom and Elaine developed more tolerance for hearing each other's feelings. Elaine began talking about how ashamed she was of the inexplicable bouts of depression that had plagued her almost all her adult life. She described how drinking used to soothe that shame, until it got so out of control that it became an additional source of embarrassment, thereby deepening her depression. Tom shared how lonely he used to feel when his schedule kept him away from his family and how personally he used to take Elaine's negative moods when he did see her. Both expressed gratitude for her sobriety, for her relief from depression, and for their willingness to be honest with each other and work through the pain.

As the weeks of their conjoint sessions continued, Elaine maintained her sobriety and intermittently kept her commitment to AA. In line with the CALM promise of completing assignments agreed to, the therapist worked with Elaine on clarifying her commitment to AA, which she reduced to one meeting per week. She found that going to AA was an important reminder to her of why she did not want to go back to drinking, and it was also useful in helping her navigate the feelings that Tom's affair had brought up. Eventually she increased her AA commitment to attending two groups per week, and also began a relationship with a sponsor. This was a huge accomplishment for her, given her battle against depression, alcoholism, and isolation.

Elaine and Tom joined the behavioral marital therapy group with three other couples after completing ten conjoint sessions. They stated that they gained significant understanding of their problems and of each other from these sessions, along with a greater ability to change what needed to be changed in order to strengthen their relationship. Elaine also felt that it was tremendously helpful to have Tom involved in supporting her recovery efforts this time. She stated that she was now able to talk to him freely about herself for the first time. Tom appreciated her willingness to take these risks and found that he too became more vulnerable and direct with his feelings. For them, the group was a continuation and elaboration of the work they started in their pregroup sessions.

As it turned out, the other couples in this group were also very committed to each other and actively involved in their treatment. Although it does not always happen in the group, couples brought in some of the more sensitive issues they had been working on in pregroup sessions. Elaine and Tom found that they were not the only couple who had struggled with infidelity, nor was Elaine the only alcoholic also struggling with depression. In fact, three out of the four alcoholics in the group, two of them women, were also on antidepressant medication. Their ability to see that they had two distinct but related disorders which they had been battling, that they were not alone, that they were not "bad" or "morally defective" people, and that effective treatment was available for both illnesses, was supremely validating for these clients and their partners.

At the end of the ten-week group, Elaine and Tom, along with the other couples, negotiated a continuing recovery plan. Elaine agreed to continue her commitment to attend two AA meetings per week and to speak with her sponsor at least once a week. Tom agreed to try an Al-Anon meeting, encouraged by the offer of another group member to accompany him. They both enthusiastically agreed to continue their daily sobriety trust discussion and to have a weekly communication session to make sure that they continued sharing their feelings and ideas with each other. By this time, they had increased their shared rewarding activities to twice per week and often included other friends or relatives. Elaine planned to continue her individual therapy, but the couple felt they did not need to have further couples therapy—at least not right away. The group as a whole, having bonded quite strongly, decided to continue meeting informally once a month at someone's house.

STRENGTHS AND LIMITATIONS

CALM is a structured BCT approach that brings the power of behavioral-systems thinking to bear on intractable disorders such as alcoholism and major depression. The approach is flexible enough to be adapted to many different settings and client populations. The program's impact is systemic rather than individualistic because it validates the far-reaching effects substance abuse and psychological disorders have on family functioning, emphasizes sobriety and strengthening of dyadic relations, and incorporates the potential for change inherent in multiple couples group therapy.

CALM is also a treatment model supported by empirical research. This fact is clinically reassuring and, perhaps just as important, an asset in the era of accountability and managed health care. Three broad conclusions about BCT are noteworthy in this regard. First, BCT produces more abstinence, happier relationships, and fewer separations than does individual-based treatment for both alcoholism and drug abuse. Second, domestic violence is substantially reduced after BCT for alcoholic and for drug-abusing patients (O'Farrell and Murphy, 1995). Finally, cost outcomes after BCT are very favorable for both alcoholism and drug abuse and superior to individual-based treatment for drug abuse, with reduced hospital and legal system costs after BCT saving more than five times the cost of delivering BCT.

Perhaps the most important limitation is that the impact of BCT on the couple's children is not known. The children of alcoholic and drug-abusing patients are not involved in BCT, and we do not have data showing the impact on the children of their parents' participation in BCT. We can argue that children likely are helped by their parents' participation in BCT; the reductions in violence and the improvements in marital adjustment observed after BCT support this argument, as does Moos's work suggesting that parental sobriety is associated with improved child functioning (Moos, Finney, and Cronkite, 1990). Still, we do not know whether or how BCT impacts these children. Thus, research is needed to find out whether BCT for a substance-abusing parent, with its demonstrated reductions in domestic violence and reduced risk for family breakup, has beneficial and preventive effects for the children in the family, reducing their risk for mental health and substance-abuse problems (O'Farrell and Feehan, 1999). In any case, a more comprehensive whole-family assessment and treatment package, which includes services for children of alcoholics and dual-diagnosed clients, can be developed.

Couples in which both partners are active substance abusers also present a challenge to BCT. Couples in which both partners abuse alcohol or drugs have been excluded from most BCT studies. Our clinical experience suggests that current BCT models may not be as effective as individual treatment for such individuals, but we need to study this important subgroup of patients.

CULTURAL AND GENDER ISSUES

Another important limitation of the model is that BCT needs to be more thoroughly studied among women and minority clients with alcohol and drug problems. The CALM program, originally utilized with white, male alcoholics and their partners, has recently been extended and is in use with female and minority alcoholics. For instance, the "BCT for Women and Minorities Study," led by Tim O'Farrell of the Harvard Families and Addictions Program, will oversample women and obtain a reasonable number of minority alcoholics to see if earlier findings obtained primarily with male alcoholics generalize to broader treatment populations and to learn whether predictors of outcome vary as a function of gender or minority status. The Rutgers University Women's Study, under the direction of Barbara McCrady and Elizabeth Epstein (Epstein and McCrady, 1998), is testing the effectiveness of BCT for low-income women with alcohol problems.

Furthermore, researchers at the Research Institute on Addiction in Buffalo, New York, are conducting a study on BCT and individual treatment for an equal number of men and women with low- to moderate-severity drinking problems. This is an important endeavor because studies to date have focused on patients with more chronic and severe problems and have not examined the impact of patients' gender on BCT outcomes. Female alcoholics are more likely to have a heavy-drinking male partner than male alcoholic patients are to have a heavy-drinking female partner (Wilsnack and Beckman, 1984). Heavy-drinking male partners of female alcoholic patients may not be supportive of the women staying sober, and partner support for abstinence is important for BCT to be effective. In this regard, Dick Longabaugh at Brown University examined variability in outcomes after treatment and found that for alcohol abusers who were highly invested in a relationship that provided low social support of abstinence, individually focused therapy produced more abstinence than relationship-enhanced therapy similar to BCT (Longabaugh et al., 1993). To summarize, it appears couples therapy can effectively be used for women and dual-diagnosed clients, as evidenced by the previous case illustration, but studies with sizable samples are not yet completed.

INTEGRATION WITH PSYCHIATRIC SERVICES
AND ROLE OF MEDICATION

Even when working exclusively with substance-misusing clients, it is common that co-occurring mental health issues arise that necessitate crisis intervention, psychiatric evaluation, medication evaluation, and referral for more comprehensive psychological assessment or testing. Project CALM commonly utilizes psychiatrists to prescribe Antabuse, naltrexone, and psychiatric medications (typically antidepressants), monitor clients during the detoxification process; and monitor physiological functioning (e.g., liver function tests) of clients maintaining a medication regimen. Due to the close proximity to more traditional mental health personnel in affiliated hospital and outpatient settings, it has been fairly easy for CALM staff to consult and work with interdisciplinary mental health staff. As described previously, the Antabuse contract is an important part of the treatment model and clearly functions to increase medication compliance. Psychiatric medications are also used by our couples in the context of a dyadic contract or daily ritual, which therefore enhances the active pharmacological and response expectancy effects of these drugs (Kirsch and Lynn, 1999).

FUTURE DIRECTIONS

It is essential to view clients and their family systems holistically. In our experience at Project CALM, the high prevalence of dual-diagnosed clients, couples with a history of domestic violence, and couples experiencing other psychosocial stressors has necessitated that therapists be versed in identifying the need for and providing generalized psychological services, as well as addictions assessment and treatment. The complexity of addictions treatment and high frequency of comorbid disorders demands well-trained therapists competent in assessment of (1) other addictions besides alcohol dependence (e.g., cocaine, pain medications, food, gambling); (2) psychological disorders (e.g., PTSD and other anxiety disorders, major affective disorders, personality disorders); (3) suicide risk and dangerousness; and (4) domestic violence. Because many referrals to the program come from mental health clinics, psychiatric inpatient units, PTSD programs, veterans centers, and child and family clinics, it can be argued that the need exists to export the CALM program into these various settings, tailoring the protocol to be compatible with a particular service delivery system and clinical population. At the very least, clinicians in all settings must display a readiness to work with multiproblem couples and families and refer to adjunctive therapies when integrative programs are not available.

Another line of reasoning that argues for a generalist approach and broad clinical training is the empirical support BCT methods have with various clinical problems such as depression (e.g., Halford and Markman, 1997; Jacobson, Holtzworth-Munroe, and Schmaling, 1989). Regardless of the specific disorder, altered functioning of a spouse can similarly affect family processes such as communication, role performance, trust, and cohesion. This highlights the utility of the couples therapy procedures noted previously. For example, Project CALM clinicians are familiar with alcohol-specific themes and practice issues but must also demonstrate flexibility within the program structure. Since alcoholics' family functioning in the early recovery period looks much like that of other nonalcoholic but distressed couples, the clinician can become more focused on general family processes and relationship repair and less focused on specific addictions.

Couples and family therapy of alcohol problems and other biopsychosocial disorders has emerged as a field of practice with theoretical and empirical underpinnings. Although the prevailing norms of practice in the addictions field and in community mental health centers have traditionally not emphasized or fully utilized interventions based on outcome research, there is now a growing need for quality and cost-effective programming that bridges the gap between treatment research and therapy. Marital and family therapy approaches to alcohol problems have produced positive and cost-effective outcomes and reflect the usefulness of behavioral-systems perspectives that routinely include family members in the treatment of chemically dependent and dual-diagnosed clients.

Why not export and expand this model to more substance-abuse centers and general mental health settings? Before doing so, we need to identify and overcome barriers to implementation of BCT and other couple and family treatment methods that have been shown to be effective in outcome studies. Even more than additional research, we need technology transfer so that patients and their families can benefit from what we have already learned about BCT for alcoholism and drug abuse. The Institute of Medicine (1998) has documented a large gap between research and practice in substance abuse treatment. BCT is one example of this gap. BCT programs such as CALM have relatively strong research support, but have not yet become widely used. Hopefully the next few years will see progress in closing this gap.

REFERENCES

Epstein, E. E. and McCrady, B. S. (1998). Behavioral couples treatment of alcohol and drug use disorders: Current status and innovations. *Clinical Psychology Review, 18*, 689-711.

Halford, W. K. and Markman, H. (Eds.) (1997). *Clinical handbook of marriage and couples intervention.* New York: Wiley.

Institute of Medicine. (1998). *Bridging the gap between practice and research: Forging partnerships with community-based drug and alcohol treatment.* Washington, DC: National Academy of Sciences Press.

Jacobson, N., Holtzworth-Munroe, A., and Schmaling, K. (1989). Marital therapy and spouse involvement in the treatment of depression, agoraphobia, and alcoholism. *Journal of Consulting and Clinical Psychology, 57*, 5-10.

Kessler, R., McGonagle, K., Zhao, Z., Nelson, C., Hughes, M., Eshelman, S., Wittchen, H., and Kendler, K. (1994). Lifetime and 12-month prevalence of DSM-III-R psychiatric disorders in the United States: Results from the National Comorbidity Study. *Archives of General Psychiatry, 51*, 8-19.

Kirsch, I. and Lynn, S. J. (1999). Automaticity in clinical psychology. *American Psychologist, 54*, 504-515.

Longabaugh, R., Beattie, M., Noel, N., Stout, R., and Malloy, P. (1993). The effect of social investment on treatment outcome. *Journal of Studies on Alcohol, 54*, 465-478.

Moos, R. H., Finney, J. W., and Cronkite, R. C. (1990). *Alcoholism treatment: Context, process, and outcome.* New York: Oxford University Press.

O'Farrell, T. J. (Ed.) (1993). *Treating alcohol problems: Marital and family interventions.* New York: Guilford Press.

O'Farrell, T. J. and Bayog, R. (1986). Antabuse contracts for married alcoholics and their spouses: A method to maintain Antabuse ingestion and decrease conflict about drinking. *Journal of Substance Abuse Treatment, 3*, 1-8.

O'Farrell, T. J., Choquette, K. A., and Cutter, H. S. G. (1998). Couples relapse prevention sessions after behavioral marital therapy for male alcoholics: Outcomes during the three years after starting treatment. *Journal of Studies on Alcohol, 59*, 357-370.

O'Farrell, T. J., Cutter, H., Choquette, K., Floyd, F., and Bayog, R. (1992). Behavioral marital therapy for male alcoholics: Marital and drinking adjustment during the two years after treatment. *Behavior Therapy, 23*, 529-549.

O'Farrell, T. J., Cutter, H., and Floyd, F. (1985). Evaluating behavioral marital therapy for male alcoholics: Effects on marital adjustment and communication from before to after therapy. *Behavior Therapy, 16,* 147-167.

O'Farrell, T. J. and Feehan, M. (1999). Alcoholism treatment and the family: Do family and individual treatments for alcoholic adults have preventive effects for children? *Journal of Studies on Alcohol,* Supplement 13, 125-129.

O'Farrell, T. J. and Murphy, C. (1995). Marital violence before and after alcoholism treatment. *Journal of Consulting and Clinical Psychology, 63,* 256-262.

O'Farrell, T. J. and Rotunda, R. (1997). Couples interventions and alcohol abuse. In W. K. Halford and H. Markman (Eds.), *Clinical handbook of marriage and couples intervention,* (pp. 555-588). New York: Wiley.

Regier, D., Farmer, M., Rae, D., Locke, B., Keith, S., Judd, L., and Goodwin, F. (1990). Comorbidity of mental disorders with alcohol and other drug abuse. *Journal of the American Medical Association, 264,* 2511-2518.

Rotunda, R., Scherer, D., and Imm, P. (1995). Family systems and alcohol misuse: Research on the effects of alcoholism on family functioning and effective family interventions. *Professional Psychology: Research and Practice, 26,* 95-104.

Stuart, R. B. (1980). *Helping couples change: A social learning approach to marital therapy.* New York: Guilford Press.

Wilsnack, S. and Beckman, L. (1984). *Alcohol problems in women.* New York: Guilford Press.

Chapter 13

Family Therapy of Brain Injury: Basic Principles and Innovative Strategies

Laurence Miller

INTRODUCTION

The Brain-Injured Patient in the Family System

In the United States, traumatic brain injuries (TBIs) account for an estimated 400,000 new hospital admissions per year, of which 99,000 will suffer lifelong disability (MacFarlane, 1999). Approximately one million people suffer from the effects of brain injury at any given time (Slagle, 1990). Medical technology has made possible the survival of many patients who even a decade earlier might have died as a result of their injuries. As a consequence, more of these patients are returning home to be cared for and reintegrated into their families.

Major traumatic events and the recovery process never occur in an interpersonal vacuum; brain injury in a family member is a major traumatic event for both patient and family (MacFarlane, 1999; Miller, 1991b, 1993a, 1993c, 1998b, 1999c). From the first acute stages of the injury to the eventual long-term resolutions that are reached, the patient's "significant others"—spouse and in-laws, children and parents, friends and lovers—play a crucial role in determining the kind of life that person will have postinjury. Clinicians working with brain-injured patients generally tend to focus their evaluative, remediative, and therapeutic efforts on the patient, to the neglect of that patient's larger social world. But, consistent with a more comprehensive psychotherapeutic approach to the brain-injured patient (Miller, 1990c, 1991a, 1993b, 1999b), our efforts must also include the family system. At the same time, marriage and family therapists must gain the necessary clinical knowledge and experience to be able to recognize and screen for brain injury syndromes as they now do for substance abuse, sexual abuse, and domestic violence (MacFarlane, 1999).

Major Patient Problems

Family members, despite the best intentions, may be ill-equipped to handle the variety of unanticipated difficulties presented by the returning brain-injured patient. In many cases, the emotional and interpersonal problems are a result of the cognitive impairments incurred during the brain injury (Miller, 1992a, 1993b), and the family therapist should become familiar with this syndrome.

Brain-injured patients' organic disorientation for time and place may make them unmindful or oblivious to their actual surroundings. In a restaurant or movie theater they may walk around, talk loudly, and otherwise act as if at home. In addition, an immature, childlike egocentricity may develop in which patients fail to regard people as distinct personalities with needs and feelings in their own right (Lezak, 1988). A previously healthy, mature, and self-sufficient adult man or woman who now habitually acts like a complaining, demanding child can quickly exhaust the goodwill of even the most devoted caretaker.

But even children eventually learn which behaviors lead to adverse consequences and, therefore, avoid doing them. However, because of deficits in learning and memory, brain-injured patients typically fail to learn from their mistakes. They do not remember the consequences of their actions (or indeed, even the actions themselves); therefore, they tend to get into the same kinds of difficulties repeatedly. The family eventually realizes that they must always remain vigilant for potential trouble and be prepared to intervene repeatedly in the same kinds of situations (Brooks, Campsie, and Symington, 1987; Lezak, 1988; Livingston and Brooks, 1988; McKinlay and Hickox, 1988).

A variety of emotional changes occur in the patient after brain injury that families may find difficult to comprehend or tolerate. These include apathy, silliness, irritability, anger, and depression (Lezak, 1988). Compounding the situation is the frequent assumption by family members that these emotional displays are in some way deliberate, even spiteful, and could be controlled by the patient if he or she really wanted to. In fact, in some cases this kind of willful motivation may actually lie behind the obnoxious emotionality. The patient, in effect, "uses" the symptom to express anger or resentment over enforced dependency or feelings of neglect by the caregivers. The same use of symptoms as weapons may result in the development and/or entrenchment of chronic pain and somatization syndromes (Miller, 1990a, 1993b, 1999a).

Brain-injured patients may no longer be able to comprehend their world and to respond to it as before. The internal disorientation produced by cognitive impairment and the patients' self-consciousness and insecurity over their altered mental status may produce a tremendous degree of anxiety (Lezak, 1988). This further serves to erode patients' self-confidence and may cause them to be overly cautious or hypervigilant. This, in turn, fosters feelings of inadequacy, confusion, and fears of "going crazy."

Probably the most common response to brain injury is depression. Organic depressions can result directly from focal or lateralized brain damage; for example, agitated, anxious, and angry depressions may occur with injury to the left frontal lobe (Robinson, 1986; Robinson et al., 1984; Robinson, Lipsey, and Price, 1985), while more apathetic, amotivational depressions may be seen with right hemisphere damage (Ross, 1981; Ross and Rush, 1981; Ross and Stewart, 1987). In addition, depression is a natural psychological reaction to impairment of function, and this, perhaps more than any other emotional response, tends to erode family members' self-esteem and fuel their feelings of guilt and inadequacy (Lezak, 1988), since depressed mood and behavior are so refractory to their best efforts to relieve it: "We've done everything humanly possible and more, so why doesn't he snap out of it already?"

A change in the patient's personality—"He's not the same person"—is another common problem voiced by families. Such changes can be long standing. They have been reported by up to three-fourths of families as long as five or more years postinjury (Brooks, Campsie, and Symington, 1986, 1987), and they typically constitute more of a burden on the family than physical disability or impairment in intellect, memory, or speech (Brooks, 1984; Fahy, Irving, and Millac, 1967; Livingston and Brooks, 1988). The most frequently reported problems are irritability, temper, lack of spontaneity, restlessness, and overall "childishness" (Brooks, 1984; McKinlay et al., 1981;

Thomsen, 1974). Lack of spontaneity and interpersonal indifference have been reported to be among the most frequent and intense contributors to caregiver stress, as the patient "just doesn't seem to care" (Groom et al., 1998).

One common personality change after brain injury is increased impulsivity. In some cases, this results from focal frontal lobe damage, but it may be seen to some degree with almost any kind of injury to the brain. In addition, the relationship of premorbid impulsive personality traits and behavioral disorders to posttraumatic impulsivity and dysfunctional behavior is a complex one. Impulsive behavior and a corresponding lack of judgment may be seen in a number of spheres, such as food, sex, money, and abuse of drugs and alcohol (Miller, 1989, 1990b, 1992b, 1993b, 1994a, 1994d, 1998b).

Postinjury aggression can occur for a number of reasons, such as episodic dyscontrol syndrome, frontal lobe disinhibition, or exacerbation of premorbid personality traits (Miller, 1990b, 1994d, 1998a). Many patients are frustrated, frightened, and angered by their condition. They may feel that they are an unworthy and unwanted burden on their families. They may feel demeaned and humiliated by the care they need, yet fearful of losing it, and their self-loathing may be projected onto caretakers and clinicians. As the ever-present reminders of their dependency and incompetency, caretaking family members may become the focus of the patient's resentment, which may take the form of belittling, rejection, smoldering hostility, endless complaints and demands, and accusations of unfaithfulness and neglect (Lezak, 1978). Although verbal outbursts are the most common expression (Lezak, 1988), physical violence may occur, especially when brain injury is combined with a postinjury pattern of alcohol or drug abuse (Bond, 1984; Galasko and Edwards, 1974; Galbraith et al., 1976; Jamieson, 1971; Potter, 1967; Rosenbaum and Hoge, 1989; Schmidt and Heinemann, 1999).

Even if not overtly hostile, many patients develop increased suspiciousness, sometimes to the point of paranoid delusions. Patients with left hemisphere damage, often accompanied by aphasia, may develop organic paranoid syndromes (Benson, 1977; Leftoff, 1983), but for most brain-injured patients, perceptual deficits, impaired insight, feelings of worthlessness, and fear of rejection combine to create the perfect setup for the development of paranoia (Lezak, 1988). Sexual fidelity and financial matters form the bulk of the content of most postinjury paranoid preoccupations. In some cases, this may even lead to protracted legal action and expanding webs of family intrigue that extend far beyond the patient and immediate family (Miller, 1993b, 1994b).

Reactions of Family Members

Although reactions to the returning brain-injured loved one are unique to each family, certain clusters of family reaction patterns may be observed. At least in the beginning stages, denial is common. Most families want to believe that their loved one will ultimately "return" to them in some semblance of his or her former self. Denial may be adaptive when it preserves family stability, keeps the family members from being overwhelmed, and maintains appropriate role functioning within the family. In such cases, trying to force the family to "face reality" at too early a stage may serve only to entrench the denial and stiffen resistance to further clinical recommendations. Denial becomes maladaptive when it impedes progress toward functional independence or when it prevents realistic planning for the future (Rosenthal and Young, 1988). Families may collude with the patient's own denial system in accepting no less than complete and miraculous recovery. This leads to endless shopping for new doctors, treatment facilities, and "breakthroughs" (McKinlay and Hickox, 1988; Romano, 1974). The inevitable shattering of these unrealistic hopes may be followed by a classic grief reaction on the part of family members who mourn the patient's premorbid self (MacFarlane, 1999; Padrone, 1999).

Family members frequently feel trapped and isolated by their caretaking role, which may seem like an interminable sentence (Lezak, 1978). Families forgo vacations, put moving and career plans on hold, and sharply limit activities. Patients whose behavior is disturbing to others may turn even a simple dinner date with friends into an embarrassing ordeal, and the family eventually decides that it is just easier to stay home. Moreover, guests and visitors to the patient's home tend to drift away in the face of obnoxious, embarrassing, or boring behavior. Even if not actually offensive, patients with language disorders, orientation problems, or childish dependency may hardly be able to fulfill the role of normal companion when going out with their spouses. Eventually, even extended family members may fail to keep in touch.

The patient's dependency may provoke a number of reactions in family members. Spouses, in particular, sooner or later come to resent their enforced caretaking role, while parents typically persevere longer out of a greater sense of obligation; some may actually be gratified to "have their child back again." Battles may rage when parents clash with spouses over the "best way" to treat the brain-injured family member, although in some cases, the spouse (usually the wife) will welcome the increase in authority bequeathed by the patient's incapacity, and spouse and parents may then collude in the patient's progressive infantilization, ostensibly for his or her "own protection" (Brooks, 1984; Lezak, 1988).

Family members not directly involved in the care of the brain-injured patient may envy and resent the attention the patient receives, while at the same time feeling guilty about being jealous of someone who is obviously so impaired as to need continuous aid (Livingston and Brooks, 1988; McKinlay and Hickox, 1988). This vicious cycle of anger and remorse may lead to depression in family members, and the family's mood may become yoked to that of the patient, with rollercoaster ups and downs sometimes oscillating daily. It is the symptomatology of depression—anxiety and agitation, obsessive rumination, lethargy and fatigue, disturbed sleep and appetite—that otherwise stable family members may interpret as signs of "going crazy" (Lezak, 1978). Clearly, at this point, therapeutic help is needed.

SETTING

The treatment recommendations in this chapter are appropriate for rehabilitation and mental health clinicians who work with brain-injured patients and their families in inpatient hospitals, outpatient day treatment facilities, and office practice settings. The difference in setting is usually determined primarily by the severity of injury and stage of recovery of the patient. The case examples described below are drawn from the author's experience in a private practice and outpatient clinic, where he specializes in the treatment of brain-injured individuals and their families.

TREATMENT MODEL

Principles of Family Therapy of Brain Injury

In general, family therapy of brain injury should maximize the family's capability in managing the patient's activities, while also encouraging the family to give the patient as much autonomy as possible and—equally important—helping the family members to utilize one another as sources of strength (McDaniel, Hepworth, and Doherty, 1992; Miller, 1991b, 1993a).

Educative and Supportive Measures

A crucial but often neglected component in the psychorehabilitative process is the education and training of the family in the nature of brain injury and its treatment. More than half of relatives in one survey (Panting and Merry, 1972) reported that medical personnel did not supply sufficient information, particularly with regard to the patient's prognosis and to the kinds of difficulties that the family should anticipate. Indeed, by far the most common complaint I hear in daily practice is, "Why didn't my doctor tell me that?" Do not underestimate the anxiety-relieving power of clear, simple, accurate explanations (Acorn and Roberts, 1992; Miller, 1993b; Padrone, 1999).

While the patient is still in the hospital, and during the first few "honeymoon" weeks or months after returning home, the family may ignore, deny, and resent well-intended professional advice as to the nature of the task ahead, since they may be unwilling to let go of the optimistic anticipation of boundless progress by their loved one (Lezak, 1978). Supportive family therapy is intended to assist the family in dealing with feelings of loss and helplessness and to help the family adapt itself to the patient's disability. Family members should be given the opportunity to work through their feelings of sadness, loss, guilt, and anger, while being helped to accept a realistic picture of the brain injury (Acorn and Roberts, 1992; MacFarlane, 1999; McCown and Johnson, 1993; Rosenthal and Young, 1988).

Lezak (1978) delineates several basic points about life after brain injury that all families should be helped to understand:

1. Anger, frustration, and sorrow are natural emotions that relatives of brain-injured patients should expect to experience.
2. Caretakers must take good care of themselves if they expect to be of continued benefit to the patient.
3. In the inevitable conflicts with the patient and disagreements with other family members, the primary caretaker must ultimately rely on his or her own conscience and judgment.
4. All family members should try to understand that the family role changes often necessitated by the patient's brain injury can be emotionally distressing for everyone concerned.
5. There are realistic limits to what the family members can do to change the patient's personality or behavior, so they need not feel guilty or ineffective when their care does not result in dramatic improvement.
6. When the welfare of dependent children is at stake, the family must face tough but necessary choices about where the best placement for the patient may be.

A large part of educative and supportive counseling involves dealing with unrealistic expectations the family may have about the patient's future and theirs (McLaughlin and Schaffer, 1985). Families may harbor expectations of a complete personality overhaul, especially when premorbid behavior has been impulsive, antisocial, or disruptive. In these cases, some families may expect the patient to have been "scared straight" or to have had "some sense knocked into him," and thus may actually feel relieved that life will now be more calm and trouble-free—an illusion that is typically shattered when the patient's impulsive behavior escalates now that even the meager prior restraints on behavior have been further impaired by brain injury.

Many patients go through a recovery period that seems to replicate normal development: learning to walk, talk, acquire self-care skills, and so on. Recovery may therefore be seen by the family as a fortuitous opportunity to nurture the patient back toward becoming the "right" kind of person, a "second chance" at parenting—especially when there is guilt or regret over having misused the first chance. In such cases, the therapist may need to gently discourage the family from trying to effect a total psychological makeover of the patient; instead, they should be encouraged to proceed at the patient's own pace in developing his or her realistic potential (McLaughlin and Shaffer, 1985).

Family Psychotherapy

Many families carry emotional baggage that has nothing to do with this particular injury, for which they may turn to a family therapist for help. Brain injury in a family member can stretch the adaptive capacity of the family system to its limits, compounding whatever problems already exist and often becoming the key issue around which family pathology crystallizes. Where educative and supportive measures are not in themselves sufficient, more extensive and intensive family therapy approaches may be indicated.

When the brain injury impacts on a premorbid history of family dysfunction, and/or where the family's reaction to the brain injury results in maladaptive interactional patterns, family therapy can help resolve dysfunctional communication that may be causing problems among the family members and between the family and the patient. Rosenthal and Young (1988) emphasize several approaches to and goals of family therapy in brain injury. First, the family members must be encouraged to assume mutual responsibility for the family's problems and must learn how to shift the burden of causality from the identified patient to the dysfunctional areas of the family system. Second, the positive, adaptive, and healthy aspects of the family system should be strengthened and capitalized upon. Third, dysfunctional interaction patterns can be explored by the reenactment of family conflicts and by assisting the family members to substitute conflict resolution strategies that are appropriate to their particular family system. Finally, cognitive-behavioral strategies during the sessions and practice exercises or "homework assignments" outside the sessions can be assigned to foster generalization of behavior change (Smith and Godfrey, 1995).

One key task of family therapy is to ease the transition of the patient into his or her new role within the family and to facilitate adjustment to changed roles on the part of the other family members (Lezak, 1988). This usually requires some reworking of each family member's old feelings, expectations, and reaction patterns so that new, more realistic perceptions and understanding can take their place. Such dissolution and reintegration can be a difficult task and is rarely accomplished right away (Pasnau, Fawzy, and Lansky, 1981).

Interventions introduced at too early a stage of the adjustment process must run interference through a host of unrealistic expectations, fantasies, denial, raw shame, guilt, and catastrophic reactions on the part of the family. The family healing process takes both time and skill.

Guilt, reactive blaming, and demandingness are often found in family members, along with marked anxiety about disclosing and discussing these difficulties directly (Pasnau, Fawzy, and Lansky, 1981). These reactions tend to contribute to splitting among family members, as well as to the bombardment of the therapist and other clinicians with demands and complaints of inadequate care. This, in turn, may lead to the pitting of doctors against one another, clinicians dumping and referring to avoid the patient, the family becoming angrier and more desperate, and the therapist finally coming to believe that the case is hopeless because of "reality issues."

In such cases, the therapist must try to ensure that families do not perceive intervention as a humiliating, accusing, or demanding interrogation or trial. Rather, empathic contact with each family member, including the brain-injured patient, should be used to draw out and explore the fears and fantasies that may be getting in the way of progress toward adjustment (Pasnau, Fawzy, and Lansky, 1981). For example, patients should be gently probed about their fears of the family wanting to get rid of them or conspiring to steal their money—reality issues *are* important here (Miller, 1992a, 1994b). Families should be encouraged to express their guilt for resenting the "poor, injured patient," which is often related to the inadequately faced fear that caring for the patient will exhaust the family's energy, money, and goodwill. In addition, family members may need help to get in touch with anxieties about no longer being able to depend on the injured person financially, emotionally, socially, or otherwise.

From the beginning, the therapist should empathize with such disowned fearful fantasies without attempting to discredit or dismiss them. This enables the family to work toward the time when these fantasies can be acknowledged as conscious anxieties to be openly dealt with. At some point in the process, the family should be ready to face more productively the reality-based management issues involved in caring for and living with the patient. In this regard, requirements of the family members should be made explicit and should be constructively challenged in response to uncontrolled outbursts by the patient. To this end, the patient's capacity and motivation to take responsibility for his or her actions must be examined (Pasnau, Fawzy, and Lansky, 1981).

Special problems revolve around sex. In brain injury, interpersonal difficulties tend to account for sexual problems to a far greater degree than physical incapacity, the latter being more of a concern with spinal cord injuries (Rosenbaum and Najeson, 1976). It is usually wives that report dissatisfaction with marital relations after their husband's brain injury, and this may occur for a number of reasons (Lezak, 1978, 1988; Miller, 1993a, 1994c; Rosenbaum and Najeson, 1976; Rosenthal and Young, 1988).

The loss of empathic sensitivity and the childlike emotionality and behavior of many brain-injured patients usually serve to discourage feelings of intimacy. The patient's organic egocentricity may prevent her or him from genuinely expressing affection; instead the patient may behave "like a horny monkey," as one spouse expressed it. Sexual demands may be tinged with anger at the perceived rejection by the spouse, sometimes compounded by delusional jealousy, leading in some cases to domestic violence. Even in less extreme cases, a male patient who cannot perform adequately may defensively blame the spouse, yet pursue her all the more vigorously to "prove" himself. Wives, for their part, typically find it easier to live with sexual indifference than with such compulsive but emotionally vacuous ardor. In general, however, sexual indifference is more common than rampant lust, perhaps related to depression and/or organic neuroendocrine dysfunction (Miller, 1993b, 1994c; Parker, 1990).

Rosenthal and Young (1988) maintain that it is important to address marital and sexual issues from the earliest stages of recovery. Although some spouses and significant others may be unable to confront these problems productively during this stage, raising the issue at least lets the family know that the therapist is available to discuss it at a later date when the family is ready. Often, family members are more receptive and willing to work on these issues after the patient has been home for a while and they have accommodated and accepted the reality and permanence of the changes. In other cases I have found, the marital relationship may have already been shaky before the injury, and the patient's invalidism is now used as an excuse—by either party—to avoid all further intimacy. Here the problem is less one of sexual performance than a personality-relationship issue, and it should be treated accordingly (Carter and Carter, 1998; Harmon, Waldo, and Johnson, 1998; Miller, 1993a; Weeks and Treat, 1992).

CASE EXAMPLES

Three siblings and one friend, all adolescents, were involved in an auto accident in which the oldest sibling was driving while stoned on beer and marijuana. The boy's youngest brother was killed, and his sister and the friend both suffered serious brain injury, while the driver himself escaped with a broken wrist and shoulder dislocation, but no head trauma or serious permanent injury. Not only did the driver blame himself, but the full fury of the family's existential outrage was for a time directed against the son, who came close to killing himself.

In this case, the therapist had to address the family's loss, their rage against the "guilty" member, and that member's own crippling remorse. In the course of individual and family therapy, the driver and his parents learned to deal adaptively with issues of responsibility, guilt, atonement, and forgiveness. This young man eventually became active in caring for his injured sister and in antidrug, designated-driver, and other such causes.

Another case involved a physically enormous yet premorbidly gentle teddy bear–like young male adult who, following his TBI, was repeatedly arrested for indecent exposure and attempted sexual assault and eventually had to be institutionalized on the basis of his disinhibited sexual behavior. Interviews with the patient, his family, and local officials revealed that he was not at any time physically aggressive, but rather had the disconcerting habit of crudely and blatantly (albeit politely) soliciting sexual favors from local neighborhood women. This, combined with his imposing size, made him appear particularly dangerous and led to the arrests and confinement. His father, a retired police officer, had the most trouble dealing with this son who not only would now never follow in the father's law-enforcement footsteps, but was a source of embarrassment among the father's peer group.

Surprisingly, the father was quite amenable to family therapy, if only to discover ways to "fix" the son's behavior and improve the family situation. Beginning with a very down-to-earth cognitive-behavioral problem-solving approach to therapy and focusing at first on small goals that could be realistically attained, the family learned to gain enough of a sense of control that they could explore other issues associated with their feelings of having a "defective child." Ultimately, they learned to accept that some degree of custodial control would always be required in managing their son and were able to form productive liaisons with local medical and law enforcement authorities, so that critical incidents involving their son could be swiftly and effectively handled with a minimum of trauma and disruption. In this regard, the father's law-enforcement connections in the community proved invaluable.

A third case illustrates how distressingly easy it sometimes is for painstakingly and laboriously crafted family therapy regimens to be undone by careless or deliberate (even if well-meaning) sabotage. One wife of a brain-injured man in his thirties reported numerous pitched battles between herself and her husband's parents, who repeatedly accused her of "pushing our boy beyond his limits" by expecting him to be as self-sufficient in daily tasks as possible—a therapeutic goal that had been worked on for some time. Tired of the continual backseat complaining and thinking to provide a kind of "shock treatment" cure, the wife encouraged the parents to take care of their son at the parents' house while she took her children on a two-week trip to visit out-of-state relatives. The expectation was to find, on her return, a pair of exhausted, distraught, and contrite in-laws begging her to take back their son, and forswearing any further criticism of her noble efforts.

Instead, the wife was stunned to discover her husband cheerily aslouch in a rented wheelchair, in front of the television, all rehabilitation home-practice tasks lying undone for the last two weeks, and being doted on by both parents, who had apparently devoted every waking moment since the wife's departure to making their son "comfortable," thereby setting their own example of how they expected the wife to treat their offspring from that point on. Predictably, the family situation deteriorated quickly when the wife took her spouse home, and no amount of further therapeutic intervention could prevent the marriage from ending in divorce several months later.

STRENGTHS AND LIMITATIONS

Strengths of the family therapy approach to brain injury rehabilitation include involvement of the whole family system in comprehensive, real-world, ecologically relevant rehabilitation. This approach conceptualizes rehabilitation not as a static, time-limited treatment model, but as an ongoing, integrative, and cumulative human enterprise encompassing cognitive, emotional, and social functioning. On a practical level, attention to family issues increases the overall motivation of the family system to support the patient's efforts at recovery, rehabilitation, and return to work, if possible.

Limitations of the model include the difficulty often encountered in eliciting and sustaining sufficient commitment from family members or the patient to follow through on treatment recommendations or even to regularly attend family sessions. Another limitation is that, especially in medical settings, family therapy—indeed, psychotherapy in general—is often seen as an ancillary or adjunctive treatment modality as compared to, say, physical therapy, and this lack of regard is subtly or overtly communicated to family members. Actually, this is hardly the family treatment model's fault per se, but may be correctable by better patient and family education.

INTEGRATION WITH PSYCHIATRIC SERVICES AND THE ROLE OF MEDICATION

All responsible clinicians recognize the role of appropriate psychotropic medication in the management of TBI syndromes (Zeilman, Perry, and Robinson, 1996). These include anticonvulsants, psychostimulants, antidepressants, anxiolytics, and pain medications. In the best cases, medication is used to stabilize the emotional and behavioral functioning of the patient, so that appropriate behavioral management, cognitive rehabilitation, individual psychotherapy, and family therapy can be productively applied. Not to be neglected is the role of medication in treating family members themselves, many of whom may have developed mood disorders or other psychological disorders from the stress of dealing with their brain-injured family member.

CULTURAL AND GENDER ISSUES

Cultural issues may become important in several areas. First, neuropsychological assessment needs to account for differences in language and cognitive style (Ardila, 1995; Ardila, Rosselli, and Ostrovsky, 1992). Second, certain cultures are much less tolerant of "mental problems" than others, and families from such cultures may neglect and disparage any manifestation of TBI that does not present as an obvious physical impairment. Third, many of these same cultures are resistant to the idea of "mental help" and may avoid family therapy and psychotherapeutic modalities generally; conversely, any help that *is* sought may come from religious leaders or folk medicine practitioners.

With regard to gender issues, wives of brain-injured men may show greater commitment to preserving the relationship than husbands of brain-injured women. This gender difference also intersects with age variables: older couples with more investment in the relationship may be more committed to preserving it.

FUTURE DIRECTIONS

Surveying the literature, one can get the impression that the outlook for family adjustment to brain injury is almost always poor, and my own clinical experience suggests that family therapists who require regular doses of success and gratitude steer clear of the brain-injury field. However, even if it is the exception rather than the rule, the positive results we do see as the result of our assiduous helping efforts can sustain the promise of optimism in each new case. Nor are the reports from the field uniformly grim. Even some very severely injured patients make excellent recoveries and satisfactory reintegrations into the family system (Fahy, Irving, and Millac, 1967; London, 1967; Oddy and Humphrey, 1980; Weddell, Oddy, and Jenkins, 1980).

So the good news is that it is not all bad news. The challenge is to discern the factors that contribute to good recovery, such as premorbid personality, family environment, social support, professional intervention, and so on. Perhaps clinicians who do much of their work in acute and postacute rehabilitation settings see the tough cases before time and proper treatment have enabled the situation to improve. Too often, any systematic therapeutic work ends when the family carts the patient home from the treatment facility. Aggravating this situation is the growing reluctance of third-party payers to underwrite such services as psychotherapy, family therapy, sex therapy, aggression management training, and so on, on the premise that physical and vocational rehabilitation is all that is needed to return the patient to "maximum medical improvement."

Ironically, one of the most promising future directions of family therapy after TBI is its potential integration with cognitive rehabilitation and vocational retraining. Enlisting the family as an ally in the reinstatement of a patient into the workforce will ultimately save money that would have been spent for more formal treatment or for disability payments to patients that remain unemployed and dependent on others.

The reality is that a patient whose cognitive difficulties are exacerbated by depression over his or her distorted family role, whose willingness to cooperate with treatment recommendations and follow through on work assignments is sapped by constant interpersonal bickering, who feels beaten and demoralized and unsure of what miseries each new day will bring—this person is not likely to be a reliable wage earner, no matter how much vocational rehabilitation and job site retraining is provided. The principles of effective psychotherapy of brain injury are fundamentally those of effective psychotherapy generally (Miller, 1993b, 1993d, 1999b; Prigatano, 1999). If the therapist can help turn the brain-injured patient's and family's life from disastrous defeat into at least a fighting struggle, a crucial corner will have been turned.

REFERENCES

Acorn, S. and Roberts, E. (1992). Head injury: Impact on the wives. *Journal of Neuroscience Nursing, 24,* 324-328.

Ardila, A. (1995). Directions of research in cross-cultural neuropsychology. *Journal of Clinical and Experimental Neuropsychology, 17,* 143-150.

Ardila, A., Rosselli, M., and Ostrovsky, F. (1992). Sociocultural factors in neuropsychological assessment. In A.E. Puente and R.J. McCaffrey (Eds.), *Handbook of neuropsychological assessment: A biopsychosocial perspective* (pp. 181-192). New York: Plenum Press.

Benson, D.F. (1977). Psychiatric problems in aphasia. In M.T. Sarno and O. Hook (Eds.), *Aphasia: Assessment and treatment.* New York: Masson.

Bond, M. (1984). The psychiatry of closed head injury. In N. Brooks (Ed.), *Closed head injury: Psychological, social, and family aspects* (pp. 148-178). New York: Oxford University Press.

Brooks, N. (1984). Head injury and the family. In N. Brooks (Ed.), *Closed head injury: Psychological, social, and family aspects* (pp. 123-147). New York: Oxford University Press.

Brooks, N., Campsie, L., and Symington, C. (1986). The five-year outcome of severe blunt head injury: A relative's view. *Journal of Neurology, Neurosurgery, and Psychiatry, 49,* 764-770.

Brooks, N., Campsie, L., and Symington, C. (1987). The effects of severe head injury upon patient and relatives within seven years of injury. *Journal of Head Trauma Rehabilitation, 2,* 1-13.

Carter, R.E. and Carter, C.A. (1998). Physical illness and married couples. In J. Carlson and L. Sperry (Eds.), *The disordered couple* (pp. 163-186). New York: Brunner/Mazel.

Fahy, T.J., Irving, M.H., and Millac, P. (1967). Severe head injuries: A six-year follow-up. *Lancet, 2,* 475-479.

Galasko, C.S.B. and Edwards, D.H. (1974). The causes of injuries requiring admission to hospital in the 1970s. *Injury, 6,* 107-112.

Galbraith, S., Murray, W.R., Patel, A.R., and Knill-Jones, R. (1976). The relationship between alcohol and head injury and its effects on the conscious level. *British Journal of Surgery, 63,* 128-130.

Groom, K.N., Shaw, T.G., O'Connor, M.E., Howard, N.I., and Pickens, A. (1998). Neurobehavioral symptoms and family functioning in traumatically brain-injured adults. *Archives of Clinical Neuropsychology, 13,* 695-711.

Harmon, M.J., Waldo, M., and Johnson, J. A. (1998). The sexually dysfunctional couple: Vaginismus and relationship enhancement therapy. In J. Carlson and L. Sperry (Eds.), *The disordered couple* (pp. 83-95). New York: Brunner/Mazel.

Jamieson, K.G. (1971). Prevention of head injury. In *Head Injuries: Proceedings of an International Symposium* (pp. 12-15). Edinburgh: Churchill Livingstone.

Leftoff, S. (1983). Psychopathology in light of brain injury: A case study. *Journal of Clinical Neuropsychology, 5,* 51-63.

Lezak, M.D. (1978). Living with the characterologically altered brain injured patient. *Journal of Clinical Psychiatry, 39,* 592-598.

Lezak, M.D. (1988). Brain damage is a family affair. *Journal of Clinical and Experimental Neuropsychology, 10,* 111-123.

Livingston, M.G. and Brooks, N. (1988). The burden on families of the brain-injured: A review. *Journal of Head Trauma Rehabilitation, 3,* 6-15.

London, P.S. (1967). Some observations on the course of events after severe injury of the head. *Annals of the Royal College of Surgeons, 41,* 460-479.

MacFarlane, M.M. (1999). Treating brain-injured clients and their families. *Family Therapy, 26,* 13-29.

McCown, W.G. and Johnson, J. (1993). *Therapy with treatment-resistant families: A consultation-crisis intervention model.* Binghamton, NY: The Haworth Press, Inc.

McDaniel, S.H., Hepworth, J., and Doherty, W.J. (1992). *Medical family therapy: A biopsychosocial approach to families with health problems.* New York: Basic Books.

McKinlay, W.W., Brooks, N., Bond, M., Martinage, D.P., and Marshall, M.M. (1981). The short-term outcome of severe head injury as reported by relatives of the injured persons. *Journal of Neurology, Neurosurgery, and Psychiatry, 44,* 527-533.

McKinlay, W.W. and Hickox, A. (1988). How can families help in the rehabilitation of the head injured? *Journal of Head Trauma Rehabilitation, 3,* 64-72.

McLaughlin, A.M. and Schaffer, V. (1985). Rehabilitate or remold? Family involvement in head trauma recovery. *Cognitive Rehabilitation, 3*(1), 14-17.

Miller, L. (1989). Neuropsychology, personality, and substance abuse: Implications for head injury rehabilitation. *Cognitive Rehabilitation, 7*(5), 26-31.

Miller, L. (1990a). Chronic pain complicating head injury: Recommendations for clinicians. *Cognitive Rehabilitation, 8*(5), 12-19.

Miller, L. (1990b). Major syndromes of aggressive behavior following head injury: An introduction to evaluation and treatment. *Cognitive Rehabilitation, 8*(6), 14-19.

Miller, L. (1990c). Neurobehavioral syndromes and the private practitioner: An introduction to evaluation and treatment. *Psychotherapy in Private Practice, 8*(3), 1-12.

Miller, L. (1991a). Psychotherapy of the brain-injured patient: Principles and practices. *Journal of Cognitive Rehabilitation, 9*(2), 24-30.

Miller, L. (1991b). Significant others: Treating brain injury in the family context. *Journal of Cognitive Rehabilitation, 9*(3), 16-25.

Miller, L. (1992a). Back to the future: Legal, vocational, and quality-of-life issues in the long-term adjustment of the brain-injured patient. *Journal of Cognitive Rehabilitation, 10*(5), 14-20.

Miller, L. (1992b). Neuropsychology, personality, and substance abuse in the head injury case: Clinical and forensic issues. *International Journal of Law and Psychiatry, 15,* 303-316.

Miller, L. (1993a). Family therapy of brain injury: Syndromes, strategies, and solutions. *American Journal of Family Therapy, 21,* 111-121.

Miller, L. (1993b). *Psychotherapy of the brain injured patient: Reclaiming the shattered self.* New York: Norton.

Miller, L. (1993c). The "trauma" of head trauma: Clinical, neuropsychological, and forensic aspects of posttraumatic stress syndromes in brain injury. *Journal of Cognitive Rehabilitation, 11*(4), 18-29.

Miller, L. (1993d). Who are the best psychotherapists? Qualities of the effective practitioner. *Psychotherapy in Private Practice, 12*(1), 1-18.

Miller, L. (1994a). Alcohol and drug abuse in traumatic brain injury. In A.T. DiKengil, S. Morganstein, M.C. Smith, and M.C. Thut (Eds.), *Family articles about traumatic brain injury* (pp. 121-122). Tucson: Communication Skill Builders.

Miller, L. (1994b). Competency and guardianship issues in traumatic brain injury. In A.T. DiKengil, S. Morganstein, M.C. Smith, and M.C. Thut (Eds.), *Family articles about traumatic brain injury* (pp. 167-168). Tucson: Communication Skill Builders.

Miller, L. (1994c). Sex and the brain-injured patient: Regaining love, pleasure, and intimacy. *Journal of Cognitive Rehabilitation, 12*(3), 12-20.

Miller, L. (1994d). Traumatic brain injury and aggression. In M. Hillbrand and N.J. Pallone (Eds.), *The psychobiology of aggression: Engines, measurement, control* (pp. 91-103). Binghamton, NY: The Haworth Press, Inc.

Miller, L. (1998a). Brain injury and violent crime: Clinical, neuropsychological, and forensic considerations. *Journal of Cognitive Rehabilitation, 16*(6), 2-17.

Miller, L. (1998b). *Shocks to the system: Psychotherapy of traumatic disability syndromes.* New York: Norton.

Miller, L. (1999a). Atypical psychological responses to traumatic brain injury: PTSD and beyond. *Neurorehabilitation, 13,* 13-24.

Miller, L. (1999b). A history of psychotherapy with patients with brain injury. In K.G. Langer, L. Laatsch and L. Lewis (Eds.), *Psychotherapeutic interventions for adults with brain injury or stroke: A clinician's treatment resource* (pp. 27-43). New York: Psychosocial Press.

Miller, L. (1999c). Treating posttraumatic stress disorder in children and families: Basic principles and clinical applications. *American Journal of Family Therapy, 27,* 21-34.

Oddy, M. and Humphrey, M. (1980). Social recovery during the year following severe head injury. *Journal of Neurology, Neurosurgery, and Psychiatry, 43,* 798-802.

Padrone, F. J. (1999). Psychotherapeutic issues in treating family members. In K.G. Langer, L. Laatsch, and L. Lewis (Eds.). *Psychotherapeutic interventions for adults with brain injury or stroke: A clinician's treatment resource* (pp. 191-209). Madison, WI: Psychosocial Press.

Panting, A. and Merry, P. (1972). The long-term rehabilitation of severe head injuries with particular reference to the need for the patient's family. *Rehabilitation, 38,* 33-37.

Parker, R.S. (1990). *Traumatic brain injury and neuropsychological impairment: Sensorimotor, cognitive, emotional, and adaptive problems of children and adults.* New York: Springer-Verlag.

Pasnau, R.O., Fawzy, F.I., and Lansky, M.R. (1981). Organic brain syndrome and the family. In M.R. Lansky (Ed.), *Family therapy and major psychopathology* (pp. 301-324). New York: Grune and Stratton.

Potter, J.M. (1967). Head injuries today. *Postgraduate Medical Journal, 43,* 574-581.

Prigatano, G.P. (1999). *Principles of neuropsychological rehabilitation.* New York: Oxford University Press.

Robinson, R.G. (1986). Post-stroke mood disorders. *Hospital Practice, 21,* 83-89.

Robinson, R.G., Kubos, K.L., Starr, L.B., Rao, K., and Price, T.R. (1984). Mood disorders in stroke patients: Importance of location of lesion. *Brain, 107,* 81-93.

Robinson, R.G., Lipsey, J.R., and Price, T.R. (1985). Diagnosis and clinical management of post-stroke depression. *Psychosomatics, 26,* 769-778.

Romano, M.D. (1974). Family response to traumatic head injury. *Scandinavian Journal of Rehabilitation Medicine, 4,* 1-5.

Rosenbaum, A. and Hoge, S.K. (1989). Head injury and marital aggression. *American Journal of Psychiatry, 146,* 1048-1051.

Rosenbaum, M. and Najeson, T. (1976). Changes in life pattern and symptoms of low mood as reported by wives of severely brain-injured soldiers. *Journal of Consulting and Clinical Psychology, 44,* 881-886.

Rosenthal, M. and Young, T. (1988). Effective family intervention after traumatic brain injury: Theory and practice. *Journal of Head Trauma Rehabilitation, 3,* 42-50.

Ross, E.D. (1981). The aprosodias: Functional-anatomic organization of language in the right hemisphere. *Archives of Neurology, 38,* 561-569.

Ross, E.D. and Rush, A.J. (1981). Diagnosis and neuroanatomical correlates of depression in brain-damaged patients: Implications for a neurology of depression. *Archives of General Psychiatry, 38,* 1344-1354.

Ross, E.D. and Stewart, R.S. (1987). Pathological display of affect in patients with depression and right frontal brain damage: An alternative mechanism. *Journal of Nervous and Mental Disease, 175,* 165-172.

Schmidt, M.F. and Heinemann, A.W. (1999). Substance abuse interventions for people with brain injury. In K.G. Langer, L. Laatsch, and L. Lewis (Eds.), *Psychotherapeutic interventions for adults with brain injury or stroke: A clinician's treatment resource* (pp. 211-238). Madison, WI: Psychosocial Press.

Slagle, D.A. (1990). Psychiatric disorders following closed head injury: An overview of biopsychosocial factors in their etiology and management. *International Journal of Psychiatry in Medicine, 20,* 1-35.

Smith, L.M. and Godfrey, H.P.D. (1995). *Family support programs and rehabilitation: A cognitive-behavioral approach to traumatic brain injury.* New York: Plenum.

Thomsen, J.V. (1974). The patient with severe head injury and his family. *Scandinavian Journal of Rehabilitation Medicine, 6,* 180-183.

Weddell, R., Oddy, M., and Jenkins, D. (1980). Social adjustment after rehabilitation: A two-year follow-up. *Psychological Medicine, 10,* 257-263.

Weeks, G.R. and Treat, S. (1992). *Couples in treatment: Techniques and approaches for effective practice.* New York: Brunner/Mazel.

Zeilman, C., Perry, P.J., and Robinson, R.G. (1996). Medications and their effects. In M. Rizzo and D. Tranel (Eds.), *Head injury and postconcussion syndrome* (pp. 333-350). New York: Churchill Livingstone.

Chapter 14

Women and Mental Health:
A Feminist Family Systems Approach

Carmen Knudson-Martin

INTRODUCTION

The headline of the August 4, 1999, *USA Today* proclaimed that women in every economic, age, and social category of a large international survey reported more stress than men. This is not surprising. Women experience higher rates of depression and anxiety (Anderson and Holder, 1989; McGrath et al., 1990). They continue to carry the major burden for household and relationship work and are more stressed by the performance of these demands than men (Larson and Richards, 1994; Risman and Johnson-Sumerford, 1998). Women score lower on common measures of emotional well-being such as self-esteem and personal power, and the avenues historically available to them for self-expression have been limited (Lennon, 1996). Moreover, the standard by which psychological health has been measured is male. Thus it can seem difficult to be female and psychologically healthy at the same time (Anderson and Holder, 1989).

Many practitioners today are concerned that traditional approaches to mental health treatment are biased against women (e.g., Greene, 1994; Walters, 1994). Though women are the most frequent consumers of mental health services, the theories and diagnostic systems commonly applied to women frequently have not taken into account their developmental experiences or considered the prominent role that gender socialization and inequalities play in creating and maintaining the mental health symptoms of women. As the ones held responsible for family care and well-being, women have also been disproportionately targeted for change by "systems" treatments of child and family problems.

How the construct of "self" is framed is pivotal in devising more effective, less biased approaches to mental health treatment for women. When the self is viewed as an individual property that remains static from one situation to another, diagnosis and treatment will focus on the capacities for autonomous functioning and mastery. This traditional formulation does not accurately represent the processes of self development for women (Belenky et al., 1986; Jordan et al., 1991). It devalues the relational qualities associated with the feminine, making them less likely to be highlighted or encouraged in treatment. Awareness of dependence on others and the ways that the self is influenced by one's position in the class, gender, racial, and cultural structures of society are masked (Almeida, Woods, and Messineo; 1998; McGoldrick and Carter, 1999). The changing and contextual nature of self is overlooked (Rosenbaum and Dyckman, 1995).

Family systems theory, which shifts the focus from the intrapsychic to the interactional, is a move toward a contextual conceptualization of self and provides a relational frame from which to approach women's issues. However, traditional family systems approaches were also based on the "old" separation-individuation model (Fowers and Richardson, 1996). Individualistic notions of hierarchy, boundaries, and fusion were emphasized at the expense of the capacities necessary for commitment, relationship maintenance, and interdependence—abilities for which women tend to be better socialized than men. Power differences between women and men remained buried within systemic conceptualizations that assumed equality of the players and failed to address the larger sociopolitical factors impacting relationship dynamics.

Feminist approaches integrate the experiences of women into treatment models. They place human development and relational processes within their larger sociopolitical contexts, examine the power relations that reinforce institutional and relationship structures, and ask how these structures can equally support the persons within them. Feminist approaches consider the impact of traditional gender roles on health and well-being of both women and men, make invisible inequalities visible, and avoid treatment practices that replicate them. They also empower clients within the treatment process and require that therapists examine their own roles within social and cultural systems.

This chapter presents a feminist family systems approach to women's mental health issues that helps the practitioner:

- Place symptoms within their larger social, cultural, and political contexts
- Assess functioning according to a more inclusive model of "self"
- Focus on the multisystemic nature of women's problems at three levels
- Develop treatment plans that respect and value women's experiences
- Empower women, not blame them

The model put forth in this chapter provides an expanded systems framework from which to approach mental health treatment. Though our focus here is on women's issues, the model is intended to be an inclusive one. It provides a way of thinking that allows for wide variation in the experiences of both women and men and may be integrated with a variety of other approaches. It is useful for working across multiple racial, class, economic, gender, and cultural structures and is especially valuable for groups that do not prioritize individualism.

SETTING

The model was developed within a university training clinic that provides family and mental health counseling services to the community and in a private practice specializing in women's issues, gender, and relationship problems. It may be incorporated into many different treatment settings. The case presented in this chapter is based on one from private counseling practice and included managed care oversight and referral to a psychiatrist for medication.

Attention to setting is central to the feminist family systems approach. Setting is expanded to include the societal context within which women develop symptoms and approach treatment and how the treatment system supports or reinforces institutional gender inequalities. Because a case is not understood apart from the treatment setting, specific details of the setting and the therapist will be elaborated in the case example provided later in the chapter.

Practice in the setting described here is guided by two principles: (1) symptoms must be understood within their social and interpersonal context, and (2) the context within which women present for treatment is not neutral. These principles, which expand awareness of context, provide the lens through which women's mental health treatment is viewed. They are described below.

Women's Symptoms in Context

Historical constructions of gender were based on power differences between women and men. Women were dependent on men for their identities and economic well-being. To maintain these positions, men were required to be strong, competent, and in charge; women needed to hide their strengths and competencies and develop indirect influence strategies. Women were trained to accommodate, limit, and measure their voices in a world defined by men. Though ideals about gender are rapidly changing, the gendered styles of behaving live on, often in ways that are hidden and invisible to us (see also Knudson-Martin and Mahoney, 1998).

Women are influenced by a variety of contradictory social messages. Though active participants in the labor force, they remain the primary caregivers and kin-keepers. They are judged psychologically or professionally deficient when they "focus too much" on others, but are held accountable for the health and well-being of their families. They are expected to calm and soothe men and to ensure the safety and self-esteem of their children, but they are criticized for being "overinvolved" or "controlling." Women who do not conform to dominant role stereotypes may be stigmatized; those who do are marginalized.

Some women thrive despite these contradictory pulls, but positive models are few and social structures still promote gender inequality (Dusky, 1996; Lindsey, 1997). Many of women's symptoms are best understood as normal responses to the circumstances of their lives. Feeling fatigued, overwhelmed, incompetent, and powerless is normal in situations with seemingly impossible demands and little recognition. It is difficult to develop a strong sense of one's own worth or value if it is invisible or discounted in the larger society. To the extent that what is "true" is defined by men, women learn that their experiences are not real or are wrong (Kaschak, 1992). They are likely to internalize problems and blame themselves for them.

Gender is not the only cause of women's problems. Symptoms arise from the intersection of a variety of factors. However, the ways symptoms are expressed, their meaning, their course, and the appropriate treatment are not the same for each gender (Padgett, 1997). The onset of schizophrenia, for example, is later for women. Their symptoms have a greater affective component and less cognitive and behavioral disturbance than men's. Psychotic episodes are more likely to be precipitated by real or perceived interpersonal loss than by the assaults on the self-esteem and major role functioning common to men (Anderson and Holder, 1989). Women's addictions are usually hidden, while men's are more overt. They usually have the expressed intent of diminishing a woman's impulses (Bepko, 1989) and are often associated with depression and a history of sexual abuse (Hudal, Krestan, and Bepko, 1999). Because depression affects one's capacity to be relational, depression may have a profoundly negative impact on a woman's sense of self (McGrath et al., 1990). Which psychological symptoms are associated with quality of family life vary according to gender (Knudson-Martin, 2000).

Cultural proscriptions based on gender affect us all, but how they are framed and the ways they play out depend on a variety of other factors. A "nontraditional" woman, for example, may separate herself from her partner to avoid the internalized gender message that she must "be available." Another may react assertively "so she won't be run over by men." A lesbian woman grows up in the same dominant culture as heterosexuals. She may or may not conform to the cultural stereotypes for her gender (Johnson and Keren, 1998). An African-American woman usually holds more power in her household than an Anglo woman. She is encouraged to be self-reliant. Yet she still may learn that her ultimate goal is to find a black man who will take care of her (Boyd-Franklin and Franklin, 1998). A Latina may achieve professional independence in the work world and still feel bound by her culture's rule that the only acceptable way to leave home or have sex is to marry a man (Garcia-Preto, 1998). The feminist family systems model views a woman's symptoms in relation to the current circumstances of her life and identifies the cultural values, ideals, and roles that limit and inform her behavior and choices.

A woman needs validation for her ability to adapt and respond to changing demands. Her competency increases when she recognizes the cultural and sociopolitical hurdles she leaps. If symptoms are defined as the woman's problem or as *her* illness without identifying their social and interpersonal context, mental health treatment can unintentionally contribute to a woman's sense of guilt, shame, responsibility, and incompetence.

Treatment Is Not Neutral

Most clinicians have been trained to be neutral, to avoid imparting their own values or influencing clients. Our stance toward treatment is premised in the conviction that most efforts to "be neutral" reinforce existing inequalities in the status quo; that the absence of active efforts to counteract them perpetuates gender injustices and can be harmful to women. To be truly neutral, to avoid bias against women, treatment settings must consciously create practices that support women while challenging gendered power differentials and the historical constructions of gender that maintain them.

Approaches to gender vary regarding whether they challenge or reinforce gender inequalities (see Knudson-Martin, 1997). In fact, training in gender does not necessarily result in practices that discriminate less against women (Leslie and Clossick, 1996). Models that emphasize ways that women and men are different without critically examining the social context within which reported differences arise tend to reinforce existing gender structures. There is a large overlap between the traits, skills, and abilities of women and men; variations within each gender are considerable (Lindsey, 1997; Lips, 1997). Focusing on how women and men are "wired differently" tends to exaggerate male-female differences, transforming them into female disadvantage (Bem, 1993; Hare-Mustin, 1987).

The treatment model outlined in the next section is designed to actively counteract societal-based gender inequalities. This is accomplished through:

- Self-reflexivity regarding the treatment context and process
- Commitment to validating women's strengths and experiences
- Identifying power inequalities
- Encouraging alternatives to restrictive gender constructions
- Language and theory that expand women's options

TREATMENT MODEL

The feminist family systems model described here provides an overall framework for assessment and treatment at three levels. The first level takes a metaperspective on the treatment context, questioning how the woman came to be identified as the problem and how case conceptualization and treatment processes are part of societal constructions of gender and power. The second level examines how other family members, persons, groups, or agencies are involved in the problem and how power and gender role expectations play out within these systems. The third level focuses on the development of an integrated "self" as a critical component of mental health, offering an inclusive model for assessment. At each level attention is paid to how the language and focus of treatment can identify the woman's strengths and validate her experience.

The feminist family systems model does not necessarily replace DSM diagnoses or other personal and systems assessments, but it informs how these other sources of information are interpreted and applied. Though assessment in the feminist family systems model is an ongoing process that will occur simultaneously with treatment, it is important to approach new cases with an initial assessment of context at each of the three levels. This will expand how the case is viewed and make conscious ways that gender-based habits and ways of thinking invade treatment and family structures. The order of the levels is significant. We look first beyond the individual before assessing "the self."

Level I—Context of Treatment

The model begins by assessing the treatment situation itself. It poses five questions that frame a contextual approach to the case.

1. How has the woman become defined as the problem?
2. How are gendered expectations influencing case conceptualization?
3. How is power a part of the treatment system?
4. How can treatment identify and validate the woman's strengths and experience?
5. How might treatment reinforce or challenge existing gender inequalities?

How the Woman Became Defined As the Client

Consider the circumstances surrounding a particular woman's presentation for treatment. Why is she the focus of treatment? If she was not "the problem," who else would be? Is she carrying more than her share of responsibility for others? What are her sources of support? What has caused her behavior to be labeled dysfunctional? For example, Glenda, who sought treatment following an investigation of unsubstantiated sexual abuse charges against her husband, approached therapy saying that she was "incompetent" as a parent and responsible for her family's troubles. Her internalized label followed her husband's judgment that she was "too weak to stand up for him" and the referring psychologist's counsel that she needed to learn to be less "passive."

Some women, like Glenda, quickly assume more than their share of responsibility for relationship and child-rearing issues. When their self-blaming definition of the problem or the definition of the referral agent is accepted without examining the larger context, treatment can easily reinforce cultural messages telling women they are both incompetent and responsible. Yet women who resist these messages and approach therapy from an angry or disengaged standpoint may be labeled "uncooperative" or "hostile."

How Gender Expectations Influence Case Conceptualization

Gender expectations influence our conceptualizations in three ways: (1) they limit what we see, (2) they shape how we interpret behaviors, and (3) they influence what we value or define as important. Behavior that is acceptable for men may be defined as a problem when it is expressed by a woman. Thus, a woman who stands up for her rights might be labeled "resistant" by the referring agency. Willingness to accommodate or take in another person's perspective may be negatively defined as "passive," as in Glenda's case, without crediting the important ways that her behavior contributes to relationship maintenance.

Asking how our expectations regarding appropriate behavior for women and men limit what we see helps us remove the gender blinders that are so much a part of our culture that we do not notice them. Because our field has historically labeled female qualities as pathological, questioning our assumptions helps us to consider ways that "female" behavior may be an adaptive response to cultural expectations and institutional power imbalances and to direct our thinking toward the positive functions it provides. Examining our assumptions also helps us attend to differences between the genders without exaggerating or reinforcing them (see Hare-Mustin, 1987).

How Power Is a Part of the Treatment System

When a woman such as Glenda accepts her diagnosis or follows the therapist's advice, this seems normal; we may not consider the power structures surrounding her behavior. Yet her passive "female" behavior is reflective of the societal power structures within which it is embedded. If she is a woman of color or lower socioeconomic status, additional power structures come into play. Knowing how power and powerlessness operate in a particular case is key to effective intervention. The experience of persons from groups occupying lower power positions is seldom empathically understood. Difference and pathology can become interchangeable (Hardy, 1997). To understand the ways larger forces of systemic power impinge on our work, we must consider how power affects the client's approach to authority and how therapist gender, socioeconomic status, and position in the treatment system impact the therapist's relationship with the client. Ask what barriers to trust exist and how previous efforts to "help" may have increased the client's powerlessness. Identify ways that the therapist can make the treatment relationship more symmetrical, such as involving the client in the assessment process, maintaining a less "expert" stance, and making the therapist's vulnerabilities more visible.

It is important to assess the power relations in the treatment structure itself. To whom is treatment ultimately responsible? The client? The court? The schools? An agency? The insurance company? How do economics and the scheduling of time impact the structure of therapy? Who has the power to label or diagnose the problem? Who is defined as the problem if a therapeutic relationship is difficult to attain—in other words, a "hard to engage" client or a disconnected therapist?

How Treatment Can Identify Strengths
and Validate the Woman's Experience

The ability to identify strengths evolves out of sensitivity to the woman's experience and to the obstacles or oppression she may have had to overcome in order to survive or cope. Look for strengths that are likely to remain hidden in traditional assessments. They are likely to include the skills or qualities necessary for relationship maintenance, such as being sensitive to another's needs or perspectives or the willingness to accommodate.

This question helps the therapist define a "problem" that recognizes and supports the woman's strengths. In Glenda's case, this meant validating and building upon her intelligence and deep sense of commitment to her family. Instead of focusing on her as "passive," the assessment credited her worth and asked how it happened that there was no room for her ideas in the marriage. Thus the assessment questions themselves set the stage for a nonblaming, supportive approach and directed the therapy away from individual pathology and toward issues in the relationship structure.

How Treatment Reinforces or Challenges
Existing Gender Inequality

The question of how treatment reinforces or challenges inequality makes visible an active choice on the therapist's part. He or she must consider how treatment will impact the gender status quo for this woman and be accountable for the impact of treatment decisions. For example, if treatment reinforces Glenda's view of herself as "responsible" by helping her "improve her communication skills" without examining the ways the responses of others diminish her position and worth, treatment may actually reinforce inequality. Similarly, efforts to help her by explaining male and female "styles" and helping her adjust to them will also reinforce traits that perpetuate inequality.

Gender inequality is challenged when "making room for her ideas" is framed as the *husband's* responsibility as well as Glenda's. One way to accomplish this is by involving him in the therapy with specific attention to the balance of power in their relationship. Another way is to help Glenda view her situation interactionally and devise strategies for equalizing her position. What is important is that treatment does not reinforce her position as the problem in the family or foster an increased sense of her incompetence and need for help.

Level II—Context of the Client

Level II assessment makes visible the interpersonal context surrounding the woman's symptoms and expands the focus of treatment from the individual to her relational context. Four aspects of client context are examined:

1. How other family members, persons, groups, or agencies are involved in the problem
2. How power is distributed and managed within these relationship structures
3. How gender roles and expectations within these systems help or hinder the problem
4. Specific sources of support and strength

How Others Are Involved

Asking how others contribute to the client's symptoms is critical. Though the other players do not necessarily *cause* the problems, her symptoms cannot be understood without knowing how what others do and think affect her situation. If a woman is depressed, we want to know how others help maintain her depression. We will consider whether anyone benefits from her depression and how the behavior of others may contribute to or help her symptoms. Family members are important, but other groups, such as friends, church acquaintances, coworkers, classmates, and other medical or human service providers or agencies, also play significant roles, as do legal, political, and economic systems.

This level of assessment requires that the therapist create a picture of the client interacting with others. How do others respond to her? To whom does she respond? Who notices her symptoms? How are they interpreted? Who is connected to whom in the family? In the community? What role does the woman play in the structure? The symptoms are only one part of an ongoing interaction process. What are the other components that keep the repetitive process going? If the client did not have these symptoms, how might her part be different? How would others react?

The best way to get contextual information is to ask significant others to participate in the therapy. When arrangements are being made for the initial treatment session, we ask, "Who else is affected by the problem?" and "Who is concerned?" We tell the client that it is our policy to include as many of these involved persons in the first session as possible and that we will later determine together who should actually participate in therapy on an ongoing basis. So, when Jeannie called for an appointment for herself, citing concerns about depression and anxiety, we asked that her husband, Ben, come to the first session also. When we met with Jeannie and Ben, we tried to get a detailed picture of what happens in their daily life together. We wanted to "see" the interaction, as if we were watching a videotape of it. Most important, we observed them as they interacted in the session.

If Ben had been unwilling to participate, if Jeannie had clearly not wanted to involve him, or if we believed a conjoint session would harm Jeannie, we would have needed to ask Jeannie questions that framed her symptoms within relationship processes (instead of within her). Such questioning helps to not only expand our view of the situation, but also expands hers. Seeing Jeannie and Ben together made several things immediately visible: (1) both were deeply committed to each other and happy with their marriage, and (2) Ben was much less stressed than Jeannie. Thinking contextually raised the question, "What factors made it possible for Ben to do so well and for Jeannie to be 'falling apart'?"

How Power Is Distributed and Managed
Within Relationship Structures

Institutional power differences between women and men infiltrate all kinds of relationships (among intimates, in the workplace, in the community). Although overt dominance strategies are quite easily recognized, hidden power differences are less readily noticed (see Komter, 1989). For example, a couple makes "shared" decisions that regularly support the husband's goals; a woman automatically adjusts her schedule to facilitate working with a male partner at work; or the conversation between a man and woman tends to focus more on his interests than hers.

When assessing the power distribution in a relationship, look for who accommodates to whom, who notices and attends to the needs of the other, whose needs and interests shape the relationship, and how the well-being of each is supported. When power is equally distributed, partners will share these relational responsibilities equally. Each will feel equally entitled to his or her needs, wishes, and goals. Responsibility for relationship maintenance and for lower-status tasks such as housework and child care will be shared. Because power imbalances are invisible to most people, it is necessary to ask very specific, behavioral questions, such as, "How (and when) does your partner accommodate to you?" or "How do you make your partner aware of your needs and wishes?"

Ben and Jeannie reported egalitarian ideals. They said they shared child care and household responsibilities. Ben was clearly interested in Jeannie's well-being and respected her. Yet without their awareness, culturally based hidden power flowed to Ben. For example, on his day off, Ben felt free to get a baby-sitter and go skiing. Jeannie worried that they were leaving their children with sitters too often, since both worked and Ben was gone frequently. When Jeannie had time off, she took care of the children and the household chores that she could not get to when she was working. The couple had never discussed this disparity. Remnants of old cultural socialization prevented Jeannie from feeling as entitled to personal time as Ben. They kept her from raising issues of unfairness; they allowed Ben simply not to notice. When we asked how the couple could make the stress in their relationship more equal, both partners readily made changes and Jeannie's depression lifted. Like many men today, Ben wanted to share power with Jeannie. But neither had yet fully developed the corresponding behaviors.

Despite changing gender ideals, many women still live within relationship contexts that limit a woman's voice, agency, and options and grant men the "right" to dominate women. Though women also use violent tactics, only men appear to have the ability to use violence to incite fear and control (Jacobson et al., 1994). A disproportionate number of women diagnosed with psychiatric disorders or who have attempted suicide have been victims of violence and abuse (Bograd, 1999; Padgett, 1997). In assessment of the client's context, one must be alert to violence as a possible, even probable, factor contributing to many women's symptoms.

How Gender Role Expectations Hinder or Help the Problem

Gender tends to structure relationship roles, defining appropriate behavior, who should do what, and how to respond to each other. Traditional gender-role expectations frequently contribute to women's mental health problems, but new, more egalitarian gender-role expectations can also be part of the solution. For example, Jeannie and Ben believed that their relationship should support the well-being of each of them equally, but had fallen into many traditional gender patterns that advantaged Ben's well-being at Jeannie's expense. When assessment of gender-role expectations made their unequal patterns visible, they immediately began to reorganize their relationship system. Not all cases resolve so readily, but discussion about gender arrangements and how they came to be usually helps unexamined alternatives become visible.

To assess how gender-role expectations influence the current situation, consider how cultural gender messages shape the ways partners respond to each other. How do they limit the available choices? Look for ways that "personal" traits such as "emotional" or "not talkative" are influenced by cultural constructions of gender. Do not assume that such differences in male or female behaviors are just the way men or women are. Refer to these behaviors as their habits, not their "natures." Recognize how outmoded gender-role expectations perpetuate power imbalances, contribute to violence, and limit the ability to address conflicts and attain intimacy.

Sources of Strength and Support

Women's strengths are frequently not noticed or validated within the female client's social and interpersonal contexts. Questions that help identify and credit her abilities in relation to these people are important. It is especially useful if questions or observations about her strengths can be directed to significant others. For example, "It seems that Glenda is very sensitive to the needs of others. In what ways has her sensitivity been helpful to you?" Or "Have there been times when Jeannie's automatically attending to household chores has made it easier for you to do the things you want to do?" And when significant others are not present, "How has your loyalty to your work group increased the productivity of others?" Or "How has your ability to put your own needs temporarily on hold contributed to the raising of your children?"

Within most women's contexts are persons who can or do provide support. These sources need to be identified, credited, and encouraged. Some women who readily reach out to support others hesitate to reveal their own vulnerability (Ewashen, 1997). They may feel undeserving of the caring of others or have learned to fear the consequences of their vulnerability. They may even devalue or criticize the caring they do receive. Assessment needs to identify both the available sources of support and what will help the female client feel entitled to access them. Many significant others, especially men, may want to be supportive but need help learning how to provide it. Though therapists can and should be supportive, our approach suggests that the most important forms of support are those developed outside of therapy, within the client's context.

Level III: Emotional Differentiation Within the System

Level III focuses on how the "self" functions within relational systems. We draw on Murrey Bowen's family systems theory (Bowen, 1978; Kerr and Bowen, 1988), but incorporate an updated, more inclusive view of differentiation (see Knudson-Martin, 1994, 1996). According to this way of thinking, culture and family generate an invisible emotional field that influences relational processes. The driving force within this field is the tension between the needs for individuality and the needs for togetherness. Movements toward either may raise anxiety and induce emotionally reactive responses. Differentiation is the key developmental process. When persons are well-differentiated, they experience less anxiety and are able to respond independently of the emotional field without losing connection to the persons that constitute it.

In our model, individuality and togetherness are examined as two distinct dimensions of emotional differentiation (see Figure 14.1). The *individuality* dimension represents increasing increments of the capacity to function autonomously, including the abilities to recognize one's own authority and the development of a distinct sense of self. At the low end of this continuum, individuals cannot separate the self from their perceptions and have little control over their emotional

FIGURE 14.1. Dimensions of Differentiation (Leading to Development of Self)

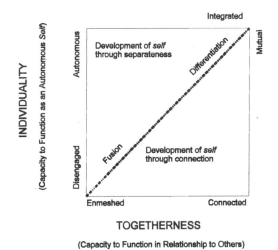

TOGETHERNESS

(Capacity to Function in Relationship to Others)

Source: Knudson-Martin, C., 1996. Differentiation and Self-Development in the Relationship Context. *The Family Journal, 4,* p. 191.   ACA. Reprinted with permission. No further reproduction authorized without written permission of the American Counseling Association.

responses. Adults may exhibit a "pseudoindependence" or self-absorption that keeps them emotionally disengaged from others. The *togetherness* dimension represents increasing increments of the capacity to function in relation to others, including being able to orient oneself to another and temporarily take on another's experience. At the low end of this continuum, anxiety about the reactions of others is high and the experience of others is confused with one's own.

Figure 14.1 shows how both of these aspects of self-development can be integrated. Well-differentiated persons demonstrate both capacities. Level of differentiation is indicated by the intersection point of each dimension. A person may be well developed on one, neither, or both dimensions. The capacities in the area of individuality are not superior to capacities in the area of togetherness. Most people, however, are more developed on one side than the other. Persons on the right side tend to experience the self through their connections to others. At low levels of differentiation they may appear "enmeshed."

Persons on the left side experience the self more separately. At low levels of differentiation they appear "detached." These differences are often, but not always, gender related.

Level III assessment includes four basic questions:

1. How well is the client able to function in relation to others?
2. How well is the client able to function autonomously?
3. In what ways does lack of differentiation from cultural constructions of gender limit development?
4. What will help the client develop a more integrated self?

How the Client Functions in Relation to Others

Assess the client's ability to show concern for and orient to another person. Does she show empathy? Can she imaginatively hold onto another person's experience? Does she recognize her own experience as subjective? Is she oriented toward reciprocal obligation and the development of a shared reality? Is she able to let others impact her? Persons who are poorly developed in this dimension tend to see others through their own experience rather than being able to apprehend the other's experience. They may confuse their own needs with those of others and experience differences as a challenge to the self.

How the Client Functions Autonomously

Assess the client's sense of her own authority and her capacity for independence and self-sufficiency. Does she have a sense of her own private world and integrity? Can she distinguish separate realities? Does she have internal control over her response to her emotions? Has she developed a personal ideology? Can she keep sight of her own position even in the presence of another's? Persons who are poorly developed in this dimension may have difficulty seeing themselves when they are aware of another's needs or interests. In order to preserve relationships they may keep important parts of themselves outside the relationship, detaching from "self."

How Lack of Differentiation from Cultural Gender Constructions Limits Development

To the extent that women and men respond according to gender stereotypes grounded in the past and reexperienced in the present, development of self is limited. Instead, both women and men automatically respond with beliefs and behaviors typical for their genders. Attempts to break these internalized rules may generate anxiety. For example, a woman may feel guilty if she does not accommodate to her partner's wishes. She may hesitate to assert her own wishes. A man may feel controlled or criticized if a female gives him advice. His dependency needs may cause him shame.

Identify ways that the client has internalized cultural messages about gender. Help the client consider where and how these messages were learned. This helps to externalize the messages and increase choice. Note the circumstances that generate anxiety. For example, Nancy, who worked in the marketing division of a major company, reacted with hurt and anger when colleagues "criticized" her marketing plans. This experience raised anxiety over two internalized constructions of gender: (1) that because she was a woman her ideas would not be respected, and (2) that women who liked her would not criticize her ideas. Rather than engage with her colleagues about the marketing issues, she shut down from them emotionally, limiting her development on both dimensions.

How to Help the Client Develop a More Integrated Self

An integrated self is well-differentiated; that is, the person has developed the capacities for both individuality and togetherness. Unlike Nancy, integrated persons are able to stay in a relationship while dealing with contested or hurtful issues. They can share their ideas and their vulnerabilities. They expect and receive mutual giving, are oriented toward reciprocal obligation, and are open to differences. They demonstrate the capacities for emotional expression and interdependence.

Individuality and togetherness tend to support and reinforce each other; the development of one can facilitate development of the other. Tension between the two, however, can sometimes create an impasse, making further movement in either direction difficult. For example, for many years Nancy had primarily developed her togetherness abilities (the connected self). More recently, she had begun to develop a sense of her own ideas (the separate self), but anxiety generated by her fears of losing relational connection limited her ability to consider the input of others without losing confidence in her own thoughts. Though she was no longer willing to sacrifice her ideas to maintain a relationship, she could not tolerate the feelings of separateness she experienced when others questioned her ideas. Nancy was caught in a stalemate. To continue to grow on the individuality dimension, she needed reassurance about her connections with her colleagues.

This model allows for considerable diversity in development. Clients need validation for the more developed side and encouragement and help managing the anxiety that arises as they take steps toward the less developed side. Therapy can and should attend to each dimension simultaneously and help move clients toward the goal of integration; that is, knowing oneself within the context of relationships. When significant others are involved in the therapy, the anxiety generated by the intersection of individuality and togetherness needs can be addressed directly.

Application

Use of this assessment model is itself an intervention. The questions introduce contextual factors into the therapy, support "female" traits that are commonly devalued, and make hidden gender constructions visible. Specific treatment goals can be developed for each level of assessment. The following general treatment goals are suggested:

1. Create a collaborative treatment context that recognizes and minimizes power differences
2. Direct therapeutic interventions toward changing the relationship patterns that maintain symptoms
3. Encourage the development of an integrated self that demonstrates capacities for both togetherness and individuality

CASE EXAMPLE

Generalized Anxiety Disorder with Depressive Symptoms

Dorothy, a thirty-five-year-old white female, called for an appointment following a divorce initiated by her. She reported being unable to relax, irritability, and feelings of anxiousness, inadequacy, and worthlessness. She was concerned about her competence in parenting her children, Danielle (age eight) and Brian (age eleven).

Level I: Context of the Treatment

Dorothy defined herself as the problem. Cultural messages that women are responsible for the success or failure of relationships made it difficult for her to reconcile herself to the decision to divorce her husband. At the same time, other, newer cultural messages said that she should not stay in a relationship that she did not find emotionally supportive. Though experiencing a great deal of distress, Dorothy did not feel entitled to receive care. She could seek help only for her children's sake.

Dorothy worked as a secretary for a local business. Though she carried much responsibility, her pay was less than ten dollars per hour. One hour of therapy cost more than seven hours' work. Because she believed joint custody was in the best interests of her children, she received almost no child support. Although her job provided her with a managed-care insurance plan that covered 80 percent of the costs of approved visits, the economic and educational differences between the therapist and the client were considerable. The therapist, also a white female who had experienced divorce when her children were school-aged, was older and more confident than Dorothy.

Dorothy approached therapy with considerable respect for the authority of the therapist. She appeared to readily accept a one-down position. Therapy needed to validate her competence and sense of responsibility as parent and her right to make decisions that supported her personal well-being. At the same time, Dorothy needed to be engaged as a partner in the therapy process, taking the therapist off the professional pedestal and exposing some of her vulnerabilities. The therapist needed to avoid the temptation to take an all-knowing position that would reinforce Dorothy's experience of inequality. The managed care company had the power to determine duration of treatments.

Level II: Context of the Client

Dorothy's relationship with her former husband, Ken, continued to play a significant part in maintaining Dorothy's anxiety and hopelessness. Traditional gender expectations had resulted in an unequal balance of attention and care in their marriage. Dorothy had learned to keep her interests and concerns to herself rather than risking disappointment or making him upset. He expected not to be questioned.

Though divorced for nearly a year, worry regarding how to raise issues with him regarding the children was a major source of distress.

Dorothy's relationship with Danielle and Brian reflected cultural expectations for mothers. They expected her to be available and understanding. They were willing to ask for what they wanted and argue for it. Dorothy's parenting style was "feminine." She sought the children's input and involved them in day-to-day decisions such as what to eat. She balanced sensitivity to their feelings and concerns with firmness regarding homework and household chores. She cared what they thought about her.

Dorothy and Gabe (age forty-five), the new man in her life, wanted a relationship based on equality. Yet hidden power flowed to Gabe in many ways. When Dorothy was distressed, Gabe would offer advice. Because he was older and appeared certain of himself, Dorothy viewed him as "more knowledgeable" than she. She more readily accommodated to his schedule than he did to hers, even though she had more demands on her time. When the children resisted accommodating him, she thought he could have bent to them more frequently, but had difficulty holding her own in this argument.

Gabe was also a major source of support and encouragement for Dorothy. He wanted to help, but had never learned to listen from the perspective of another. So he attempted to help her without really understanding her. Gabe was willing to participate in therapy. Dorothy's sister was her other major source of support. Though she lived in anoher state, she was available for lengthy phone conversations and appeared to value Dorothy's strengths. Since Ken shared parenting responsibilities on alternate weeks, Dorothy had some freedom from the constant pressure of child-care responsibilities. In addition, the appropriate supportive role provided by the children should not be discounted. She enjoyed their company and derived much pleasure from her interactions with them. Though she reported no close friendships, she talked with other women at work, and several of them were potential sources of support. Neither of Dorothy's parents were alive.

Level III: Differentiation and Integration of Self

Like many women, Dorothy was more developed on the togetherness dimension. She was able to apprehend what others needed and be responsive to them. She appreciated and valued the skills and tal-ents of others and was willing to give much of herself to relationships. Her decision to divorce was an assault on her sense of being the one who maintains relationships. The lack of mutual attending in the marital relationship had been destructive to her.

The individuality aspect of self was more poorly developed for Dorothy. Though she had an active mind and many thoughts, she had never learned to trust that others would respect her ideas or that she had a right to them. Movements toward individuality provoked guilty feelings. Further development on the togetherness dimension was hampered by her doubts regarding her worth to others. Thus, she would keep significant parts of herself hidden, limiting the growth of individuality. Periodically, however, she would explode with anger or retreat altogether.

Treatment Goals and Strategies

The overall goal was for Dorothy to claim a more equal position in relation to others. Related goals included the following:

1. Increasing Dorothy's feelings of worth and competence by validating her "connected self" and her relationship with her children
2. Decreasing the anxiety experienced when expressing her thoughts or concerns to others, especially Gabe and Ken
3. Realigning the power between Gabe and Dorothy by encouraging him to listen to her and accommodate more frequently

Therapy included twenty sessions over fifteen months and seven sessions two years later. Early sessions included one with Dorothy and the children, one with the children alone, and one with Dorothy, Ken, and the children. These sessions helped to give the therapist information about the significant persons in her life and credibility to validate Dorothy's competence as a parent. They helped her better collaborate with Dorothy in devising strategies to engage with Ken.

Individual meetings with Dorothy were alternated with couples sessions with Gabe. Being listened to and taken seriously was a new experience for Dorothy and raised some anxiety. Similarly, though Gabe was quite willing to help Dorothy with "her" problem, attention to his contributions raised anxiety for him. Individual sessions helped Dorothy clarify her experience and needs. The couples sessions helped them manage the anxiety that arose as they tried new behaviors that would redistribute the power and attention in their relationship more equally.

Though Dorothy clearly liked the therapy sessions, she struggled with entitlement to time and resources directed toward her own well-being. Two outside "authorities" helped give her permission to continue. First, the case manager from the managed-care company took Dorothy's issues seriously. She encouraged Dorothy to attend therapy sessions *more* frequently. Second, after a discussion of her options, Dorothy decided to seek a psychiatric consultation for possible medication. Though prescribing medication, the psychiatrist also encouraged the therapy sessions. Medication was framed as a way of helping her achieve the personal and relationship goals she was working on in therapy.

The first series of sessions focused on helping Dorothy develop a more equal position in relation to others. She decided to stop the therapy sessions when she felt confident that "she knew what to do" and was now able to work on it at home. By supporting this decision, the therapist respected Dorothy as the expert on herself and validated her as a competent person. The possibility of coming back in the future was framed positively as something she might decide to do when new issues came up in her life, rather than as a sign of failure.

When Dorothy returned two years later, she approached therapy from a more empowered position. She knew what issues she wanted to address and what she was hiring the therapist to do. She had ideas about what would help. The therapist was a source of support and information, but not the only one. Dorothy decided that psychotropic medication was no longer the answer for her and selected a female physician who would work with the biological side of her issues more holistically. The goal for these therapy sessions (all individual) was to help Dorothy develop a process for taking charge of change in her life. Now remarried, with children growing older, she was ready for there to be more room for her in her relationships.

STRENGTHS AND LIMITATIONS

The strength of the feminist family systems approach is that it provides a broad framework for the treatment of mental health issues that may readily be integrated and employed within a wide range of settings. It offers an inclusive model for assessment that encourages positive, affirming, systemic treatment plans but does not limit the kinds of techniques and interventions that may be used. It helps the practitioner consider political and contextual questions that frequently are not addressed in traditional therapy; but it leaves the choices for how to respond to these issues to the practitioner. The model values traditionally "feminine" traits and behaviors without devaluing the "masculine." Issues of gender and power are externalized within the social context and can be addressed without blaming individuals.

Use of the model will suggest treatment goals, but it does not provide a step-by-step intervention plan. Treatment methods and outcomes are therefore difficult to standardize or measure. Our clinical experience suggests that the model is effective and affirming of clients. Research testing the effectiveness has not yet been completed.

INTEGRATION WITH PSYCHIATRIC SERVICES AND ROLE OF MEDICATION

This model may be successfully integrated with psychiatric services and medication. Psychiatric diagnoses must, however, be examined within dimensions addressed by the model. We cannot assume that standard diagnostic practices are gender neutral. Women are more readily diagnosed with mental disorders than men and more likely to receive medication (Padgett, 1997). Psychiatric decisions must give consideration to the context within which the symptoms arise, and in particular to the questions addressed in Level I (context of treatment). There is also evidence that women and men differ in their response to psychotropic drugs. Optimal doses for many women are often lower, the risk of side effects higher, and the likelihood of a favorable response may be less (Padgett, 1997). For all the reasons outlined in this chapter, we must ask how often women are medicated while the social factors that contribute to their problems remain unexamined.

For our clients to be empowered, they must have access to knowledge and be the final arbitrator of decisions regarding their treatment. It is therefore consistent with the feminist family systems approach to inform clients of the treatment options available to them, including the pros and cons of medication. In some cases, we may request a psychiatric consultation as a source of more information. If the client is already on medication, we ask questions about how that decision was made and how it is working for her. Discussion that helps the client integrate the use of drugs into a multisystemic approach to her issues is important. Without this discussion, use of medication can lead to the assumption that the problem is a medical one only, and that it resides within the woman rather than in a social and interpersonal context.

CULTURAL AND GENDER ISSUES

The feminist family systems model does not assume that there is a single female experience and apply it to women. Instead, it raises questions that help the clinician determine how gender is a factor is each particular case. The goal is to understand each client within her meaning, to be respectful of her experience, and to recognize the many ways societal differences in power and position impede us. Two aspects of gender are addressed—gender as a power difference and gender as a socially constructed set of attitudes and behaviors. Because many constructions of gender are based on power differences between women and men, the challenge is to validate each woman's values and ideals without reinforcing inequalities, to empower women while respecting the ways they may be culturally different from us.

Gender roles and relationships are not equivalent from one culture to another. For example, African-American women and men have both been victims of racism and abuse. Women are taught not to depend on men (who have more difficulty finding employment and are treated less well in the work world). Yet African-American men receive messages similar to men in the dominant culture—that they *should* be in charge and *should* be providers, complicating the dynamics of power and gender (Boyd-Franklin and Franklin, 1998). Women who live within cultures that place high priority on loyalty to the family or group may be ashamed to share family stories or to reveal abuse, even when they are the victims (Bograd, 1999). Many women must walk the fine line between two cultures, both of which are changing. (See Garcia-Preto, 1998, for an excellent example of how to help Latina women bridge cultures and find their strengths within the cultural values and roles that are important to them.)

Gender is only one of the social categories that influences expectations and shapes the available opportunities. A person may be privileged as the result of membership in one category while stigmatized and oppressed in another. A white woman may hold more power, for example, than a black man. Those with the least economic power are the ones whose experience is least often understood (Taffel and Masters, 1989). Membership in a dominant category makes it more difficult to be sensitive to the needs and concerns of subordinate groups. Sensitivity requires more than "awareness"; it requires exposure outside of therapy that helps us experience our differences at a gut level (Hardy, 1997). We must admit our discomfort, acknowledge our differences, and be willing to discuss issues of race, class, and culture with clients. When we do, we create an opportunity for deeper knowledge of ourselves and others.

FUTURE DIRECTIONS

Mental health professionals are increasingly aware of the ways traditional approaches to mental health treatment may be biased against women. Yet we have only begun to document the ways gender impacts the onset and course of specific mental health problems and to develop treatment approaches based on this information. Surprisingly little is known about the gender-specific efficacy of treatments, including psychotropic drugs (Padgett, 1997). There is also a substantial need for qualitative study regarding the client's experience in treatment. The mental health needs of many groups of women remain invisible or poorly understood. Many never receive services at all. We need information from all of these sources to be able to provide appropriate health-enhancing services to women from all socioeconomic and cultural backgrounds.

Gender consciousness also raises new ethical questions such as the meaning of neutrality, client welfare, and therapist power. As we examine the socially constructed nature of mental health delivery systems, the practices and position of the therapist in relation to these time-honored principles is less clear. Grappling with these questions will force us to examine the very nature of therapy itself and the role of mental health treatment in relation to the larger society.

REFERENCES

Almeida, R., Woods, R., and Messineo, T. (1998). Child development: The intersection of race, gender, and culture. In R. Almeida (Ed.), *Transforming gender and race.* Binghamton, NY: The Haworth Press, Inc.

Anderson, C. and Holder, D. (1989). Women and serious mental disorders. In M. McGoldrick, C. Anderson, and F. Walsh (Eds.), *Women in families: A framework for family therapy* (pp. 381-405). New York: Norton.

Belenky, M., Clinchy, B., Goldberger, N., and Tarule, J. (1986). *A woman's way of knowing: The development of self, voice, and mind.* New York: Basic Books.

Bem, S. (1993). *The lenses of gender: Transforming the debate of sexual inequality.* New Haven: Yale University Press.

Bepko, C. (1989). Disorders of power: Women and addiction in the family. In M. McGoldrick, C. Anderson, and F. Walsh, (Eds.), *Women in families: A framework for family therapy* (pp. 427-450). New York: Norton.

Bograd, M. (1999). Strengthening domestic violence theories: Intersections of race, class, sexual orientation, and gender. *Journal of Marital and Family Therapy, 25,* 275-290.

Bowen, M. (1978). *Family therapy in clinical practice.* New York: Jason Aronson.

Boyd-Franklin, N. and Franklin, A. (1998). African American couples in therapy. In M. McGoldrick (Ed.), *Revisioning family therapy: Race, culture, and gender in clinical practice* (pp. 268-281). New York: Guilford.

Dusky, K. (1996). *Still unequal: The shameful truth about women and justice in America.* New York: Crown Publishers.

Ewashen, C. (1997). Devaluation dynamics and gender bias in women's groups. *Issues in Mental Health Nursing, 18,* 73-84.

Fowers, B. and Richardson, F. (1996). Individualism, family ideology, and family therapy. *Theory and Psychology, 3,* 353-377.

Garcia-Preto, N. (1998). Latinas in the United States: Bridging two worlds. In M. McGoldrick (Ed.), *Revisioning family therapy: Race, culture, and gender in clinical practice* (pp. 330-344). New York: Guilford.

Greene, B. (1994). Diversity and difference: Race and feminist psychotherapy. In M. Mirkin (Ed.), *Women in context: Toward a feminist reconstruction of psychotherapy* (pp. 333-351). New York: Guilford.

Hardy, K. (1997). *Race, class, and gender in family therapy.* Presented at the American Association for Marital and Family Therapy Annual Meeting, Atlanta, GA, September.

Hare-Mustin, R. (1987). The problem of gender in family therapy theory. *Family Process, 26,* 15-27.

Hudal, J., Krestan, J., and Bepko, C. (1999). Alcohol problems and the family life cycle. In B. Carter and M. McGoldrick (Eds.), *The expanded family life cycle* (pp. 455-467). Boston: Allyn & Bacon.

Jacobson, N., Gottman, J., Waltz, J., Rushe, R., Babcock, J., and Holtzworth-Monroe, A. (1994). Affect, verbal content, and psychophysiology in the arguments of couples with a violent husband. *Journal of Consulting and Clinical Psychology, 62,* 929-988.

Johnson, T. and Keren, M. (1998). The families of lesbian women and gay men. In M. McGoldrick (Ed.), *Revisioning family therapy: Race, culture, and gender in clinical practice* (pp. 320-329). New York: Guilford.

Jordan, J., Kaplan, A., Miller, J., Stiver, I., and Surrey, J. (1991). *Women's growth in connection.* New York: Guilford.

Kaschak, E. (1992). *Engendered lives: A new psychology of women's experience.* New York: Basic Books.

Kerr, M. and Bowen, M. (1988). *Family evaluation.* New York: Norton.

Knudson-Martin, C. (1994). The female voice: Applications to Bowen's family systems theory. *Journal of Marital and Family Therapy, 20,* 35-46.

Knudson-Martin, C. (1996). Differentiation and self development in the relationship context. *The Family Journal, 4,* 188-198.

Knudson-Martin, C. (1997). The politics of gender in family therapy. *Journal of Marital and Family Therapy, 23,* 421-437.

Knudson-Martin, C. (2000). Gender, family competence, and psychological symptoms. *Journal of Marital and Family Therapy, 26,* 317-328.

Knudson-Martin, C. and Mahoney, A. (1998). Language and processes in the construction of equality in new marriages. *Family Relations, 47,* 81-91.

Komter, A. (1989). Hidden power in marriage. *Gender and Society, 3,* 187-216.

Larson, R. and Richards, M. (1994). *Divergent realities.* New York: Basic Books.

Lennon, M. C. (1996). Depression and self esteem among women. In M. Falik and K. S. Collins (Eds.), *Women's health: The commonwealth fund survey.* Baltimore: Johns Hopkins University Press.

Leslie, L. and Clossick, M. (1996). Sexism in family therapy: Does training in gender make a difference? *Journal of Marital and Family Therapy, 22,* 253-269.

Lindsey, L. (1997). *Social roles: A sociological perspective* (Third edition). Upper Saddle River, NJ: Prentice-Hall.

Lips, H. (1997). *Women, men, and power.* Mountain View, CA: Mayfield Publishing.

McGoldrick, M. and Carter, B. (1999). Self in context: The individual life cycle in systemic perspective. In B. Carter and M. McGoldrick (Eds.), *The expanded family life cycle* (pp. 27-46). Boston: Allyn & Bacon.

McGrath, E., Keita, G., Strickland, B., and Russo, N. (1990). *Women and depression: Risk factors and treatment issues.* Washington, DC: American Psychological Association.

Padgett, D. (1997). Women's mental health: Some directions for research. *Journal of Orthopsychiatry, 67,* 522-534.

Risman, B. and Johnson-Sumerford, D. (1998). Doing it fairly: A study of postgender marriages. *Journal of Marriage and the Family, 60,* 23-40.

Rosenbaum, R. and Dyckman, J. (1995). Integrating self and system: An empty intersection? *Family Process, 34,* 21-44.

Taffel, R. and Masters, R. (1989). An evolutionary approach to revolutionary change: The impact of gender arrangements on family therapy. In M. McGoldrick, C. Anderson, and F. Walsh, (Eds.), *Women in families: A framework for family therapy* (pp. 117-134). New York: Norton.

Walters, M. (1994). Service delivery systems and women: The construction of conflict. In M. Mirkin (Ed.), *Women in context: Toward a feminist reconstruction of psychotherapy* (pp. 9-24). New York: Guilford.

Chapter 15

Family Therapy and Issues of Aging

Jonathan G. Sandberg
Jason J. Platt

INTRODUCTION

As I opened the first day of class, I could sense the apprehension in the air, both my own and the students', even if it was 8:30 in the morning in the middle of winter. I casually asked the students why they chose to take this introduction to gerontology class. Of the nearly fifty students, not one had taken the class as an elective. As the semester continued, it was clear that many students, like society at large, were apprehensive talking about growing old. I conducted an informal survey and discovered many of the students were deathly afraid of the possibility of memory loss, dependence, isolation, and death itself. I can remember my own fear as I watched my grandmother struggle, along with the rest of our family, to cope with her decline due to Alzheimer's disease. I can remember wondering if all old people suffered this way. Such negative stereotypic views of aging are referred to in the literature as ageism (Eisdorfer, 1983; Walsh, 1999), a type of prejudice that must be challenged in order to provide competent treatment for older adults and their families.

These undergraduate students are not the only ones who avoid looking at issues relating to aging. Two comprehensive reviews of marriage and family therapy literature have yielded little specific information regarding aging families. Van Amburg, Barber, and Zimmerman (1996) analyzed the content of four major family therapy journals, from 1986 to 1993, in an effort to summarize the family therapy literature regarding the treatment of older clients. "Of the 873 journal articles analyzed, only 28 (3.2 percent) contained an explicit emphasis on aging issues and later life family concerns" (Van Amburg,

Barber, and Zimmerman, 1996, p. 198). A previous review of the family therapy literature from 1976 to 1985 yielded similar conclusions (Flori, 1989). Even though a number of books address the interface of family therapy and aging families, including the comprehensive and insightful work of Hargrave and Hanna (1997), this topic remains underinvestigated (see also Walsh, 1999; Hughston, Christopherson, and Bonjean, 1989). Clearly, a gerontological hole in the family therapy literature persists in spite of an increasing need for clinical information about older families.

For example, even though the potential and need for family-based treatment for those experiencing the transition to, or life in, a long-term-care facility is great, few marriage and family therapists (MFTs) seem to be working in that setting. According to Doherty and Simmons' (1996) national survey of family therapists in the United States, only .8 percent work in a medical center (inpatient) setting, with no specific reference to long-term care. Perhaps a major deterrent to MFTs and the facilities themselves is the lack of funding and reimbursement available to family therapists. Whatever the reason might be, the need for family-based consultation in long-term care settings is real and growing. To cite only one example, Mosher-Ashley (1993) reported in her study that among the primary reasons for referral of long-term-care residents to mental health services were (1) emotional problems (depression, anxiety, etc.) and (2) family conflict; two problems MFTs commonly treat.

McDaniel, Campbell, and Seaburn (1995) note an emerging trend toward the practice of MFT in medical settings. This trend, as well as an increasing emphasis on collaborative health care, will likely pave the way for increased contact for MFTs with older clients and their families. According to the national survey, over 4 percent of MFTs already work in a medical setting as their primary workplace (Doherty and Simmons, 1996). Because mental health issues in later life often present as (or are comorbid with) physical illness/symptoms (chronic pain, vision loss, cardiac illness, headaches, gastrointestinal problems, etc.; see Zarit and Zarit, 1998), marriage and family therapists in medical settings must acquaint themselves with assessment and treatment strategies aimed at aging families.

Recent demographic projections further highlight this need. Reports suggest that in the United States over the next twenty-five years the number of Americans over the age of sixty-five will literally double, representing an increase of over 30 million individuals (AARP,

1996). As early as the year 2010, some reports have estimated that people over the age of sixty-five will represent 14 percent of the total U.S. population—a trend typical of international patterns as well (see Hargrave and Hanna, 1997).

The implication of these statistics for family therapists is critical. Someone must provide mental health services for this large group of older adults and their families. The question is who? Continuing neglect of this population may prove increasingly costly for the field of family therapy, as a growing number of researchers are recognizing a relationship between family dynamics and common problems in later life (Tower and Kasl, 1996). The focus now must be on preparing family therapists in all settings to competently and compassionately treat the complex problems that can accompany aging.

Aging 101

What do you know about the aging process? (True or False)

- A gradual but constant decline in most biological processes begins approximately at age forty and continues throughout adulthood.
- Psychological processes such as memory, intelligence, and problem solving are naturally and unavoidably subject to deterioration with age and usually result in what most people call senility.
- Socially, most older adults willingly and appropriately withdraw from society as they age to maintain dignity and privacy.

The answer to each of the above questions, which were meant to challenge common ageist views, is "false." Although a number of natural and unavoidable declines in biopsychosocial processes occur due to aging, they are much less pronounced and occur much later in life than is typically represented in the popular media. Also, how individuals live their lives will have a tremendous impact on the onset and course of these declines (Rowe and Kahn, 1997). In addition, in the end it is the response to those declines that likely determines the impact on an individual's mental health (Walsh, 1999; Frankl, 1959).

Biological Aging

One of the most difficult myths to deconstruct about aging—particularly physical aging—is that aging and disease are synonymous. Because of stereotypes in the media and perhaps overgeneralized personal experience, the predominant Western view of aging is one of illness and disability. Atchley (1997), in his text, makes an important distinction between optimal, usual, and pathological aging. He suggests that in *optimal aging* the environment and genetics combine in a positive way that results in few problems relating to physical functioning. *Usual aging* is a term used to describe an interaction between the environment and genetics that results in "chronic disease and functional limitations that are noticeable and limiting in minor ways" (Atchley, 1997, p. 77). *Pathological aging,* which many people consider normal or typical, is the result of a negative combination of genetics and environmental factors that results in significant difficulty with chronic disease and functional impairment.

If pathological aging is not a normative experience for older adults, then what are some of the normal or typical biological changes that accompany the process of aging? (For an excellent comprehensive review from an MFT perspective, see Hargrave and Hanna, 1997.) Researchers have noted that with age many older adults experience a decrease in physical energy due to a decrease in their ability to get oxygen into the blood as well as changes in sleep patterns, such as frequent awakening in the night (Atchley, 1997). A decline in sensory perception, particularly sight, taste, hearing, and smell, is also a common experience for many adults as they age. Although regular physical exercise can work to offset many changes in the musculoskeletal system, loss of muscle strength and decreases in bone density due to aging can be manifested in illnesses such as osteoporosis, arthritis, and back pain (Hargrave and Hanna, 1997). And finally, it appears the immune system suffers a decline in efficiency over time, making it harder to prevent disease and disability with increasing age (Atchley, 1997).

Psychological Aging

Contrary to the popular view of older adults, substantial losses in the areas of learning, problem solving, memory, intelligence, and creativity do not occur for the majority of elders until the seventies and beyond. In fact, numerous studies across each of these areas have shown only small decrements through middle and early later life and substantial losses occurring only for a small number of adults in the latest stages of life (Atchley, 1997). On the other hand, age has been positively associated with wisdom. Although age itself does not produce wisdom, Baltes (1993) noted that the ability to use knowledge garnered over time and apply it to life's circumstances is found more often in older adults.

Again, contrary to popular stereotypes, older adults do not have or express significantly more negative emotion than their younger counterparts (Atchley, 1997). In fact, a number of studies by Carstensen, Gottman, and Levenson (1995) "suggest age-related improvements in the control of emotion and emotional understanding" (p. 140). Similarly, even though Parkinson's and Alzheimer's diseases impact (in such a cruel and dehumanizing way) only a small minority of older adults, they are frequently equated with aging because these illnesses are more common in later life (Zarit and Zarit, 1998).

Social Aspects of Aging

One of the key concepts in the study of social aspects of aging is the importance of social roles. As Atchley (1997) points out, "social roles have great significance because individuals often define themselves in terms of roles" (p. 133). Perhaps, as at no other time in life, older adults face numerous and significant changes in the roles they play. Starting in the earliest stages of later life (fifty-five to sixty-five), older adults experience role changes in their family (grandparenthood, child launching, and empty nest) and society (preparing for retirement). In the middle stages (ages sixty-five to eighty), older adults and couples can experience profound role strain and loss as they cope with postretirement life, issues of decreased independence, and perhaps bereavement due to the death of one's partner. For those who can remain functionally independent in the later stages (eighty-five-plus), it is often the sense of extreme isolation and loneliness that becomes so difficult.

Loss can often become one of the most common themes and problems facing older adults. Not only must they cope with the tangible loss of a spouse or a job, but they must also deal with the less visible, yet extremely difficult, loss of power, prestige, and social influence (Hargrave and Hanna, 1997). As can be seen, successful aging requires a tremendous ability to adapt and cope with both role changes and loss. Factors identified in the literature that seem to aid in coping with these challenges are social support from friends and family, as well as personal and family resiliency (Walsh, 1999; Sandberg and Harper, 1999). In conclusion, it is important for family therapists to recognize and remind others that the stereotype of a physically frail, cognitively impaired, and socially withdrawn older adult is not the normative experience for most people over age fifty-five.

The Family and a Biopsychosocial Approach to Aging

Because aging is a complex combination of biological, psychological, and social issues, we strongly encourage family therapists to assess for and treat problems and strengths in each of these key areas. However, attention to these three key areas alone is insufficient. As leading gerontologists have noted, it is still the family that provides the majority of connection and support in the lives of older adults (Bengston, Rosenthal, and Burton, 1996). Family functioning is influenced when an older adult experiences physical illness or frailty, when cognitive impairment sets in, or when role strain or loss becomes unbearable. As the following summary of common presenting problems shows, the family becomes the context for treating these biopsychosocial issues.

Depression

Research on the prevalence of depression in later life has suggested that over 5 percent of community-dwelling older adults who present to outpatient clinics could be diagnosed as experiencing a major depressive disorder (MDD) according to DSM-IV criteria (Blazer, 1994). The literature also states that 10 to 20 percent of older adults experience significant depressive symptoms while not meeting the full criteria for MDD (Blazer, 1994; Blazer, Hughes, and George, 1987). Coupled with the fact that depression is so commonly presented with or masked by other illnesses or symptoms (Zarit and Zarit, 1998), it is vital that MFTs know how to assess and treat depression in later life.

First and foremost, MFTs must recognize that depression in later life is nonnormative and treatable (Reynolds et al., 1994). Second, MFTs must be aware that depression in later life can be deadly. The rate for suicide deaths among the elderly is nearly two times the national average, and they account for nearly 20 percent of all suicide deaths; depression is a major player in this frightening statistic (Zarit and Zarit, 1998). Third, particular attention should be paid to issues of loss when treating depression (Hargrave and Hanna, 1997; Zarit and Zarit, 1998). Finally, treatment of depression in later life is almost completely devoid of a family dynamics perspective (Sandberg and Harper, 2000; Hinrichsen and Zweig, 1994; Sandberg and Harper, 1999)

This neglect of a family dynamics perspective is troublesome because it is clear that depression has an impact on family functioning at all ages (Joiner and Coyne, 1999). In addition to working with the depressed older adult, family therapists may be asked to help family members work through anxiety and role strain as they attempt to help their loved one cope with depression. Family therapists may also be sought to help couples deal with the relationship dissatisfaction that can accompany depression (Sandberg and Harper, 1999), such as lack of emotional or sexual intimacy or prolonged conflict. In any case, family therapists must explore the reciprocal relationship between depression and family dynamics.

Issues Related to Caregiving

As stated previously, family members still provide the majority of care for functionally dependent older adults. Without question, caregiving for a dependent family member is stressful and can result in numerous symptoms for the caregiver, including stress, anger, and depression (Zarit and Zarit, 1998). Therefore, because of our training in family dynamics, MFTs could be called upon to work with those struggling to deal with the strains and rewards of caregiving. This work may or may not include the impaired older adult; nevertheless, each case requires knowledge of the disease and how it impacts the aging family. An understanding of the aging process and systems theory may be particularly valuable in cases in which aging spouses care for each other (Wilken, Altergott, and Sandberg, 1996) and adult children care for parents. A number of articles now exist that advocate for a family dynamics/therapy lens in this area as well as demonstrating initial evidence of an interactional description of caregiver depression (Benbow et al., 1993; Shields, 1992; Zarit, Anthony, and Boutselis, 1987).

Adjustment Issues

As mentioned previously, later life is a time of tremendous role strain and transition. Issues relating to retirement, illness and death, child launching, and changes in housing can cause tremendous intrapsychic and interpersonal strain (Atchley, 1997). These adjustment issues may result in older adults and their families presenting for MFT with problems such as depression and family conflict, or referred by a physician for somatic complaints.

Although little has been written regarding specific treatment modalities for adjustment disorders in later life, Zarit and Zarit (1998) emphasize the importance of the core skills of empathy, warmth, and genuineness. Walsh's (1999) description of a resilience-based approach in *The Expanded Family Life Cycle* also seems appropriate for dealing with adjustment issues in later life. Her model "engages elders collaboratively, affirms their strengths and personhood, encourages their optimal functioning, and builds social network resources" and can be applied to the family unit (p. 320).

Intergenerational Issues

This broad category may include issues ranging from intergenerational conflict and strain (Framo, 1976) to the unique struggles of grandparent-headed families (Miller and Sandberg, 1998). Perhaps it is these problems that traditional family therapy models are best structured to treat. As will be discussed in the next section, Boszormenyi-Nagy's theory of contextual therapy, as applied by Hargrave (Hargrave and Anderson, 1992), is especially well suited to address the complex issues of loyalty and equity that are so prevalent in later life. For example, issues regarding end-of-life decision making or the transfer of property after death are two examples of difficult and often conflictual family processes in later life (Sandberg, 1999). Similarly, multigenerational conflict about such topics as the role and involvement of grandparents, who plays the role of caregiver, or the need for long-term care are also likely presenting problems for older adults seeking help from MFTs.

SETTING

Although it is conceivable that MFTs would work with older adults in any setting, we have chosen to place an emphasis on community mental health centers, which may become the treatment setting for mature couples and individuals over the next twenty years. Our fictionalized case example in subsequent sections is set in a community mental health center (CMHC).

Although there is clear existing legislation in the United States requiring mental health centers to provide specialized programs to the elderly, older adults continue to be underserviced in these settings (Mosher-Ashley, 1993; Goldstrom et al., 1987). This neglect may be due to major roadblocks facing the centers, the clinicians, and the older adults themselves. For example, centers may struggle with issues relating to funding, reimbursement, staffing issues, and client transportation issues. Similarly, clinicians can face barriers due to lack of training in issues of aging, internalized stereotypes of older adults, and fears about facing their own issues. Finally, the older adults themselves may need to overcome the stigma of mental health treatment or the belief that mental health problems are a normal part of aging, as well as mobility and safety concerns.

Overall, the underutilization of mental health services by older adults has been a long-standing, deeply concerning, national problem (Hagebak and Hagebak, 1983; Goldstrom et al., 1987). Even with the roadblocks currently in place preventing treatment of elders in a CMHC setting, we believe that treating issues of aging in the rising generation of older adults, particularly the baby boomers, will be substantially different. For many reasons, it is likely that over the next thirty years family therapists in CMHC settings will see a substantial increase in older clients and their families.

First and foremost, demographic studies show a tremendous trend toward increasing numbers of older adults. Not only are there more older adults, they are living longer and healthier (Rowe and Kahn, 1997). Second, the stigma surrounding mental health services may likely be a cohort (or generational) effect. Because so many of the baby boomers have sought treatment during earlier stages of life, it is probable that doing so in later life will not be as new and stigmatizing as it was for their parents (Hagebak and Hagebak, 1983). Third, because of movement away from costly inpatient treatment, outpatient treatment will likely be the only realistic option for functionally independent older adults. Fourth, a number of researchers have already labeled CHMCs as "the most promising approach to providing psychological treatment for the elderly" (Mosher-Ashley, 1993, p. 5). If these trends hold true and more MFTs will be treating older adults and their families, what kinds of issues should we prepare for?

TREATMENT MODEL

A Family-Based Treatment Approach

This approach to treating problems in later life employs multiple systems theory concepts, which reflects a desire for intervention that impacts the family and larger systems (i.e., medical), as well as the older adult. This method also seeks to help aging individuals and their families negotiate the transition into later life, reduce unnecessary suffering, and create room for continued meaningful living. The treatment approach itself is conceptualized as three stages or areas of focus: (1) establishing a therapeutic relationship, (2) exploring meaning through a narrative life review, and (3) exploring and negotiating intergenerational relationships. These areas of focus are listed as stages but are more circular and overlapping in actual clinical application.

Stage 1: Establishing a Therapeutic Relationship

To begin with, it is important to note that there generally exists a significant difference in age between therapists and elderly clients. "It is not unusual for a therapist to be 50 or 60 years younger than the member of the oldest generation" (Hargrave and Anderson, 1992, pp. 73-74). Therefore, therapists must be aware of potential roadblocks due to cohort and age differences that may prevent the forming of a therapeutic relationship.

Of primary importance in this stage is for therapists to be aware that older adults live their lives in a societal context dominated by ageist views. Therapists must identify their own biases, deconstruct them, and show genuine respect for their older clients. Ageist views can be manifested in therapy when "older persons sense that they are obliged to wait longer for appointments because the caregiver assumes unemployed persons have unlimited time" (Burlingame, 1995,

p. 32), or a clinic is not easily accessible or when the only reading material is *Seventeen* magazine or *Parents*. These experiences justifiably may lead older adults to feel leery of a therapist's understanding of the problems in their lives.

Once an effort is made to address age differences and ageism, it behooves the clinician to begin the interaction by allowing "the older person to be the teacher when it comes to his or her life" (Hargrave and Anderson, 1992, p. 74). This stance is similar to the one-down position advocated by the Mental Research Institute (MRI) approach to therapy and "most often involves a 180-degree shift (U-turn) in that the majority of professionals of any sort, by nature, take a one-up or expert stance" (Cohen, 1995, p. 213). Assuming a one-down stance begins with initial contact and the affording of common courtesies and builds trust and confidence in the therapeutic relationship. "Being respectful, using polite language, and acknowledging the experience and learning that their years have acquired, will enhance your elderly client's acceptance of you and your services" (Burlingame, 1995, p. 35).

To illustrate, Blazer suggests that therapists not prematurely address older clients by their first name; instead, a therapist should "wait for a cue that familiarity is permissible rather than assuming it is permissible because the elder is no longer in a professional role" (Blazer, 1998, p. 27). This is a therapeutic position that extends beyond assumptions about the use of familiar names and should be thought of as a therapeutic stance or way of being that should hold throughout therapy. Gafner (1987) does an excellent job of describing how this one-down approach can be used during assessment to engage with clients and build trust, a process that requires a slower and more tentative pace when working with older clients who tend to be more private and discreet.

*Stage 2: Exploring Meaning Through a Narrative
Life-Review Approach*

Once clients enter therapy, engaging them in a process of life review would be a useful place to begin. Clinicians can utilize the life-review process in joining, as an assessment, and as an intervention. Life-review interventions (Butler, 1963) are based upon the concept that older adults will naturally undergo a period of reflection about the purpose and meaning of their existence as death approaches. Erik

Erikson (1963) described this process of self-evaluation and review in his eighth and final stage of human development, *integrity versus despair*. During this stage, such questions as "Have I lived a full life or have I failed?" typify older adults' experience as they attempt to make meaning regarding themselves in the past, present, and future. This theory states that those who find contentment, purpose, and meaning in their review will feel a sense of integrity, and those who do not will feel despair.

It is important, therefore, that therapists allow space for older clients to tell their stories by listening intently and respectfully, which is also a powerful method of joining. Older adults are often met with rejection as they attempt to engage in the process of life review. Because of the prevalent "idea that older people . . . are always living in the 'good ole days' . . . reminiscence has often been devalued as merely the aimless meanderings of an increasingly decrepit mind" (Scrutton, 1989, p. 100). Therefore, active and respectful listening will likely be a new and therapeutic experience for them.

Even though providing an attentive ear has genuine therapeutic benefit, a skillful family therapist will also see this unfolding of a life story as the seedbed for intervention. For example, numerous family therapists have already creatively and skillfully proposed models that naturally integrate the use of storytelling and reminiscence into assessment and treatment plans for older clients (Gafner, 1987; Hargrave and Anderson, 1992). As Butler (1963) noted, this sharing of life history and the making of meaning can be seen as a "basic ingredient of the curative process" in the treatment of older adults (p. 495).

Step 3: Exploring Intergenerational Issues

During the process of life review, it is likely that numerous problematic patterns will emerge. We believe family therapy and systems theory provide a framework for understanding how these problems are experienced by older adults and their families. We also believe a family perspective can shed light on how problems may have their roots or be maintained within a relational context, as well as how those problems impact the entire system.

When family therapy was still in its infancy, many of the founding parents of the field saw the value and utility of including older adults in family therapy sessions (Minuchin et al., 1967; Haley, 1976;

Framo, 1976; Bowen, 1978). However, with a few notable exceptions, family therapy theory has not been applied and tested with problems facing the older adults themselves. The most notable of these exceptions is Boszormenyi-Nagy's contextual theory and therapy (Boszormenyi-Nagy and Spark, 1973), as applied by Hargrave and Anderson (1997, 1992).

Contextual theory is primarily organized around the concept of relational ethics (Boszormenyi-Nagy and Krasner, 1986). Relational ethics are concerned "with the subjective balance of trustworthiness, justice, loyalty, merit, and entitlement among members of a relationship" (Hargrave and Anderson, 1997, p. 63). When family members can interact in a balanced or fair manner, where both can give and take without manipulation, trustworthiness is developed. According to this theory, trustworthiness is the key to family loyalty and strength across generations (Hargrave and Anderson, 1997). Conversely, when trust erodes, family dysfunction often follows (Anderson and Hargrave, 1990).

Symptoms of intergenerational conflict or dysfunction can be seen as a sign of an unbalanced relational account. These accounts or ledgers are described as ongoing legacies of emotional commitments and obligations (Boszormenyi-Nagy and Spark, 1973; Everett, Russell, and Keller, 1992). Simply put, multigenerational ledgers are accounts of relational charges (hurts) and credits (benefits) accrued by family members over time (Boszormenyi-Nagy, 1974). It follows that when a family member is hurt or neglected, it goes down in an ongoing, implicit relational account. To avoid relational bankruptcy, this same member then attempts to rebalance his or her account with other family members.

As therapy begins with older clients, the inclusion of other family members can have a number of benefits. For example, Wolinsky (1986) includes partners and combines the common practice of learning about marital history with the life-review process. Other members of the family might also be invited at the life-review stage. Because issues of fairness, loyalty, and entitlement become evident as past experiences are recalled through the life review, important details regarding the family's intergenerational ledger can be gleaned in this process. With this increased awareness of how and when injustices first occurred, the older adults are able to better understand their own relationship with both the past (their own parents) and the future (their children).

However, it is not enough that the older adult experience this new perspective; other family members must also experience themselves differently in their relationship with the older adult. When older adults are able to explore their own past in the presence of their children, all parties are allowed to view more clearly the disappointments and suffering of the elder's life. Although such a process can trigger painful emotions, it is important that adult children are able to see and better understand the "charges" or injustices in their parents' lives. Upon doing so, they are more likely to recognize their parents' "human dignity and suffering" and have the chance to view the relationship in a new light (Boszormenyi-Nagy, 1974, p. 267).

CASE EXAMPLE

To illustrate the three stages of this treatment approach, the following fictionalized case example, based on the work of Dr. Dan Blazer, is used. The case was chosen because of the broad range of clinical issues facing Mr. Paxton and his family, issues that are typical for many older adults.

Mr. Paxton was seventy-three years old when he was hospitalized, once again, for shortness of breath and fatigue. He was seen by his primary care physician almost weekly because he suffered chest pains (secondary to two previous heart attacks) and heart failure. A diuretic and nitroglycerin alleviated the symptoms to some extent.

Mr. Paxton complained that he was just about ready give up because he could no longer help around the house. Actually, there was no need for him to continue his former handiwork around the house, nor for him to attend to his large garden. His wife had assumed these responsibilities as he became more ill. Nevertheless, he felt useless and found himself spending many hours watching television. He was discouraged with the results of cardiac bypass surgery two years earlier following an acute heart attack, and he was frustrated that he was no longer the man that he once had been.

Mr. Paxton did not seek treatment for his depression, for he did not view his depression as abnormal or serious enough to require help. He became more animated when talking to his doctor, especially when he talked about his family and his many interests. He admitted he was watching too much television, yet he was an avid sports fan and he especially enjoyed basketball games. Visits from his children and grandchildren, who lived near him, were the highlight of the week, yet they did tend to tire him after an hour or so (Blazer, 1998, pp. 64-65).

Imagine now that Mr. Paxton, through the encouragement of his family and his physician, has been referred to you as a client. A number of simple steps could be taken to join with Mr. Paxton and his wife long before they come to the first appointment. Following a courteous phone intake process, the clinical setting could be assessed to determine if it will help build trust and confidence. For example, arrangements could be made to increase accessibility or to accommodate specific needs. Due to Mr. Paxton's problem with shortness of breath and tendency to become fatigued easily, a special parking pass might be mailed to him in advance, or a wheelchair could be made available for getting from the car to the clinic.

Once inside the clinic, arrangement could be made so that he—and other older clients—could observe pictures and reading materials that acknowledge and validate older adults. In the initial therapist contact, he would be referred to as Mr. Paxton, "Sir," or some other polite term. Once therapy begins, the therapist would adopt a tentative and questioning stance aimed at inviting Mr. Paxton to tell about his life. This invitation marks the beginning of the second stage, in which a student-teacher relationship continues while exploring the meaning Mr. Paxton has made of his life.

To further the illustration, the first sessions with Mr. Paxton could be spent actively listening to and encouraging him to share the story of his life. It is clear from the intake that Mr. Paxton is struggling with feelings of uselessness and depression as his heart problems prevent him from being involved in home life the way he would like to be. What was his home life like before his bypass surgery? His work life? What was his work and family life like in his twenties or his forties? What societal forces impact him now that did not in his twenties and forties? These types of questions draw forth information about the meaning he has carved out from his life events.

Although as MFTs we can do little for chronic coronary disease, we can do a great deal to help shape and define how our older clients and their families see their problems and the impact of this meaning on family functioning. Once this information is gathered and understood, it may be useful to help Mr. Paxton reexamine or restory the meaning he has created around work, retirement, and health problems (White, 1995). In addition, as his therapist you could "draw on those historical experiences that may be useful in enabling movement toward a more satisfying future state" (Mittelmeier and Friedman, 1993, p. 159). The details provided by Mr. Paxton about past events, therefore, can be used to create new meaning about his future with chronic health problems. As new meaning and purpose is developed, space is created so that he can relate in ways that would have previously been incongruent with his understanding of life circumstances.

It appears that Mr. Paxton's sense of hopelessness and depression is linked to a perceived inability to function in a fair and equitable manner in his relationship with his wife, children, and grandchildren (step 3). In many instances like the Paxtons', partners and children of ailing older adults are called upon to provide care, an act that requires great emotional and physical resources. As caregivers are required to give more and recipients receive more, old relationship accounts are rebalanced. How will Mr. Paxton cope with his increased dependence? Can he still feel valuable in the relationship with a less active giving stance? Where will Mrs. Paxton find the deposits necessary to balance her account? How will adult children cope with a father who cannot be as physically active and present as he previously had been? Clearly, these questions would be best asked in the presence of Mrs. Paxton and any adult children, where a dialogue regarding expectations and fairness could occur.

So often it becomes the therapist's job to help renegotiate these relationship accounts and help balance the ebb and flow of give and take (Sandberg, 1999). Now that traditional means of finding his purpose and utility in relationships (i.e., through breadwinning and/or physical activity) are not as available to Mr. Paxton, how will he feel a valuable part of his relationships? Already he has stated that he is "about ready to give up" because there is "no need for him." Now that he may perceive his role as less fulfilling for him and others in the relationship, can he see his interactions with others as fair and equitable? This concept is vital from a contextual therapy approach because "the breakdown of . . . the relationship through disengagement from multilateral caring and accountability sets the stage for symptom development" (Boszormenyi-Nagy and Ulrich, 1981, p. 171).

A therapist working from this approach may, in addition to including Mrs. Paxton and adult children in the life-review session, want to invite family members to discuss how Mr. Paxton's health problems will change the balance of their interactions. In this delicate process, a therapist will encourage members to talk openly about existing charges (hurts) and credits (benefits) in their relationships. Acknowledging past hurts and injustices, including reparation where possible (Sandberg, 1999; Hargrave and Anderson, 1992), can serve to help the family eliminate as much "unfinished business" as possible as current relationships are adjusted realtive to present and future circumstances. It may be that a great deal of Mr. Paxton's hopeless and depressed condition is connected with his natural review of past and present relationship quality. Family therapists are uniquely trained and required by necessity to address these intergenerational conflicts, which can and do impact biological and psychological functioning.

In conclusion, through the three-stage process of establishing a therapeutic relationship, conducting a life review, and exploring and treating intergenerational issues, it is likely that a family therapist could have a major, positive impact on Mr. Paxton and his family. Specifically, a family therapist would be ideal for helping the family work with and adjust to the changes brought on by age and illness. However, family therapists must also know how and when to seek help with issues beyond their ability to treat.

STRENGTHS AND LIMITATIONS

The clear strengths of this intergenerational model lie in its ability to provide support and services for the entire family, its focus on how the family copes with problems of aging (as well as how the aging adult copes), and its theoretical appropriateness for end-of-life issues. The model is very respectful and client focused. It incorporates a developmental perspective that addresses both individual life-cycle development and family life-cycle issues. It addresses the key individual life-cycle task of a life review and provides specific narrative techniques for exploring life-review issues. The contextual therapy component of the model allows therapists to embed the individual life review in a family relationship context and, through the therapy process, to resolve outstanding conflict and "unfinished business" between family members.

The model is limited to some extent in that it does not provide a strong framework for addressing biomedical issues and their impact on aging. This can be compensated for to some extent through collaboration between family therapists and other treatment providers (i.e., family physicians, psychiatrists, geriatricians) as described subsequently. A further limitation of the model is the lack of clinical research regarding its effectiveness. This is an area that clearly needs to be further addressed.

INTEGRATION WITH PSYCHIATRIC SERVICES AND ROLE OF MEDICATION

"One of the biggest differences in the treatment of older people is the importance of coordinating psychotherapy with medical care" (Zarit and Zarit, 1998, p. 178). Whether the medical care is focused on mental health issues or broader physical ailments, clinicians "should know [their] client's particular medical diagnoses and also their intensities, prognoses, costs, and how they are perceived and handled by patient and family. Frank communication with your client, the physician [or psychiatrist], and the family together . . . will help you" (Burlingame, 1995, p. 56). Hargrave and Anderson (1992) also state that "medical facts constitute the most common assessment done for older people in our society. Indeed, these facts are important, because they will have a great impact on how the individual feels about himself or herself and how the rest of the family interacts" (p. 79). Therefore, there may be value in considering a disorder or physical ailment as a new member of the system and observe what it contributes and how others in the system organize around it.

Furthermore, because so many older adults already take medication for medical conditions, and because these medications often impact mental health, family therapists must either become experts on the side effects of such medications or consult with those who are. Some antidepressants can adversely impact heart patients (Zarit and Zarit, 1998) or influence sexual functioning. Other medications for health problems (for instance, cardiac medications) may contribute to depression or depressive symptoms (e.g., lack of energy or sleeplessness) or to sexual dysfunction, which may result in marital problems, reduced intimacy, or lowered self-esteem. Because these issues can be so prevalent yet hidden in cases such as Mr. Paxton's, family therapists must regularly assess clients' experience with medications. These issues should be addressed through collaboration with other health care providers rather than simply adopting an ageist perspective that sexual difficulties or depression are normal in older adults.

In addition, the physiological impact of medication on an older person's body is different than on those of their younger counterparts. It is important to note that medications generally "are absorbed, distributed, metabolized, and eliminated more slowly . . . [and] remain in the body longer . . . [increasing the] risk that drugs will build up to toxic levels" (Zarit and Zarit, 1998, p. 180). This biological fact has many important implications for MFTs. First, medications must be monitored more carefully. Second, psychotropic medications may be started at lower doses and require more frequent adjustments. Third, simply because of the sheer number of different medications many older adults take, the potential for dangerous drug interaction is greater (Zarit and Zarit, 1998). If MFTs have concerns regarding how an older client is responding to medications, they should consult with the client's family physician, psychiatrist, or other prescribing physician.

These powerful biomedical facts carry great clinical import. Clinicians carry the responsibility to gain a basic understanding of common illnesses and medication. In addition to this understanding, Zarit and Zarit (1998) suggest that therapists develop the ability to speak about mental health issues in a nonjargon way and clearly present treatment plans, two keys to successful collaboration with the medical community. It should also be noted that a number of outstanding, MFT-based writings already exist on how to collaborate effectively (Seaburn et al., 1996; McDaniel, Campbell, and Seaburn, 1995). This collaboration is the key to ethically and effectively dealing with the interface between medication and mental health issues in the lives of older clients.

In addition to family physicians, physical and occupational therapists, religious leaders, residential-care providers, and government agencies are all examples of systems that may also be having an impact on older clients. Beyond serving as a gateway for older adults' participation in therapy, these systems also provide services and advice, which, when taken together, can appear confusing and contradictory. Because these systems are a major force in the making of meaning for older adults, it is vital that MFTs learn which systems are most important to their clients and learn how to help them work through the barrage of information they will receive.

Once the different systems have been identified, it is often useful to initiate contact promptly. In the case of Mr. Paxton, his primary care physician would be an important first contact. A conversation with the family doctor could provide a background on depressive symptoms, attempted treatment approaches, the comorbidity of symptoms, current medications, and a second opinion on his comments that he is "about ready to give up." In many cases, a joint appointment can be made in which Mr. Paxton can see both parties working together. This unified approach can eliminate confusion, duplication of services or contradictory treatment, and unnecessary suffering on his part.

CULTURAL AND GENDER ISSUES

The publication of *Ethnicity and Family Therapy* by McGoldrick, Pearce, and Giordano in 1982 resonated with many therapists. Similarly, Virginia Goldner's (1985) landmark article "Feminism and Family Therapy" challenged many therapists to consider issues of gender more intently in their work. Since the publication of these and other seminal articles, the field of family therapy has taken initial strides toward recognizing how cultural structures and unexamined assumptions impact the lives of clients and therapists, as well as therapy itself. Unfortunately, discussions about diversity often remain disconnected from discussions of aging. Therapy with older adults is enhanced when efforts are made to identify and address salient issues of diversity.

A simple awareness of these issues is not enough, however. Hardy and Laszloffy (1995) explain that "awareness is primarily a cognitive function; an individual becomes conscious of a thought or action and processes it intellectually. Sensitivity, on the other hand, is primarily an affective function; an individual responds emotionally to stimuli with delicacy and respectfulness" (p. 227). Not only must clinicians become aware of these issues but also learn to respond with genuine sensitivity. For the purpose of this project, the three main areas of invisible differences to consider in later life are age, gender, and ethnicity.

The first area of invisibility is age. In most instances, older adults are spoken about as if they were one homogenous group. It should be recognized that a broad span of age is included within the term "older adults." Neugarten and Neugarten (1986) developed distinctions within the "old age" category that can be useful for therapists. These categories distinguish between the young old (ages fifty-five to seventy-five), the middle old (ages seventy-five to eighty-five), and the old old (ages eighty-five-plus). Walsh (1988) observed that "more 'young old' couples at retirement age with diminishing resources will be involved in caring for their 'old old' parents" (p. 327). Given this, it is important to realize that two different couples within the "older adult" category would have very different needs.

In addition to differences in the present, members in the various age categories would also have had very different experiences as youths. A child born during the Great Depression and a child born during World War II would have been socialized in two very different worlds; these important cohort differences will impact every part of the therapeutic experience, from how clients view their problems to what they think of mental health services. Therefore, therapists must be aware of and sensitive to diversity by age and experience among older adults.

The second area of "invisible differences" is gender. The fact that men and women have different experiences at all ages of the life cycle is basic yet absolutely vital to consider when working with older clients. To illustrate, women of all ages are forced to deal with the inequity of male privilege on a daily basis. However, this inequity is greatly increased for an older woman who experiences double jeopardy because of her age and gender and who grew up in a time when gender inequality was even more pronounced. Therefore, family therapists must be sensitive to this inequality as they conduct life reviews and attempt to establish fairness and justice across intergenerational ledgers.

Another significant gender difference is that women tend to live longer then men. Therefore, women are much more likely to experience widowhood and periods of being alone. Older women are also less likely to remarry then are men. This may be partly due to the unbalanced percentage of men and women in later life. The United States Census figures for 1987 reported, "For every 100 men in the 65-69 age-group, there were 120 women, but for every 100 men in the 85 years and older age bracket, there were 256 women" (Cocker-ham, 1991, p. 18).

Due to this fact, women are much more likely to the face the challenges of later life without a partner. Among the many challenges that can be exacerbated by isolation in later life are health problems. Cockerham (1991) states that "women are sick more often (with less serious health problems), but live longer; men, in contrast, are sick less often, but die sooner from more life-threatening diseases" (p. 18). Therefore, although a woman may have been there to care for her husband during serious health problems, when a more life-threatening illness impacts her later in life, she may not have the support he did. Therapists informed by these facts will explore potential issues of isolation and support with female clients or issues of morbidity with younger-old male clients.

Therapists should also be conscious about the differences in how men and women have been socialized relative to gender in our culture. An additional layer to explore is the messages they have received at different periods in their lives about what it means to be a man or a woman. These socially acceptable roles will inform their definition of self as an older adult. In the example of Mr. Paxton, his feelings of being useless may be tied to socialization about men and work. How will Mrs. Paxton feel if she is unable, at some point, to provide care for Mr. Paxton—a role she has likely played for over fifty years?

As in all age groups, there is also a gender discrepancy in terms of financial stability. Women are more likely than men to experience financial difficulty in old age. Hargrave and Anderson (1992) observed that "widowhood may mean profound changes for the family. First, aside from the grief associated with the passing of a member, widowhood may bring on financial problems that affect the surviving spouse's lifestyle and even cause the spouse to be dislocated from the home" (p.15). These financial concerns are extremely salient in a time of rapidly changing federal and state laws regarding financial support of older adults. Accordingly, therapists should be aware of how gender impacts financial security in later life.

The third area of invisibility to explore is ethnicity. "The United States is at the threshold of two very dramatic demographic changes: the aging of its population and the increasing ethnic and racial diversification of its population" (Mui, Choi, and Monk, 1998, p. 1). The ethnicity of clients should be given greater importance in our work with older adults. Mui, Choi, and Monk (1998) describe an ethnic group as any "group [that] may be composed of any racial or religious . . . members [who] share a common history and common cultural norms and identities and experiences that differentiate them from other groups in the society" (p. 5). An important first step in this process is to explore how both the client's and the therapist's ethnicity influences the therapy process. It is vital to recognize that older adults who have experienced oppression and discrimination from the dominant culture may understandably be reluctant to discuss certain issues with a therapist from a privileged group. An open dialogue about potential differences and conflicts such as these can be very helpful and demonstrate respect.

A second step toward becoming aware of and sensitive to ethnic differences is therapist education. Therapists can and should do two things to increase their understanding of how ethnic and cultural difference impact therapy with older adults. Family therapists must read about multicultural issues in later life to build a basic understanding, but also, and more important, adopt a student position in their relationship with the older adult. It is more important to know about an older adult's individual experience within a cultural group than it is to know what a text says about that group.

For example, the research says that many cultures and religions have strong values about aging (Atchley, 1997). In Asian and Latin cultures, older adults are revered as wise and seasoned. However, what does it mean to Korean or Dominican immigrants with U.S.-born children to age in a country and culture that is not their own? Will they receive the respect they feel they deserve from the acculturated children? Similarly, the research says that, in some cultures, particularly African-American, religiosity and spirituality are a major source of social and psychological support in later life (Atchley, 1997). However, is that experience more or less true for African Americans born after the Great Depression or from different socioeconomic status (SES) groups? In short, therapists should develop awareness and sensitivity to how the experiences of older adults of different ethnic background lead to different clinical needs.

FUTURE DIRECTIONS

In this chapter, we have attempted to present an accurate view of potential clinical needs of older adults and their families as well as the need for MFTs to more adequately prepare to serve this population. In order for MFTs to be more adequately prepared for this work, we must accomplish two major goals. First, basic family therapy models must be theoretically and practically expanded to fit the needs of older families. Second, these models must then be tested for their effectiveness. This research, conducted in real-life clinics, with typical, community-dwelling older adults and families, will provide valuable information as to what works and what does not. Only then will we be clinically and empirically prepared to work with this growing population. Because aging occurs in a family context, and because aging has the potential to trigger so many symptoms in even the most functional families, MFTs have the opportunity and responsibility to provide competent and caring family-based treatment. It is our hope that as a profession we will rise to the occasion.

REFERENCES

American Association of Retired Persons (AARP). (1996). *A profile of older Americans* [Brochure]. Washington, DC: Author.

Anderson, W. T. and Hargrave, T. D. (1990). Contextual family therapy and older people: Building trust in the intergeneration family. *Journal of Family Therapy, 12,* 311-320.

Atchley, R. C. (1997). *Social forces and aging: An introduction to social gerontology* (Eighth edition). Belmont, CA: Wadsworth Publishing Company.

Baltes, P. B. (1993). The aging mind: Potential and limits. *The Gerontologist, 33,* 580-594.

Benbow, S. M., Marriott, A., Morley, M., and Walsh, S. (1993). Family therapy and dementia: Review and clinical experience. *International Journal of Geriatric Psychiatry, 8,* 717-725.

Bengston, V., Rosenthal, C., and Burton, L. (1996). Paradoxes of families and aging. In J. E. Birren (Series ed.), R. H. Binstock, and L. K. George (Volume ed.), *Handbook of aging and the social sciences* (Fourth edition) (pp. 253-282). New York: Academic Press.

Blazer, D. (1998). *Emotional problems in later life: Intervention strategies for professional caregivers*. New York: Springer.

Blazer, D. G. (1994). Epidemiology of late-life depression. In L. S. Schneider, C. F. Reynolds, B. D. Lebowitz, and A. J. Friedhoff (Eds.), *Diagnosis and treatment of depression in late life: Results of the NIH Consensus Development Conference* (pp. 9-19). Washington, DC: American Psychiatric Press, Inc.

Blazer, D., Hughes, D. C., and George, L. K. (1987). The epidemiology of depression in an elderly community population. *Gerontologist, 27,* 281-287.

Boszormenyi-Nagy, I. (1974). Ethical and practical implications of intergenerational family therapy. What is psychotherapy? *Psychosomatic, 24,* 261-268.

Boszormenyi-Nagy, I. and Krasner, B. (1986) *Between give and take: A clinical guide to contextual therapy.* New York: Brunner/Mazel.

Boszormenyi-Nagy, I. and Spark, G. (1973). *Invisible loyalties: Reciprocity in intergenerational family therapy.* New York: Harper and Row.

Boszormenyi-Nagy, I. and Ulrich, D. N. (1981). Contextual family therapy. In A. S. Gurman and D. P. Kniskern (Eds.), *Handbook of family therapy* (pp. 159-186). New York: Brunner/Mazel.

Bowen, M. (1978). *Family therapy in clinical practice.* New York: Aronson.

Burlingame, V. S. (1995). *Gerocounseling: Counseling elders and their families.* New York: Springer Publishing Company.

Butler, R. N. (1963). The life review: An interpretation of reminiscence in the aged. *Psychiatry, 26,* 65-76.

Carstensen, L. L., Gottman, J. M., and Levenson, R. W. (1995). Emotional behavior in long-term marriage. *Psychology and Aging, 10(1),* 140-149.

Cockerham, W. C. (1991). *The aging society.* New Jersey: Prentice-Hall.

Cohen, W. (1995). A physician's view: On one-downmanship and treating the complainant. In J. H. Weakland and W. A. Ray (Eds.), *Propagations: Thirty years of influence from the Mental Research Institute* (pp. 207-225). Binghamton, NY: The Haworth Press, Inc.

Doherty, W. J. and Simmons, D. S. (1996). Clinical practice patterns of marriage and family therapists: A national survey of therapists and their clients. *Journal of Marital and Family Therapy, 22,* 9-25.

Eisdorfer, C. (1983). Conceptual models of aging: The challenge of a new frontier. *American Psychologist, 38(2),* 197-202.

Erickson, E. H. (1963). *Childhood and society* (Second edition). New York: Norton.

Everett, C. A., Russell, C. S., and Keller, J. (1992). *Family therapy glossary* (pp. 1-40). Washington, DC: The American Association for Marriage and Family Therapy.

Flori, D. E. (1989). The prevalence of later life family concerns in the marriage and family therapy journal literature (1976-1985): A content analysis. *Journal of Marital and Family Therapy, 15,* 289-297.

Framo, J. L. (1976). Family of origin as a therapeutic resource for adults in marital and family therapy: You can and should go home again. *Family Process, 15,* 193-210.

Frankl, V. (1959). *Man's search for meaning.* New York: Simon and Schuster Pocket Books.

Gafner, G. (1987). Engaging the elderly couple in marital therapy. *The American Journal of Family Therapy, 15,* 305-315.

Goldner, V. (1985). Feminism and family therapy. *Family Process, 24,* 31-47.

Goldstrom, I. D., Burns, B. J., Kessler, L. G., Feuerberg, M. A., Larson, D. B., Miller, N. E., and Cromer, W. J. (1987). Mental health services use by elderly adults in a primary care setting. *Journal of Gerontology, 42,* 147-153.

Hagebak, J. E. and Hagebak, B. R. (1983). Meeting the mental health needs of the elderly: Issues and action steps. *Aging* (January/February), 26-31.

Haley, J. (1976). *Problem solving therapy.* San Francisco: Jossey-Bass.

Hardy, K. V. and Laszloffy, T. A. (1995). The cultural genogram: Key to training culturally competent therapists. *Journal of Marital and Family Therapy, 21,* 227-237.

Hargrave, T. D. and Anderson, W. T. (1992). *Finishing well: Aging and reparation in the intergenerational family.* New York: Brunner/Mazel.

Hargrave, T. D. and Anderson, W. T. (1997). Finishing well: A contextual family therapy approach to the aging family. In T. D. Hargrave and S. M. Hanna (Eds.), *The aging family: New visions in theory, practice, and reality* (pp. 61-80). New York: Brunner/Mazel.

Hargrave, T. D. and Hanna, S. M. (1997). *The aging family: New visions in theory, practice, and reality.* New York: Brunner/Mazel.

Hinrichsen, G. A. and Zweig, R. (1994). Family issues in late-life depression. *Journal of Long-Term Home Health Care, 13(3),* 4-15.

Hughston, G. A., Christopherson, V. A., and Bonjean, M. J. (Eds.) (1989). *Aging and family therapy: Practitioner perspectives on Golden Pond.* Binghamton, NY: The Haworth Press Inc.

Joiner, T. and Coyne, J. C. (1999). *The interactional nature of depression.* Washington, DC: American Psychological Association.

McDaniel, S. H., Campbell, T. L., and Seaburn, D. B. (1995). Principles for collaboration between health and mental health providers in primary care. *Family Systems Medicine, 13(3/4),* 283-298.

McGoldrick, M., Pearce, J.K. and Giordano, J. (1982). *Ethnicity and family therapy.* New York: Guilford.

Miller, R. M. and Sandberg, J. G. (1998). Interventions in intergenerational relations. In M. Szinovacz (Ed.), *Handbook on grandparenthood* (pp. 217-229). Westport, CT: Greenwood Press.

Minuchin, S., Montalvo, B., Guerney, B., Rosman, B., and Schumer, F. (1967). *Families of the slums.* New York: Basic Books.

Mittelmeier, C. and Friedman, S. (1993). Toward a mutual understanding: Constructing solutions with families. In S. Friedman, (Ed.), *The new language of change: Constructive collaboraton in psychotherapy.* New York: Guilford.

Mosher-Ashley, P. (1993). Referral patterns of elderly clients to a community mental health center. *Journal of Gerontological Social Work, 20(3/4),* 5-23.

Mui, A. C., Choi, N. G., and Monk, A. (1998). *Long-term care and ethnicity.* Westport: Auburn House.

Neugarten, B. L. and Neugarten, D. A. (1986). Age in the aging society. *Daedalus, 115,* 31-50.

Reynolds, C. F., Schneider, L. S., Lebowitz, B. D., and Kupfer, D. J. (1994). Treatment of depression in elderly patients: Guidelines for primary care. In L. S. Schneider, C. F. Reynolds, B. D. Lebowitz, and A. J. Friedhoff (Eds.), *Diagnosis and treatment of depression in late life: Results of the NIH Consensus Development Conference* (pp. 463-490). Washington, DC: American Psychiatric Press, Inc.

Rowe, J. W. and Kahn, R. L. (1997). Successful aging. *The Gerontologist, 37,* 433-440.

Sandberg, J. G. (1999). "It just isn't fair": Helping older families balance their ledger before the note comes due. *Family Relations, 48(2),* 177-180.

Sandberg, J. G. and Harper, J. M. (1999). Depression in mature marriages: Impact and implications for marital therapy. *Journal of Marital and Family Therapy, 25,* 393-406.

Sandberg, J. G. and Harper, J. M. (2000). In search of a marital distress model of depression in older marriages. *Aging and Mental Health, 4(3),* 210-222.

Scrutton, S. (1989). *Counseling older people: A creative response to aging.* London: Hodder and Stoughton.

Seaburn, D. B., Lorenz, A. D., Gunn, W. B., Gawinski, B. A., and Mauksch, L. B. (1996). *Models of collaboration: A guide for mental health professionals working with health care practitioners.* New York: Basic Books.

Shields, C. G. (1992). Family interaction and caregivers of Alzheimer's disease patients: Correlates of depression. *Family Process, 31,* 19-33.

Tower, R. B. and Kasl, S. V. (1996). Gender, marital closeness, and depressive symptoms in elderly couples. *Journal of Gerontology: Psychological Sciences, 51B(3),* 115-129.

Van Amburg, S. M., Barber, C. E., and Zimmerman, T. S. (1996). Aging and family therapy: Prevalence of aging issues and later family life concerns in marital and family therapy literature (1986-1993). *Journal of Marital and Family Therapy, 22,* 195-203.

Walsh, F. (1988). The family in later life. In B. Carter and M. McGoldrick (Eds.), *The changing family life cycle.* New York: Gardner Press.

Walsh, F. (1999). Families in later life: Challenges and opportunities. In B. Carter and M. McGoldrick (Eds.), *The expanded family life cycle: Individual, family, and social perspectives* (pp. 307-326). Boston: Allyn & Bacon.

White, M. (1995). *Re-authoring lives: Interviews and essays.* Adelaide, South Australia: Dulwich Centre Publications.

Wilken, C. S., Altergott, K., and Sandberg, J. (1996). Spouses' self-perceptions as caregivers: The influence of feminine and masculine sex-role orientation on caring for confused and non-confused partners. *American Journal of Alzheimer's Disease* (November/December), 37-42.

Wolinsky, M. A. (1986). Marital therapy with older couples. *Social Casework: The Journal of Contemporary Social Work, 67(8),* 475-483.

Zarit, S. H. Anthony, C. R., and Boutselis, X. (1987). Interventions with care givers of dementia patients: Comparison of two approaches. *Psychology and Aging, 2,* 225-232.

Zarit, S. H. and Zarit, J. M. (1998). *Mental disorders in older adults: Fundamentals of assessment and treatment.* New York: Guilford.

Index

AAMFT Code of Ethics, 193
Abraham, B., 208
Abuse and BPD, 138-139, 146
Acorn, S., 317
Adamce, C., 6, 7
Adler, G., 217
Affective involvement in family
    functioning, 86, 88, 98
Affective responsiveness
  in family functioning, 86, 88
  stage in PCSTF, 94, 98
Ageism, 361
Aging
  adjustment issues, 368
  aging process, 363
  apprehension of aging, 361-363
  biological, 364
  biopsychosocial approach, 366-368
  caregiving, 367
  case example, 374-377
  cultural and gender issues, 380-383
  depression in later life, 366-367,
      374-377
  family-based treatment model, 370-374
  future directions, 384
  intergenerational conflict and strain,
      368, 372-374
  medication integration with
      psychiatric services, 378-380
  optimal, 364
  pathological, 364
  psychological, 364-365
  social aspects, 365-366, 382
  treatment setting, 369-370
  treatment strengths and limitations,
      377-378
  usual, 364
Agoraphobia. See also Panic disorder
  complex, 115-116, 130

Agoraphobia (continued)
  and interpersonal relationships, 113-116
  simple, 115, 130
Agras, W. S., 118
Agresta, J., 64
Akiskal, H. S., 176
Alarms, 110, 112
Albers, M., 189
Albro, J., 86
Aletti, A., 186
Alexander, J. F., 18
Allen, J. G., 218, 222
Allmon, D., 145
Almeida, R., 332
Alter, Jane G., 289
Altergott, K., 367
Alves, James W., 83
American Association for Marriage and
      Family Therapy, 193
American Association of Retired
      Persons (AARP), 362
American Psychiatric Association
    borderline personality disorder,
      135, 215
  diagnoses of mental problems, 31
  diagnosis of panic disorder, 129
  obsessive-compulsive disorder, 155
  schizophrenia, 207
American Psychological Association
      Division of Family
      Psychology, 18
Amir, E., 204
Amundson, J., 266, 270, 275
Andersen, T., 271
Anderson, C., 189, 197, 331, 335
  family treatment, 58
  partnership model, 28, 38
  psychoeducational therapy, 12, 188,
      191, 205, 208
Anderson, H., 166

Anderson, W. T., 368, 370, 371, 372, 373, 377, 378, 382
Andrews, G., 157
Ansel, M., 189
Antabuse contract, 293-294, 306
Anthony, C. R., 367
Antonuccio, D. O., 245
Antony, M. M., 115
Anxiety disorders, prevalence of, 14
Aponte, H. J., 281
Apostal, R. A., 224
Apter, S., 136, 141
Ardila, A., 325
Armstrong, H., 145
Arnow, B. A., 118
Arrindell, W., 103, 113
Ash, P., 18
Asnis, G. M., 112
Assessment stage in PCSTF, 90-91, 96-99
Asylum period of institutionalization, 5
Atchley, R. C., 364, 365, 368, 383
Atkinson, S. D., 191
Attribution of mental illness, 32-33
Auciello, P., 76
Auerbach, C. F., 245
Austin, M., 138
Averill, P. M., 163, 177
Avery, A. W., 221
Azrin, N. H., 3, 186

Babcock, J., 343
Bachrach, L., 7, 189
Baldwin, D. S., 127
Baldwin, L., 85
Bale, R., 176
Ballenger, J. C., 112
Baltes, P. B., 365
Bamrak, J. S., 72
Bannigan, K., 3, 186
Barber, C. E., 361-362
Barlow, D. H.
    obsessive-compulsive disorder, 156
    panic disorder, 110, 111, 112, 113, 114, 115, 117, 127
Barnes, S., 208
Barone, D., 76
Barrowclough, C., 58, 72

Barth, J. C., 19
Basoglu, M., 127
Bateson, G., 10, 27, 57
Baucom, D. H., 73
Bayog, R., 293, 298
Beach, S. R. H., 83, 87
Bearden, S., 174
Beattie, M., 305
Bebbington, P., 186
Beck, A. T., 102, 163, 230, 245, 247
Beck Depression Inventory, 247-248, 255
Becker, D., 59, 73, 216, 217, 218
Beckman, L., 305
Becvar, D. S., xxi
Becvar, R. J., xxi
Behavior control
    dimension of family functioning, 86, 89
    stage in PCSTF, 94, 98
Behavioral couples therapy (BCT), 289-290. See also Harvard Counseling for Alcoholics' Marriages Project
Behavioral family therapy (BFT)
    case example, 68-72
    cultural issues, 74-75
    future, of, 76-77
    gender issues, 75-76
    integration with psychiatric services, 73
    limitations, 73
    logistics, 61
    medication, 73
    model components
        assessment, 62-63
        communication skills training, 64-66
        education, 63-64
        engagement, 62
        problem-solving training, 66-68
        special problems, 68
    overview, 60
    setting for treatment, 59-60
    strengths, 72-73
    treatment model, 60-68
Beigel, D. E., 4, 186
Belenky, M., 332
Bell, John Elderkin, 8
Bellack, A. S., 64, 72, 75, 77

Belotti, G., 186
Bem, S., 336
Benbow, S. M., 367
Bengston, V., 366
Benson, D. F., 314
Bepko, C., 335
Berg, I. K., 271
Bergman, A., 216
Berkowitz, D., 139
Bernheim, K. F., 28
Berry, S., 238
Bevilacqua, P., 186
Biegel, D. E., 187
Billett, E. A., 164
Biopsychosocial model of disease, 10
Bipolar disorder
    Mood Disorders and Family
        Research Programs, 84, 86
    treatment of, 57-59. *See also*
        Behavioral family therapy
Birley, J. L., 11, 28
Birtwistle, J., 57, 127
Bishop, D., 83, 85, 86, 89
Blaauw, E., 158
Blashfield, R. K., 215
Blazer, D., 218, 366, 371, 374, 375
Blum, H., 138, 140
Bodin, A. M., 19
Bograd, M., 343, 355
Boigo, I., 138
Bond, G. R., 185
Bond, M., 313, 314
Boney-McCoy, S., 76
Bonjean, M. J., 362
Borderline Personality Disorder (BPD)
    background of treatment, 135-136
    biological contribution, 137
    borderline couples, 140-141
    case example, 147-149
    caused by physical and sexual abuse,
        138-139, 146
    criteria for diagnosis, 136
    cultural and gender issues, 150
    defined, 136, 215
    enabling factors in treatment, 143-144
    evaluation and family assessment,
        142-143
    familial transmission of
        characteristics, 140

Borderline Personality Disorder (BPD)
        (continued)
    family pathology, 137-138
    family therapy, 144-147
    future directions, 150-151
    genetic etiology, 136-138
    history of, 216-219
    integration with psychiatric services
        and medication, 149
    medication for, 137, 149
    parental neglect and overprotection,
        139-140
    parental pathology, 140
    RE therapy. *See* Borderline
        personality disorder
        relationship enhancement
        therapy
    setting for study, 141-142
    treatment. *See also* Borderline
        personality disorder relationship
        enhancement (RE) therapy
    goals, 143
    model, 142-147
    strategies, 144, 218
    strengths and limitations, 149
Borderline personality disorder
        relationship enhancement
        (RE) therapy
    background, 215-219
    case example, 225-229
    cultural and gender issues, 231-232
    expresser role, 222-223
    financial considerations of
        treatment, 220
    future directions, 232
    listener role, 222-223
    medication integration with
        psychiatric services, 230-231
    setting for treatment, 219-220
    strengths and limitations of
        treatment, 229-230
    treatment model for RE therapy,
        221-225
Boscolo, L., 165, 265
Boszormenyi-Nagy, I., 9, 368, 373,
        374, 376
Bourne, E. J., 163
Boutselis, X., 367
Bowen, Murray
    aging issues, 372-373

Bowen, Murray (continued)
    borderline personality disorder, 224
    committee on GAP, 9
    psychoeducational model, 187
    women and mental health, 345
Bowlby, John, 8
Bowler, A. E., 32
Bowling, J., 159
Boyd, J. L., 28, 58, 59, 188
Boyd-Franklin, N., 335, 355
Brain injury
    case examples, 322-323
    cultural and gender issues, 325
    denial by family members, 315
    effect on families, 311-312, 315-316
    future directions, 325-326
    medication integrated with
        psychiatric services, 324
    patient problems
        aggression, 314
        cognitive impairment, 313
        depression, 313
        emotional changes, 312-313
        impulsive behavior, 314
        learning and memory deficits,
            312
        paranoia, 314-315
        personality changes, 313-314
    principles of family therapy, 317
    treatment model
        educative and supportive
            counseling, 317-319
        family psychotherapy, 319-322
        intervention perceptions, 320-321
        marital and sexual issues, 321-322
        premorbid family dysfunction,
            319
        transition patient roles, 319-320
    treatment setting, 316
    treatment strengths and limitations,
        324
Brekke, J. S., 186, 189
Brock, G. W., 221
Broderick, C. B., 8
Brooks, N., 312, 313, 316
Brown, G. W., 11, 28
Brown, J. C., 241
Brown, S., 57
Brown, T. A., 115
Bruce, T. J., 127

Bryer, J. B., 138, 139
Bucy, J. E., 242
Buie, D., 217
Buiker-Brinker, M., 192
Burck, C., 282
Burgess, J., 137
Burke, J. D., 155
Burlingame, V. S., 370, 371, 378
Burnam, M. A., 238
Burnham, A., 155
Burns, B. J., 369
Burton, L., 366
Burton, T., 114
Butler, R. N., 37, 372
Butzlaff, R. L., 58, 64

CALM Project. See Harvard
        Counseling for Alcoholics'
        Marriages Project
Calvocoressi, L., 158
Campbell, T. L., 362, 379
Campeas, R., 127
Campsie, L., 312, 131
Canadian mental health movement, 6-7
Capponi, P., 15
Caregiving of aging adults, 367
Carpenter, D., 73
Carpentier, N., 57
Carson, R., 112
Carstensen, L. L., 365
Carter, B., 135, 283, 332
Carter, C., 121, 128, 322
Carter, J., 150
Carter, Michele M., 20, 109, 111,
        112, 113, 117, 121, 128
Carter, R. E., 322
Carver, C., 208
Cascardi, M., 76
Case examples
    aging and family therapy, 374-377
    behavioral family therapy, 68-72
    borderline personality disorder,
        147-149
    borderline personality disorder
        relationship enhancement
        therapy, 225-229
    brain injury, 322-323

Case examples *(continued)*
couples therapy for alcohol
dependence and depression,
299-303
generalized anxiety disorder with
depressive symptoms, 349-353
obsessive-compulsive disorder,
167-172
panic disorder, 116, 119-126
partnership model, 40-45
Problem-Centered Systems Therapy
of the Family, 95-102
psychoeducational model and case
management, 198-202
suicidal client treatment, 253-256
traumatic loss, 274-276
walk-in mental health centers, 272-276
women and mental health, 349-353
Case management, 189-190, 205. *See
also* Psychoeducational model
and case management
Cassano, G. B., 176
Causation theories of mental illness, 9-10
Cecchin, G., 165, 265
Cerny, J. A., 114, 115, 117, 127
Chambless, D. L., 111, 115, 128, 130,
162
Charney, D. S., 167
Charny, I. W., 19
Chesler, P., 218
Chevron, E. S., 102
Choi, N. G., 382, 383
Chopra, M., 165
Choquette, K. A., 298, 299
Christensen, A., 14
Christopherson, V. A., 362
Clark, R. E., 59, 73
Clarkin, J., 73, 137, 142-143
Clinchy, B., 332
Clossick, M., 336
Closure stage in PCSTF, 90, 95, 101
Coalition on Family Diagnosis, 18
Coccaro, E., 136, 137, 141
Cockerham, W. C., 382
Cognitive-behavioral interpersonal
approach to treatment of panic
disorder, 116-118. *See also*
Panic disorder
case example, 119-126
cultural and gender issues, 128-129

Cognitive-behavioral interpersonal
approach to treatment of panic
disorder *(continued)*
future directions, 129-130
integration with psychiatric services,
127-128
role of medication, 127-128
strengths and limitations, 126-127
Cognitive behavioral therapy (CBT) for
obsessive-compulsive
disorder, 161-162
Cognitive restructuring, 123
Cohen, B., 140
Cohen, S., 114, 115
Cohen, W., 371
Colapinto, J., 35
Colson, D. B., 218, 222
Colson, L., 159
Communication
in family functioning, 86-87
skills training, 64-66
stage in PCSTF, 93-94, 97
Community Mental Health Act (1963),
6
Community support movement, 7
Community therapists, 263-264
Comorbid substance abuse treatment.
See Behavioral couples
therapy
Comorbidity, 115, 157
Comos-Diaz, L., 74
Compulsions, 156. *See also* Obsessive-
compulsive disorder
Confidentiality by mental health
professional, 48, 193-194
Consumer-driven therapy approach,
268-269
Contracting stage in PCSTF, 90, 91-92,
99-100
Cook, B., 127
Cornelison, A. R., 10
Cornelius, J., 144
Corney, R. H., 83
Correddu, G., 176
Countertransference, 146
Coverdale, J. H., 208
Coyne, J. C., 87, 367
Coyne, L., 218, 222
Craske, M. G., 114, 115, 117, 127
Crilly, J., 38, 73, 77

Crino, R. D., 157
Cromer, W. J., 369
Cronkite, R. C., 304
Culbertson, J. L., 18
Cultural issues
    aging, 380-383
    behavioral family therapy, 74-75
    borderline personality disorder
        treatment, 150, 231-232
    brain injury treatment, 325
    CALM Project, 305
    cognitive-behavioral interpersonal
        treatment, 128-129
    Eastside Family Centre, 281-282
    feminist family systems approach,
        355-356
    invisible differences, 380-383
    obsessive-compulsive disorder,
        176-177
    partnership model, 48-49
    Problem-Centered Systems Therapy
        of the Family, 103-104
    psychoeducational model and case
        management, 206-207
    schizophrenia, 206-207
    suicidal clients, 258
Curran, P. J., 71
Cutter, H., 298, 299

Dadds, M. R., 58
Dai, Q., 72
Daiuto, A. D., 73
D'Angelo, E., 140
Daniels, M., 238
Davenport, R., 156
Davidson, M., 136, 141
Davies, S., 127
Davis, K. L., 136, 137, 141
de Beurs, E., 116
de Haan, E., 158, 160
de Haan, L., 208
de la Gandara, J. E., 19
de Shazer, S., 270
Deakins, S. A., 73
Deegan, P. E., 15
Deering, C. G., 18
DeGiralomo, J., 76
Deinstitutionalization, 6-7
Delle Femine, A. L., 186

DeMaso, D., 140
Denial of mental illness, 191
Depression. *See also* McMaster Model
    of Family Functioning;
    Suicidal client treatment
    and alcohol abuse, 299-303
    and brain injury, 313
    effect on dimensions of family
        functioning, 86-89
    and family dysfunction, 83-84
    family influence, 242
    in later life, 366-367, 374-377
    model of, 239-241
    Mood Disorders and Family
        Research Programs, 84, 86
Developmental approach in partnership
    model, 33-34
*Diagnostic and Statistical Manual of
    Mental Disorders* (DSM-IV)
    borderline personality disorder
        (BPD), 215
    classifications of mental problems,
        31-32
    diagnosis of BPD, 136
    narrow focus of diagnosis, 18, 19
    obsessive-compulsive disorder, 155
    panic disorder with agoraphobia,
        129
Diaphragmatic breathing, 117, 122
Dickstein, S., 84, 85
Differentiation, 345-349, 351-352
DiNardo, P. A., 156
Dingemans, P., 208
DiNicola, V., 282
Dix, Dorothea, 5
Dixon, L., 4, 77, 187
Doane, J. A., 28
Dobson, K., 84
Doherty, W., 17, 37, 317, 362
Dohrenwend, B., 218
Double-bind hypothesis of
    schizophrenia, 10
Draguns, J. G., 128
Draine, J., 4, 187, 190, 191
Drake, R. E., 59, 73, 76, 185
Droogan, J., 3, 186
Drop-back period in developmental
    process, 38-39

Drugs. *See also* Medication integration
  with psychiatric services;
  Substance abuse
  dual diagnosis, 43, 64
  major force of deinstitutionalization,
  6
  SSRI medications, 127, 175
  substance use disorder, 41-42, 64
Drummond, L. M., 176
DSM-IV. *See Diagnostic and
  Statistical Manual of Mental
  Disorders*
Dual diagnosis, 43, 64
Dual thrust approach to incorporating
  partnership model, 31, 49
Dunne, E. J., 73
Dushay, R., 38, 73, 77
Dusky, K., 334
Dworkin, J., 76
Dyckman, J., 332
Dysfunctional family patterns
  and relationship diagnosis, 18-19
  resulting from family functioning
  disturbances, 86, 89
Dysfunctional transactional patterns,
  86, 89, 98-99
D'Zurilla, T. J., 94

Eastside Family Centre. *See* Walk-in
  mental health centers
Eckman, T., 58
Edwards, D. H., 314
Eisdorfer, C., 361
Eisen, J. L., 155, 157, 176
Ellis, A., 163
Emery, G., 102, 245
Emmelkamp, P. M. G., 113, 114, 117,
  158, 160
Emotional disturbance
  as symptom of frustration, 33
  vs. mental illness, 31-33
Empathic listening, 221
Engel, George L., 10
Epidemiological Catchment Area
  (ECA) Survey, 155
Epstein, E. E., 305
Epstein, N., 83, 85, 86, 89

Epston, D., 166, 167, 176
Ericksonian models of intervention,
  270
Erikson, E. H., 371-372
Escobar, J., 60, 72
Eshelman, S., 289
Estrada, A. U., 244
Eth, S., 60, 72, 192
Ethnicity. *See* Cultural issues
Ethnicity and Family Therapy, 380 ·
Evans, J. R., 188
Evans, R., 86
Everett, C. A., 8, 373
Ewashen, C., 345
Exposure
  exercises, 117
  imaginal, 117, 162
  in vivo, 117, 124, 127, 162
  interoceptive exposure, 117
Exposure/response prevention (EX/RP)
  behavioral therapy, 159-160,
  162-164, 170, 173, 177
Expressed emotion (EE)
  background, 27-28
  in OCD, 158
  in schizophrenia, 11

Fadden, G., 186
Fahy, T. J., 313, 325
Falloon, I. R., 28, 58, 60, 72, 78, 188,
  208
False alarms and panic disorder, 110
False suffocation alarm theory, 112
Family Assessment Device (FAD), 85
Family dysfunction and depression. *See*
  Depression
Farley, O. W., 189
Farmer, M., 14, 75, 289
Fawzy, F. I., 319, 320, 321
Feehan, M., 304
Feminist family systems approach,
  331-333
  case example, 349-353
  cultural and gender issues, 355-356
  future directions, 356
  gender expectations and case
  conceptualization, 338-339
  gender role expectations, 344
  identifying strengths, 340

Feminist family systems approach
    (continued)
    medication integration with
        psychiatric services, 354-355
    neutral treatment, 336
    power structures, 339, 342-343
    sources of strength and support,
        344-345
    treatment and gender inequality,
        340-341
    treatment model, 337-349
        application, 349
        context of client, 341-345, 350-351
        context of treatment, 337-341, 350
        emotional differentiation,
            345-349, 351-352
    treatment setting, 333-336
    treatment strengths and limitations,
        353-354
    women as clients, 338
    women's symptoms in context,
        334-336
Feuerberg, M. A., 369
Fielding, A., 204
Finney, J. W., 304
Fiorillo, A., 186
Fisch, R., xix, xxi, 271
Fischer, S. C., 162
Fisher, H., 193
Fishman, H. C., 35
Fleck, S., 10, 27
Fleischmann, R. L., 167
Flori, D. E., 362
Floyd, F., 298
Foa, E. B., 158, 162, 163
Folstein, M. F., 176
Fontana, G., 186
Fowers, B., 332
Fox, L., 75
Foy, D. W., 76
Framo, J. L., xix, 368, 372-373
Frances, A., 72, 77
Frandsen, K. J., 238
Frank, E., 230
Frank, H., 139
Frank, M., 155
Frankenberg, F. R., 139, 140
Frankl, V., 363
Franklin, A., 335, 355
Franklin, M. E., 162, 163

Frazer, H. J., 127
Freeman, H., 72
Frey, J. III, 109
Friedel, R., 144-145
Friedman, A. S., 83
Friedman, S., 376
Frieswyk, S. H., 218, 222
Fristad, M., 85
Fromm-Reichmann, F., 10, 27, 57
Fruzzetti, A. E., 84
Fry, R., 208
Fry, W. F., Jr., 111
"Functionality hypothesis," 111
Furlong, M., 193
Fyer, A. J., 127

Gabbard, G. O., 218, 222
Gafner, G., 371, 372
Galasko, C. S. B., 314
Galbraith, S., 314
Gallagher, S. K., 4, 186
Garcia-Preto, N., 335, 355
Garvey, M. J., 127
Gatz, M., 242
Gawinski, B. A., 379
Gender issues
    aging, 380-383
    behavioral family therapy, 75-76
    borderline personality disorder
        treatment, 150, 231-232
    brain injury treatment, 325
    CALM Project, 305
    cognitive-behavioral interpersonal
        treatment, 128-129
    Eastside Family Centre, 282-283
    feminist family systems approach.
        See Feminist family systems
        approach
    invisible differences, 380-383
    obsessive-compulsive disorder,
        176-177
    partnership model, 49
    Problem-Centered Systems Therapy
        of the Family, 103-104
    psychoeducational model and case
        management, 206-207
    schizophrenia, 207-208
    suicidal clients, 258

Generalized anxiety disorder (GAD), 130
George, L., 218, 366
Gerontology. *See* Aging
Gersons, B., 208
Gibbons, J., 137
Gilchrist, P., 159
Gilderman, A. M., 188
Gingerich, S., 64
Giordano, J., 74, 380
Given, B., 205
Gladstone, G., 138
Glick, I., 72, 73, 77, 135
Glickauf-Hughes, C., 18
Gluhoski, V. L., 18
Glynn, S. M., 58, 59, 60, 64, 66, 68, 72, 192
Godfrey, H. P. D., 319
Goetz, D., 127
Goldberg, R., 139
Goldberg, S., 144-145
Goldberger, N., 332
Goldfried, M. R., 94
Golding, J. M., 155
Goldman, H., 4, 7, 57, 187
Goldman, S., 140
Goldner, Virginia, 380
Goldstein, A. J., 111, 115, 130
Goldstein, M. J.
    effects of treatment, 3, 4
    family treatment, 58, 59, 73
    partnership model, 28
    psychoeducational therapy, 11-12, 186, 188, 189, 190
Goldstrom, I. D., 369
Gollan, J. K., 18
Gonso, J., 94
Goodman, L., 76
Goodman, W. K., 158, 167
Goodpaster, W., 138
Goodwin, F., 14, 75, 289
Goolishian, H. A., 166
Gore, Kristie L., 20, 109
Gorham, D. R., 71
Gorman, J., 127
Gortner, E. T., 18
Gottesman, I., 204, 206
Gottman, J., 94, 343, 365
Goulet, I., 57
Grad, J., 186

Graham, R., 6-7
Grantham, D., 174
Granvold, D. K., 221
Grauer, L., 83
Greenberger, D., 163, 164, 177
Greene, B., 331
Greenfield, S., 238
Greenwald, D. P., 38, 188
Gregg, S. F., 127
Greist, J. H., 176
Grief and mental illness, 191
Griffin, J. M., 224
Griffith, J. L., 174
Griffith, M. E., 174
Grob, G. N., 5
Groom, K. N., 314
Gross, R., 165
Group for the Advancement of Psychiatry (GAP), 9
Gruenberg, E., 155
Grunes, M. S., 157
Guerney, B., 221, 372
Guilt of mental illness, 191
Gunderson, J., 139, 140, 145, 219
Gunn, W. B., 379
Gustin, Q., 138

Hafen B. Q., 238
Hafner, R. J., 114, 158, 159, 176
Hagebak, B. R., 369
Hagebak, J. E., 369
Hageman, W., 103
Haley, J.
    aging issues, 372
    double-bind hypothesis, 10
    history of treatment, 8
    schizophrenia, 10, 27, 57
    walk-in mental health centers, 261, 270
Halford, W. K., 307
Hamby, S. L., 76
Hamer, R., 144-145
Hand, I., 159
Hanna, S. M., 362, 363, 364, 365, 367
Harding, C., 15
Hardy, K., 339, 356, 380

Hare-Mustin, R., 336, 339
Hargrave, T. D., 362, 363, 364, 365,
        367, 368, 370, 371, 372, 373,
        377, 378, 382
Hargreaves, W. A., 72, 77
Harman, Marsha J., 215, 216, 219, 221
Harmon, M. J., 322
Harper, J. M., 366, 367
Harper-Jacques, S., 271
Harris, M., 158
Harrison, C. A., 58
Harvard Counseling for Alcoholics'
        Marriages (CALM) Project,
        290
Harvard Counseling for Alcoholics'
        Marriages (CALM) Project
        (continued)
    case example, 299-303
    cultural and gender issues, 305
    future directions, 306-308
    medication and integration with
        psychiatric services, 306
    purpose of, 291
    setting, 290
    treatment model
        CALM promises, 292-293
        couples group objectives, 295-298
        feedback, 295
        limitations, 304
        outcome data, 298-299
        sobriety contract, 293-294
        strengths, 303-304
        therapeutic relationships, 295
Hatfield, A. B.
    history of treatment, 5, 7
    integrating of perspectives in mental
        illness, 3
    partnership model, 27, 28
    psychoeducational therapy, 11, 12
    schizophrenia, 10, 11, 57
Hay, L. R., 114
Hayden, L., 84, 85
Hays, R. D., 238
Heavey, C. L., 14
Hegel, M. T., 127-128
Heinemann, A. W., 314
Helzer, J. E., 155
Henderson, J. G., 155
Heninger, G. R., 167
Hepworth, J., 37, 317

Herkov, M. J., 215
Herman, J., 138
Hickox, A., 312, 315, 316
Hill, C. L., 167
Himadi, W. G., 114, 115
Hinchcliffe, M., 87
Hinrichsen, G. A., 367
Hiss, H., 158
Historical overview of family therapy,
        3-4, 7-9, 12
    integrated approach, 20-21
    marital and family therapy, 15-18.
        See also Marital and family
        therapy
    movements from eighteenth century
        to present, 5-7
    relationship diagnosis and
        dysfunctional family patterns,
        18-19
    theories of causation of mental
        illness, 9-10
    treatment of schizophrenia, 11-12
    U.S. Surgeon General's Report on
        Mental Health, 12-15
Hoffart, B., 279, 283
Hoffart, I., 279, 283
Hoffman, L., 166, 265
Hogarty, G. E.
    family treatment, 58
    partnership model, 28, 38
    psychoeducational therapy, 12, 188,
        191, 205, 208
Hoge, S. K., 314
Holder, D., 331, 335
Holding environment in BPD
        treatment, 141, 147
Hollon, S. D., 112
Holtzworth-Monroe, A., 307, 343
Hoogduin, C. A. L., 158, 160
Hooley, J., 29, 58, 64, 83
Hooper, D., 87
Hoover, C. F., 158
Horen, B., 73
Horvath, T. B., 136, 141
Horwitz, L., 218, 222
Howard, N. I., 314
Hoyt, M., 278
Hu, X., 72
Hudal, J., 335
Hudson, J., 140

Hughes, D. C., 366
Hughes, M., 289
Hughston, G. A., 362
Hull, J., 73
Humphrey, M., 325
Huxley, G., 138

Imaginal exposure, 117, 162
Imm, P., 290
In vivo exposure, 117, 124, 127, 162
Insel, T., 158
Institute of Medicine, 308
Institutionalization
    asylum period, 5
    deinstitutionalization, 6-7
    mental hospital period, 5-6
Integrated approach for mental health
        treatment, 20-21
Integrated self, 348-349, 351-352
Interdisciplinary team and case
        management, 205-206
Interoceptive conditioning, 110
Interoceptive exposure, 117
Invisible differences, 380-383
Irving, M. H., 313, 325

Jackson, D. D., 10, 27, 57
Jackson, R., 189
Jacobs, H. E., 58
Jacobs, M., 72, 77
Jacobson, N., 18, 84, 118, 307, 343
Jamieson, K. G., 314
Javna, C. D., 188
Jefferson, J. W., 127
Jenkins, D., 325
Jessee, R. E., 221
Joanning, H., 221
Johannessen, J. O., 208
Johnson, B., 86
Johnson, Eric D., 4, 27, 29, 48
Johnson, J., 221, 317, 322
Johnson, T., 335
Johnson-Sumerford, D., 331
Joiner, T., 367
"Joining" with the family in therapy,
        145
Jonas, J., 140

Jordan, J., 332
Jorgensen, S. R., 221
Judd, L., 14, 75, 289
Julian, J., 176
Jutras, S., 4, 187

Kabacoff, R., 85
Kagan, J., 137
Kahn, J., 87
Kahn, R., 112, 363, 369
Kalucy, R., 159
Kane, J. M., 72, 77
Kanter, Joel, 189, 194, 203
Kaplan, A., 332
Karanci, A. N., 186
Karls, J. M., 189
Karno, M., 155
Karp, J. F., 230
Kaschak, E., 334
Kasl, S. V., 363
Kaslow, Florence W., 18, 19
Kaslow, N. J., 18
Kazak, A. E., 18
Kee, K., 75
Keefler, Joan, 3, 185, 189, 195
Keita, G., 331, 335
Keith, S., 14, 72, 75, 77, 289
Keitner, G., 19, 83, 84, 85, 86, 104
Kellam, S., 205
Keller, J., 373
Kellner, R., 231
Kendler, K., 289
Kennedy, J. L., 164-165
Kent, S., 189
Keren, M., 335
Kernberg, O. F., 216
Kerr, M., 345
Kessler, L. G., 369
Kessler, R., 289
Kinney, R., 189
Kirby, M., 127
Kirsch, I., 306
Kirschner, D. A., 19
Kirschner, S., 19
Klar, H., 136, 141
Klein, D., 112, 115, 127, 137
Klein, M., 216
Klein, R., 231
Kleinman, A., 72

Kleinman, J., 72
Klerman, G. L., 102
Kloek, J., 158
Knill-Jones, R., 314
Knudson-Martin, Carmen, 331, 334,
     335, 336, 345, 346
Koch, A., 141
Koedam, W. S., 19
Kohn, R., 83
Komter, A., 342
Kopelowicz, A., 208
Koponen, H., 127
Koran, L. M., 156
Koritar, E., 189, 195
Kornblith, S. J., 38
Kornbluth, S. J., 188
Kozak, M. J., 162, 163
Krasner, B., 373
Krestan, J., 335
Krol, P. A., 138, 139
Kubos, K. L., 313
Kuch, K., 127
Kuipers, L., 58, 186
Kunovac, J. L., 176
Kupfer, D. J., 366
Kydd, R. R., 208

Lachkar, J., 216, 222
Laidlaw, T. M., 208
Lalonde, P., 57
Lam, D., 58
Lange, A., 116
Langle, S., 193
Language issues as limiting factor in
     utilizing resources, 49
Lansky, M., 3, 319, 320, 321
Larson, D. B., 369
Larson, R., 331
Last, C. G., 114, 115
Laszloffy, T. A., 380
Latimer, E., 204
Lawson, A., 261, 266
Lebowitz, B. D., 366
Leete, E., 15
Leetz, K., 150
Lefcoe, D., 208
Leff, J., 11, 28, 58, 188
Lefley, H. P., 11, 27, 28, 29, 57
Leftoff, S., 314

Leggatt, M., 193
Lehman, A., 4, 28, 77, 189
Lehman, S., 187
Lehto, H., 127
Leinonen, E., 127
Leliott, P. T., 127
Lenior, M., 208
Lennon, M. C., 331
Lensi, P., 176
Leon, A. C., 156
Leong, G. B., 60, 72, 192
Lepola, U., 127
Lesage, A., 57
Leslie, L., 336
Levenson, H., 217, 218
Levenson, R. W., 365
Levin, A., 127
Levin, S., 85, 86
Levine, P., 19
Levinson, D. F., 7
Lewinsohn, P. M., 245
Lewis, B., 158
Lezak, M. D., 312, 313, 314, 315,
     316, 317, 319, 321
Liberman, R. P., 28, 58, 60, 72, 208
Lidz, T., 10, 27
Lieberman, J. A., 72, 77
Liebowitz, M., 127
Life-cycle issues in mental illness
     diagnosis, 192
Life-review therapy approach, 371-
     372
Lindsey, L., 334, 336
Linehan, M., 145
Link, B., 15, 38, 73, 77
Links, P., 138, 140
Linzen, D., 208
Lips, H., 336
Lipsey, J. R., 313
Livingston, M. G., 312, 313, 316
Locke, B., 14, 75, 289
London, P. S., 325
Long, J., 189
Longabaugh, R., 305
Looper, K., 204
Lopez, S. R., 58
Loraas, Emily L., 135
Loranger, A., 140
Lorenz, A. D., 379
Loukissa, D. A., 186

Lukens, E., 73, 191
Lyles, A., 4, 187
Lynn, S. J., 306

MacFarlane, Malcolm M.
  brain injury therapy, 311, 312, 315, 317
  historical overview, 3, 20
  obsessive-compulsive disorder, 155, 165
Macias, C., 189
MacLaurin, B., 266, 275
Madanes, C., 10, 270
Madonia, M. J., 188
Magana-Amato, A., 28
Magliano, L., 186
Mahler, M. S., 216
Mahoney, A., 334
Maj, M., 186
Malangone, C., 186
Malloy, P., 305
Mance, R., 72, 77
Mann, Horace, 5
Mann, L., 139
Marchal, J., 38, 73, 77
Margolin, G., 87
Margolis, R. B., 155
Marino, M., 139, 140
Marital and family therapy (MFT)
  alcohol use disorder, 290
  efficacy of, 15-18
  internships, 209
  treatment of chronically mentally ill, 185, 187
  treatment of obsessive-compulsive disorder, 159, 160
Markman, H., 94, 307
Marks, I. M., 114, 127, 159
Marriott, A., 367
Marsh, D. T., 189, 205
Marshall, M. M., 313
Martinage, D. P., 313
Marziali, E., 137, 138, 142-143, 218
Massel, H. K., 58
Masters, R., 356
Masterson, J., 217
Mathiesen, S. G., 186
Matthews, S. M., 72, 77
Mattis, S., 192

Maucioni, F., 186
Mauksch, L. B., 379
Mavissakalian, M., 114
May, P. R. A., 188
Mazure, D., 167
McClearn, G. E., 242
McCorkle, B. H., 159
McCormack, C., 141
McCown, W. G., 317
McCrady, B. S., 305
McDaniel, S. H., 37, 317, 362, 379
McDermut, Wilson, 83
McDougle, C. J., 158
McElheran, N., 261, 266, 271
McFarlane, W. R.
  family treatment, 58, 73, 77
  partnership model, 29, 38
  psychoeducational model, 187, 191, 205, 206
McGill, C. W., 28, 58, 59, 188
McGlashan, T., 139, 208
McGlynn, E., 4, 187
McGoldrick, M., 74, 135, 332, 380
McGonagle, K., 289
McGrath, E., 331, 335
McHugh, P. R., 176
McHugo, G. J., 71
McKay, D., 157
McKinlay, W. W., 312, 313, 315, 316
McLaughlin, A. M., 318, 319
McLean, P., 83, 237, 243
McMaster Clinical Rating Scale (MCRS), 85
McMaster Model of Family Functioning (MMFF)
  background, 83-84
  dimensions of family life
    affective involvement, 86, 88, 98
    affective responsiveness, 86, 88, 94, 98
    behavior control, 86, 89, 94, 98
    communication, 86-87, 97
    dysfunctional transactional patterns, 86, 89, 98-99
    problem-solving, 86, 87, 94, 97
    roles, 86, 87-88, 94, 97-98
  future of, 104

McMaster Model of Family
      Functioning (MMFF)
      (continued)
   Problem-Centered Systems Therapy
      of the Family (PCSTF). *See*
      Problem-Centered Systems
      Therapy of the Family
   research, 85-86
McMaster Structured Interview of
      Family Functioning
      (McSIFF), 85
McNamee, G., 127
Measey, L. G., 113
Mechanic, D., 4, 186
Medication integration with psychiatric
      services
   aging, 378-380
   behavioral family therapy, 73
   borderline personality disorder, 149,
      230-231
   brain injury, 324
   CALM Project, 306
   cognitive-behavioral interpersonal
      approach to treatment of panic
      disorder, 127-128
   feminist family systems approach,
      354-355
   obsessive-compulsive disorder,
      174-176
   partnership model, 47-48
   Problem-Centered Systems Therapy
      of the Family (PCSTF),
      102-103
   psychoeducational model, 205-206
   suicidal clients, 257
   walk-in mental health centers,
      279-280
Mehta, M., 160, 176
Meissner, W. W., 27
Meltzer-Brody, S., 127
Mental hospital period of
      institutionalization, 5-6
Mental hygiene movement, 5-6
Mental illness
   chronic. *See* Psychoeducational
      model and case management
   described, 12-15
   vs. emotional disturbance, 31-33
Merry, P., 317
Merry, S., 208

Messineo, T., 332
Meydrech, E., 174
Meyer, R. G., 215
Miklowitz, D. J.
   effects of treatment, 3, 4
   family treatment, 58, 59, 73
   partnership model, 28, 29
   psychoeducational therapy, 11-12,
      186, 188, 189, 190
Milan team treatment for OCD, 165
Millac, P., 313, 325
Miller, F. E., 191
Miller, I., 19, 83, 84, 85, 86, 104
Miller, J., 138, 139, 266, 271, 278, 279,
      282, 332
Miller, Laurence, 311, 312, 313, 314,
      315, 317, 320, 321, 322, 326
Miller, Lynn, 237
Miller, N. E., 369
Miller, R., 76, 368
Miller, S., 150, 271
Milligan, D. W., 4
Milligan, S. E., 186, 187
Millward, J., 139, 140
Milton, F., 114
Mintz, J., 58
Minuchin, S., 35, 372
Mishler, E. G., 27
Mitchell, P., 138
Mittelmeier, C., 376
Mitton, J., 138
Models
   aging, 370-374
   behavioral family therapy, 60-68
   biopsychosocial model of disease, 10
   borderline personality disorder
      treatment, 142-147, 221-225
   brain injury, 317-322
   CALM project, 291-299
   cognitive-behavioral interpersonal
      treatment, 116-118
   depression, 239-241
   feminist family systems approach,
      337-349
   McMaster. *See* McMaster Model
      of Family Functioning
   obsessive-compulsive disorder,
      161-167
   partnership. *See* Partnership model

Models *(continued)*
  psychoeducational. *See*
    Psychoeducational therapy
  relationship enhancement therapy,
    221-225
  stress-diathesis, 12, 28, 185
  suicidal client treatment, 245-253
  walk-in mental health centers,
    266-272
Mohs, R. C., 136, 141
Monk, A., 382, 383
Monking, H. S., 192
Monoamine Oxidase Inhibitors
    (MAOIs), 127
Montalvo, B., 372
Monteiro, W., 114
Mood disorder, 147, 148
Mood Disorders and Family Research
    Programs, 84
Moos, R. H., 304
Moral treatment approach, 5
Morales-Dorta, J., 74
Morgan, A. C., 221
Morley, M., 367
Morosini, P., 208
Morris, T., 103
Morrison, R. L., 75
Mosher-Ashley, P., 362, 369, 370
Moss, H. B., 188
Mueser, K.
  family treatment, 57, 58, 59, 60, 64,
    66, 68, 71, 73, 75, 76, 77
  historical overview, 3
  psychoeducational model, 185, 186
Mui, A. C., 382, 383
Multiple-family behavioral treatment
    (MFBT), 159
Munroe-Blum, H., 137, 142-143, 218
Murphy, C., 304
Murray, W. R., 314
Murrin, M., 76

Najeson, T., 321
Narcissistic personality disorder
    (NPD), 216
National Alliance for the Mentally Ill
    (NAMI)
  accountability to clients and
    relatives, 58

National Alliance for the Mentally Ill
    (NAMI) *(continued)*
  borderline personality disorder, 151
  criticism of EE studies, 11, 28
  focused groups, 29
  history of, 7
  insurance coverage for mental
    illness, 32
  psychoeducation and family
    therapy, 35
National Center for Health Statistics, 238
National Committee on Mental
    Hygiene, 6
National Mental Health Association, 6
National mental health movement, 6-7
Neider, D. M., 19
Nelson, B. A., 138, 139
Nelson, C., 289
Nelson, K. A., 58
Nesselroade, J. R., 242
Nestadt, G., 176
Network therapy, 37
Neugarten, B. L., 381
Neugarten, D. A., 381
Neurobiological model of panic
    disorder, 112
Newmark, M., 73
Newsom, G. E., 218, 222
Neziroglu, F. A., 157
Nichols, W. C., 3, 8
Ninan, P. T., 72, 77
Noel, N., 305
Norman, W., 83
Noshirvani, H., 127
Notarius, C., 94
Noyes, R., 127
Nuechterlein, K. H., 28
Nuzzarello, A., 127

Oakander, M., 266, 275
O'Brien, G. T., 114, 115
Obsessions, 155-156
Obsessive-compulsive disorder (OCD)
  behavioral treatment approach,
    162-163
  biological approach, 164-165, 174

Obsessive-compulsive disorder (OCD)
  (continued)
  case example, 167-172
  cognitive treatment approach,
    163-164
  compulsions, 156
  cultural and gender issues, 176-177
  family etiology, 158
  family impact, 157-158
  family treatment, 159-160
  future directions, 177-178
  medication integrated with
    psychiatric services, 174-176
  obsessions, 155-156
  rituals, 156, 157-158
  setting for treatment, 160-161
  symptoms, 155-156
  systemic approach, 165-167
  treatment model, 161-167
  treatment strengths and limitations,
    173-174
O'Connor, M. E., 314
Oddy, M., 325
O'Farrell, T. J., 289, 290, 291, 293,
    298, 299, 304
Ogtron, K., 83
Ohaeri, J. U., 186
O'Hanlon, W., 270
Oldham, J., 140
O'Leary, K. D., 83, 87
Oppenheimer, K., 109
Orley, J., 83
Orvaschel, H., 155
Osher, F. C., 76
Ostrovsky, F., 325
O'Sullivan, G., 127
Otto, M. W., 127
Overall, J. E., 71
Ozarow, B. J., 162

Padesky, C. A., 163, 164, 177
Padgett, D., 335, 343, 354, 356
Padrone, F. J., 315, 317
Panic disorder
  agoraphobia and interpersonal
    relationships, 113-116
  background, 109-110
  case example, 116, 119-126

Panic disorder *(continued)*
  cognitive-behavioral interpersonal
    treatment model. *See*
    Cognitive-behavioral
    interpersonal approach to
    treatment of panic disorder
  cultural and gender issues in
    treatment, 128-129
  etiological theories, 110-112
  future directions, 129-130
  panic control treatment (PCT), 117
  strengths and limitations, 126-127
Panting, A., 317
Papp, P., 283
Parental neglect and overprotection and
    BPD, 139-140
Paris, J., 139
Parker, G., 138
Parker, R. S., 321
Parle, M., 58
Partnership model
  case example, 40-45
  cultural issues, 48-49
  development of, 29-30
  developmental approach, 33-34
  dual thrust approach of
    incorporation, 31, 49
  future of, 50-51
  gender issues, 49-50
  limitations of the model, 46-47
  medication integration with
    psychiatric services, 47-48
  mental illness vs. emotional
    disturbance, 31-33
  programs and settings, 30-31
  psychoeducation and family
    therapy, 35-37
  role of medication, 47-48
  strengths of the model, 45-46
  team, 37-40
Pasnau, R. O., 319, 320, 321
Patel, A. R., 314
Pato, M., 157, 159
Paul, Norman, 9
Pauls, D. L., 164
Paz, G., 60, 72, 192
Pearce, J., 74, 380
Pedersen, N. L., 242
Pedersen, T., 127
Pedersen, V., 127

Pederson, J., 60, 72
Pedraza, A., 19
Penn, D. L., 3, 186
Penn, P., 165, 265
Penttinent, J. T., 127
Perel, J., 144
Perlick, D., 192
Perlmutter, R., 3
Perry, J., 138
Perry, P. J., 324
Pesocolido, B., 15
Petrila, J. P., 193, 194
Pharmacotherapy. *See* Medication
     integration with psychiatric
     services
Phelan, J., 15
Phillips, M. R., 72
Physical abuse and BPD, 138-139, 146
Pickens, A., 314
Pigott, T. A., 165, 175
Pine, F., 216
Pinkham, L., 141
Pinsof, W. M., 11, 12, 15, 17, 20, 244
Pitts, W., 138
Platt, Jason J., 361
Plomin, R., 242
Pollack, M. H., 127
Pollard, C. A., 155
Pope, H., 140
Porceddu, K., 72
Portera, L., 156
Postrado, L., 4, 187
Post-traumatic stress disorder
     (PTSD), 76
Potter, J. M., 314
Practice Patterns Survey, 17
Prata, G., 165
Price, L. H., 158, 167
Price, T. R., 313
Prigatano, G. P., 326
Problem-Centered Systems Therapy of
     the Family (PCSTF), 85-86,
     89-95
  assessment, 90-91, 96-99
  case example, 95-102
  closure, 90, 95, 101
  communication, 93-94, 97
  contracting, 90, 91-92, 99-100
  cultural and gender issues, 103-104
  future of, 104

Problem-Centered Systems Therapy of
     the Family (PCSTF)
     (continued)
  integration with psychiatric services,
     102-103
  role of medication, 102-103
  roles, 94, 97-98
  strengths and limitations of, 102
  treatment, 90, 92-95, 100-101
Problem-solving
  in family functioning, 86, 87
  stage in PCSTF, 94, 97
  training, 66-68
Project CALM. *See* Harvard
     Counseling for Alcoholics'
     Marriages Project
Protinsky, H., 266, 271, 278
Prusoff, B., 83, 87
Pruyn, N. A., 157, 158
Psychiatric services and medication.
     See Medication integration
     with psychiatric services
Psychodynamic theory on the etiology
     of panic, 111-112
Psychoeducational model and case
     management, 185-186
  case example, 198-202
  case management, 48, 189-190
  confidentiality, 193-194
  contribution of MFT, 187-188
  cultural issues, 206-207
  family and chronic mental illness,
     186-187
  future directions, 208-209
  gender issues, 207-208
  integration, 190-193
  interdisciplinary team, 205-206
  limitations of the model, 203-204
  medication and psychiatric services,
     206
  psychoeducational model, 188-189
  strengths of model, 202-203
  treatment model, 195-198
  treatment setting, 194-195
  workshop, 197-198
Psychoeducational therapy
  background of, 28
  borderline personality disorder, 148
  defined, 11
  and family therapy, 35-37

Psychoeducational therapy *(continued)*
  schizophrenia treatment, 11-12
  treatment model, 195-198
Psychopharmacologic treatment, 13,
  137
Psychopharmacotherapy, 12, 13
Psychotherapy
  background of term, 8
  for children, 14
  interpersonal psychotherapy
    approach, 125
  intervention, 13
Public health movement, 5-6
Pugh, C. A., 18

Racial diversity. *See* Cultural issues
Rae, D., 14, 75, 289
Ramm, E., 114
Randolph, E. T., 60, 72, 192
Rani, S., 176
Rao, K., 313
Rapee, R., 112, 242
Raphael, F. J., 176
Rasmussen, S., 84, 85, 155, 157, 167,
  176
Ravagli, S., 176
Raymond, C. L., 164
Razani, J., 188
Rea, M. M., 73
Reciprocal behavioral agreements in
    treatment of suicidal clients,
    249-251
Reciprocity hypothesis, 245
"Reframing" in family therapy, 145
Regier, D., 14, 75, 155, 289
Rehabilitation of patients, 48
Reiser, D. E., 217, 218
Reiss, D., 19
  family treatment, 58
  partnership model, 28, 38
  psychoeducational therapy, 12, 188,
    191, 205, 208
Reiter, S. R., 127
Relationship diagnosis and
    dysfunctional family patterns,
    18-19
Relationship enhancement (RE) therapy
    for BPD
  case example, 225-229

Relationship enhancement (RE) therapy
    for BPD *(continued)*
  cultural and gender issues, 231-232
  empathic listening, 221
  expresser role, 222-223
  financial considerations of
    treatment, 220
  future directions, 232
  listener role, 222-223
  medication integration with
    psychiatric services, 230-231
  setting for treatment, 219-220
  strengths and limitations of
    treatment, 229-230
  treatment model, 221-225
Relaxation training for OCD, 162
Renaud, M., 57
Resnick, R., 144-145
Reynolds, C. F., 366
Rezneck, J., 137
Richards, M., 331
Richardson, F., 332
Richter, M. A., 164
Ridley, C. A., 221
Riggs, D. S., 158
Risman, B., 331
Rituals, 156, 157-158. *See also*
    Obsessive-compulsive
    disorder
Roberts, E., 317
Roberts, F. J., 87
Robertson, M., 164
Robins, L. N., 155
Robinson, R. G., 313, 324
Rodnick, E. H., 188
Rogers, Carl R., 221
Rogers, W., 238
Roles
  expresser, 222-223
  in family functioning, 86, 87-88, 94,
    97-98
  gender, 344
  listener, 222-223
  stage in PCSTF, 94, 97-98
Rolland, J. S., 37
Romano, M. D., 315
Romanoski, A. J., 176
Rosen, A., 18
Rosenbaum, A., 314
Rosenbaum, J. F., 127

Rosenbaum, M., 321
Rosenbaum, R., 278, 332
Rosenberg, S. D., 76
Rosenthal, C., 366
Rosenthal, M., 315, 317, 319, 321
Rosman, B., 372
Ross, D. C., 115
Ross, E. D., 313
Rosselli, M., 325
Rossi, A., 186
Rotunda, Rob J., 289, 290, 291
Rounsaville, B., 83, 87, 102
Rowe, J. W., 363, 369
Rudin, E., 155
Ruiwen, W., 72
Rush, A. J., 102, 230, 245, 313
Rushe, R., 343
Russell, C. S., 373
Russo, N., 331, 335
Ryan, C., 19, 83, 86, 104

Sachs, G. S., 127
Sadoff, R. L., 193, 194
Sainsbury, P., 186
Salesperson "consumer-driven"
    service, 268-269
Salusky, S., 84
Sameroff, A., 84, 85
Samuels, J. F., 176
Sandberg, Jonathan G., 361, 366, 367,
    368, 376, 377
Sandeen, E. E., 87
Sanderman, R., 113
Santa-Barbara, J., 85
Sasson, Y., 165
Satir, Virginia, 221
Saunders, J., 203
Sbrocco, T., 121, 128
Schaffer, V., 318, 319
Schear, S., 136, 141
Scherer, D., 290
Schiller, M., 84, 85
Schizophrenia
    cultural issues, 206-207
    diagnosis problems, 208
    gender issues, 207-208

Schizophrenia *(continued)*
    theory of causation, 10
    treatment of, 11-12, 14, 57-59. *See
        also* Behavioral family
        therapy
Schizophrenic Research Project, 12
Schizophrenogenic mother, 10
Schmaling, K., 84, 307
Schmidt, M. F., 314
Schneider, L. S., 366
Schooler, N. R., 72, 77
Schrader, S. S., 8
Schultz, P., 144-145
Schulz, S., 144-145
Schumer, F., 372
Schwartz, E., 139, 140
Scott, J., 4, 187
Scripted behavior, 87
Scrutton, S., 372
Seaburn, D. B., 362, 379, 379
Seay, S., 165, 175
Segal, E., 139
Seifer, R., 84, 85
Selective serotonin reuptake inhibitors
    (SSRIs), 127, 175
Self-help groups, 14-15
Selvini Palazzoli, M., 165
Sengun, S., 127
Sengupta, A., 77
Severe, J. B., 72, 77
Sexual abuse and BPD, 138-139, 146
Shaner, A. L., 60, 72, 192
Shapiro, E., 139, 146
Shapiro, L. J., 114
Shaw, B. F., 102, 245
Shaw, T. G., 314
Shelton, R. C., 112
Shields, C. G., 367
Shoham, V., 73
Siever, L. J., 136, 137, 141
Silk, K. R., 219
Silovsky, J. F., 18
Silverman, J. M., 136, 141
Silverstein, L. B., 245
Silverstein, O., 283
Simmons, D., 17, 150, 362
Simmons, S., 205
Simms, S., 18
Simpson, G. M., 72, 77
Singer, M. T., 27

Singh, H., 75
Sjodin, I., 127
Slade, E., 189
Slade, M., 205
Slagle, D. A., 311
Slipp, S., 146
Slive, A., 261, 266, 271, 275, 278
Smith, G., 58
Smith, L. M., 319
Snidman, N., 137
Snyder, K. S., 28, 58
Snyder, S., 138, 215
Sobriety contract, 293-294
Sobriety-trust discussion, 293-294
Soloff, P., 139, 140, 144
Solomon, D. A., 86, 104
Solomon, M., 4, 18, 216
Solomon, P., 4, 187, 190, 191
Song, L., 4, 186, 187
Sorenson, S. B., 155
Spaniol, L., 193
Spark, G., 373
Speed, B., 282
Spiegel, D. A., 127
Spiral pattern in developmental
        process, 38-39
Spring, B., 58, 185
Stanley, M. A., 163, 177
Staroste, A., 192
Starr, L. B., 313
Stastny, P., 192
Stayton, W. R., 18
Steer, R. A., 247
Stein, M. B., 112
Steinberg, M. R., 188
Steiner, M., 138
Steinmetz, J. L., 245
Steinwachs, D. M., 189
Steketee, G., 114, 156, 157, 158, 159,
        160, 162, 163, 164, 175, 176
Stewart, A., 238
Stewart, R. S., 313
Stickle, T. R., 73
Stiver, I., 332
Stockman, R., 157
Stone, M., 137, 138
Stout, R., 305
Strachan, A., 28, 60, 72, 192
Strauman, T., 112

Straus, M. A., 76
Strauss, J. S., 15
Stress-diathesis model, 12, 28, 185
Strickland, B., 331, 335
Strickle, T. R., 73
Stroke patients telephone-
        administered intervention,
        86
Structural family therapy
        intervention, 35-36
Stuart, R. B., 245, 296
Stueve, A., 15
Suarez, A., 145
Substance abuse, treatment for. See
        Behavioral couples therapy
Sue, D., 128
Suelzer, M., 127
Sugerman, D. B., 76
Suicidal client treatment, 237-238
    case example, 253-256
    cultural and gender issues, 258
    depression as cause of suicide,
        238-239
    family therapy, 241-244
    future directions, 258-259
    inherited depression, 242
    job of therapy, 241
    limitations of treatment, 256-257
    medication integration with
        psychiatric services, 257
    psychosocial model of
        development of depression,
        239-241
    setting for treatment, 244-245
    strengths of treatment, 256
    suicide demographics, 238-239
    treatment model, 245-253
        action steps, 250-253
        acute stage assessment,
            246-247
        comprehensive assessment
            stage, 247-248
        educational intervention,
            249-253
        reciprocity hypothesis, 245
Sullivan, H. S., 57
Surgeon General's Report on Mental
        Health, 12-15

Surrey, J., 332
Swartz, M., 218
Swinson, R. P., 127
Symington, C., 312, 313

Taffel, R., 356
Talmon, M., 277, 278
Tarrier, N., 58, 72
Tarule, J., 332
Task evaluation stage in PCSTF, 95
Taylor, C. B., 118
Taylor, E. H., 32
Taylor, S., 243
Teasdale, J. D., 83
Teichner, G., 3, 186
Telch, M. J., 118
Telfer, L. A., 112
Teresi, J., 192
Teri, L., 245
Thienemann, M. L., 156
Thomsen, J. V., 313-314
Thornicroft, G., 159
Todaro, J., 157
Tomm, K., 165
Tompson, M. C., 73
Toran, J., 73
Torgersen, S., 130
Torpy, D. M., 113
Torrey, E. F., 32
Tower, R. B., 363
Transference, 146
Traumatic brain injury (TBI). *See*
Brain injury
Travi, M., 186
Treat, S., 322
Treatment stage in PCSTF, 90, 92-95,
100-101
Trepper, T. S., 19
Tricyclic antidepressants, 127
True alarms, 110
Trufan, S. J., 158
Trumbetta, S. L., 76
Tulis, E., 140
Turner, R. M., 162
Turovsky, J., 113
Turtonen, J., 127

U. S. Department of Health and Human
Services (USDHHS), 5, 6, 7,
10, 12, 238
U. S. Surgeon General's Report on
Mental Health, 12-15
Uhde, T. W., 112
Ulrich, D. N., 376
Ulrich, R., 38, 144

Van Amburg, S. M., 361-362
van Balkom, A. J. L. M., 175
van der Kolk, B., 138
van Dyck, R., 175
Van Noppen, B., 157, 159
Van Praag, H. M., 112
Van Vort, W., 60, 72
Vaughn, C., 11, 28, 72, 188
Vaughn, P. J., 87
Veilleux, F., 4, 187
Vermilyea, B. B., 156
Vidaver, R., 76
Vos, B., 189

Wade, A., 127
Waldinger, R. J., 218, 219
Waldo, M., 215, 216, 219, 221, 322
Walker, L. E. A., 18
Walk-in mental health centers, 261
case examples, 272-276
community therapists, 263-264
cultural issues, 281-282
demographic and political context of
setting, 262
future directions, 283-284
gender issues, 282-283
medication and integration with
psychiatric services, 279-280
philosophy, 262-263
research findings, 278
service structure, 264-265
setting, 262-266
training programs, 265-266
treatment model
consumer-driven approach,
268-269
follow-up, 272
interventions, 270-271

Walk-in mental health centers
    (continued)
    limitations, 278-279
    questions to answer, 267-268,
        269-270
    relationships, 266-267, 271
    setting parameters, 267
    strengths, 276-277
    therapy as consultation, 271-272
Wallace, C. J., 58
Walsh, F., 9, 10, 361, 362, 363, 366,
        368, 381
Walsh, S., 367
Walters, M., 283, 331
Waltz, J., 343
Wandrei, K. E., 189
Ward, M., 76
Ware, J., 238
Waring, E. M., 208
Watts, S., 72
Watzlawick, P., *xix, xxi*, 271
Waxler, N. E., 27
Weakland, J., *xix, xxi*, 10, 27, 57, 271
Webster, A. S., 111
Weddell, R., 325
Weeks, G. R., 322
Weiner, D., 86
Weiner-Davis, M., 270
Weinstein, M., 189
Weissman, M., 83, 87, 102, 155, 156
Welfare, A., 159, 160
Wells, K. B., 238
Wenniger, W., 103
Wetzler, S., 112
Whisman, M., 83
White, K., 176
White, M., 166, 167, 171, 176, 270,
        376
Whitford, D., 264
Whybrow, P. C., 32
Wickwire, K., 127
Wilhelm, K., 138
Wilken, C. S., 367
Williams, K. E., 128
Williams, T. G., 19
Williamson, M., 188
Wilner, P., 73
Wilsnack, S., 305
Winfield, I., 218
Wing, J. K., 11, 28

Wise, T., 139
Wittchen, H., 289
Woerner, M. G., 72, 77, 115
Wolinsky, M. A., 373
Women and mental health. *See*
        Feminist family systems
        approach
Wood's Homes, 261, 264
Woods, R., 332
Woodward, C., 85
Workshop for psychoeducation, 197-198
Wright, L. M., 270
Wynne, Lyman C., 9, 10, 11, 12, 15,
        17, 20, 27

Xie, H., 77
Xiong, W., 72

Yadalam, K. G., 75
Yale-Brown Obsessive-Compulsive
        Scale (YBOCS), 167
Yalom, I., 147
Yarnold, P. R., 75
Yaryura-Tobias, J., 157
Yellowlees, P., 189
Young, J. E., 18
Young, T., 315, 317, 319, 321

Zanarini, M., 139, 140, 216, 217
Zanus, P., 186
Zarconi, V., 137
Zarit, J. M., 362, 365, 366, 367, 368,
        378, 379
Zarit, S. H., 362, 365, 366, 367, 368,
        378, 379
Zeilman, C., 324
Zhao, Z., 289
Zimmerman, T. S., 361-362
Zipple, A. M., 193
Zitrin, C. M., 115
Zlotnick, C., 85
Zohar, J., 165
Zubin, J., 15, 28, 58, 185
Zweig, R., 367

Order Your Own Copy of
This Important Book for Your Personal Library!

FAMILY THERAPY AND MENTAL HEALTH
Innovations in Theory and Practice

_____in hardbound at $69.95 (ISBN: 0-7890-0880-7)

_____in softbound at $39.95 (ISBN: 0-7890-1589-7)

COST OF BOOKS_____

OUTSIDE USA/CANADA/
MEXICO: ADD 20%____

POSTAGE & HANDLING_____
(US: $4.00 for first book & $1.50
for each additional book)
Outside US: $5.00 for first book
& $2.00 for each additional book)

SUBTOTAL_____

in Canada: add 7% GST

STATE TAX____
(NY, OH & MIN residents, please
add appropriate local sales tax)

FINAL TOTAL____
(If paying in Canadian funds,
convert using the current
exchange rate, UNESCO
coupons welcome.)

❑ **BILL ME LATER:** ($5 service charge will be added)
(Bill-me option is good on US/Canada/Mexico orders only;
not good to jobbers, wholesalers, or subscription agencies.)

❑ Check here if billing address is different from
shipping address and attach purchase order and
billing address information.

Signature_____

❑ **PAYMENT ENCLOSED: $_____**

❑ **PLEASE CHARGE TO MY CREDIT CARD.**

❑ Visa ❑ MasterCard ❑ AmEx ❑ Discover
❑ Diner's Club ❑ Eurocard ❑ JCB

Account # _____

Exp. Date_____

Signature_____

Prices in US dollars and subject to change without notice.

NAME_____

INSTITUTION_____

ADDRESS_____

CITY_____

STATE/ZIP_____

COUNTRY_____ COUNTY (NY residents only)_____

TEL_____ FAX_____

E-MAIL_____

May we use your e-mail address for confirmations and other types of information? ❑ Yes ❑ No
We appreciate receiving your e-mail address and fax number. Haworth would like to e-mail or fax special
discount offers to you, as a preferred customer. **We will never share, rent, or exchange your e-mail address
or fax number.** We regard such actions as an invasion of your privacy.

Order From Your Local Bookstore or Directly From
The Haworth Press, Inc.
10 Alice Street, Binghamton, New York 13904-1580 • USA
TELEPHONE: 1-800-HAWORTH (1-800-429-6784) / Outside US/Canada: (607) 722-5857
FAX: 1-800-895-0582 / Outside US/Canada: (607) 722-6362
E-mail: getinfo@haworthpressinc.com
PLEASE PHOTOCOPY THIS FORM FOR YOUR PERSONAL USE.
www.HaworthPress.com

BOF00